◇◇◇

Setsuko's Secret

Setsuko's Secret

❖❖❖

Heart Mountain and the Legacy of the Japanese American Incarceration

Shirley Ann Higuchi

The University of Wisconsin Press

The University of Wisconsin Press
728 State Street, Suite 443
Madison, Wisconsin 53706
uwpress.wisc.edu

Gray's Inn House, 127 Clerkenwell Road
London EC1R 5DB, United Kingdom
eurospanbookstore.com

Printed in the United States of America

This book may be available in a digital edition.

Library of Congress Cataloging-in-Publication Data
Names: Higuchi, Shirley Ann, author.
Title: Setsuko's secret: Heart Mountain and the legacy of the Japanese American incarceration / Shirley Ann Higuchi.
Description: Madison, Wisconsin: The University of Wisconsin Press, [2020]
| Includes bibliographical references and index.
Identifiers: LCCN 2019055415 | ISBN 9780299327804 (cloth)
Subjects: LCSH: Higuchi, Shirley Ann—Family. | Heart Mountain Relocation Center (Wyo.)
| Japanese Americans—History. | Japanese Americans—
Evacuation and relocation, 1942–1945—Biography.
Classification: LCC D769.8.A6 H54 2020 | DDC 973/.04956—dc23
LC record available at https://lccn.loc.gov/2019055415

To
Amelia
and
little William

Remember the past to help you shine brightly in the future.

Contents

Contents

Illustrations

On the barren windswept corner of northwestern Wyoming there is a rocky outcropping called Heart Mountain, a bleak formation made up of limestone and ancient dolomite. It has little scenic or geologic appeal, but it is a sentinel for a profoundly shameful time in American history.

Heart Mountain overlooks the site of what can only be described as an American concentration camp.

On the barren prairie leading up to it, the US government in 1942 hastily constructed a prison for Japanese Americans who were forcibly removed from their homes on the West Coast because they were thought to be potential agents for Tokyo's warlords during World War II.

More than ten thousand American citizens of Japanese lineage arrived here in 1942 with only what they could fit on the train that transported them.

Families of merchants, business owners, teachers, fishermen—the woof and warp of American life—were assigned living quarters in rudimentary barracks barely heated by smoky coal-burning stoves. Each resident was given an army cot and two blankets.

A hospital was established with outside medical personnel. One of the prisoners—euphemistically called "detainees"—had been a journalist, so he organized a weekly newspaper.

In a culture known for its enterprise, the Japanese prisoners on their own established schooling for the children and recreational opportunities. They organized schools, sports, Boy Scout troops, hobby clubs, and gardens.

Reflecting its warped sense of values, the US government decided that draft-age young men should report for military duty.

When sixty-three resisters refused to serve until their constitutional rights had been restored, they were put on trial and sentenced to three years in prison.

One young man jailed as a resister served his time, and when he was released, he joined the Army.

Who was the more authentic American? His jailers or this Nisei volunteer?

But in these deplorable conditions the Nisei maintained their dignity and their historic sense of family and community.

They found entertaining ways to beat the draconian rules and manage the primitive conditions.

When the war was over, they were released to go home, where many found their businesses taken over or so depleted it took years to restore their economic health.

The US Navy seized the entire tuna fleet of an enterprising Long Beach fisherman, and he was never compensated.

Now, in a new century, the descendants of those confined to Heart Mountain have brought the story to contemporary Americans and the world by establishing a study center and restoring some of the old buildings.

Most important, they are determined that the stories, the legal and physical abuse suffered, the heritage of American citizens subjected to such an outrage, shall always be a part of our history, however painful the acknowledgment.

Since my first trip to Heart Mountain it has been deeply imbedded in my consciousness.

Setsuko's Secret

◆

Prologue
Setsuko's Secret

◇◇◇

When my family asked my mother, Setsuko Saito Higuchi, where she wanted the *koden*, the traditional Japanese condolence money gift, sent when she died, we expected her to say Johns Hopkins University Hospital. That was where she was being treated for the pancreatic cancer that had ravaged her body.

"Heart Mountain," she told us.

Why? My two remaining brothers and I knew of Heart Mountain, this mysterious place in my parents' past, as where they had first met. Beyond that, we knew almost nothing.

My father, Bill, knew exactly what my mother wanted. Heart Mountain, Wyoming, was the camp to which my parents, their families, and about fourteen thousand other Japanese Americans, two-thirds of them US citizens, had been exiled by the federal government following the 1941 attack on Pearl Harbor. There my parents had first met in the seventh-grade classroom of the camp's makeshift school. The photo from their ninth-grade class shows them together in the middle of the front row. My mother, a beautiful and unusually poised city girl from San Francisco, sits next to my father, the young and ruggedly handsome young man who had helped his parents and older brothers run the family truck farm in what is now Silicon Valley. They and their families endured the cold, snowy days on that flat, wind-scoured plain sixty miles east of Yellowstone National Park. Each day, they faced the barbed wire penning them inside the camp, where the guards' machine guns faced inward, not out.

My mother maintained a reserve typical of her generation among the Nisei, as the first US-born generation of Japanese Americans is known.

3

Classmates Bill Higuchi and Setsuko Saito sit next to each other in the center of the front row in the photograph of their ninth-grade class at Heart Mountain High School. (Higuchi family collection)

Despite being American citizens by birth, Nisei were rounded up and incarcerated in what the government euphemistically called "relocation" or "internment" camps. Many of those willing to accommodate camps for Japanese forced from their homes, such as the governors of Idaho and Wyoming, identified them for what they were—concentration camps meant to isolate Japanese Americans from the rest of "real" Americans. Like at least 120,000 of her fellow people of Japanese ancestry, my mother spent almost four years as a prisoner in her own country.

My mother referred to the Nisei as the "quiet Americans," a silence that masks a multitude of scars from the incarceration and its accompanying racism. This silence meant keeping up appearances to convince white America it had nothing to fear. For my mother, the silence meant turning Heart Mountain into little more than a speed bump on her upwardly mobile trajectory.

She never talked about her time at Heart Mountain.

That was not because I did not want to know. While a student at the University of Michigan, I took a philosophy class in which I worked on a project about the Japanese American incarceration camps. I interviewed my mother and another former prisoner. Afterward, I prodded her about the experience and its essential unfairness.

"Hey, Mom, tell me something about how it was in the camp," I asked her at our home in Ann Arbor.

"It was where I met Dad. It was a fun place to be," she said.

"Oh, come on, Mom, were you sad?"

"No, I was happy," she said.

"Really? Wasn't it hard?"

"I was happy! I was happy!" she answered.

"Mom, why are you yelling?"

It was *her* experience, not mine. "You don't know what it was like," she said. I could not have an opinion about her incarceration experience, she thought, because "I was there, not you." She made it very clear by the look on her face and by her body language that she did not want to answer any questions. Setsuko's account of her life resembled one of the intricate lacquer boxes the Japanese create to hold keepsakes. Instead of being open about what being imprisoned as a child did to her, she hid her unhappy memories in this lacquer box modeled after the postwar American ideal of single-family homes, a fresh Detroit-made car every two years, and Madison Avenue–driven conspicuous consumption. She pushed me into that world. I played softball, captained my high school cheerleading squad, worried about homecoming and prom dates and how I could get into Dooley's bar despite being underage. Instead of being alarmed when her hairdresser told her that she had seen me dancing at Dooley's late at night when I was not old enough to be there, she was excited and almost proud — this was a sign that I fit into this American slice of life.

I thought of Heart Mountain as a place of love, a rural Stardust Ballroom that brought together people who were meant to be with each other. My mother spoke only about the activities there, like playing volleyball, and about the boys who liked her — all the same things I cared most about as an adolescent, so those were the only things I focused on. I never saw any of the photos of Heart Mountain's tarpaper barracks or the dusty, muddy, and rutted walking paths that connected the barracks to the public showers. I did not know it as the source of shame or sadness that it was for so many of my older family members and their friends, who spent the rest of their lives trying to understand what they had done to deserve being imprisoned by the same US government that was claiming to be fighting a war to liberate the rest of the world. My mother spent the remaining sixty years of her life trying to sugarcoat or cover up her experience, all the while surreptitiously trying to bear witness to what had happened to her and so many like her.

When my mother looked at me, I felt she was looking into a mirror. She gave me all the material goods to create the image of what she wished she had had as a child, buying me an excessive quantity of clothes, perming my hair, and lacing that experience with frequent criticisms about my weight and appearance and telling me I was not "ladylike" enough. When she died, the mirror shattered, and it created an opening for me to investigate what had actually happened to her at Heart Mountain and how it might have shaped the way she was as my mother.

I knew virtually nothing of that world or my mother's struggle other than what I learned from that one class at Michigan; however, Setsuko, whom my father and their friends called "Sets," spoke often of some of the people she knew from Heart Mountain, including Raymond Uno, who went on to become the first minority judge in Utah and a columnist in the *Pacific Citizen*, the Japanese American newspaper we subscribed to at home. "Raymond Uno used to have a crush on me," she would say to me each time she saw his column, much to my amusement, because it was one of the few times she ever let her guard down. I would soon learn that and far, far more, such as how the Heart Mountain authorities had tried to change her name to Shirley, which she had rejected but decided to pass on to me.

So much of Setsuko's life revolved around doing what society expected of her. At home, she ran everything. She cooked, managed my father's life outside work, and made sure my brothers and I did what we were supposed to at school and elsewhere. Until she died, I never saw my father write a check, cook a meal, or take out the garbage. That was her world, and she dominated it. It was only when she learned she had pancreatic cancer, which is virtually incurable, that we started to learn of her own dreams, which included "building something" at Heart Mountain.

Fulfilling my mother's dream meant more than raising money and trying to build a museum in the remote plains of northwestern Wyoming. It meant a journey into my past and mind, a mission to understand the forces that had shaped my community and myself. My generation, the Sansei, or third generation of Japanese Americans, were born with the need to assimilate, excel, and be better than the rest of "ordinary" Americans—we were the "Model Minority." We had to get good grades in school, find great jobs, and raise equally successful children. Failure meant shame and embarrassment for our families. I now call it the Sansei Effect, the condition in which my generation of Japanese Americans strives to achieve perfection while knowing it is not possible. We grew up with the expectation that we would remain quiet, humble, and presentable, but some of us crumbled under the pressure. They succumbed to drugs or alcohol, and their parents often pretended not to notice.

Although my mother never talked about the negative experiences of incarceration, I instinctively knew that something bad had happened to my parents and grandparents. Instead of hugging, nurturing, or telling me she loved me, my mother tried to fill the void created by her childhood incarceration with the latest fashion and shiny silver dollars as bingo game prizes for children during parties she hosted. Something about it seemed as if she were covering a deeper damage, but I just could not put my finger on it.

My education about her experiences at Heart Mountain started with a telephone call after she died, on April 21, 2005. Pat Wolfe, who was part of the small cadre of people trying to restore Heart Mountain, was inviting me to the June dedication of a walking trail named after my mother. At first, I was skeptical, like any good Japanese American, wondering if this stranger was exploiting my mother's death to get me to support a cause that I knew nothing about. My mother had never talked about her work at Heart Mountain. I agreed to go, because it seemed proper to acknowledge those who honor your deceased mother. My son, Bill, agreed to accompany me, because he wanted to support me during this difficult time. I was curious about this part of my mother's history.

That weekend changed my life. When I met the people who had been working with my mother on this project for all of these years, I finally opened the lacquer box that she had worked to create for most of her life. I felt her commitment to something more substantial than buying clothes or a succession of larger and more expensive homes. This was the something real about her life, not the artificial world she had created to hide a painful part of her history.

I met Norman Mineta, then the US secretary of transportation, who had been incarcerated as a child at Heart Mountain. Also there was Senator Alan K. Simpson, the three-term Republican from Wyoming. This bighearted man of unparalleled grace and courtesy has been linked with

Heart Mountain since the day he met Mineta at a Boy Scout jamboree inside the camp. Another Heart Mountain prisoner, Bill Hosokawa, was also at the dedication. Bill was editor of the *Heart Mountain Sentinel*, the camp's newspaper, and he eventually became an editor at the *Denver Post*. His book, *Nisei: The Quiet Americans*, gave me one of my first glimpses into the lives of my parents and their community. I would not have known anything about the Nisei if it had not been for that book. Yet here he was at ninety, a legend in the Japanese American community, honoring my mother and Heart Mountain, of which I knew little.

I was finally starting to understand why my mother had sent anonymously at least $100,000 to turn her experience into something that would stir the consciences of the millions of Americans who knew nothing about the incarceration. My first trip to Heart Mountain was the missing key to open the door to my history and to truly define who I was. As a lawyer in Washington, DC, I was always chasing the next big legal cause and trying to reach the top professional legal committees, but somehow, many of those activities made me feel empty. At times, I felt as if I were just going through the motions and checking boxes on a list. I decided to do something bigger than just honor my mother. I was not alone; my relationship with my mother was not unique. There were other Sansei daughters like me.

When Pat Wolfe asked me to finish my mother's three-year term on the board of the Heart Mountain Wyoming Foundation (HMWF), I agreed. Through Heart Mountain, as I got to know the people who had known her as a child and through the years, I realized how she had let down her guard with her former Heart Mountain incarcerees and showed her passion about her experience. Educating the residents of Wyoming also gave her permission to talk openly, because she was helping them build something that had meaning for all of them. This gave me an understanding of my mother that had always eluded me. Together, the board and I dedicated ourselves to fulfilling my mother's dream of building a museum and interactive center to teach people about the incarceration. Eventually, Doug Nelson, who had led one of the nation's most successful nonprofit foundations, the Annie E. Casey Foundation, nominated me to chair the foundation. As a graduate student, Doug had studied the incarceration and Heart Mountain, which led to a book on America's concentration camps. He knew how to turn my mother's dream into reality and to memorialize what had happened at Heart Mountain for all the families who suffered. I agreed again, not knowing how deeply I would be immersed in the

After years of fundraising, the Heart Mountain Interpretive Center opened in 2011.
With Shirley Ann Higuchi are Tom Brokaw, Norman Mineta, and Alan Simpson. (Don
Tanguilig / Heart Mountain Wyoming Foundation)

life that my mother had hidden from me. As I tried to fulfill her dream, I
became steeped in the complexity of a community that has been fractured
and divided for almost eighty years.

On August 21, 2011, with the opening of the Heart Mountain Interpretive Center, accompanied by Senator Alan Simpson, Secretary Norman
Mineta, the journalist Tom Brokaw, and Senator Daniel Inouye, of Hawaii, I knew we had accomplished the first part of my mother's dream. My
relationship with Senator Inouye had started nine years earlier, when he
swore me in as the president of the District of Columbia Bar. Heart Mountain was a more genuine and real experience for him than anything in
Washington. At the Heart Mountain dedication, Inouye surveyed all of
the challenges faced by the Japanese American community and the sacrifices it has made to earn its place in society and asked all of us, including
himself, "Was it all worth it?" It was, but it was not a perfect triumph. My
journey has involved navigating the complicated terrain of the Japanese
American community, which can be as paternalistic as a pride of lions. It
meant understanding the Sansei Effect. Most of us carry some residual
damage, such as the drive to be better than everyone else, predicated always

on the fear that someone would tell you that you were not supposed to be here. I had to understand and then master these dynamics to achieve Setsuko's vision.

That meant learning the history, not just of my parents but of all Japanese Americans, their incarceration and then their attempts to deal with its effects. But first I had to research the lives of some of the most influential people in my life now—Daniel Inouye, Takashi Hoshizaki, Clarence Matsumura, Norman Mineta, and Raymond Uno. I needed to understand their experiences so that I would know not just their professional accomplishments but also the pain and racism that had shaped them into who they became.

Inouye was born in Hawaii, served in the Army's 442nd Regimental Combat Team, was recognized for his heroism in the war, and then served in Congress for more than fifty years.

Hoshizaki grew up in Los Angeles and was sent to Heart Mountain as a teenager. While there, he resisted the military draft and was sent to prison. He was drafted again during the Korean War and served.

Matsumura went from Heart Mountain to the Army, where he helped rescue Jewish prisoners kept in a Nazi labor camp. His grandniece serves on the Heart Mountain board with me.

Mineta left Heart Mountain, where he befriended the future senator Alan Simpson, and served in the House and then in the cabinets of a Democratic and a Republican president.

A classmate of my parents at Heart Mountain, Raymond Uno was born in Utah, moved to California during the 1930s, and later served during the Korean War before returning to Utah, where he became the state's first minority judge.

When I was younger, these men were peripheral figures I had seen only on TV or in the *Pacific Citizen*, like Inouye, Mineta, or Uno, or were completely unknown to me, like Matsumura and Hoshizaki. Today I know their lives join with mine like the silk, gold, and silver strands in a Japanese *tsuzure* tapestry. Since men have dominated Japanese American life over the past century, that meant I dealt mostly with the men who had shaped the community's and the Heart Mountain experience. All, except for Matsumura, had been instrumental in the creation of our lasting Heart Mountain memorial, although Matsumura's legacy lives on through his grandniece who serves on our board. In *Setsuko's Secret*, I use them to trace the arc of the Japanese American experience in the United States and how a government that had once promised liberty was responsible for putting them behind barbed wire. If I understood this history, I could understand my-self. I knew there had to be more to the incarceration than the explanation that Japanese Americans accepted it with an old Japanese saying: *shikata ga nai* or "It cannot be helped." Much of what happened *could* have been helped, and I needed to know how.

Heart Mountain brought my family together after my mother's death. It took her deathbed revelation about the *koden* and her secret commit-ment to the cause to get me involved. Now it is the biggest gift for me and my father. My years working with psychologists have shown me that classic coping tools for dealing with traumas like incarceration include workahol-ism and perfectionism, two traits that describe my father almost perfectly. He spent most of my childhood working in his laboratory, which made him an almost distant figure to me. We now have something to talk about when we had little before. We never used to talk much; now we talk often. As heartbreaking as it was for me to accept, my mother's death gave me the space to have more of a relationship with my father than I did when I was growing up. Our work together for Heart Mountain has allowed me to see a totally different side of my father and all of the Nisei.

Now my mother's dream is mine, and it has taken me ever deeper into the history of the Japanese American community and into an understand-ing of how hysteria and fear can force Americans to turn on each other. My mother's mission is now mine, a calling from which I can never turn away.

1

The Issei

Or, Where It All Begins

<><><><><><><><><><><><><><><><><><><><><><><><><><><><><><><><><><><><><><><>

Higuchi Family

My paternal grandfather, Iyekichi Harada, prepared to leave the country of his birth for a second time in 1915. A few years earlier, he had sailed across the Pacific Ocean from his home in Saga prefecture on Kyushu, the southernmost of Japan's four home islands, to South America, where he worked on the farms of Peru. But the conditions there were too harsh, even for the stubborn and resilient Iyekichi, the middle of three sons, so he left for home. He knew, however, that he would have to leave Saga again for the same reason he had left before—times were hard and opportunities limited for all but a family's first-born son. His second voyage across the Pacific was to California, but he did not go alone. Days before he embarked, he had married another villager, Chiye Shiki, who was eleven years his junior. Her family considered her so intelligent that they had prepared her to be one of the few women in Japan to attend college, but she cast her lot with Iyekichi instead. Bound for a strange new country, both bore a new name—Higuchi, the surname of his mother's family, which had no male heir. When they landed in California, Iyekichi and Chiye Higuchi joined the tens of thousands of other Issei, first-generation Japanese immigrants, trying to coax a living out of the state's rich soil.[1]

My paternal grandparents, like thousands of other Japanese immigrants, gravitated to Santa Clara County, a lush agricultural region south of San Francisco. What the world now knows as Silicon Valley was then marked by small vegetable farms and orchards. The Higuchis first rented a farm from a white family in Los Altos, where their oldest son, James, was born in 1915, followed by Kiyoshi a year later and Takeru on New Year's Day 1918. The entire family struggled to make a living as they tried to raise prunes and save enough money to buy their own farm. Iyekichi would pick the fruit and then dip them in a lye solution to prepare them for drying. A heavy storm in 1919 washed out the crop, leaving Iyekichi shaking his head and muttering, "*Zen metsu, zen metsu*"—total loss, total loss. By 1922, the family had moved to Mountain View, where they lived in a home built of redwood planks with newspaper layered over the walls to cover the cracks. Their home held one symbol of Japan—the large wooden bathtub Iyekichi had built and that was heated by a wood-burning stove.[2]

Their children soon attended the local school in Mountain View, but because the Higuchis spoke only Japanese at home, James, Kiyoshi, and Takeru understood virtually no English. When James started first grade, he did not know what his teacher or any of his fellow students were saying. One day, James had to take a bowel movement, but he did not know how to ask his teacher for permission to go to the bathroom. "I finally let go in my pants," he said, "and I remember the agony of having to walk home with poop running down my legs."[3]

The immigrants, known as Issei, and their children, the second generation, or Nisei, began to thrive. American farmers envied how the Japanese turned marginal land profitable through intensive farming techniques that required them to tend to each plant by hand. However, banks still refused to lend money to Japanese businesses, and Issei and Nisei alike still needed help navigating a legal and political system rigged against them. They created dozens of organizations to help them cope, and by 1929 the Japanese American Citizens League (JACL) was created by merging three groups together. The JACL aimed to protect the citizenship rights of Japanese Americans, and its leader was Saburo Kido, a San Francisco lawyer and Hawaii-born Nisei.[4]

When my grandfather Higuchi needed to buy his first farm in San Jose, he and his two oldest sons, James and Kiyoshi, went to Kido's office, where he drafted the documents that put the Higuchi farm, for Iyekichi the symbol of his thirteen years of toil as a sharecropper, into the ownership of his thirteen- and twelve-year-old sons, who, not yet old enough to drive, now owned a fourteen-and-a-quarter-acre farm in San Jose. They left, as James recalled, "the relatively carefree life of sharecropper" for the greater responsibility of owning a farm.[5] I had never understood why my grandfather put the farm in the names of his children. Only later did I learn that the discriminatory Alien Land Law of the time had made it necessary.

My grandfather Higuchi's raspberry farm succeeded beyond his dreams, and he shared his prosperity by allowing some of the Mexican families who worked on the nearby farms to live on the family's fourteen acres rent-free. Their children, particularly those of the Briones family, became some of the first playmates for my father, who was born on March 16, 1931, thirteen years after his brother Takeru. Unlike his older brothers, he grew up speaking more Spanish than Japanese.

By 1936, when my aunt Emily was born, the older sons had begun to leave home. James finished high school and headed to San Jose State University and then to medical school. The third son, Takeru, followed suit and then went to graduate school at the University of Wisconsin to study chemistry. But Kiyoshi, the second son, fell ill with pleurisy. Although it is now easily treatable with antibiotics, the illness confined Kiyoshi to bed for four years. My grandmother Chiye treated him with love and her nurturing home remedies and often wheeled him into the sun to watch Bill play with the Briones children.

The Higuchi family around the time they bought their first farm in San Jose. From left to right are Takeru, Iyekichi, James, Chiye, and Kiyoshi. (Higuchi family collection)

Saito Family

Three years after the Higuchis arrived in California, seventeen-year-old Yoshio Saito, my maternal grandfather, left his home near Tokyo on a ship bound for San Francisco. He moved in with his brother Ryoichiro, who was twenty-two years older, and found a job as a houseboy. Like most of the Japanese in the city, they lived in Japantown, a seventy-three-block enclave west of San Francisco's financial district. The age difference between Yoshio and Ryoichiro seems to have caused some confusion for the US government. The 1920 Census lists Yoshio Saito as living at 1521 Geary Street as the adopted son of Ryoichiro, who was forty-one and married with two children. Their home was the Nankaiya Hotel and Tokyo Bath House, of which Ryoichiro was listed as the proprietor.[6] In 1930, their relationship,

The Saito family lived in San Francisco's Japantown, where Yoshio Saito ran several stores. From left to right are Fumio, Yoshio, Setsuko, Hiroshi, Fumi, and Yoshiro. (Higuchi family collection)

at least in the eyes of the US Census, changed, as Ryoichiro and Yoshio were listed as brothers on the subsequent census.[7] Yoshio worked during the day, studied English and business at night school, and eventually became a treaty merchant importing products from Japan.

Yoshio arrived like most Japanese immigrants—as a single man. Many lived in labor camps or crowded boarding houses in Japantown and other enclaves. These men, including Yoshio, eventually wanted to settle down and start families. To find wives, they either relied on family connections back in Japan or pored through books of photographs of young Japanese women willing to marry men who had emigrated to the United States. This new iteration of the Japanese tradition of *oimai*, or arranged marriages, resembled today's online dating. Between 1868 and 1924, twenty thousand "picture brides" came to the United States. Many came alone and were processed into the country through Angel Island, the Ellis Island of the West. They often encountered future husbands far older than they expected, because the men often sent old or doctored photos to Japan.[8]

When my grandfather Saito traveled back to Japan to find a wife in early 1924, he had little time to waste. Congress was about to pass a new immigration law freezing immigration from Japan. My uncle Fumio "Al" Saito explained that Yoshio "had selected a woman in Nagoya," but on visiting the Hattori family, "He got a glimpse of the lady's younger sister who was fantastically better looking, so he immediately chose the younger sister as his bride." It is clear to me, now that I have learned more about my grandfather, that he would never leave such a major decision to chance. He always wanted to get the best deal, and when he saw he had a better alternative than his original match, he went for it. With Fumi, his then seventeen-year-old wife, Yoshio boarded the *Empress of Canada* in Japan and disembarked in Vancouver, British Columbia. They eventually settled on Geary Street with Ryoichiro and his family.[9]

Yoshio used his business school education to start managing a series of retail stores that sold Japanese ceramics, stationery, tableware, and some food in the Bay Area, starting with City of Tokyo on Grant Avenue near Bush Street and then Asahi, which was on Market Street near the Warfield Theater. He and Fumi started a family. Their first child, Yoshiro, was born in 1928, followed a year later by Fumio, my uncle Al. My mother, Setsuko, was born on January 2, 1931. Hiroshi, the youngest son, was born in 1933 and was called Taisho, which means "general," because he was bossy and imperious. Tragedy struck in 1940 when Yoshiro died after a long illness that the family believed had started when he attended a YMCA summer camp in 1938. Doctors initially thought it was spinal meningitis, but Al later said it was a brain infection that wore Yoshiro down physically and mentally.[10]

My grandparents were among the 125,000 Japanese who made the journey from Japan to the United States or Hawaii—until 1898 an independent nation—between 1868 and 1924. They left Japan because of the economic and social upheavals of the Meiji Dynasty and came to the United States in search of riches and work, often after reading glowing reports in books like *How to Succeed in America*.[11] Unlike European immigrants, they were of a different race, spoke an unfamiliar language with an unrecognizable alphabet, and practiced a religion—Buddhism—that clearly marked them as "the other." White Americans, many of them recent immigrants themselves, saw the Japanese as the successors to the Chinese immigrants who had helped build the transcontinental railroad before their immigration was banned by the 1882 Chinese Exclusion Act. A *San Francisco Chronicle* editorial in 1905 called the Japanese "the worst immigrant we have," citing no reason but clearly indicating the root cause was pure racism.[12] Whites created anti-Japanese leagues to discourage immigration and sought to deny the newcomers the rights of citizenship and land ownership. "I am opposed to the Japanese immigration, just as I am opposed to the coming in of any race that injures our working man," a local businessman said in March 1905.[13] It was a repeat of the same "yellow peril" argument that had led to the Chinese Exclusion Act, this time transferred to the Japanese immigrants who were allegedly competing with the white European immigrants heading West.

Inouye Family

Daniel Inouye's grandfather Asakichi Inouye left Fukuoka prefecture on Kyushu in 1899 with his wife and two-year-old son, Hyotaro, to work in Hawaii. He had to settle a family debt incurred when his father, Wasaburo, accidentally started a fire that burned down their village. Asakichi signed with one of the labor contractors roaming through rural Japan looking for young men willing to cut sugar cane or pick pineapples in the rapidly expanding plantations of Hawaii, which had just become a US-controlled territory. By 1900, more than twenty-five thousand Japanese lived in Hawaii.[14] In 1922, Hyotaro met a local woman, Kame Imanaga, at a church social. One year later, they married and moved to the teeming Queen Emma Street neighborhood in Honolulu, where their son, Daniel, was born in 1924. He would eventually join the US Army, fight and lose his right arm in Italy, and serve in the United States Senate for almost fifty years.[15] For many Sansei such as myself growing up in the 1960s and 1970s, Daniel Inouye was the exemplar of a successful Japanese American.

The Hawaii in which the Inouyes settled was relatively free of the racial tensions faced by the Japanese on the West Coast. For one thing, Japanese immigrants and their descendants made up at least one-third of the population. By 1941, 158,000 people of Japanese descent lived in Hawaii, which was also home to large concentrations of Chinese and Filipino immigrants.[16] Japanese immigrants enjoyed the diversity and freedom that Hawaii offered, Daniel Inouye recalled later, because they had escaped the rigid social system that dominated Japan. "They, for the most part, were not successes in their communities," he said. "If they were, they wouldn't be here. They would have stayed back there. Why should they want to move out to a strange land not knowing what is in the future?" Working conditions in the United States were better, too; even if the work in the cane fields was hard, the workers were treated with respect.[17]

As the Inouyes' fortunes improved, they gradually adopted American customs. Kame Inouye encouraged Daniel to take the best of Japan and the United States. "When we ate chicken and beef, we used knives and forks," Daniel said. "When we ate sukiyaki or tempura, we used chopsticks. Although I went to a Japanese school every afternoon, it was never permitted to interfere with my American education." When Daniel was four, he watched at home as his family celebrated his grandfather finally paying off his family's debt back in Japan. After settling such a serious obligation, Asakichi Inouye could have returned to Japan a hero, but, like so many Japanese who had come to the United States, he had no intention of returning to Japan. He would remain in Hawaii, as would his son and grandson. They were Americans now.[18]

Japanese Americans eventually took their places among Hawaiian society as teachers, policemen, and government officials. Still, they remained stuck between cultures. As a teenager, Daniel objected to the demands of a teacher in Japanese school that he proclaim loyalty to the emperor. Daniel also resented some of his Japanese neighbors who "behaved as they were white, too. They bought automobiles beyond their means, were sensitive to any change in *haole* [white person] fashion and mimicked them, and bitterly resented those of us who refused to conform to their twisted notions of what made an American."[19] Inouye would always be proud of his Japanese heritage and act as a bridge between the community's dissenting factions after the war.

Mineta Family

California's sugar industry also drew Japanese immigrants, who were needed to pull and top the sugar beets that grew in farms along the West Coast. Norman Mineta's father, Kunisaku Mineta, the second son of a farmer in Shizuoka prefecture located south of Tokyo, boarded a ship in 1902, when he was fourteen. He landed in Seattle and worked his way south until he reached his uncle, who was working in the sugar beet fields near Salinas, California.[20] His uncle told him that to move beyond work as a simple laborer he would have to learn to speak English like an American. That meant studying English in elementary school with first graders. "That was the most humiliating thing he'd ever done," said his youngest son, Norman, who would end up imprisoned at Heart Mountain with my parents before becoming mayor of San Jose, a member of the US House of Representatives, and a cabinet member for Presidents Bill Clinton and George W. Bush.[21] Midway through the second grade, Kunisaku decided he had learned enough English, so he left school for a job with the Spreckels Sugar Company in Santa Clara County.[22]

Kunisaku would have worked in the sugar industry longer, but he fell ill during the cataclysmic 1918–19 influenza epidemic and spent months in the hospital. After doctors told Kunisaku he could not return to farming, he worked as a correspondent for a Japanese newspaper and translated for Japanese immigrants in the county courthouse. One day two men approached him and asked if he was interested in the insurance business. "I have no idea what insurance is about," Kunisaku said, but he trained and then took two of the business cards he had been given and went to San Francisco and got a job selling insurance in San Jose, California.[23]

Like the Inouyes in Hawaii, the Minetas maintained their Japanese values while avidly embracing those of the United States. In San Jose, Kunisaku Mineta bought his own home with the assistance of J. B. Peckham, a white lawyer who helped dozens of Japanese American families. The Minetas had also achieved the kind of success that transcended the Japanese American community. "In those days, virtually all insurance companies put a surcharge on the premiums of 'Orientals,' as we were then called," Norman Mineta said. "For example, if you could buy life insurance for

$10 per thousand, I would be charged $12 per thousand," because the Japanese were believed to carry a higher risk. Kunisaku became the first agent for a company called West Coast Life, which sold policies without the surcharge, which "made them very popular," his son said.[24] That propelled the Minetas into the upper middle class, enabling them to send a daughter to college and to vacation each year at Lake Tahoe. Young Norman, born in 1931, was the last of five Mineta children. He spent his days going to school and playing baseball; he was such a fan that he constantly carried a ball with him.

The family's place among the Japanese American elite took on a more political turn when their daughter Etsu began dating a young Nisei activist named Mike Masaoka, who would become the first executive director of the Japanese American Citizens League (JACL) and a figure of enduring controversy in the Japanese American—Nikkei—community for the role he played in the wartime incarceration. However, Norman remembered hiding behind the couch in the family living room when Masaoka came to visit Etsu at the family home in San Jose and how Masaoka would give him a nickel or a dime to go away. "One time, I guess he must have been so short of change that I even got a quarter out of him," Norman said. "What a deal!"[25]

Matsumura Family

The 1882 Chinese Exclusion Act did not curb the appetite in the United States for cheap foreign labor, and Japanese laborers stepped into the vacuum. Railroad crews spent days at a time away from home, pounding spikes between the heavy rails and ties they had lugged into place. Families moved where the work took them. By 1906, more than thirteen thousand Japanese immigrants had taken jobs with the railroads.[26] One was Clarence Matsumura's father, Rokuazem "Roy" Matsumura, who arrived that year from Japan and found work building the Union Pacific Railroad line that ran from Wyoming to Oregon. His wife, Takeko, arrived in 1915, and they soon started a family. In 1921, Clarence was born in Bryan, Wyoming, and two years later his younger sister, Susan, was born across the state line in Devil's Slide, Utah. Eventually the family settled in Granger, Wyoming, while Roy continued to travel up and down the railroad line for his work.

Roy's age and his growing family made staying in Granger and the railroad industry too difficult. The one-room schoolhouse in Granger took students only through the eighth grade. If the Matsumura kids were going to progress beyond doing manual work on the railroad, they would need better schooling than a remote railroad town in Wyoming could provide. In 1935, Roy took his savings and moved the family to Los Angeles, where he bought a market in the Silver Lake neighborhood that he named "Wyoming," after the state where he had lived for close to thirty years.

Clarence thrived in the California schools. He graduated from John Marshall High School and then attended UCLA, where he studied electronics. He wanted to work in radio, and the growing entertainment industry in Los Angeles provided plenty of opportunities. Twenty in 1941, Clarence saw a world of opportunities awaiting him when he graduated. But after Pearl Harbor, he and the rest of his family were sent to Heart Mountain. Only after I started working with the Heart Mountain Wyoming Foundation did I learn how Clarence had worked in camp, struggled to leave, and then was drafted from college to serve in the all-Nisei military units that fought bravely in France, Germany, and Italy. I learned how Clarence went on to rescue Holocaust victims from a forced death march in Germany.

Hoshizaki Family

Not all Japanese immigrants arrived in the United States as laborers. Takashi Hoshizaki's father, Keijiro Hoshizaki, was a college graduate. Born in 1895, he was the last son in a farming family of thirteen children—three sons and ten daughters—in the small village of Yahagi in Kanagawa prefecture, forty-five miles southwest of Tokyo. The firstborn son, Sadagoro, was educated until he reached his early teens, when he was forced to join his father in the fields. But by the time Keijiro reached the age his brother had been when he finished school, enough children had come before him that his father did not need him on the farm. Instead, he went to Waseda University in Tokyo. It was unusual for young men to attend college in early twentieth-century Japan; few young men made it off the farms and into the classroom. Keijiro excelled and managed to graduate second in his class.

Second wasn't good enough.

"You're only number two," his father said. "You can come home now."

While the top student was given a position at a large corporation, Keijiro moved back to Yahagi. He had squandered his chance at a life outside the village. He found a job working on a fishing boat.

One day, a boy came running up to Keijiro's boat with news that the top student from Waseda had passed on the job. Keijiro was offered the job, and he accepted.

The corporation sent Keijiro to a mining operation in the frigid and windy Chinese province of Manchuria, where he pushed papers in the company office. Sadagoro, his oldest brother, had already emigrated to Los Angeles, where he owned a market and trading company. He urged Keijiro to join him, so, in 1915, after three months in Manchuria, twenty-year-old Keijiro boarded a ship to the United States.

By 1923, he also wanted to start a family. Keijiro contacted friends back in Japan, and they arranged a marriage with Name Hirano, whose family owned a store in Tokyo. Name almost did not make it. On September 1, 1923, an earthquake registering 7.9 on the Richter scale struck off the coast of Tokyo, devastating that city and many others and killing up to 140,000 people. The Hirano family's store collapsed around her, but the peculiar layout of its shelves protected her. Her neighbors ripped open the roof of the store and rescued her.

After their wedding, Keijiro and Name raced the clock to return before Congress passed a new immigration law banning all Japanese immigration to the country. A previous "gentleman's agreement" had limited the immigration of men to the United States, but it allowed for picture brides to join those men already in the country. Anti-foreigner sentiment had erupted after World War I, accompanied by a revival of the Ku Klux Klan, and Name and other women like her had little time to wait. She and Keijiro made it back just before the bill became law.

Back in Los Angeles, Keijiro tended to Fujiya, his store in Hollywood, and he and Name began a family. Takashi, their oldest son, was born in 1925, and five other children followed. Takashi, who would be incarcerated at Heart Mountain, resist the military draft, and be sent to federal prison, remembers a childhood spent playing in vacant lots near the family store and growing up in a Japanese American ghetto in that part of Los Angeles. He helped translate English into Japanese for his mother at the store, and, as he grew older, he bulked up by carrying one-hundred-pound sacks of rice.[27]

By 1941, Keijiro had determined that tensions between Japan and the United States had reached a breaking point. He had owned stock in several Japanese companies, including Tokyo Electric. When he heard that the United States had placed an embargo on oil sales to Japan that August, he immediately sold his shares in Tokyo Electric and expected the worst.

Uno Family

Raymond Uno has been a force in my life since I was a young child, although I knew little about him other than what I gleaned from the columns I would see in the *Pacific Citizen*, the JACL newspaper. I did not know until much later how much of his character came from his father, Clarence, who had first arrived in the United States in 1910. In Chico, California, Clarence worked in his mother's family's flower business, quickly learned English, and demonstrated his skills at organizing and selling to his fellow immigrants. By 1917, when the United States entered World War I on the side of the Allies—which then included Japan—Clarence had joined the US Army and fought with the Rainbow Division in France and Belgium.[28] After the war, he moved to Ogden, Utah, opened a store where he sold dry goods to the local Japanese community, and eventually married a Japanese woman, Osako Teraoka, who had stopped in Utah to see family on her way to graduate school at Columbia University in New York. She met Clarence and forgot about school, Raymond said.[29]

Each year following World War I, Clarence had appealed unsuccessfully to the government to become a US citizen.[30] In 1935, however, Congress passed a law granting citizenship to about five hundred Asian immigrant veterans of World War I. Clarence Uno was now a citizen of the country he had served honorably during the war.[31] His niece Amy Uno Ishii remembers that he "always held that over my father, saying 'Aha, you may have been here in America before I came and you may be older than me, but I am an American citizen. And America will always be closer to me than it is to you.'"[32]

Citizenship, however, did not help Clarence save his business, and he eventually had to close the store in 1937. A friend in El Monte, California, offered him a job as secretary of the San Gabriel Japanese Association. Clarence and two friends packed the Uno family into trucks, with Raymond and his sister Elma laid out in the open air in the back of one pickup, which had been padded into a kind of bed. Like the Okies who trekked West after the Dust Bowl, the Unos traveled down the quiet roads from Ogden at night, "and I still remember the lights as we pulled out of Layton and still remember the trip to Las Vegas and then we went to the Hoover Dam and then we went to El Monte," Raymond remembers.[33]

At the San Gabriel Japanese Association, Clarence helped the local members of the Japanese community navigate the property, tax issues, and other challenges of American life. Such organizations, along with the

Buddhist Church, provided the kind of glue the Nikkei community needed to weather the prejudices and racism that faced them. It also made them the targets of suspicion by the law enforcement and intelligence organizations that monitored Japanese Americans, particularly as tensions increased with Japan.

Raymond attended the Lexington School, where the students were Mexican, Chinese, and Japanese immigrants whose families worked on the farms in the San Gabriel Valley. There he met a fellow Nisei, Harumi Sakatani, whom everyone called "Bacon," because his friends had once held him over a fire like a piece of bacon as a child. Thus began an eighty-year friendship that lives on with the Heart Mountain Wyoming Foundation, where Bacon is known as "Mr. Heart Mountain" for his work creating the original organization. "I had just started school, and this Mexican guy that was a year ahead of me started a fight with me, and I didn't know anything about fighting at the time," Raymond said. "Bacon happened to be right there, and he got a hold of his leg and arm and the guy couldn't do anything. So, I always say, 'Bacon, you saved my life! Because that guy would have killed me since I don't know how to fight!'"[34]

Brewing Tensions

Tensions between the United States and Japan grew throughout the 1930s as Japan strengthened its hold over China, a US ally. When President Franklin Roosevelt started his third term, in 1941, he knew war between the United States and Japan was inevitable, a feeling he had had since he served as assistant Navy secretary during World War I. But the United States lacked any significant intelligence capability; no CIA existed to spy on foreign governments. Only the military intelligence services, specifically the Office of Naval Intelligence, monitored foreign governments and potentially dangerous groups. Naval intelligence officers had already broken a spy ring that operated out of the Japanese consulate in Los Angeles. Lieutenant Commander Kenneth Ringle had broken into the building, as local police kept watch outside, to look for evidence of a spy ring whose members included a Japanese naval officer who had pretended to be a student. US intelligence used the documents to identify all of the Japanese spies on the West Coast and deport them. The same documents, however, showed that the Japanese government considered the Issei and Nisei unreliable and useless in a war against the United States.[35]

It seems inconceivable now that the president of a budding superpower would officially sanction, as Roosevelt did, having a syndicated newspaper columnist take on an official role as an intelligence officer. John Franklin Carter was a forty-three-year-old author of thrillers and a column called "We, the People," which he wrote under the name Jay Franklin, when he enthusiastically supported Roosevelt's unprecedented run for a third term in 1940. After Roosevelt's victory, Carter was repaid for his support by being made an unofficial intelligence clearing house with about a dozen agents funded by the State Department. Carter's eclectic assortment of operatives carried out assignments in the Caribbean and South Africa. In the summer of 1941, Roosevelt asked Carter to study the Japanese community on the West Coast. Carter assigned the job to an unlikely agent—Curtis Munson, a Republican industrialist from Detroit. No expert in Asian affairs or anthropology, Munson had a gift for gathering information and reporting it back clearly and colorfully. On the West Coast, Munson visited with Saburo Kido of the JACL, other community leaders, and Ringle, who told Munson the local community was not dangerous. Munson also detected the Nisei's strong desire to prove their patriotism and the Issei's general lack of pro-Japanese sympathies. Munson did note that "there are still Japanese in the United States who will tie dynamite around their waist and make a bomb out of themselves," but the overall tone of his report was that the Japanese community in the United States did not pose a threat. When Carter passed the report to Roosevelt, he highlighted in a one-page cover sheet the sensational finding about dynamite. It's not clear whether Roosevelt read much more, particularly the part of the report that spelled out that "there is no Japanese 'problem' on the coast. There will be no armed uprising of Japanese." Neither Munson nor Carter knew of Roosevelt's long-held suspicion of the Japanese, evidenced by a 1936 memo to the chief of naval operations in which he recommended the establishment of concentration camps for Japanese Americans in Hawaii who were suspected of collaborating with the Japanese.[36]

Munson himself saw a Japanese community intensely loyal to the United States, one that was motivated to prove itself in spite of decades of suspicion and ostracism. Japanese Americans, Munson reported, knew that they were "in a spot" between their love for their new home and their ethnic origin. Munson observed that the Issei "have made this their home. They have brought up their children here, their wealth accumulated by hard labor is here, and many would have become American citizens had they been allowed to do so. They are for the most part simple people."[37] The overwhelming majority of Japanese Americans just wanted to work, provide for their families, and be treated as Americans, he noted.

Most Japanese Americans had no inkling of how much of a spot they were in. The FBI was already compiling lists of suspect members of the community, starting with Buddhist priests, Japanese-language teachers, and leaders of various social organizations. Munson did single out one group of Japanese Americans—US-born Nisei who had been sent by their parents to Japan for school. These students were known as the Kibei, and Munson said they were "considered the most dangerous element and closer to the Issei with especial reference to those who received their early education in Japan." His opinion foreshadowed the tougher treatment of the Kibei during wartime, as they fell under suspicion as potential saboteurs. Munson noted, however, that insular Japanese society often rejected the Kibei as tainted by foreign influence. "In fact, it is a saying that all a Nisei needs is a trip to Japan to make a loyal American out of him."[38]

This was the best intelligence Roosevelt had at his disposal on December 7, 1941. Fears of sabotage in Hawaii led military commanders to lash together the ships of the 7th Fleet in port and to park the military aircraft in Hawaii closely together in the middle of their runways. Such precautions protected the ships and planes from sabotage but left them vulnerable to sabotage from the sky.

On the morning of December 7, 1941, as he prepared to go to church, Daniel Inouye heard a local radio newscaster excitedly announce the attack on Pearl Harbor, just a few miles from his home in Honolulu. He saw the smoke rising and heard explosions and machine gun fire. He thought it was the end of his world, because "the men who piloted those planes looked like us, looked like me." Inouye and his fellow members of a local first aid station rushed into Honolulu's neighborhoods to find any wounded. They encountered victims of friendly fire from inexperienced anti-aircraft crews who had failed to arm their shells properly; some of these had exploded in neighborhoods. "I led the stretcher team that picked up this elderly Japanese lady who was just having her breakfast at that time, I think, oblivious to the fact that an attack was in progress, and a shell just went through the roof and sliced her head."[39]

The people of Japanese descent killed by the surprise attack on Pearl Harbor were the first innocent victims among the Japanese American community in the United States. Within months, there would be almost

120,000 more victims, two-thirds of them US citizens, singled out as the government reacted by labeling an entire group of people as potential saboteurs without evidence. Now, almost eighty years later, the Japanese American community is still coping with the effects of these acts.

2

Executive Order 9066
Forcing People Out of Their Lives

◇◇

In the nine weeks between December 7, 1941, and February 19, 1942, the day President Roosevelt signed Executive Order 9066, authorizing the exclusion of Japanese Americans from the West Coast, government officials fought a battle between racism and reason. Racism won. No evidence existed that the people of Japanese descent living on the West Coast endangered national security, but FBI director J. Edgar Hoover believed his detention of thousands of community leaders had neutralized any potential threat of sabotage and the need for a large-scale removal of the Japanese American population.[1] However, too many other Americans cast a blanket of blame on Japanese Americans and believed that the 120,000 people of Japanese descent living on the West Coast, mostly in California, had to go.

Inside the Roosevelt administration, the sides formed quickly. Although Curtis Munson's report had included two sentences that implied the presence of potential saboteurs, it contained nothing that detailed a specific plot or even loose talk about Japanese American efforts to assist in a Japanese attack. That lack of evidence did not stop some officials from imputing the worst motives to Japanese Americans. Navy Secretary Frank Knox went to Hawaii on December 9 and returned six days later to claim that Japanese Americans in Hawaii had aided the Pearl Harbor attack. "I think the most effective Fifth Column work of the entire war was done in Hawaii with the possible exception of Norway," where local Nazis had overthrown the legitimate government in 1940. He told Roosevelt the United States needed to "take all the aliens out of Hawaii and send them off to another island."[2]

Major General Allen Gullion, the Army's provost marshal, led the military push for evacuation, mixing racism and authoritarianism into a toxic brew that aligned him with Knox.[3] Gullion had to persuade the top general on the West Coast, Lieutenant General John DeWitt, to act. DeWitt had been the quartermaster in the same Rainbow Division that Clarence Uno had fought in during World War I, and DeWitt had remained in the Army, where he rose to lead the Western Defense Command (WDC), based in San Francisco's Presidio. At first, DeWitt warned against a mass removal of Japanese Americans, believing it was a logistical problem that meant "we are going to have an awful job on our hands."[4] Soon, DeWitt caved to the pressure, but not enough to satisfy Gullion, who dispatched one of his most gung-ho aides, Karl Bendetson, a lawyer with the rank of captain and a history of whitewashing his own biography, to San Francisco.[5] By ancestry a Lithuanian Jew, Bendetson had claimed to be Danish in order to join an anti-Semitic fraternity at Stanford, and by February 4 he had furthered that fraud by changing the spelling of his last name, substituting an "e" for the "o," changing the spelling to "Bendetsen."

Bendetsen, DeWitt, and Gullion all reported to War Secretary Henry Stimson, who had held the same job thirty years earlier in the administration of Republican president William Howard Taft. At seventy-four, Stimson worked about four hours a day and delegated the handling of the West Coast security situation to his deputy, forty-six-year-old John McCloy, a Republican Wall Street lawyer who saw saboteurs everywhere, the result of the ten years he had spent investigating the World War I "Black Tom" sabotage case. His biographer noted, "McCloy was now psychologically prepared to be a ready believer in all spy rings."[6]

Japanese victories in battles that took place after Pearl Harbor heightened fears that the Japanese would soon strike the US mainland. The Japanese invaded Malaya, Burma, Midway Island, Burma, Wake Island, Hong Kong, the Philippines, and Guam, and by Christmas they controlled Hong Kong, Guam, and Wake Island. Manila fell on January 2. US soldiers were holed up on the small island of Corregidor under constant shelling. Japanese submarines patrolled off the coast of California and had sunk three ships by Christmas.

To sixteen-year-old Takashi Hoshizaki, it seemed the United States could actually lose the war. He saw the maps showing a spreading red zone controlled by the Japanese. He shared his fears with his father, Keijiro. "No, Japan is going to lose the war," Keijiro said. His reasoning drew on history as well as his experience and knowledge of Japan's industrial capabilities. Japan's lightning victory in its 1905 war with Russia, Keijiro said, masked its weaknesses. The Japanese lacked the raw materials and industrial capacity to build and sustain a war machine and occupy a wide swath of the Pacific. Because he had worked for a Japanese company in Manchuria, he knew the limits on what Japan could do over the long term.[7]

Most American officials and commentators lacked Keijiro's vision. Instead, they fueled the rising hysteria. The columnist, broadcaster, and author Damon Runyon falsely claimed in a January 4 broadcast that a transmitter had been discovered in a Japanese boarding house. "It would be extremely foolish to doubt the continued existence of enemy agents among the large alien Japanese population," Runyon said.[8] Feeding on the fear, politicians and newspapers called for Japanese Americans to be placed in inland concentration camps, in part so they could show their sacrifice and loyalty.[9] In Washington, the dependably racist factions in Congress demanding drastic action were led by a Democratic representative from Mississippi, John Rankin. "This is a race war," Rankin said. "I say it is of vital importance that we get rid of every Japanese, whether in Hawaii or the mainland. . . . Damn them! Let's get rid of them now." Jed Johnson, a Democratic congressman from Oklahoma, called for the forced sterilization of all Japanese living in the United States.[10]

As the feeling against Japanese Americans continued to build along the West Coast, Roosevelt ordered another study of the Pearl Harbor attack, this time led by Supreme Court Justice Owen Roberts, whose hurriedly appointed panel issued its report on January 23, 1942. Roberts's commission laid the blame for the catastrophic defeat on two commanders in Hawaii, Admiral Husband Kimmel and General Walter Short, who had little chance to defend themselves. The commissioners also made vague and unsupported references to possible Japanese American collaborators in Hawaii.[11]

"There were, prior to December 7, 1941, Japanese spies on the island of Oahu," the report found. "Some were Japanese consular agents and others were persons having no open relations with the Japanese foreign service. These spies collected and, through various channels, transmitted information to the Japanese Empire respecting the military and naval establishments and dispositions on the island."[12] Japanese agents inside the consulate had thoroughly analyzed the military weaknesses on Oahu as part of their jobs for the Japanese government. The commissioners, however, provided no evidence of support for Japan among Hawaii's Japanese American community. Nevertheless, the claim of potential saboteurs set afire the dry tinder of anti-Japanese hysteria that had been gathering since the Pearl Harbor attack.[13]

Meanwhile, Lieutenant Commander K. D. Ringle of the Office of Naval Intelligence had been assigned to analyze the potential threat posed by the West Coast Japanese community. Ringle knew the Japanese government did not trust the Issei and Nisei, considering them "cultural traitors" tainted by Western influence. Ringle had spent eight years working in the US embassy in Tokyo and read and spoke Japanese fluently; he knew Japanese culture like few other white Americans. He wrote that the Japanese government preferred recruiting "communists, labor union members, Negroes, and anti-Semites" as spies rather than drawing from the Japanese living in the United States.[14]

Ringle wrote his superiors in Washington that the "entire 'Japanese problem' has been magnified out of its true proportions, largely because of the physical characteristics of the people." A mass evacuation made no sense. "It should be handled on the basis of the individual, regardless of citizenship, and not on a racial basis." Ringle concluded that the Issei were "passively loyal" to the United States and would not knowingly hurt it, just as they would not do anything to hurt Japan. But, he noted, some Issei "might well do surreptitious observation work for Japanese interests if given a convenient opportunity." At most, Ringle's report said, maybe three hundred Issei or Nisei living in the United States posed a possible sabotage threat, but most of them, he noted, had already been rounded up by the FBI, while the rest were benign.[15]

Ringle knew that the young and ambitious leaders of the JACL were encouraging Nisei to cooperate with the government and to inform law enforcement of any signs of subversive activity. Japanese government officials working in the United States did not trust the Nisei, he wrote, but the US government had done little or nothing to "develop their loyalty to the United States, other than to permit them to attend public schools." If the United States wanted to tap the resources of the Nisei, Ringle warned, that attitude had to change.[16] In the end, Ringle was an unheard prophet. Ringle's official report arrived in Washington on January 29, just days after Roberts's report, and its one provocative sentence about possible saboteurs stole public attention. His report, overshadowed by Roberts's, was forgotten. Only years later would it resurface and change the course of a legal case that would expose the incarceration of Japanese Americans as a fraud.

The Evacuation Order

Some elected officials, such as Earl Warren, California's Republican attorney general, had initially adopted a moderate approach. But as his party's odds-on favorite to challenge incumbent Democratic governor Culbert Olson in the fall, Warren knew the majority of his voters favored coming down hard on the Japanese Americans.[17] Warren had received no new evidence of possible sabotage, because none existed, but DeWitt had been feeding him false information.[18] On January 29, Warren reversed his position and called "the Japanese situation . . . the Achilles Heel of the entire civil defense effort. Unless something is done it may bring about a repetition of Pearl Harbor."[19] Warren's new stance legitimized the rising hysteria, and Olson quickly joined in with trite claims about the inscrutability of Japanese Americans, which made it impossible for authorities to separate the loyal ones from the disloyal.

The pressure from West Coast politicians and the military proved too much to bear. Opponents of forced removal, such as Attorney General Francis Biddle and FBI director J. Edgar Hoover, were outnumbered. Those in the middle, such as Stimson and McCloy, were inclined to give the military what it wanted. "You are putting a Wall Street lawyer in a helluva box, but if it is a question of safety of the country, [or] the Constitution of the United States, why, the Constitution is just a scrap of paper to me," McCloy said.[20]

The final vote in favor of the forced removal was cast on February 12 by the newspaper columnist Walter Lippmann, who for more than fifty years had spoken for the liberal establishment elite. The founder of the Council on Foreign Relations and the influential *New Republic* magazine, Lippmann through his writings had shaped the foreign policies of presidents Woodrow Wilson and Franklin Roosevelt. Lippmann met in California with DeWitt and other military officials in early February, and DeWitt easily persuaded Lippmann, who took to print with his opinion. "The enemy alien problem on the Pacific Coast, or much more accurately the Fifth Column problem, is very serious and it is very special," Lippmann wrote. "What makes it so special is that the Pacific Coast is in imminent danger of a combined attack from within and from without." Japanese ships, he continued, have been "reconnoitering the Pacific Coast more or less continually and for a considerable period of time, testing and feeling out the American defenses." There had been some incidents involving Japanese ships, but Lippmann's greater point—that there existed a serious danger of sabotage—had sprung directly from DeWitt's fevered imagination, along with DeWitt's creative explanation for why no sabotage had yet happened. "It is also a fact that since the outbreak of the Japanese war there has been no important sabotage on the West Coast," Lippmann wrote. But that was not because there was no danger. "It is a sign that the blow is well-organized and that it is held back until it can be struck with maximum effect."[21] Lippmann's column swayed the doubters, asserts Bill Hosokawa, a Heart Mountain prisoner, journalist, and author. "Almost anyone of any influence read Lippmann," Hosokawa said. "He was as responsible as anybody in swaying public opinion."[22]

By then, Biddle knew he had lost. In a February 12 letter to Stimson, Biddle washed his hands of whatever evacuation was coming. Roosevelt had already ordered the Justice Department to round up enemy aliens from Germany, Italy, and Japan, but those proclamations, Biddle wrote, did not "include American citizens of the Japanese race; therefore, the Department of Justice has no power or authority to evacuate American-Japanese." Noncitizens, Biddle wrote, could be evacuated, "but American citizens of Japanese origin could not, in my opinion, be singled out of an area and evacuated with the other Japanese." That was a matter for the Army to worry about, and "these problems are so serious that I urge you to give them immediate and careful consideration."[23]

The result, issued on February 19, was Executive Order 9066. Its brevity and vagueness reflected skilled drafting by McCloy, one of the nation's most able lawyers. The order stipulated that military leaders had the power "to prescribe military areas in such places and of such extent as he or the appropriate Military Commander may determine, from which any or all persons may be excluded." Roosevelt had effectively stripped the Justice Department of any authority over the evacuation. Nowhere did the document contain the terms "Japanese," "Japanese Americans," or "US citizens," but everyone involved knew exactly the identities of the intended targets of the order—the 120,000 people of Japanese descent, immigrants or US-born citizens, who lived on the West Coast.[24] This order forever changed the lives of my grandparents, parents, extended family, and many friends.

Japanese Americans on the West Coast knew little or nothing of the deliberations inside Washington about their lives, but they knew from the moment they learned about the Pearl Harbor attack that things for them would change dramatically. All had experienced the various types of racism directed at them from the white majority, who they believed might get violent. Many of the Japanese living outside Hawaii had no idea where Pearl Harbor was or the purpose it served. They knew, however, that the country of their ancestors had attacked the United States and that that would make the prewar discrimination seem tame.

The Saitos

My maternal grandfather, Yoshio Saito, was working in his Oakland store, the Golden Pagoda, when he heard about the attack on Pearl Harbor. He called my grandmother at home, and Fumi knew that any man with a Japanese face was at risk of being attacked by an angry mob. She grabbed my mother, who was ten, and her two brothers, twelve-year-old Al and eight-year-old Hiroshi, and headed for Oakland. My grandmother knew that escorting my grandfather with three children would protect him, because she believed vigilantes would not hurt a family with small children. "When we finally got over to Oakland," Al remembered, "my mother had a brisk, a very brisk walk and she told us not to look even left or right, just walk straight ahead and follow quickly." They found Yoshio and escorted him home without incident.[25]

Fears of violence against Japanese citizens were confirmed almost immediately by actions taken of FBI agents, who had long tracked suspected Japanese American saboteurs or spies. They swooped in to detain community leaders, such as Buddhist priests, members of pro-Japan groups, and men such as Raymond Uno's father, Clarence Uno, the secretary of the San Gabriel Valley Japanese Association, who spent most of his days helping local farmers translate documents and navigate the US bureaucracy.[26] The FBI, which had already detained Clarence's older brother, George, soon descended on Clarence's home, witnessed by ten-year-old Raymond, who saw the bulge of a gun in one agent's pocket.[27] The agents took sixteen receipt books from the San Gabriel Valley Japanese Association, lists of Japanese American organizations, a copy of *Ten Proverbs for a Good Life*, a pamphlet for a Showa Japanese textbook, and two copies of the family census.[28] Clarence Uno remained free, however, while other Japanese Americans, such as his brother, would spend years in FBI detention centers without trial. The main criterion for FBI detention was a person's status in the community, so Buddhist priests, teachers, community group leaders, and others were taken away, which effectively decapitated the Japanese American population when it needed its elders the most.

The Minetas

At home in San Jose, meanwhile, Norman Mineta's family had returned from church to gather around the radio when a news bulletin about the Pearl Harbor attack interrupted the regular music program. Soon thereafter, they sat stunned as they watched the police take away their next-door neighbor. Kunisaku, Norman's father, called the local police chief, who told him of the roundup of leaders of the Japanese community. "My father was rather insulted," remembered Norman, chuckling. "He assumed he was one of the leaders."[29]

The next day, a Monday, President Franklin Roosevelt entered the chamber of the House of Representatives to address a joint session of Congress, where he spoke these famous words:

> Yesterday, December 7th, 1941—a date which will live in infamy—the United States of America was suddenly and deliberately attacked by naval and air forces of the Empire of Japan. . . . With confidence in our armed forces, with the unbounding determination of our people, we will gain the inevitable triumph. So help us God. I ask that the Congress declare that since the unprovoked and dastardly attack by Japan on Sunday, December 7th, 1941, a state of war has existed between the United States and the Japanese Empire.[30]

Japanese American schoolchildren listened to the speech in school that day. My uncle Al said that none of the two dozen Japanese American students in his class in San Francisco's Roosevelt Junior High School were clapping after the speech.[31] In the San Gabriel Valley, Raymond Uno listened with his fifth-grade class. "I wasn't sure what was happening," he said. "I had no idea where my dad was, but he became very busy," helping members of the local Japanese American community communicate with government officials and arrange for the harvesting and storage of their crops.[32]

Fear and Loss

Fear surged through the Japanese American community during the weeks between the attack and the executive order. In Southern California, Bacon Sakatani's mother put away anything Japanese and placed a picture of Abraham Lincoln on the mantel.[33] Inside my grandparents' farmhouse in San Jose, my grandmother stuffed large newsprint photographs of Emperor

Hirohito in the wood-burning stove, along with anything else that indicated loyalty to Japan. She wanted FBI agents who came knocking on her family's door to see an all-American home. My grandfather Higuchi had already noticed signs of vandalism around their fourteen-and-a-quarter-acre raspberry farm, and a family owning neighboring land had already asked whether the Higuchis wanted to sell their farm. Around San Jose, other Japanese farmers felt the same pressure.[34] My grandmother Chiye was right to worry. No person of Japanese descent living on the West Coast could count on the white politicians to save them.

The signing of Executive Order 9066 and the imminent expulsion of the Japanese Americans thrust Setsuko into a reality for which she was unprepared. Perhaps this was the seed for her future passion for real estate and home buying. Being yanked from her home, losing her possessions, and being tossed into a prison camp proved to her how important it was to have a home of your own that could never be taken away. Adding to the pressure she must have felt was the reality that Setsuko's beauty was in many ways a commodity for her father that was expected to contribute to the family's success. In the Japanese American community, as in Japan, marriage to the right family would help further one's own family, and that message was constantly pressed upon my mother. Executive Order 9066 heightened the pressure that was already there for her.

3

Forced Removal, Exclusion Zones, and Assembly Centers

<><><><><><><><><><><><><><><><><><><><><><><><><><><><><><><><><><><><><>

President Franklin Roosevelt's issuance of Executive Order 9066 shattered the Japanese American community and scattered families hoping to avoid imprisonment across the country. As much as anything else, the order forced the separation of the two generations, as the older Nisei with options to leave rushed to the Mountain West, the Midwest, or the East Coast for jobs or school, while their older Issei parents remained rooted where they had settled. The order, so firmly rooted in paranoia, was the first step in a kind of ethnic cleansing. The pressure on the Japanese American community ruptured families up and down the West Coast. It also blew my family apart, sending my aunts and uncles scrambling to avoid incarceration.

Roosevelt's order, following the FBI's detention of community leaders, empowered the JACL and its assimilationist Nisei leaders. Most of the elders who held the community together were in FBI and Justice Department camps, their whereabouts unknown to their families and friends. The JACL collaborated with the government ostensibly to minimize the damage to the Japanese Americans, many of whom considered those leading the organization sellouts and collaborators. In turn, the JACL, backed by the federal government, persecuted Japanese Americans who dared resist incarceration or their subsequent treatment. At a time when the community needed to be unified, it was divided between the assimilationist JACL and those who believed they were being treated unfairly. In fact, these divisions have lasted for decades, hampering the community's ability to work together.

Meanwhile, Congress scrambled to pass laws to create the legal framework to enable Executive Order 9066. Money had to be appropriated to build and staff the series of temporary assembly centers that would serve as waystations to more permanent concentration camps. Other legislation was drafted that would enable the government to identify and remove Japanese Americans more easily. In the Presidio, the brass of the Western Defense Command developed maps and plans to remove 120,000 people without consulting the people who would have to move, an oversight that exacerbated the emotional and financial toll of the forced removal.

The Tolan Committee

The House Select Committee Investigating National Defense Migration began to study the ramifications of the evacuation with a series of hearings beginning on February 21, 1942. It took its unofficial name, the Tolan Committee, from its chairman, Representative John Tolan, a liberal Democrat from northern California. It was charged with examining the need to remove "enemy aliens" with ties to Japan, Germany, and Italy from their homes on the West Coast to locations inland. They started with an executive session at the Presidio with Lieutenant General John DeWitt, who continued his baseless calls to protect military installations from imminent sabotage, and heard from state and local officials, the military, and law enforcement.[1] Attorney General Earl Warren of California, who belonged to the Native Sons of the Golden West, an anti-Asian group of white Californians, also argued for the forced removal of Japanese Americans from the West Coast. California and the West Coast, Warren said, had "an alien problem" that had to be solved quickly, like a kitchen with a cockroach infestation. The Japanese, he argued, were unable and unwilling to integrate. He had assembled a collection of evidence packed with unsubstantiated claims designed to scare. Among these, he asserted that Japanese settlements near oil fields were part of a larger conspiracy to sabotage the United States and that Japanese farmers lived and worked "within a grenade throw" of US military outposts. Warren went on to frame the popularity of organizations in the Japanese American community as a mechanism for "a widespread simultaneous campaign of sabotage."[2] This hugely influential figure—the only person to be elected governor of California three consecutive times and a civil libertarian whose tenure as chief justice of the Supreme Court changed millions of lives—greased the path for forced removal based only on supposition and a racist belief in the existence of inherent racial differences between Americans of Japanese descent and the rest of the US population. He, along with dozens of other officials, referred to a so-called fifth column of potential saboteurs who were quietly biding their time until called to action.

Tolan anointed Mike Masaoka as a leader of the Japanese American community, although the JACL represented only a fraction of those subject to forced removal. The group's leadership believed it was inevitable that the government would force Japanese Americans to move, so resistance would be futile, and since most of the community's longtime leaders had already been arrested and imprisoned, the JACL was the only organization left to provide some veneer of credibility for claims that Japanese Americans had been allowed to testify. Masaoka told the committee and federal authorities what they wanted to hear. He willingly traded away the rights of Japanese Americans in the name of shared sacrifice, which he, as a resident of Salt Lake City, Utah, did not have to make. He lived outside the exclusion zone.

Masaoka was desperate to separate the JACL and himself from those of Japanese descent who could be considered suspicious. "Just to show you how Americanized we are I have an English name," Masaoka said, before entering into the record his support of an evacuation based on national security needs, even if it targeted Japanese Americans. When asked if Japanese Americans would cooperate with being removed from their homes, "Oh, yes; definitely," he said. "I think that all of us are called upon to make sacrifices. I think that we will be called upon to make greater sacrifices than any others. But I think sincerely, if the military say, 'Move out,' we will be glad to move, because we recognize that even behind evacuation there is not just national security but also a thought as to our own welfare and security because we may be subject to mob violence and otherwise if we are permitted to remain."[3]

The committee members knew any evacuation would devastate the Japanese Americans financially, so it recommended the government establish a property custodian for the evacuees. Evacuation and resettlement, the Tolan Committee report said, meant resettling the Japanese Americans on agricultural projects and possibly allowing them to bring their livestock with them.[4] However, no federal agency, not the Federal Reserve nor the Treasury Department, stepped forward with a way to save my family's farm in San Jose or any of the other homes, businesses such as my grandfather Saito's store, or farms of the Japanese Americans subjected to forced removal. Instead, the federal government, cheered on by local officials across the area, focused more on the removal of the Japanese Americans than on protecting their property; financial concerns took a back seat to national security. After all, according to the chorus coming from the military, a war was on. Eventually, the scope of the financial losses for those forced to evacuate became obvious.

Exclusion Zones

On March 2, Public Proclamation No. 1, citing Executive Order 9066 as the justification, declared the states of California, Oregon, and Washington, as well as part of Arizona, off limits to people deemed a potential threat. The proclamation relied on vague language to announce that members of suspect ethnic, primarily Japanese Americans, would be subject to removal. By singling out Western states, the proclamation was designed to hit Japanese Americans particularly hard.[5]

Events unfolded rapidly following Public Proclamation No. 1. DeWitt was the leading authority on all military matters on the West Coast, and on March 11 he created the Wartime Civil Control Administration (WCCA), which would handle the removal and relocation of Japanese Americans. The WCCA, which DeWitt put under the command of Colonel Karl Bendetsen, would operate fifteen assembly centers in West Coast states. These centers would be the first stops for Japanese Americans on their way to as yet undetermined sites elsewhere in the country.

The sites would be run by the War Relocation Authority, which was created on March 18. The authority would run ten camps: Heart Mountain in Wyoming; Gila River and Poston in Arizona; Jerome and Rohwer in Arkansas; Manzanar and Tule Lake in California; Amache in Colorado; Minidoka in Idaho; and Topaz in Utah. For the War Relocation Authority's first director, Roosevelt turned to Milton Eisenhower, the director of information at the Agriculture Department and the younger brother of Brigadier General Dwight Eisenhower, who was destined to lead Allied forces in Europe. Milton Eisenhower was an unlikely choice; a serious academic, he lacked the zeal to uproot so many people from their homes and put them in camps. Nevertheless, the momentum for creating the centers built each day, as DeWitt and his civilian allies continued to broadcast the threat of imminent sabotage.[6]

Just where the Japanese Americans would go remained unclear. Governors of the states to the east did not want them, especially if the displaced people would be allowed to move about freely. After all, multiple military officials had deemed the Japanese Americans too dangerous to remain in their homes. If they were sent to Idaho or Wyoming, where my family ended up, the governors of those states said, the evacuees had to be put in camps under armed guard. Arizona governor Sidney Osborn, whose state would house two camps, said Arizona would reject any attempt to put Japanese Americans there, arguing that they should be put in concentration camps east of the Rocky Mountains.[7] Many of the governors said they would accept the evacuees if they were housed in armed camps separate from the rest of their citizens.

Colorado governor Ralph Carr, a Republican, welcomed the Japanese Americans, however. "They are as loyal to American institutions as you and I," Carr said on February 29. "Many of them have been born here—are American citizens, with no connection with or feeling of loyalty toward the customs and philosophies of Italy, Germany and Japan."[8] Some Japanese Americans did manage to move to Colorado and find sanctuary, though the state eventually became home to the camp called Amache. Carr would lose a Senate bid later in 1942 in part because of his support for Japanese Americans.

Officials in Hawaii, where people of Japanese descent made up 37 percent of the population, told the Tolan Committee there had been no acts of sabotage on the islands before or after December 7. They debunked a rumor that Japanese collaborators had deliberately blocked the roads between Honolulu and the base to slow or stop those responding to the attack, a claim that some committee members had recited as gospel during the hearings.[9] There would be no evacuation or incarceration there, the actual site of the worst attack on US soil since the Civil War. The Tolan Committee's March 19 report notes these inconsistencies with almost a shrug, as if its authors realized they were a party to something that made no sense but that they were powerless to stop. "A profound sense of certain injustices and constitutional doubts attending the evacuation of the Japanese cannot shake the committee in its belief that no alternative remains," the report said.[10]

Lieutenant General DeWitt created military exclusion zones in early March. The affected Japanese Americans got the news of their mandated departures through a series of signs that quickly appeared throughout their neighborhoods. "Instructions to all persons of Japanese ancestry," read the signs that first appeared on March 24. The first of 108 separate exclusion orders issued by the Western Defense Command targeted the Japanese American community of Bainbridge Island, Washington, where 227 people were given six days to gather as many belongings as they could carry and report for transfer to a hastily arranged assembly center.[11]

Evacuation orders were shaped by Census Department records that identified Japanese Americans living on the West Coast. Every ten years, the census tallies the number of people living in the United States and lists their country of origin. The Higuchi family's 1940 Census listing details where Iyekichi and Chiye lived in San Jose, along with their nation of origin—Japan—just as it also listed the Italian origins of their neighbors. The census also showed that three of the Higuchi children—Kiyoshi, William, and Emily—lived at home with them.[12] Using census records enabled the military to identify quickly how many Japanese Americans lived in each town. A February 7, 1942, *New York Times* article reported, "The census data . . . would be of material aid in mopping up those who eluded the general evacuations orders."[13] Though the federal government had promised as recently as 1940 that census information would not be used to pry into the personal lives of Americans, Congress passed the Second War Powers Act in March 1942, specifically giving the government the power to use census information to help round up Japanese Americans. While previous census directors had blocked law enforcement accessing their data, the new leadership had no objections. Census officials backed the new law and turned over the data to the military.

Tom Clark, who was the Justice Department's civilian coordinator of the Enemy Alien Control Program on the West Coast, said he worked with DeWitt's team on the evacuation plans with census officials. "We took over this hotel and put these people in there and the census people began to ask where the citizens of Japanese descent lived," Clark said. "Fortunately, the census had only been taken the year before, 1940, and so they brought their own files out there. We got some big sample tables like salesmen use and they put the raw reports out on the table. Inside of, oh, sixty days they could tell us exactly the city blocks where the people of Japanese descent lived. It was amazing, their office figures from the 1940 census was within half of 1 percent of the actual figures."[14] For decades, the Census Department and its leaders lied about these actions, until academic researchers proved otherwise in 2000 and forced a formal apology from the Census Bureau.[15]

Preparing for Exile

Within hours of the evacuation order, my mother's family, the Saitos, began debating whether to remain in the country where my grandfather had lived since 1918, my grandmother since 1924, and their three children since birth. By then their oldest son, Yoshiro, had died, leaving thirteen-year-old Fumio the oldest; my mother, Setsuko, was eleven, and Hiroshi (Taisho, or "General") was eight. My grandfather seriously considered moving the family to Japan, where he traveled often for his job and where he still had relatives, including his older brother, Ryoichiro, who had returned there with his family just a few years earlier. My mother and her siblings, born in California, had never been to Japan, however. Furthermore, only a few ships owned by neutral countries such as Sweden were permitted to carry passengers from the United States to Japan; gaining a berth for five people required careful planning and fast action. Ultimately, the idea of moving my mother's family to Japan proved more daunting than the prospect of heading with their Japanese American neighbors to the assembly centers.

My grandfather Saito had luck through friends in finding a storage warehouse in the basement of the Japanese Church of Christ at 1732 Buchanan Street in San Francisco. There he stashed cabinets, wicker chairs, a vacuum cleaner, pieces of linoleum and carpet, and assorted tables, while my grandmother packed the rest of the bags to take with them. My mother, who always took particular care of her appearance, fretted about what to pack. Wherever they were going, she wanted to look her best, a standard she would strive to meet for the rest of her life. She took some of her best dresses and shoes.[16]

On March 24, my paternal grandparents, Iyekichi and Chiye Higuchi, received the news that they had anticipated for weeks. They had already been victims of racially motivated vandalism—gasoline tanks emptied, branches dragged across the driveway, chicken coops damaged—and realized they had few options besides evacuating. Unlike other Japanese Americans farmers in the area, they did not know any white families who could manage their farm while they were detained. My uncle James, who held the title to the farm with his younger brother Kiyoshi, was stationed at an Army hospital at Camp Chaffee in Arkansas. James began receiving repeated letters from his father and his attorneys begging him to release the property so they could sell it. Within two weeks, James was granted leave from his base and met with a notary in nearby Fort Smith, Arkansas, where he signed papers authorizing the sale of the Higuchi farm to Italian American neighbors. "The property we had held together for twelve years through some of the toughest times was practically given away," James wrote.[17] Iyekichi and Chiye's arguments about the farm were five-year-old Emily's first real memories of the evacuation period. My grandmother thought they should sell, because there was so much uncertainty about their future and there was no guarantee they would return to San Jose. She believed the farm would be vandalized while they were incarcerated. My grandfather was more of a risk taker and was willing to take a chance on coming back. For him, Emily said, the farm was more than a home; it was the family's livelihood.[18]

During that time, James wrote to Amy Iwagaki, the twenty-year-old daughter of Jugoro and Tsuchiye "Bessie" Iwagaki, who also owned a farm in San Jose. James and Amy had first met in May 1941, when she was invited to attend his graduation ceremony at the medical school at the University of California at Berkeley. Shortly afterward, he entered the service, and Amy had heard little from him since. But the Higuchis and the Iwagakis had plans for Amy to escape incarceration. "Unbeknownst to me, my parents and Jim's parents were thinking seriously of getting us together," Amy recalled. "Jim was as innocent as I was. His parents indoctrinated him, too." Amy received a letter from James around the time the farm was sold in April. Would she marry him? "Well, you can imagine my surprise," she said. "Considering the time and what was happening, my future was pretty much ordained." Amy and her family rushed to get her a permit to travel east to Arkansas. In early May, she boarded the train to Arkansas alone. An older white couple on the train adopted her for the journey and protected her from harassment by soldiers and angry passengers. When Amy arrived at the Fort Smith station, James was not there. He had gone to the wrong station, and Amy spent an hour waiting for the fiancé she barely knew, alone and 2,080 miles from home. They were married on May 16 in an Army chapel at Camp Chaffee with some of James's fellow officers and their wives in attendance; it had been less than a month since the Iwagakis had received their evacuation order. Surrounded by smiling white Army officers throwing rice, James and Amy rushed from the chapel and into their new lives as a married couple.[19]

James and Amy Higuchi rush from the chapel at Camp Chaffee, Arkansas, where they were showered with rice by white Army officers in James's unit. Amy had taken the train alone from California to Arkansas to avoid being sent to Heart Mountain with the rest of her family. (Higuchi family collection)

"Did I love Jim?" Amy would later write. "That word was not used in my family. We didn't say, 'Mom, I love you,' as we freely do today. We know what trust and respect means. I believe I trusted and respected Jim. Love, trust, and respect have sustained our marriage."[20]

Dorothea Lange and Estelle Ishigo: Documenting Injustice

In March, the Western Defense Command hired the noted photographer Dorothea Lange, whose 1936 *Migrant Mother* remains one of the indelible images of the Great Depression, to chronicle the evacuation and placement of Japanese Americans in assembly centers. Based in Berkeley, Lange never believed the evacuation and incarceration made sense. Nevertheless, Lange believed "a photographic record could be valuable, might possibly even make the process more humane," wrote Lange's biographer. Whoever hired Lange most likely had no idea of her previous work as a liberal social activist and simply thought she lived in California, was available, and wanted the work.[21]

Lange started shooting on March 22, working sixteen-hour days, often seven days a week, for four and a half months. She drove across California to find families piling their belongings on the sidewalks in front of their homes and visited schools where Japanese American children studied, ate lunch, and played with their Caucasian classmates. She spent at least one day in the Raphael Weill School in San Francisco, where my mother attended fifth grade, and listened to President Roosevelt's declaration of war on Japan. One of Lange's indelible images from the school showed a young Japanese American girl, hand over her heart, saying the Pledge of Allegiance. That girl would eventually meet and marry one of the Saitos' neighbors, fellow Weill student Sam Mihara, who would go on to become an ardent lecturer and activist working to preserve the memory of Heart Mountain. Lange's talent and dedication to showing the Japanese Americans within the overall context of life in California produced stunning results. "She was able thereby to demonstrate the respectability, Americanism, work ethic, good citizenship, and achievements of these people now being treated as criminals," her biographer wrote.[22]

Documenting the evacuation required stealth and endurance to evade the limits set by the military. Lange was forbidden to shoot photographs of the guard towers or machine guns. Guards often forced Lange to provide her press credentials or followed her as she worked. This harassment earned her sympathy from the prisoners, who reacted by cooperating and providing access to the cataclysmic disruption of their lives.

Though Lange's work would be of tremendous historical value, it was a disaster for the WDC. Once officials realized the depth of her work, the human pain it captured, and the corruption of American ideals it exposed, they would not allow the photographs to be a public contradiction of government propaganda in support of the evacuation. When she accepted the job, Lange agreed to give the government all her negatives, prints, and undeveloped film and to sign away her rights to access them. The government impounded Lange's project and hid the photographs from the rest of the world for the duration of the war. Lange would not see her own photographs until more than twenty years after she had taken them, on a visit to the National Archives in 1964.[23]

Another artist hired by the government was Estelle Ishigo, who joined the twenty-three thousand or so people at Santa Anita and Pomona assembly centers with her Japanese American husband, Arthur, before they were placed at Heart Mountain. Short and dark, Arthur, a Nisei, radiated an intense energy and good cheer. Estelle, a tall strawberry blonde, was the only child of an artistic older couple. She met Arthur, an aspiring actor, and fell in love, although for their 1929 wedding they had to travel to Tijuana, Mexico, to circumvent the US antimiscegenation laws, which prohibited interracial marriages in the United States. Back in Los Angeles, Arthur worked in the film industry, while Estelle practiced and taught art. When the Japanese bombed Pearl Harbor, Arthur was fired and so was Estelle, just for the crime of having the last name "Ishigo."

They faced a choice when they received their relocation notice: Arthur could go alone, or Estelle could join him. Arthur was Estelle's whole life; her family had disowned her after their wedding, and her Japanese surname made her the target of racism. She gathered her art supplies and boarded the bus to the assembly center, where she made an immediate impression. She sketched the train ride to Heart Mountain with the huddled Japanese Americans peering out the window toward the mountain.[24] Bacon Sakatani, who was thirteen when he first saw her at Pomona, remembers her as a tall and pretty woman with unmistakable white hair. Forty years later, he would rescue Estelle from poverty and revive her story, which to Heart Mountain incarcerees is a testament to the power of love and devotion. Seventy-six years later, her drawings would hang on the walls at the Heart Mountain museum, the site where she was imprisoned with my family.[25]

Forced from Home

After the Higuchi family sold its farm for pennies on the dollar, family members packed their belongings for the forced removal. Ken Iwagaki, the brother of Uncle James's new wife, Amy, came to their home with a can of paint to stencil their name and assigned family number—32206—on a duffel bag that would hold what they could take with them. My Uncle Kiyoshi removed the head of one of young Emily's hollow rubber dolls and hid a small pair of sewing scissors inside. "My mother felt she had to have scissors to keep our clothes mended," Emily said.[26] To me, it shows that Kiyoshi understood his mother enough to realize that hiding the scissors gave her the tools to nurture her children. In camp, she would use the scissors to make a purse from an old dress that Emily had outgrown and the zipper from an old pair of pants. Emily kept the purse for almost eighty years before she gave it to me.

On May 29, it was the Mineta family's turn to board the trains from San Jose. Kunisaku Mineta had already sold his prized Packard Clipper sedan, which he had bought for $1,100 in November 1941, for $3 in March 1942. "My dad's proudest possession at that point was his car," his son, Norman, recalled. Kunisaku's connections in San Jose's business community had made his family's life a little easier than were the lives of most of his fellow Issei. A business associate agreed to watch the family home, and their Caucasian friends the Linderoths picked them up and drove them to the freight yards. "They wouldn't even let us board the trains at the passenger terminal," Norman said, adding that the freight yards were four blocks from the elementary school he attended. "We were going to leave about 1 o'clock, so the kids from the school came down around lunchtime, 12 o'clock to see us off; that was fun to see them at that time. But I always thought, 'They wouldn't even let us board the trains from the passenger terminal—had to be from the freight yards.'"[27]

A devoted Cub Scout and baseball fan, Norman wore his scout uniform and carried his baseball bat and glove. The scouts wore their uniforms, because they were enlisted to carry messages on the train—separated family members were not allowed to move freely from car to car. An MP confiscated Norman's bat as he boarded the train. "I went running to my father, crying, saying, 'The MPs took my bat away!' He said, 'That's all right, we'll get it replaced.' As we were pulling out of San Jose and we were by the Santa Clara County Fairgrounds, I looked and saw these tears just streaming out of my dad's face. And I'll always remember that." That MP

Shirley Ann Higuchi holds the purse her grandmother Chiye Higuchi made in Heart Mountain using fabric from an old dress and a zipper from an old pair of pants. (Julie Abo / Higuchi family collection)

had no idea he was harassing a child who would become a cabinet official for two presidents—one a Democrat and the other a Republican.

In Hollywood, the Hoshizakis were one of the lucky families, because they had built and owned their own home and had supportive neighbors, particularly the Marshalls, an African American family who lived across the street. Keijiro Hoshizaki rented the home to the principal of the neighborhood elementary school, and the Marshalls agreed to watch over the home. With those arrangements made, the family gathered with their neighbors at the Hollywood Independent Church. They did not know where they were going, Takashi said, so his father tried to prepare for whatever they would face. "So, the word went around that everybody was buying these, I guess you would call them engineering boots, and so everybody was buying that type of footwear. And then my dad went out and bought canteens . . . well it may come to a point where we need to really move around or so on, so fill that thing up with water and it will boost our survival probability," he recalled. Japanese Americans in Los Angeles had already heard that some of their friends and neighbors had gone to the assembly center in the Owens Valley east of the Sierra Nevada mountains, which was later called Manzanar, so the Hoshizakis believed that could be their destination. "Other than that, we had no idea," Takashi said. Instead, the bus took them to the county fairgrounds in Pomona.[28]

Takashi—"Tak"—had witnessed the displacement in his neighborhood, but once in Pomona, he would hear terrible stories that hardened his outlook. He heard how some of the farmers who had been sent to

Pomona had been forced to grow and tend their crops and were sent to the assembly centers before they could be harvested. "Others harvested and sold their crops instead," he said. "That's when I started to think, 'Hey, this isn't quite right.' So, I wrote a letter back to my homeroom at high school about what had happened. That was the first seed of my 'protest.'"[29] It was also Takashi's first act of resistance, his first time standing up for his rights, a personality trait that he still practices today.

Living Conditions at the Assembly Centers

Families from San Jose, such as the Higuchis and the Minetas, arrived at the huge racetrack at Santa Anita in Arcadia, California, about twenty miles from downtown Los Angeles. Many families from Los Angeles went to Pomona, about twenty miles from Santa Anita and forty miles from downtown Los Angeles. My mother's family was an anomaly. As San Franciscans, they should have gone to the assembly center at the Tanforan racetrack south of the city and then to the camp at Topaz, Utah. But Tanforan was too crowded, and they were diverted to Pomona. This quirk of fate made it possible for my parents to meet as eleven-year-olds in their seventh-grade class at Heart Mountain. At the time, my father was intimidated by my mother's sophisticated city look, while my mother would later joke to me that she thought my father was a rugged-looking farm boy from San Jose.

They arrived to conditions that few could have imagined. The earliest arrivals at each center were stuffed into quarters that had only days earlier held the horses that raced at the tracks. Decades later the stench of the horse stalls remained stuck in their nostrils. "We were led to this stable, and there was nothing there," said Toyoko Okumura, whose family came from Los Angeles. "They just had an asphalt floor, and, oh, it smelled terrible." The Okumura family had to sleep that first night on the cement. "I thought we were coming to the end," she said. "Just lost all hope, you know." Large black insects crawled out of the stall's floors, while some stalls still had manure layered under the hay, which made shoes sink deeper into the muck.[30]

The families that arrived later received quarters in hastily built barracks located in the parking lots at each center. These were far preferable to the stalls reeking of manure and urine. However, the construction crews used green wood that shrank as it matured, leaving gaps between the planks that allowed people to see into the barracks from the outside. The barracks had

Freshly forced from their homes, a trainload of Japanese Americans disembark at the assembly center at Santa Anita, California. (National Archives)

only one light bulb, "no screens on the window, open ceilings where you could hear the noise of your neighbors, and in fact they had those boards that you could see through to your neighbor," said Bacon Sakatani.[31]

For my father's family, the Santa Anita camp was so vast and so confusing they immediately faced a crisis soon after their arrival. Five-year-old Emily went to the latrines shortly after the family arrived. Having grown up on an isolated fourteen-and-a-quarter-acre farm in San Jose, Emily had never seen so many Japanese. When she walked out of the latrine, she did not see her brother Kiyoshi and started walking to the family's barracks alone. But the rows of barracks all looked the same, and so did the thousands of Japanese American faces. Overwhelmed and confused, Emily got lost. "My mother was in really bad shape," my father, Bill, recalled. "She was scared to death of what could happen. She was going crazy." When Bill finally spotted Emily and ran toward her, she ran away, unable to recognize him amid the crowd. It was an inauspicious start to their time at Santa Anita. Soon, Emily would begin her first day of kindergarten under the bleachers at the Santa Anita racetrack, along with the future actor and television star George Takei.[32]

Knowing how my father is—so stoic and scientific—his account of his younger sister getting lost stuck with me because of his account of my grandmother's emotion and fear. It showed me a side of my grandmother Chiye Higuchi that I never knew. She had always been so durable and resilient. Knowing how scared she must have been about the potential loss of her only daughter, just hours after losing the farm they loved, fills me with anger even now.

Fumi Saito, my maternal grandmother, faced her own scare not long after arriving at Pomona. Around 5 p.m. on July 3, she began vomiting, having trouble breathing, and feeling numbness in her hands and feet. She was rushed to the center's hospital, where the doctor, Wilfred Hanaoka, a thirty-four-year-old Nisei from Hawaii, diagnosed her with a bad reaction to medicine she had taken earlier. "This patient," Hanaoka wrote in Fumi's chart, "was perfectly well until tonight at 5:10 p.m. She had some headache so she took some white pills which were prescribed for her in San Francisco," her home until six weeks earlier. "She also became extremely nauseated, began to vomit. She also became very dyspeptic and also became deaf in both ears."[33] Yoshio, her husband, told Hanaoka that Fumi's face had turned blue, and the doctor noted that she was sweating profusely.

When I think back to how my mother used to say that camp was a fun experience, I think of how she, as an eleven-year-old girl, had to watch the mother she loved so dearly wracked by vomiting and numbness. I know that this moment, amid the stench of manure and sweat at Pomona, is when the posttraumatic stress that may have affected my mother later in her life got its start. The helpless feeling that my mother must have felt, knowing that she could not help her own mother, was most likely the impetus for her need to control everything around her and for her hypervigilance.

No Comfort, Privacy Lost

Stripped of their homes and livelihoods, the newly confined prisoners steadily lost any sense of privacy they had had. They lived in either stalls or barracks with several other families, whose activities they had no choice but to listen to and see. To bathe or go to the bathroom, they had to walk yards to the latrines and showers, where the men sat at open toilets with no barriers and where both sexes had to shower in the open. "We showered at first in the shower house where the horses were showered," said Toshi Nagamori Ito, who was sixteen when she first arrived at Santa Anita. "And so there was a wall in the middle to separate the men's side from the women's side and absolutely no partitions in the shower room. So, all of us had to go there and undress, and there were all these naked women showering together." For Toshi, a Nisei who had grown up in a single-family home in Los Angeles, it was a shock. "It didn't faze my mother at all, who was used to public bathing in Japan. She just chided me all the time, 'Don't be shy. You have to take a shower, so take a shower.'"[34]

Along with the lack of privacy in the living quarters and shared bathrooms came a steady degradation of family ties caused by the system for feeding the thousands of new prisoners. Most Japanese Americans lived in homes in which the wives cooked the meals and the families ate together every day. At the assembly centers, however, each barrack was assigned to a color-coded mess hall—blue, green, orange, red, white, or yellow. Families that had eaten all or most of their meals together now were shunted individually into the mess halls, and children gathered as they would have in school. Frank Omatsu worked in the red mess hall in Santa Anita, but his family ate in the green mess hall. "That's when the family order broke down," he said. "You know, before, we all used to eat together at home, right? And we used to talk about everything. When we went into camp, we ate with our friends, and we just hoped that my dad and mother were able to eat."[35]

Military leaders responsible for the assembly centers knew they lacked the amenities necessary for any quality of life. "Assembly centers are not designed to provide suitable semi-permanent housing and other facilities," Colonel Karl Bendetsen wrote in an April 22, 1942, memo to Milton Eisenhower, the War Relocation Authority director. "They are temporary in nature. Their facilities are transitory only." When it came to the care and well-being of the newly imprisoned Japanese Americans at the centers, it would have cost too much money to provide decent facilities. Most of the centers remained open for about three months before the incarcerees were sent to their respective camps. "Assembly centers are not and cannot, without the expenditure of tremendous sums of money . . . be designed to permit the development and maintenance of a vocational, educational, recreational and social program," Bendetsen wrote. "Long residence in an assembly center is bound to have a demoralizing effect."[36] Because of his actions during the deliberations leading up to Executive Order 9066 and after its promulgation, Bendetsen has earned his place in the ranks of historical villains. The memo to Eisenhower showed his callous disregard for the lives of the people in his charge. Bendetsen cared only for the fulfillment of the mission that he knew was unjust and unnecessary.

Culture Shock in the Camps

Japanese Americans who were not used to being surrounded by so many of their own kind found the camps fascinating and somewhat frightening. Farm kids confronted kids from Los Angeles. George Yoshinaga, a high school student from Santa Clara County, remembers his arrival at Santa Anita: "When I got there it was really an experience, not just being in camp but being thrown together with people from Los Angeles, and people from Los Angeles were a lot different from those of us from places like Mountain View and San Jose, the whole lifestyle."[37] Bacon Sakatani recalls that "those Los Angeles people were really different. Boys and men, they wore zoot suits, you know the pegged pants and long coats and pachuco haircut, long haircuts, and so those people really stood out and made us even afraid of them, like they were gangsters or what."[38]

At Pomona, Shig Yabu, a ten-year-old from San Francisco, learned he had to protect himself from bullying by some of the other young prisoners who teased him for coming from Frisco or Fog City. "I thought, 'Fog City'? No, I'm really from San Francisco." One of the bigger boys from Los Angeles tried a judo move on him, and Shig managed to use the boy's size and move against him. "I wasn't trying to be a tough guy, I just wanted to keep from being beaten up." For the rest of his time at Pomona and Heart Mountain, the larger boy gave Shig a wide berth. "I think he respected me because of the fact that he thought I was wiry and strong, but I let him think that I was strong, but that's a way to protect yourself, you know."[39]

Eventually at Santa Anita, the tensions caused by the heat and by the stress of having eighteen thousand people crammed into one place boiled over. Camp administrators encouraged the prisoners to inform on each other, which exacerbated the problems among the various groups inside the camp. One prisoner, a Korean-Japanese American named Harry Kawaguchi, was suspected as one of the main informers. On August 4, after camp police started inspecting the barracks looking for allegedly stolen contraband and Japanese-language phonograph records, a fight broke out in the orange mess hall. An FBI investigation revealed the crowd had beaten Kawaguchi, who was cornered in an office and had numerous items thrown at him, including several typewriters. The riot started just as more than three thousand prisoners, including mess hall workers, makers of camouflage netting, and warehouse workers, went on strike. Another two hundred women had also converged on the police chief's office seeking an end to the snap inspections of the barracks, which were mandated in a manual written by Bendetsen.[40] Eventually, MPs stopped the riot, which also had the effect of stopping the shakedown inspections.[41]

Occasionally the monotony of the assembly centers was broken by the arrival of visitors from outside. At Santa Anita, Joe Teresi, a friend of my uncle Kiyoshi Higuchi's from San Jose State, drove from Northern California to visit. Even that bit of kindness was tinged with bitterness. "We had to meet in a special room with a table between us and Joe," recalled Emily. "When my brother and his friend reached to shake hands, the soldier standing by lowered his rifle between them, saying nothing, preventing contact. It was startling to me and made clear that we were now forcibly separated from others."[42]

At Pomona, the Marshalls, the family that was watching the family home, met the Hoshizakis along the fence on the outside of the camp with apple pie and ice cream. It was, Takashi said, "almost a shock, to see, wow, they had gone to the effort of bringing this apple pie, that pie à la mode, and bring it all the way up and having it in the nice frozen state."[43] Ike Hatchimonji remembered when a neighbor from home brought a box of chicken that he, his brother, and sister took back to the barrack and devoured. "It was delightful to have chicken, fried chicken," he said. "But my mother saw that and she was overcome"—with emotion about their generosity.[44] A visitor to Frank Sumida at Santa Anita provided a grim view of what the Japanese Americans faced. A Jewish supplier to Sumida's father's market stopped by the camp to "see us off," Sumida said. "He said, 'This is what they're doing in Germany right now to the Jews. Don't forget it.'"[45]

Leaving the Assembly Centers

By August, workers had completed building the relocation centers for the Japanese Americans, so trains full of prisoners pulled out of the stations at Pomona and Santa Anita in darkness to make the long ride. Almost eleven thousand Japanese Americans were designated for life in a place few knew anything about—Heart Mountain, Wyoming.[46] The camp newspapers presented the news about the prisoners' new destination, but the name meant little to them. Most had never been to Wyoming, and few knew anything about it.

Soldiers herded people with their scant belongings onto trains that tracked the length of California into Oregon, then east through Idaho on to Wyoming or else headed east through Arizona and north through Utah and then Wyoming. Some trains, such as the one that carried Amy Uno Ishii and her husband, even traveled as far east as Texas and Arkansas and then moved back west.[47] Any route meant at least four days riding through searing summer heat in dark cars illuminated only by the faint bulbs inside. The authorities forbade the incarcerees to open the windows or the shades, especially when they were going through towns or cities where the local residents might see inside and cause a disturbance. The prisoners sat on hard wooden seats; no one had a sleeper car; the toilets were often backed up from overuse. Toilets on other trains just emptied through a hole in the bottom of the car and onto the tracks. "Hours lagged into days," Estelle Ishigo wrote. "Then hopeless depression filled the cars. Children cried while their elders, hollow-eyed and weary, remained silent with heart-sinking despair."[48] Some of the black Pullman porters working the trains who lived each day with the reality of racism in America "were very sympathetic toward us," said Takashi Hoshizaki, who was then sixteen.[49]

Trains containing the prisoners were often diverted to sidetracks to let the higher-priority trains carrying military essentials go by. While the Western Defense Command considered the Japanese Americans too dangerous to allow them to live on the West Coast, they seemed in little hurry to move them along. The delays left the passengers wondering where they were going and whether they would ever get there. They often sat silently, as if they were awaiting a death sentence.[50]

Some of the families, such as the Unos, were traveling without their men. Clarence Uno had left Pomona early; the government wanted him to help the Issei who spoke little English adjust to the new camp. The nation that Clarence had served in World War I, whose citizenship he had fought so hard to gain, was now relying on him to help make it easier to imprison his family and fellow Japanese Americans. "It seemed like every time we moved that my mother and the kids were the only one that were there," Raymond Uno said. "My father had already gone on."[51]

The terrifying episode at Pomona when her mother had fallen ill, writhing in pain on the barracks floor, led Setsuko to stay close to her mother's side as they left the fairgrounds for the train trip. She mostly kept a watchful eye on her mother as they rode in the darkness, afraid that something bad would happen to her. As I reflect on her life now, I realize my mother grew up living with fear that started the moment she and her family left San Francisco for Pomona and then Heart Mountain.

The Higuchis remained together on the train ride north. Kiyoshi worked as an assistant in their train car. Their train stopped in Salt Lake City, where my father, Bill Higuchi, would head the University of Utah's pharmaceutical sciences department forty years later. My father remembers looking out of the window at the mountains surrounding the city.[52] No one on their train knew their final destination. Nor did Takashi Hoshizaki's fellow passengers. He peered once through the blinds to see the train had pulled into the station in Pocatello, Idaho. Only then did he realize they were going north.[53]

The trains rolled through the prairie of Wyoming's Bighorn Basin. Young Bill Shishima, eleven, looked out the windows, from which the shades were finally lifted. In this remote area, there were no townspeople to look in through the windows to see the people inside. "Big open space, looked like the middle of nowhere, just countryside," he said. "Never saw such big open space. But then when we saw the black, tarpapered barracks, I thought, uh oh, is this where we're gonna live now?"[54]

4

A New Home
in the Dust and Wind

◇◇◇

Almost fourteen thousand people of Japanese descent ended up imprisoned in northwestern Wyoming, in part because of the grandiose dreams of one of the greatest showmen of the second half of the nineteenth century—William "Buffalo Bill" Cody. He and his partners founded a town there, which they named eponymously—Cody. His new town sat on a twenty-eight-thousand-acre tract near the Shoshone River, which spilled eastward out of the Absaroka Mountains and the nascent Yellowstone National Park. Cody and his partners envisioned a resort and fertile farmland that would be irrigated by the river's abundant waters, turning the high desert soil into an agricultural paradise. Cody leveraged his show's popularity to attract residents and investors, but he could not complete the irrigation projects, and disappointed investors sued him repeatedly. Congress bailed out Cody's failed investment when it passed the Reclamation Act in 1902, creating a system of water projects that aimed to make the West open for farming and development by damming rivers throughout the West. By 1910, the Shoshone was finally dammed, and the federal government sought to lure homesteaders to the area with land grants and promises of access to water. A handful of those immigrant farmers were Issei, who first came to Wyoming to work on the railroad and stayed to farm.[1] It is hard to believe that more than one hundred years later, I spend so much time in this area that it has almost become my second home.

The War Relocation Authority (WRA) reviewed more than three hundred potential camp sites before choosing ten that would hold more than 120,000 people. The WRA's main requirement for the sites was that they consist of government-controlled land in areas that had access to water and railroad transportation but were far from major population centers. Arizona (Gila River and Poston), Arkansas (Jerome and Rohwer), and California (Manzanar and Tule Lake), held two camps each, while Colorado (Amache), Idaho (Minidoka), Utah (Topaz), and Wyoming (Heart Mountain) had one each. Heart Mountain's new residents came mostly from Los Angeles, Santa Clara County, and San Francisco. About 1,500 came from the agricultural Yakima Valley in Washington. Among the approximately 650 from San Francisco were the Saitos, my mother's family. From Los Angeles came the Uno, Matsumura, and Hoshizaki families. The Higuchi and Mineta families came from the San Jose area in Santa Clara County. Heart Mountain, along with Minidoka and Tule Lake, was located on Bureau of Reclamation lands. Heart Mountain ostensibly had access to irrigation systems, but only after the prisoners themselves finished building the irrigation channel. Even then, access to water did not guarantee successful farming. The Bighorn Basin's soil was fine and dusty, like sifted flour, and lacked nutrients. The area's few successful farmers grew mostly grain crops or sugar beets or raised cattle.[2]

On April 7, the WRA held a meeting in Salt Lake City with the governors of ten Western states who, Milton Eisenhower and the other WRA officials hoped, would agree to create "reception centers" from which the Japanese Americans could come and go freely. It quickly became obvious the governors would not cooperate. Wyoming governor Nels Smith said that if Japanese Americans were allowed to roam freely, there "would be Japs hanging from every pine tree."[3] The region's governors demanded that any Japanese Americans relocated to their states be kept in camps surrounded by armed guards. Such opposition forced the WRA to convert the intended "reception centers" into the ten camps surrounded by barbed wire.

Some Wyoming communities, however, welcomed the idea of a camp that would bring workers who could help with local irrigation projects; other communities had already lived with Japanese American railroad workers. The Heart Mountain site was equidistant from Cody, fourteen miles southwest, and Powell, fourteen miles northeast. The 2,500 residents of Cody and the 1,900 in Powell would not be too accessible to the allegedly dangerous Japanese Americans who would live there. Plus, locating the camp there would create a mini-boom in an undeveloped area, as thousands of workers, flush with cash from their paychecks, would drink in local bars, eat at local restaurants, and buy clothes in the stores that lined the main streets in Cody and Powell.[4]

My family was still in the assembly centers in Pomona and Santa Anita when work started on the camp in the second week of June 1942. Building the camp itself further delayed the completion of the Heart Mountain irrigation canal—the jobs to build the rows of barracks at Heart Mountain paid twice as much as the Bureau of Reclamation was paying workers to work on the irrigation canal. Soon, more than three thousand men had arrived from across the country to build the camp, including John and Henry Kessel, who came from Billings for jobs hauling lumber to the building site. Velma Berryman, John's girlfriend, signed on as one of the first nurses at the camp hospital after a nursing shortage forced her hospital in Billings to close.[5]

W. Lindsay Suter, an architect, moved his family from Winnetka, Illinois, to Wyoming to design and supervise the camp's construction. Suter was a perfectionist, even when it came to building rudimentary barracks for a prison community. His daughter, Alice, whom I interviewed for this project, remembered his obsessively checking with contractors on the telephone and spending long days and nights on the job site. He never, however, talked with his family about his work, which Alice believed demonstrated his special shame about building a prison camp. He kept his silence until he died at age ninety.[6] I met Alice on one of the Heart Mountain pilgrimages when we first had our multigenerational trauma discussions and realized that she, too, suffered from the mirror image of the fear that afflicted my mother's family, who felt that white people had put them in camp because they hated Japanese Americans. Now, seventy-seven years later, Alice felt that the descendants of the Japanese Americans whom her father helped imprison would hate her, too.

Near the road that ran between Cody and Powell was the railroad line that connected northwestern Wyoming with the wider world. A road perpendicular to the main road ran uphill from the lower level of the camp and included the rows of barracks that stretched toward Heart Mountain, the eight-thousand-foot peak that loomed in the distance. Those who viewed it from the south, such as from Cody, saw a heart shape, while the prisoners viewing it from the east saw a mountain that looked more like an anvil.[7] In her mind, my mother never saw the anvil, only a heart, because that was where she met my father.

Upon completion, the camp had 450 barracks arrayed on twenty blocks. Each block had two mess halls, and two twenty-by-one-hundred-foot recreation halls. The barracks had apartments that were sixteen-by-twenty

Heart Mountain rises in the distance behind the camp. One of the nine guard towers is on the right, just behind the barbed wire that surrounded the camp. (Camp, Heart Mountain and Guard Tower: Okumoto Collection, HMWF 2010.099.230, Heart Mountain Wyoming Foundation)

feet, or twenty-four-by-twenty feet for families with children. A crew working at regular speed could build a barrack in an hour, but the green wood they used shrank when it dried, just as it had at the assembly centers, and left cracks between the planks on the walls. The tar paper covering the planks did little to keep out the wind and the dust that swirled across the plain.[8] Heart Mountain was a camp—a dusty, wind-whipped prison that filled its residents with despair. They wondered when or if they would leave. "We got off that train and looked up there at the camp that was to be our home for the next—I don't know how many months—and most of the people who got off the train shed tears like you've never seen before," said Amy Uno Ishii, who was twenty-two when she and her husband arrived at Heart Mountain. Raymond Uno's cousin, her father, George, had been arrested by the FBI in the hours after Pearl Harbor and was taken to a series of detention centers without most of his family.[9] George spent the entire war in FBI detention separated from his wife and most of his children.

Camp Life

Surviving by Your Wits

The "welcome" bulletin given to new prisoners arriving at Heart Mountain on August 25, 1942, displayed the hyperbole and enthusiasm of a real estate developer's pitch for a new subdivision. The area's history with Buffalo Bill and his failed irrigation project was prominently featured, and the next spring the bulletin peppily announced that "thousands of acres now abandoned to sagebrush and cottontail rabbits will also be green and productive through the efforts of the ten thousand or more colonists from the Pacific coast who have come to play this pioneering role as their part in the nation's war effort."[10] Prisoners at all camps would have to work building irrigation channels, farming the available land, and maintaining the basic operations of the camps. Thousands were used as cheap labor on farms throughout the west to replace the young men who had gone off to war. For the Mineta family and thousands of others, this was part of the sacrifice that the JACL's Mike Masaoka had foretold. At the core of their Heart Mountain experience was a distinctly "do it yourself" component for the new prisoners in this dry, high desert. About 27,800 of the camp's 46,000 acres were considered irrigable, but only if the new residents made them so. "Much of the work to be done this winter will be in preparation of irrigation canals so that water will be available in the spring," the bulletin said. Working during the winter months on those canals promised to be grueling; workers were told that "outdoor work will be somewhat restricted during about 100 days" in which the temperatures could reach "35 degrees below zero." Not only would prisoners have to dig the irrigation ditches to supplement the meager six to eight inches of rain that fell annually on the area but they also would have to fix their own houses. "This great barracks-city, which will be the fourth or fifth largest city in Wyoming when it is filled, is the result of an intensive works program begun last May," the bulletin said, "when extensive surveys were made to explore the feasibility of the location for a project of this sort. The camp is not yet completed. Much of the finishing work will be done by the colonists themselves." The prisoners would get insulation material for the bare wood used for the walls of the barracks, which would also get screen doors and windows—ordinary amenities for the homes they had been forced to abandon were now presented to them as luxury features. The bulletin went on: "a great deal of work remains to be done in preparing barracks and opening mess halls. Everyone's cooperation will be necessary."[11]

A crew of more than 250 local men was finishing five barracks a day by September 17 and was on track to finish the entire camp by the end of that month. Inside each apartment was a wood stove vital to keeping the prisoners warm, particularly since their barrack walls provided little insulation. The stoves installed in each apartment also created a fire hazard. "Officials state that fires may be built in the stoves after installation and inspection is completed," the camp announced on September 17.[12] After the new ceilings were installed in each barrack, the residents were to nail a piece of asbestos, as far back as the 1930s a known carcinogen, "above the stove pipe before fires are built."[13] After I joined the Heart Mountain board, Bacon Sakatani asked me to help him pursue a lawsuit regarding the use of this carcinogen. Knowing that I was a lawyer, he hoped I could use my legal skills to hold the government accountable for what appeared to be the careless poisoning of the residents. I told him it would be too difficult to prove.

At Pomona and Santa Anita, the prisoners had thought the lack of privacy, the shared latrines and showers, and the mess halls that broke up the family way of eating meals were all temporary. At Heart Mountain, they realized they would have to live this way for the foreseeable future. Inside the barracks, the walls separating the family apartments did not extend to the ceilings, meaning that a crying baby in one family meant one for its neighbors. Physical intimacy proved difficult. The new beds and mattresses creaked during sex, a telltale sign that most prisoners soon recognized and tried to ignore. My maternal grandparents conceived my aunt Kathleen in the first few months at Heart Mountain. As I learned more about the details of the barracks, I wondered how they managed that while sharing such a small place with three children. Soon, families started nailing celotex to extend the walls to the ceilings. Alarmed camp administrators said that doing so prevented the workers from finishing the rest of the barracks. "Colonists who are taking celotex . . . are reminded that a number of residents are still living in unlined barracks," a camp bulletin on October 8, 1942, announced. "In the interest of common comforts they are asked to stop this practice."[14]

Women had to walk dozens of yards from their barracks to get to the shower rooms, often under the glare of the spotlights ringing the camp,

An unidentified man sits in his barrack at Heart Mountain. Many incarcerees managed to turn their spartan housing into something more livable. (Man inside his barrack room, Okumoto Collection, HMWF 2010.099.366, Heart Mountain Wyoming Foundation)

and then shower surrounded by their neighbors. Often, the new shower heads broke, leaving camp administrators to plead with residents to take better care of them or "have to forgo the luxury of shower baths." Men using the toilets sat in open rooms with no barriers, forced to defecate in front of their neighbors. The women's latrines, just like in the assembly centers, had walls but no doors. The last stall closest to the wall became the most popular, as women would wait to use that latrine only to find their neighbors had the same idea. At first, the prisoners took out their frustrations on the latrines, often punching holes in the celotex walls, scratching the windows, and taking the stoppers and chains from the wash basins.[15] Learning about these conditions showed me how little control my family members had over their surroundings and the stripping of their privacy. I often wonder how these experiences were passed down to me. Like my parents, I need my space and privacy and plenty of room around me.

With five hundred or so new incarcerees arriving each day, Heart Mountain reached its maximum population—10,767 prisoners—on

September 17, after 532 people arrived that day. "This group concluded the main bulk of the inductees," a camp bulletin announced that day. Watching over them was the 331st Escort Guard, which had 124 soldiers and three officers. While a total of almost fourteen thousand people would call Heart Mountain their home during some part of the war, there would never be more than 10,767 in camp at one time.[16]

Settling in and Living with the Elements

Many of the new arrivals found fault with their new quarters, even if they were better than the assembly center's hastily cleaned horse stalls. The tar-paper walls of the barracks provided neither insulation from the summer heat nor protection from the dust constantly whipped up by the wind. The soil that could not hold any vegetation besides grass and sagebrush blew through the air into their newly built homes. "The dust was everywhere," said Raymond Uno.[17] Takashi Hoshizaki, another of the early arrivals, explained that the construction crews building the camp had broken the sod, so "when the wind comes up the dust blows and so it was dust everywhere." Prisoners used whatever materials they could scrounge from around camp to shore up their barracks and keep out the dust.[18]

"When we got to the site, we saw that it was really a no man's land," said Frank Emi, who had owned a grocery store in Los Angeles. He, his wife, and their baby daughter arrived on a day when the wind was whipping through the camp, sending dust everywhere.[19] Amy Uno Ishii was horrified when she arrived in mid-September. "You couldn't open your mouth because all the dust would come in," she said. "You could just barely see, and the only way to keep your eyes clean was just to cry and let the tears wash your eyes out. Inside your ears, up your nostrils, you could just feel the grit and grime, and when you rubbed your teeth together, you could feel all this sand."[20]

The Higuchi family arrived at Heart Mountain from Santa Anita on September 14. "We got to Heart Mountain in the late afternoon," my father said. "We got off the train and our family was on a truck going to our barracks. We started out on block 6. That day my father fell ill." The family thought Iyekichi had suffered a heart attack. "He was lying on the floor of the barracks for a while," Bill said. "The ambulance came and took him to the hospital. That started our first day at camp." Iyekichi, however, had only acute gastroenteritis, not a heart attack.[21] Even though my parents did not know each other at the time, they were almost simultaneously experiencing their parents' distress at their new conditions; my mother had watched my grandmother collapse, while my father witnessed the physical effects of the incarceration on my grandfather.

The hospital in which Iyekichi Higuchi spent his first two nights at Heart Mountain epitomized the triumphs and the turmoil of the incarceration. At its peak, it was one of the best hospitals in Wyoming, despite its remote location and staff shortages. It had seventeen wings, five wards, three operating rooms, 150 employees, nine doctors, ten nurses, and dozens of nurse aides, but when it first opened, in August 1942, the hospital resembled a battlefield first-aid tent more than a working hospital. "We were giving baths in fire buckets," one nurse said. There was only the chief medical officer, an incarceree doctor, a senior medical student, a registered nurse, and an incarceree student nurse. Some of the most routine hospital procedures were deemed worthy of note in the first few weeks the camp was open. The *Sentinel* dutifully printed stories about the first successful appendectomies performed at the hospital.[22]

The camp hospital also made plenty of mistakes. Tsunegoro Mihara was seventy when he arrived at Heart Mountain suffering from some type of cancer, his grandson Sam Mihara remembers. The doctors thought he was getting too hydrated, so they cut off his fluids, essentially dehydrating and killing him. "They starved him to death," Sam Mihara said. Their misdiagnosis stripped the Mihara family, neighbors of the Saitos in San Francisco, of their patriarch—a loss that would be compounded when Sam's father, the journalist and editor Tokinobu Mihara, went blind from too much exposure to the sand and high winds that swept through Heart Mountain.[23]

Most of the hospital administrators were white Americans who oversaw a staff that rapidly turned over. By the end of September, the hospital had already lost its chief nurse and had limited supplies of critical medicines, which hospital administrators augmented with those bought from local businesses.[24]

Velma Berryman, the child of homesteaders in nearby Deaver, Wyoming, recalled how in the early months at Heart Mountain the hospital's poorly insulated buildings made it a "furnace—hot in the summer and icy cold in winter." Her first glimpse of the nurses' quarters almost drove her away. "It was practically empty, containing an army cot, two sheets, one blanket, one pillowcase and pillow, a nail keg to sit on and no curtain or shades on the one window." She decided to stick it out, safe in the knowledge she could always live with her parents until she found another job in Cody or Powell. "I wondered what the Japanese thought when they first laid eye on their new homes in Wyoming," she wrote in her diary. "It must have been sad. Unlike me, they had no choice but to stay."[25]

Education First

Milton Eisenhower had wanted to quit as director of the WRA from almost the moment he started the job; he objected to the entire concept of forced removal and incarceration. Before he did, however, he responded to the pleas from the presidents of the universities of California and Washington that the government do something for the Japanese American students ejected from their studies. On May 5, Eisenhower contacted the American Friends Service Committee, an arm of the Quaker Church, to create the National Japanese American Student Relocation Council.[26] He had the support of one of the incarceration's architects—Assistant Secretary of War John McCloy. "Anything that can legitimately be done to compensate loyal citizens of Japanese ancestry for the dislocation to which they have been subjected, by reason of military necessity, has our full approval," McCloy wrote to Clarence Pickett, the executive secretary of the Friends Committee, on May 21. "In particular, the suggestion for the establishment of a committee of distinguished educators to work out a program of university education in other parts of the country for Japanese-American citizens evacuated from the Pacific Coast meets with my hearty approval."[27] With that, McCloy authorized the transfer of the Nisei students to universities around the country. Heart Mountain's leaders encouraged students to apply for relocation and trumpeted their acceptance and departures to the universities that had accepted them. By July 1943, 949 students had left the camps for college in thirty-eight states; 92 came from Heart Mountain.[28]

My uncle Kiyoshi Higuchi had finished all but the last year of his studies at San Jose State University before his family was forced to sell its farm and go to the Santa Anita racetrack assembly center and then on to Heart Mountain. He planned to be a chemist, like his younger brother, Takeru, who attended the University of Wisconsin and was exempt from the evacuation. Kiyoshi had been sick during college and could not finish on time, or else he would have been in graduate school like Takeru or out of school and working like his older brother, James, a doctor in the Army. Instead, he remained on the farm, gradually regaining his strength while being nursed with home remedies by my grandmother. While the council could not spare Kiyoshi incarceration, he was able to maintain hope that he would not have to remain imprisoned for the duration of the war. He soon found a sanctuary at the University of Utah in Salt Lake City.

The Higuchis had entered the assembly center at Santa Anita on May 28, and in July my uncle Kiyoshi had received a notice that his bank balance exceeded $2,500, which was more than enough to fund his travel to and enrollment at the University of Utah.[29] Kiyoshi learned he was accepted by Utah on September 10, just three days before the family arrived at Heart Mountain. University officials were eager to show they did not share the racism that had driven Japanese Americans from the West Coast. "We believe that the attitude of this university community is such that American Citizens of Japanese ancestry, fully accepted for admission at this university, may reside here without being molested," the university's registrar wrote to Kiyoshi. By the end of the war, dozens of Japanese Americans were studying at the University of Utah.[30]

When he packed for Salt Lake City, Kiyoshi used the duffel bag on which his neighbor Ken Iwagaki had stenciled the Higuchi name and family number before the family went to Santa Anita. Before he left, Kiyoshi asked Emily if he could get her anything from Salt Lake City. She asked him to get her a doll that walked and talked, because she thought if he was out of camp, he could do anything. Kiyoshi, however, had little money to spare. I recall seeing photo albums held by Uncle James and Aunt Amy that contained letters from Kiyoshi to James asking for money to help him get through school. Higher education was critical to the Higuchis and to many other Japanese Americans, and while the family valued Kiyoshi's presence, they knew he had to finish his education. With Kiyoshi's absence, by the beginning of 1943 the Higuchis were down to four family members at Heart Mountain—Iyekichi, Chiye, William, and Emily.[31]

Norman Mineta's older brother, Albert, who had two years of college behind him before the family was sent to Heart Mountain, engineered a similar escape. The *Heart Mountain Sentinel* announced in its October 13 edition that Albert Mineta had been accepted to Drew University in Madison, New Jersey. Two other Heart Mountain prisoners left with Albert, one for the University of Wyoming in Laramie and the other for the University of Utah.[32] Some of those incarcerated at Heart Mountain continued to depart for Laramie, Salt Lake City, and the University of Nebraska, a state whose governor had resisted taking large numbers of Japanese Americans but one where officials of the educational system did not feel the same. Other students departed for universities in Minnesota and South Dakota. Even more headed to Oberlin College in Ohio, whose president sought to enroll as many Nisei students as he could.[33]

While college officials were eager to show the Nisei students that they were welcome on their campuses, some of the students had reservations. Marjorie Matsushita said she and another incarceree left on the same train to Minnesota "with a lot of GIs and their wives or girlfriends. And one lady said, 'I hear that the Japs are cutting off people's heads.' And then one lady said, 'I lost my wallet, but some Japanese person found it and returned it.' So, she was a little bit more, you know, friendly than the others. But we really kind of stayed as quiet as possible because we really felt the hostility."[34]

On October 8, James Ito, who handled the college applications at Heart Mountain, announced that he had successfully processed the applications for another group of students to leave for college. One student went to the University of Cincinnati, which started a connection between Heart Mountain and that university. Ito's announcement was auspicious, too, because Toshiko Nagamori, a student whose application he had processed, was leaving for the National Training School for Christian Girls in Kansas City, Missouri, where forty Nisei women studied during the war. Nagamori would become his wife in July 1945.[35]

The prisoners' arrival at the camps coincided roughly with the beginning of the school year, and Heart Mountain's school was slightly less improvised than those in Pomona and Santa Anita. Some of the teachers arrived from the Cody-Powell area; others came from all over the West and even as far east as New Jersey. Some prisoners also taught at the school. My uncle Kiyoshi briefly taught eighth grade before he left for the University of Utah. My uncle Al Saito, fresh from San Francisco's sophisticated schools, said "the quality of the teachers varied from very good to some that were not too good." Some of the teachers who came in were drawn to the camp because they felt an affinity for Japanese culture and had taught in Asia.[36]

Many students from rural areas found themselves competing with children who had studied in the more competitive schools in California cities. Issei parents who had already drilled the need to get an education into their children doubled down on doing so while in camp. I know that my grandmother Higuchi constantly emphasized the need for education to all

An eighth-grade homeroom class at Heart Mountain High School posing outside the school for the yearbook. *First row:* Seichi Yano, Earl Santo, Takashi Okamoto, Don Ikebe, Tom Main, William Ujiiye, Eddie Chikasuye, John Murata, Raymond Uno; *second row:* June Nakamura, Mary Tono, Amy Takano, Setsuko Saito, Meiko Sawa, Fumie Hiuga, Lilly Taketa, Chieko Nakanishi, Clara Yoshihara, Mary Ikegami, Yuriko Jio, Dorothy Nakano, Reiko Horita, Mary Ochi; *third row:* Yae Miyahara, Hiroko Morioka, Rose Sugiyama, Setsuko Teramoto, Yoshiko Kajiyama, Mae Kurasaki, Dorothea Yokota, Yuriko Nakazawa; *fourth row:* Jack Ishikawa, Richardo Ritchie, George Higa, John Ikebe, Howard Otamura, Tom Yasumi, Edward Kawahara, Toshio Dio. (Frank Hirahara / George and Frank Hirahara Collection, Washington State University)

of her children. Exhausted after working all day on the farm, my father said, she would still read to him before he went to bed. My impression was that while behind barbed wire my mother spent each day at school on high alert; she tried to impress her teachers and maintain her appearance. School was another stressful environment, and, from examining her WRA file I could see how she, my father, and the other students were constantly examined and evaluated as if they were subjects in a giant experiment, which in a way they were.

Stanley Hayami of Los Angeles, a member of the Heart Mountain High School class of 1944, wrote in his diary often about his grades and the need to excel.[37] "I think if I worked a little bit harder I might be able to get all A's," he wrote. "I always got all A's. Of course, the competition is harder here." That need to compete was heightened by the rating system for students developed by camp administrators, who ranked the students by groups based on letters of the alphabet. The most talented students were in the A category, while others were rated in categories B, C, and D. For some, the categories caused feelings of shame. Even now, as a retired judge in Salt Lake City, Raymond Uno remembers being slotted in the B group of students, while his fellow seventh graders Setsuko Saito and Bill Higuchi were in the A group. Even at the age of eleven, Raymond knew that he was being labeled once again.[38]

School administrators used a rating system called the Jones Personality Rating Scale to determine each student's placement in classes. They noted my mother's "personal grooming and physical appearance" with the highest rating of "attractive personal appearance and exceedingly careful of appearance." She also scored in the highest categories for dependability, cultural refinement, leadership, industriousness, mental alertness, thoroughness, and the ability to get along with others, in which she was rated "sociable, responsible, tactful, and adaptable to new situations." My father received high ratings, as did my uncle Al Saito.[39]

The first school at Heart Mountain opened on September 30, with 205 students in grades one through six huddling in one barrack. Because the walls did not reach the ceilings, noise from one classroom floated into the others, making it difficult to teach or learn. Some classrooms lacked blackboards. "And they pushed in, what, about twenty-four chairs with arms on them into a [barrack] room, and some of those rooms were so small that it was really a tight fit," one student said.[40] Many of the white teachers understood their subjects well but struggled to pronounce their students' names, which could explain why some of them wanted to call my mother Shirley and not Setsuko. Sprinkled among the Japanese Americans were a few Caucasian students, the children of the camp administrators and workers, whose parents elected to have them attend the camp schools because the intelligence of the Japanese American students improved the quality of the education.[41]

Since so many teachers came from outside Wyoming, the turnover rate was high. Between October 1942 and December 1943, turnover was 42 percent, and it exploded to 203 percent for the last eighteen months the camp was open. Incarceree teachers would leave when they found jobs elsewhere in the country, and Caucasian teachers often left for the service and because of the stress of being so far removed from their homes.[42]

In one of the seventh-grade classes for the A group of students were Setsuko and Bill, my parents. Two years later, in their ninth-grade class picture, both sat in the front row next to each other, a coincidence arranged by the teachers and the class photographer. Bill leans slightly away from my mother. He is wearing a cardigan, a white shirt, and work boots. My mother sits upright, wearing a white blouse, cardigan, and dark skirt, staring straight at the camera with a composure beyond her fourteen years. They both had the need to learn burned into them by their parents.

The high school opened in early October, in six buildings that made up half of block 7. A permanent high school building was under construction. More than 1,200 students were registered for classes in the junior and senior high schools. Eventually, 2,394 students were enrolled in all Heart Mountain schools. Students could take classes in twenty-five subjects ranging from US and general history to advanced mathematics and science. Most of the teachers at the high school were Americans from other parts of the country, just as in the elementary school. Takayoshi Kawahara, who had bachelor's and master's degrees from the University of Southern California, was the sole Nisei teacher. Another twelve Nisei worked as apprentice teachers for the white staff.[43]

My aunt Emily had her first three years of education at the Heart Mountain school and remembered the white teachers. One, Faye Clark, "was tall, gray-haired, friendly, and wore lots of gaudy jewelry that I admired." Sometimes she would go into Cody and buy candy for her students. One day, however, a car came for Clark, because her son Jack had been killed in the war. "She was gone for several days, and I was afraid she would not like us anymore [when she returned] but she was just the same as before."[44]

As Stanley Hayami wrote in his diary, the competition among Japanese Americans students at Heart Mountain was intense. The schools may have lacked adequate supplies and had overcrowded classrooms, but the students were pushed to excel. Some of my parents' classmates, such as Raymond

Uno and Jeanette Misaka, remember the competition and how they were not rated as highly as my parents by school administrators, even though both of them have gone on to have distinguished careers and have been honored by the Japanese government with the Order of the Rising Sun for their contributions to US-Japan relations.

Eating as a Family

After eating in the mess halls at Pomona and Santa Anita, the prisoners knew what they could expect at Heart Mountain. Few remembered fondly the institutional food from military stockpiles, such as a mysterious "three-boned fish that nobody could eat," said Frank Emi, who owned a grocery store in Los Angeles before the war. "It was terrible, and I didn't like fish anyway, so I don't think I ate maybe one or two bites of that, and that was it."[45] Other prisoners remembered getting nothing more than canned tomatoes piled on rice. Without irrigation, the land around Heart Mountain was not ready yet to produce anything to improve or supplement the dreadful food.

Family ties continued to erode, as children often chose to eat separately from their parents. "These kids or youngsters eat by themselves," said Eiichi Sakauye, who was a thirty-year-old farmer from Santa Clara County when he entered camp. "There's no child-sized plate or men-sized plate, it was all one size. You can see the amount of food is placed on the plates. It was very sad that the custom, table manners were not kept up. You can see just the children are eating by themselves, and later on, you see parents eating by themselves."[46] Dillon Myer would later report that "family meals are almost impossible in the dining halls, and children lack the normal routine home duties which help to build good discipline."[47]

The Higuchi family, my father recalled, tried hard to eat together as a family, but there were times when he would eat with the classmates who lived on his block. Most children did not care if they did not eat with their parents or about the quality of the food.[48] They would run wild from one mess hall to the other to get enough to eat, said Ike Hatchimonji, who was fourteen when he got to Heart Mountain.[49] The Saito family, however, kept their children on a much tighter leash than many in camp. They ate their meals together, just as they had done back in San Francisco. Sakauye and his fellow farmers would eventually grow enough produce to improve the food choices, but they could do nothing to improve the food that first year.[50]

Sometimes the prisoners tried to make their own food on hot plates in their barracks, which overtaxed the inadequate electrical systems. Fuses blew routinely and had to be replaced. By the beginning of October, fifty fuses were blowing out each day. In September, camp officials said one hot plate per barrack could be used, but they peeled that back to four hot plate permits per block. "Since overloaded wiring constitutes a serious fire hazard, colonists are asked for their cooperation to prevent enforcement of drastic measures," administrators warned. Camp officials required residents to apply for permits for hot plates. "Before such permit is issued," a camp announcement said, "the person should determine the need of such appliance from a doctor at the hospital," and after that they were to contact an administrator who would see if the block's circuits were overloaded.[51]

Keeping Busy in Confinement

From the time the camp opened, administrators had started various activities to keep the prisoners occupied. Many of them, particularly the older Issei, had worked almost constantly from the moment they arrived in the United States. Now many had nothing but time. Some of them, such as my grandmother Chiye, began to enjoy their enforced vacations and developed new hobbies. Chiye took English classes regularly, which improved her spotty English skills, her two surviving children, Bill and Emily, recall. Soon, there were hobby clubs devoted to carpentry, quilting, and artwork.[52] Estelle Ishigo, the Caucasian artist who had arrived in camp with her Japanese American husband and worked for the WRA depicting scenes in camp, taught art. Artists offered classes in costume drafting and fashion illustration, while class offered by a visiting ceramicist from New York drew up to three hundred people. Another woman began using the camp kiln to create pottery showing the mountain and the barracks below it. Various prisoners, both men and women, carved wooden *geta*, the traditional Japanese sandals, out of whatever wood they could scrounge in camp. Ishigo began to paint scenes of children going to school, prisoners working, and landscapes with Heart Mountain looming in the background. Frank and George Hirahara, a father and son from the Yakima Valley in Washington, started to dig under their barracks to build a darkroom where they could develop the photos they shot of camp life—a hobby in violation of the loosely enforced policy against having cameras.[53] My father recalled that Kiyoshi had brought him a camera when he visited from college, and he began shooting photographs, too. They all started to create an artistic representation of life inside the barbed wire that the government, unlike the situation with Dorothea Lange's photographs of the evacuation, could not censor.

Feeding Heart Mountain

The completion of the Heart Mountain division of the Shoshone irrigation project enabled the prisoners to start growing crops of their own to supplement and, they hoped, replace the mediocre food provided by the government. Few populations were better equipped to feed themselves. Before the war, many of the prisoners had farmed land throughout California and the Yakima Valley of Washington, raising crops that often required intense and detailed cultivation. Iyekichi Higuchi had had a raspberry farm in San Jose. James Ito, a young Nisei, had an agricultural science degree from the University of California, Berkeley. Eiichi Sakauye, who was thirty when he arrived at Heart Mountain, had run farms in Santa Clara County. Others, such as Roy Matsumura and Keijiro Hoshizaki in Los Angeles, had owned grocery stores that catered to the Japanese American community. In short, the Japanese American community knew good food and how to produce it, often coaxing profitable crops from marginal land. They now had the water to enable them to succeed.

The previous fall, Ito and two other prisoners had tested 250 soil samples from around the camp property to determine the best areas for certain crops. This matching of soil with seeds enabled the farm crew to do more than the local farmers, who often planted crops unsuitable for the area, often believing that enough water could make anything grow, even in bad soil. Ito and his team analyzed the average crop yields in Wyoming and matched them with a projected population of six thousand people at Heart Mountain, about 75 percent of the population. They also studied the Cody and Powell weather reports to determine the exact length of the growing season. They concluded that the Heart Mountain soil lacked nitrogen and "certain organic matter, as is the case in most desert areas." Ito's team solved the problem by planting legumes, using manure as fertilizer, and analyzing the soil with lime and pH tests.[54]

Prisoners and camp administrators cleared about 1,100 acres of virgin land on which the few cattle in the area had grazed previously. Guided by the prisoners who came from the Yakima Valley, which had a growing season similar to Heart Mountain's, they built small greenhouses they called "hotbeds" that were heated by sunlight and decomposing manure produced

A group of Japanese American farmers prepare the fields with Heart Mountain behind them. Many of them had owned farms in California and Washington state before going to Heart Mountain, and their skilled use of fertilizer and seeds helped make the Heart Mountain farm productive. (Farmers working on fields, Okumoto Collection, HMWF 2010.099.094, Heart Mountain Wyoming Foundation)

by the local livestock. They planted broccoli, cabbage, cauliflower, eggplant, peppers, and tomatoes inside the hotbeds and then transplanted them in May to avoid the late frosts that killed young plants. They augmented the soil with manure to add extra nitrogen. Whatever their specific methods, they grew 2.1 million pounds of produce from forty-five different crops on 638 acres of land in 1943. One of their staples was daikon, the Japanese-style white radish that glows a radioactive yellow when pickled. The next year, the farmers took 108,000 pounds of daikon, turnips, takana, and napa cabbage for pickling in one of the giant vats, which were six feet deep and eight feet in diameter, in one of the warehouses. Often, these crops went into the camp's root cellar, which stretched more than one hundred yards under the camp and had been built with logs harvested from near Yellowstone National Park, about fifty-five miles to the west of the camp. Teams of prisoners had had just seven weeks to cut trees and bring the logs back for the roof of the cellar. More than 900,000 pounds of produce were stored in the root cellar, starting with 516,000 pounds of potatoes of ninety-eight varieties. Toshi, Ito's wife, told me that the cellar was so huge they could drive a truck through it. Many of the former prisoners proudly looked back at their time at Heart Mountain as a time when they had turned desert lands green. In many ways, the ability to farm the land successfully was therapeutic for the incarcerees, because it let them believe they could control at least part of their destiny.[55] Years later, the Heart Mountain Wyoming Foundation would restore the root cellar with the help of the National Park Service and donations from private foundations and individuals. The garden at the museum is now named after James and Toshi Ito.

Heart Mountain farmers learned the extent of the area weather's unpredictability that September, when an early frost wiped out twenty-five acres of crops, including eggplant, peppers, and cabbage. For Californians, the frost proved just how short the growing season in northwestern Wyoming could be. "While the full extent of the damage is not known definitely, some crops were lost entirely, while the yield on others will be reduced because immature plants will fail to develop," Sakauye told the *Sentinel*.[56] There were many reasons why so few farmers had thrived in the Bighorn Basin, starting with the soil and lack of water and, of course, the cold snaps that could wipe out a summer's work overnight. Annual rainfall often came accompanied by violent thunder, and hailstorms could pound crops into pulp out in the fields. By late October 1943, the need to harvest the crops still in the field was urgent. Camp administrators suspended work on virtually every other project, except for the hospital and the mess halls, to send workers into the fields. By the end of their work, they had harvested the potatoes, turnips, and daikon that went into the root cellar. Without their help, agricultural chief Glen Hartman said, "It would have been virtually impossible for the regular agricultural workers to complete the harvest."[57]

Care and Controversy

On July 18, 1943, my mother, twelve-year-old Setsuko, felt feverish and had a tremendous pain in the lower right side of her abdomen. Having lost a child, their eldest son, Yoshiro, to a mysterious illness three years earlier, my grandparents took no chances. Setsuko walked hundreds of yards in the heat of the summer from the family's barrack at 2-14-B to the camp hospital, where the doctors diagnosed her with acute appendicitis and operated on her. Her doctor, Motonori "Morton" Kimura, noted that Setsuko had had a similar attack three years earlier. Setsuko and her mother, I later learned, never seemed to pay much attention to their health until it became a crisis.

My mother said very little about being in the hospital, as if it had been a blip on the screen. "I had my appendix out," she proudly told me when I was a child, and that was that. Sam Mihara, a neighbor from San Francisco, told me later that the Saito family's barrack was one mile from the hospital and that Setsuko had had to walk there doubled over in pain. I would learn from reading her WRA file that Setsuko remained in the hospital for sixteen days, causing her to get a D in physical education because of her absence and her inability to move easily afterward.[58] But she never talked about those details afterward. Two weeks later, at 7:30 a.m. on August 16, her mother, Fumi, would return to the hospital's maternity ward to deliver her fifth child, a daughter they named Yoshiko but who would later be known as Kathleen.[59]

The hospital that cared for Setsuko and Fumi had dramatically improved from the tent that first treated the prisoners when they arrived at Heart Mountain a year earlier. By the summer of 1943, it ranked among the best in sparsely populated Wyoming. Nevertheless, tensions rippled between the Caucasian medical staff and the Japanese American physicians and sometimes between the Japanese American doctors themselves, who had struggled to gain acceptance in the medical community before the war. These highly educated and well-trained physicians, who had lost their practices because of the incarceration, often resented the less-qualified white doctors and nurses who ran the hospital. The younger Nisei doctors also chafed at the authority of their Issei colleagues. Doctor Kimura, who was licensed in 1941 shortly before Pearl Harbor, criticized the skills of Doctor Fusataro Nakaya, a fifty-six-year-old Issei from Los Angeles who had received his license in 1918.

By February 1943, the hospital had a new chief nurse, Anna Van Kirk, who had spent nineteen years in Japan as a missionary before returning to the United States. She had genuine medical and administrative skills, but she also had an ability she hid from the prisoners and Japanese American staff—she spoke Japanese. "This she did not tell anyone for several weeks since she wanted to know what the Japanese were saying about the hospital," nurse Velma Berryman Kessel said. When her ability was revealed in the March 23 edition of the *Sentinel*, the prisoners believed they had a spy in their midst, and the suspicion between the staff and patients increased.

The problems boiled over on June 24, when the Japanese American medical staff went on strike. A Nisei doctor central to the strike was transferred, and the troubles subsided. The hospital resumed operations on a more even keel, but an uneasy truce remained. Just days later after the resolution of the strike, the WRA designated Tule Lake as the camp to which all of the alleged malcontents and their families would be sent. "I felt sorry for the Niseis that had to go," Kessel wrote. "We were losing a lot of our trained nurses' aides," who had to leave with family members considered disloyal.[60] Nevertheless, the hospital continued to gain more equipment and staff. By August 1944, it had seven physicians, five of whom were incarcerees; four dentists; one optometrist; eight registered nurses; three graduate nurses who were prisoners; fifty nurse's aides; and three orderlies.

Sports and Community

Starting with the assembly centers, the military and then the WRA knew that sports would help the prisoners stay busy and relatively calm. They built baseball and softball diamonds, where players from all over came together for games. Many of the Nisei had grown up watching and playing American sports, starting with baseball, and they had the time and passion to develop their games. Young prisoners like Bacon Sakatani remember watching the softball players who could deftly turn double plays as they glided around the field.[61] My father recalled that he and his friends from San Jose would watch the San Jose Zebras baseball team play in the camp's six-team baseball league.[62]

It was the Heart Mountain High School football team, the Eagles, that bound the community together the most. Football was an alien sport to the Issei, who at least had a passing familiarity with baseball in Japan, but it was the quintessentially American sport for the Nisei. It also depended on an attribute for which most Japanese Americans were not known—size. The team's coaches, led by Ray Thompson and Jack Kawasaki, emphasized game plans featuring speed and discipline, which soon paid off in a series of surprising wins against local opponents. Thompson had been a football star at the University of Wyoming, while Kawasaki had coached teams in California before his imprisonment. It took a while for the Eagles to find enough opponents willing to play them at Heart Mountain, because travel restrictions for the prisoners meant that any team playing the Eagles had to travel to Heart Mountain and play inside the barbed wire. In 1943, the team played only three games and won all three after only three weeks of practice before the season started. Not only did their coaches drill the Eagles well, but also their opponents played at a disadvantage, as they looked from the field into a sea of Japanese faces. The Eagles' one loss in 1944 came at the hands of the team from Casper, which featured a 210-pound fullback, Leroy Pierce, who outweighed each of the Eagles players by at least sixty pounds.[63]

Heart Mountain had multiple baseball fields, an ice-skating rink in the winter, and a series of basketball teams. Each issue of the *Sentinel* had an ample collection of sports stories. Some prisoners found a way to play golf, and the camp had multiple golf tournaments. For some prisoners, camp provided a chance to participate in sports they never would have encountered living on the West Coast. Kerry Cababa, the daughter of prisoners Masa and Jack Kunitomi, recalled her mother taking her and her siblings to the Polar Palace ice-skating rink in Hollywood as a child. "Later, I had an epiphany," Cababa said. "She learned to skate and had fun with it at Heart Mountain. I finally put two and two together. How else would a Nisei woman take her kids to a place in Hollywood where they skated?"[64]

My mother often talked about how she was a good volleyball player at Heart Mountain, but I wonder how much she actually played. Her hospitalization certainly limited her physical activity to the extent that it had caused her to get a D in physical education. She also stayed close to her mother, especially after her sister Kathleen was born shortly after Setsuko returned home from the camp hospital. Most of the time, Setsuko spent time mostly with her family members. I believe at some level the Saitos, as sophisticated and polished city people, felt superior to the other incarcerees, so they kept to themselves. Since my mother never really talked about camp or about relationships formed there, I believe her family remained her social circle.

The Bonds of Boy Scouts

Just as the American Legion created a bond between the veterans of World War I inside the camp and those in Cody and Powell, so too did the Boy Scouts of America. The 1940s were perhaps the highwater mark of American scouting. Troop 379, from Little Tokyo's Koyasan Buddhist Temple in Los Angeles, which was recognized as the nation's most outstanding troop by President Franklin Roosevelt in 1935, included future Heart Mountain prisoners and soldiers Kei Tanahashi and Yoshiharu Aoyama, respectively scoutmaster and an Eagle Scout.[65] Heart Mountain had several troops, as did nearby Cody. My father was a scout, and his younger sister Emily was a Brownie. Most outside troops wanted to have nothing to do with those inside the camp. Their parents either blamed the prisoners somehow for what the Japanese troops were doing to their relatives and friends fighting in the Pacific or feared an unknown danger from prisoners thought to be dangerous. But Boy Scout troop leader Glenn Livingston thought differently. He brought his scouts from Cody to Heart Mountain for one of their periodic jamborees and in so doing helped shape the history of the Japanese American incarceration and its aftermath.[66]

Livingston, Alan Simpson remembered, had said, "We're going to go out there" to Heart Mountain. "'There are three troops there,' Livingston said. 'We're going to have a jamboree and do knots. Work on our merit badges. If any of your parents don't want you to go, you tell me.' There was only one parent who didn't allow their kids to go." At the jamboree, Alan, a tall, chubby eleven-year-old, was paired with Norman Mineta. Their task was to pitch the pup tent in which they would sleep. Alan suggested digging a small moat around the base of their tent to drain any rain away from the tent, because he wanted to flood the tent of another boy he disliked. "It was no skin off my goat so I said, 'Sure,'" Norman said, "So we did, so we cut our moat and the water to exit that way. And it rained, and our moat worked perfectly, and the rainwater went to the tent below, and the tent pegs pulled and the tent came down. And this kid is sitting there going, 'He he he . . . ho ho ho . . . ha ha ha,' about the tent going down next door to us. I kept saying, 'Alan, will you please shut up so we can get some sleep!' Well, that was Alan Simpson, and we were both eleven years old." Seventy-five years later, both remember the other laughing uproariously, aware of the mischief they had caused.[67]

Not only did Alan meet the Japanese American scouts but he also met their families. He went into their barracks and ate with them. "We went several times," he said. "That barbed wire puzzled us all. We thought, 'How do you get friendly with someone when there's barbed wire and searchlights and guns and they're all aimed inside?' And it's the third-largest city in Wyoming."[68] Alan had learned one of the essential tenets of scouting—that we're all created equal—and knew that the incarceration was based on racism and fear.

He and Norman became fast friends that summer, writing each other often, even after the war ended and the Minetas returned home to California. "Out of that short experience came this wonderful, beautiful relationship," Norman said in 2019.[69] "I just love Alan"—a sentiment I have often heard Alan share about Norman, as well. I believe that these two men were meant to meet.

Running the Camps

Heart Mountain Administrators

Running Heart Mountain was C. E. Rachford, a veteran of the US Forestry Service, a branch of the Agriculture Department that also produced WRA director Dillon Myer and his predecessor, Milton Eisenhower, both of whom had been skeptical about the security concerns behind the military's claims that the Japanese Americans had to be forced from the West Coast. "Under him is a staff of experts, all of them specialists in their particular field," the camp bulletin said. "A great measure of self-government will be practiced and the Caucasian staff will act primarily in an advisory capacity." Not to worry, the bulletin continued, "the attitude of the resident Wyomingites has been encouraging. Splendid editorials regarding this project have appeared in both Cheyenne and Cody newspapers, the first city being the state capital and the second the largest in the immediate vicinity." Newspaper editorials were one thing, but the bulletin's author was apparently ignorant of Governor Smith's earlier warning that the people of Wyoming would hang unaccompanied Japanese Americans.

Many of the WRA officials bridled at the challenge of imprisoning their fellow citizens without trial, and Milton Eisenhower quit the WRA for that reason. Nevertheless, the last two paragraphs of the camp's welcome bulletin echoed Nazi propaganda. The prisoners, the bulletin concluded, faced "a long preparatory period before our labors begin to bear fruit. The entire nation will be looking on these camps as mighty experiments. The records that we establish here will no doubt play a great part in determining the manner in which we will return to civilian life after we have won this war. We are starting a new chapter in our lives here in the free, clean air of the West under fortunate and favorable circumstances. An able, sympathetic and co-operative Caucasian staff is here to help us. The rest lies in our hands."[70] Such an exhortation was not as stark as the Nazis' *Arbeit Macht Frei*—work will set you free—bent into the iron gates at Auschwitz and other camps, but the principle remained the same. It was up to the new prisoners at Heart Mountain to make the most of their time there, and if they did not, their future ability to return to the West Coast would remain in doubt.

Among the first wave of Heart Mountain prisoners was twenty-seven-year-old Bill Hosokawa of Seattle, whom I would meet at Heart Mountain after Setsuko had died and the walking trail had been named in her memory. A graduate of the University of Washington, Hosokawa had worked as a journalist for an English-language newspaper in Singapore and then in Shanghai. By July 1941, Hosokawa could tell Japan and the United States were hurtling toward war, so he found a berth on an American ship in Shanghai and returned home just weeks before the attack on Pearl Harbor. The next day, Hosokawa offered his services to the FBI, the Army, Navy Intelligence, and the Federal Communications Commission. Hosokawa was named head of the Emergency Defense Council of the JACL, a job in which he cooperated with government authorities as they prepared the evacuation. That was the type of assistance that led the JACL and its leaders to be branded as collaborators.

Hosokawa and his family were sent to the assembly center in Puyallup, Washington, where they remained for three months. Most Japanese Americans from Washington state were destined for the camp in Minidoka, Idaho, but shortly before the scheduled departure for Minidoka, the camp director summoned Hosokawa to his office and told him without explanation that he had four hours to leave for Heart Mountain. "There were four, five other fellows that were notified at the same time. I've never found any documents to tell me why I was separated from my group. But my conclusion is that the military saw me as a potential troublemaker who asked tough questions."[71]

In fact, Hosokawa was anything but a troublemaker. As the handpicked editor of the *Sentinel*, he supported the government's efforts to promote military service as well as the JACL's line that the Japanese American community needed to sacrifice in order to be accepted by Caucasian Americans. Hosokawa's background as a journalist likely made him the WRA's choice to edit the *Sentinel*, a weekly staffed by his fellow prisoners, just as the papers at the various assembly centers had been. As editor, Hosokawa could travel to Cody to meet with Jack Richard, the editor of the *Cody Enterprise*, whose presses printed the *Sentinel*.

The *Sentinel*, Hosokawa said, had three missions. First, it had to "provide the people with information. People need news. People need to understand what's going on. Without something like that, the camp would be just rife with rumors." Second, the *Sentinel* had to help lead and "get the people to thinking in a positive manner." Finally, it had to give the prisoners a voice, because outsiders "saw us as easy game, taking pot-shots at us." The *Sentinel* allowed the prisoners to respond and say, "That's a damn lie! That's a crock! This is the truth!" Just as important, however, was an additional goal—the *Sentinel* was a means by which the WRA could meet its goals, which were to inspire continued patriotism and to encourage the prisoners to support the government's relocation policies, which allowed them to move from the camps to parts of the country away from the West Coast. Hosokawa and his successors played that role enthusiastically.[72] When Hosokawa left Heart Mountain for a job in Iowa in 1943, the *Sentinel*'s farewell article noted "his assistance to the government," which "continued through evacuation."[73]

Clarence Uno had multiple responsibilities that put him squarely in the crossfire between the camp administrators, members of the JACL, and the prisoners who deeply opposed any connection with the military responsible for their incarceration. For one, he was the camp's Selective Service director, thus responsible for ensuring that all men between the ages of eighteen and sixty-four completed their draft registration. By October 1, he had reported that 2,600 of the 3,000 men in camp had notified him of their change of address to barracks inside the barbed wire.[74] By virtue of his American citizenship and status as a World War I veteran, Clarence had to live up to his own expectations and those of the community. He worked constantly to help the incarcerees maintain any control over their lives in camp.

That included his activism inside the American Legion, the group of which he was a proud member. The Legion, however, had not always returned the loyalty of Clarence and other Japanese American veterans. It led the whipping up of hysteria on the West Coast and advocated the incarceration of Japanese Americans. But while the Legion touted the false threat of sabotage, its members also shared a bond of service with Japanese Americans. On September 9, Legionnaires from Cody appeared at Heart Mountain to meet representatives of the camp's American Legion outpost—Hitoshi Fukui and Clarence Uno, whose service in the Great War had enabled them to become citizens. The Cody Legionnaires included Ernest Goppert, a local businessman, and Milward Simpson, a Republican lawyer who would become both governor of and senator from Wyoming. His son, Alan, would later become a three-term senator and longtime supporter of the Heart Mountain Wyoming Foundation along with Clarence Uno's son, Raymond. Neither Alan Simpson nor Raymond Uno knew this chance meeting of their fathers would be the first encounter in two lifetimes shaped by the incarceration.[75] Alan and Raymond regularly meet with each other now at events at Heart Mountain.

Camp Governance

The WRA created a system of self-governance inside the camp so that the prisoners would have some semblance of authority over themselves. Each block had its own captain, who served in a camp council. In essence, however, as my colleague Doug Nelson noted in his 1975 book, the council had little influence, because camp administrators and the WRA made all of the major decisions. To Heart Mountain incarcerees, "The realities of existence were not community involvement or meaningful work or self-government, but rather confinement, dependency and powerlessness."[76]

For the first year at Heart Mountain, noncitizens were not allowed to hold office in any of the camps, which only aggravated their loss of influence among the community.[77] During a series of block meetings that first September in camp, the prisoners voted 1,083 to 83 to create a panel of seven judges and two alternates to serve on the camp's court. The relatively low voter turnout reflected the skepticism many of the incarcerees felt toward the camp government. The judges were mostly "older, substantial" Issei, with the exception of the chief judge, Kiyoichi Doi, a Nisei lawyer who had previously practiced in Los Angeles and Salt Lake City. Courtrooms were built in one of the recreation halls, and a prosecutor, public defender, court clerk, and secretary were picked from a group of qualified incarcerees. The camp legal system handled violations of WRA policy and the criminal code written by the camp council, which included provisions against gambling, running a gambling house, operating a confidence game, and giving another prisoner a venereal disease. Anything more severe, such as a felony under state law, would be handled by state courts.[78]

The independence of the civilian courts inside Heart Mountain was subject to debate, since the white administrators in charge of internal security had tried to fire the Japanese American chief of the camp's police force, Ryozo "Rosie" Matsui, just weeks after the camp's opening (all of the other camps had white police chiefs). Matsui had arrived in the United States in 1916. He had worked for the chief cinematographer at MGM studios and then, without any police experience, became the assistant police chief at the Pomona assembly center. Matsui then became Heart Mountain's police chief, reporting to Robert Griffin, the director of internal security, who was annoyed by Matsui's lax attitude toward the prisoners' many alleged transgressions, such as drinking alcohol. Griffin fired Matsui, leading the entire Japanese American police force to quit. Camp director Rachford, who wanted to retire to his ranch, fired Griffin and reinstated Matsui, which stemmed the chaos and allowed him to retire in peace.[79]

Farm Labor

While West Coast farmers may have wanted to eliminate their Japanese competitors, those in Wyoming soon realized the Japanese American prisoners could alleviate the labor shortage caused by the absence of so many young men who had left to join the military. That eased some of their hostility toward Japanese Americans. In September 1942, hundreds of prisoners left to work in the bean fields throughout Wyoming. The WRA required that they receive the same pay as other workers, and the farmers agreed. Wyoming governor Nels Smith wanted the state to control the workers, but WRA officials refused, and the workers stayed in camp until the farmers bombarded Smith's office with letters and telephone calls saying that they would be ruined financially if he did not change his mind. Smith, who was in the middle of an unsuccessful reelection bid, gave in, and, to the relief of the farmers, Japanese American workers supervised by the WRA brought in the crops. The first wave of workers left camp on September 10, and others followed suit, shuttling from Heart Mountain to Powell to other farms throughout the state. They returned to camp after the harvest.[80]

Dozens of Heart Mountain students, along with some of their parents and older siblings, caused a delay in the start of classes because they were out harvesting that year's crops of sugar beets, a commodity vital to the war effort and grown through the West, particularly in the dry areas near the camp. The work was voluntary and paid more than the jobs inside the camp. That first October, camp director C. E. Rachford emphasized the need for the prisoners to participate. "Here is a real opportunity for boys 16 years of age and older to be of outstanding service to the nation, and at the same time to earn some spending money for the long winter months ahead," Rachford said.[81] Farmers in Colorado, Idaho, Montana, Oregon, and Wyoming had asked for help. Japanese Americans from Oregon had managed to avoid camp altogether by agreeing to work the sugar beet fields in eastern Oregon's Malheur County near the Idaho border, starting a community that would remain there after the war.

By the fall, more than 1,200 Heart Mountain "colonists" had left for the beet fields. The work was grueling. "Topping" sugar beets meant bending over a row of beets and pulling them from the ground with both hands, knocking beets together to knock off the dirt, and then cutting the tops off with a knife. Farmers paid $1.05 for each ton of topped beets, and most workers averaged three tons per day for a total of $3.15 a day. Jobs inside the camp paid either $12 or $19 a month, so a prisoner working in the fields could make in one week what he or she would make in camp in a month. The field work was a throwback to the early days of the Issei immigration, when Japanese workers often dominated the sugar beet fields, especially in California.[82] After the harvest was over, it was clear that this reluctant labor force had rescued the sugar beet crop. The farmers were "enthused by the adaptability and speed displayed by colonist workers," said the field representative of the Western Sugar company after the harvest.[83] In nearby Lovell, the local Commercial Club passed a resolution calling for "courteous treatment" and the "protection that is due any citizen of the United States" for anyone from Heart Mountain who worked in the sugar fields.[84]

Dillon Myer and the WRA leadership had a larger plan for the incarcerees beyond sending them on temporary jobs. He intended to "scatter" the Japanese American community across the country in order to "solve a serious racial problem by having them . . . bunched up in three or four states."[85] The WRA had job placement offices around the country that worked with local businesses eager to fill jobs vacated by men going overseas. Some of the first workers to leave Heart Mountain headed just outside the barbed wire for jobs in nearby Cody and Powell, despite the open anti-Japanese hostility in Cody, which was frequently displayed via signs prohibiting Japanese Americans from entering local businesses and restaurants. One incarceree went to work for a local print shop, while another worked at a furniture company. The following day, six more prisoners went to work at a Cody bakery or as domestics in local homes. While political pressures prevented the mass return of the Japanese Americans to their homes on the West Coast, Myer knew a demand for help existed throughout the country and that Japanese Americans could help meet that demand. Already, small Japanese American communities had started in Chicago, Cincinnati, Cleveland, Detroit, Milwaukee, and St. Louis.[86]

Prisoners also started new jobs inside camp, where incarcerees worked on the local police and fire departments and as teachers and janitors in the local schools. Norman Mineta's father, Kunisaku, became a captain of Block 24, where his family lived.[87] Clarence Matsumura found a job as a sound equipment operator running movie cameras for the camp theater and was the supervisor for the camp's collection of animals, which was

A janitor at Heart Mountain, Iyekichi Higuchi stands surrounded by children near one of the barracks. (Higuchi family collection)

called a zoo.[88] Takashi Hoshizaki, who was just sixteen, worked as a surveyor to lay out the final stretches of the irrigation channel.[89] My grandfather Iyekichi Higuchi was a janitor, while my grandmother Chiye worked in the mess hall.[90] Yoshio Saito, my maternal grandfather, used his experience as a store manager to run one of the Heart Mountain warehouses.[91]

Safe from Loyal Citizens. Now What?

By the end of the summer of 1942, most responsible members of the government had realized that the Japanese Americans at Heart Mountain and the other nine camps posed no threat to national security. The fears of an imminent Japanese attack on the United States mainland had subsided since the manic days following Pearl Harbor. College students, such as my uncle Kiyoshi, had been cleared to leave camp for universities outside the evacuation zone. No Japanese Americans had tried to sabotage anything, and instead many Nisei clamored for a chance to fight on behalf of their country, particularly those living in Hawaii, like Daniel Inouye, who wanted to join the Army the moment he left high school. Outside the core group of uniformed officers who pushed hardest for the incarceration—General Allan Gullion, Lieutenant General John DeWitt, and their obsequious deputy, Lieutenant Colonel Karl Bendetsen—the civilians leading the War Department wanted to allow the Nisei to enlist and to permit the nonthreatening incarcerees to leave the camps. Returning to their homes on the West Coast was not an option; too much hostility remained among their white former neighbors to allow that. Like my father's family, many had no home to return to. But other parts of the country needed and wanted skilled help, even in defense-related industries, and they welcomed the chance to free Japanese Americans from the tremendous injustice of the incarceration. But to determine who would be eligible to leave the camps, the WRA and the military would rely on a loyalty questionnaire that would eventually exacerbate the tensions inside the camps and displace thousands of people.

The year ended with a bitter cold snap, and the Christmas season held slightly less fear than the preceding one, which had come in the immediate aftermath of Pearl Harbor. At very least the Japanese Americans had the certainty of knowing where they were and not wondering whether they would be detained and shipped away. Still, the *Sentinel* noted, "Christmas this year is like no other Christmas we have known. Our surroundings are bleak and many of the things we cherished are gone." Nevertheless, the paper's editors wrote, millions of other Americans had also suffered during the first full year of the war. Hundreds of strangers had given gifts and donations to the prisoners at Heart Mountain. "It will do one's heart good to read of their kindness," the paper editorialized. "People such as they help to keep alive the Christmas spirit. The day has crept upon us almost unawares for there is relatively little other than the cold to remind us that we are nearing the end of December. But it is still not too late to wish each of the *Sentinel*'s friends a fine Christmas and better ones to come."[92] I remember, growing up, that my mother told me that her parents would never celebrate her birthday—January 2—because it was the day after New Year's Day. It is hard to understand how anyone would want to celebrate anything under the circumstances they lived with in the camps.

I do not fully understand what happened to my mother at Heart Mountain, but her need to be in control of her life and our relationships makes better sense to me now. When you have everything taken away from you as a child and are confined, control is the one thing you crave. I cannot imagine what it must have been like for my mother to start her period and go through preadolescence and adolescence while in captivity, with no privacy to take a shower or go to the bathroom. This must have manifested in some form of posttraumatic stress that I did not recognize as such until recently.

5

Establishing Loyalties

◇◇◇

In 1943, the first full year of Heart Mountain's existence, incarcerees confronted a government loyalty questionnaire that divided the community, a failed military enlistment drive, and pressure from the press and outside politicians that ended with a policy that segregated hundreds of so-called troublemakers, who were relocated to the camp in Tule Lake, California. The rifts that occurred during this year would endure for decades after the war and hampered the efforts to build a lasting museum at Heart Mountain. My mother always used the word "troublemaker" while describing someone who was different or somehow problematic. That imprinted the word on my brain, but I did not realize that it was a derogatory term applied to Japanese Americans by their oppressors, a term almost as bad as labeling someone a Jap.

The Loyalty Questionnaire
and the Nisei

On January 1, 1943, General George Marshall authorized an all-Nisei Army unit, setting off a chain reaction that widened the fissures in Heart Mountain's Japanese American community—and those of other camps—into a chasm. To assess whether the Nisei were worthy of recruitment, the War Department developed a questionnaire to determine the loyalty of all military-age men in the camps and Hawaii. Throughout January, various panels met to decide on the questions they believed would elicit answers that would enable them to ferret out potential traitors. Within days of the military's approval of the questionnaire, WRA director Dillon Myer had decided to adapt it for all prisoners, regardless of age or gender, to screen everyone who wanted to relocate from the camps to jobs throughout the country.[1] Lieutenant General John DeWitt opposed Myer's plan, believing that threats from sabotage still remained. "A Jap's a Jap," DeWitt told a House committee in April. "They are a dangerous element, whether loyal or not." Wrong at the beginning of the war about the alleged military dangers of the Japanese Americans, DeWitt remained stubbornly wrong now, refusing to acknowledge that neither the initial group of community leaders snatched by the FBI nor the 120,000 kept by the WRA had been proved to have done anything wrong.[2] The government used multiple methods to determine the loyalty of its Japanese American citizens. In late January 1943, the WRA gave each prisoner form 152a, called a "declaration of declination," which asked if incarcerees had attempted to go to Japan, which many of the prisoners had never visited. Next, in early February, Army representatives appeared at Heart Mountain with the so-called loyalty questionnaire bearing the stamp of the Selective Service for young men of draft age. The loyalty questionnaire, officially called the "Statement of United States Citizen of Japanese Ancestry," asked routine questions about date and place of birth, marital status, and family members. Some of the questions sought to determine a predisposition to support Japan. Question 14 asked about foreign travel, and question 18 wanted to know the respondent's ability to read, write, and speak Japanese. Questions 25 and 26 wanted to know if the respondent's birth had ever been registered with the Japanese government and whether the respondent had applied for repatriation to Japan.[3]

Questions 27 and 28 caused the most problems for the prisoners and the camp administrators. Question 27 asked, "Are you willing to serve in the armed forces of the United States on combat duty, wherever ordered?" To that question, Takashi Hoshizaki answered, "Qualified no. When my citizenship rights are restored and land-owning rights must be cleared." For a high school student, even one deeply skeptical of the reasons given for his incarceration, that showed a remarkable degree of maturity. At the moment that he filled out the questionnaire, he changed from a boy into a man. He used to tell this story in our board meetings, but I never really appreciated it until I read about it in his WRA file. I had an immediate sense of guilt for not always treating him with the deference he deserved. The entire experience seemed surreal to me. "For me, Question 27 asked if I was going to be serving in military," he said. "One of the guys asked, 'If I answer yes, am I volunteering for the draft?' He noted it looked like there was a selective service logo on the paper. So I thought about it and answered 'No.'"

92

Question 28 asked, "Will you swear unqualified allegiance to the United States of America and faithfully defend the United States from any or all attack by foreign or domestic forces, and forswear any form of allegiance or obedience to the Japanese emperor or any foreign government, power, or organization?" To that, Takashi answered "yes."[4] His answer to this question demonstrated that he exercised an incredible amount of critical thinking while making choices under duress.

The Perils of an Honest Answer

Whatever the War Department and Myer thought the questionnaire would help them accomplish, "It became rapidly apparent that the government had not thought through the implications of the loyalty review program," said the Commission on Wartime Relocation and Internment of Civilians in its 1983 report, *Personal Justice Denied*. "Not only was the program forced on the evacuees with no notice and with few answers to important questions, but the documents themselves were flawed."[5]

Answering no to either question 27 and 28 meant drawing the immediate scrutiny of military and WRA authorities with the possibility of detainment at another facility, perhaps one of those run by the FBI. Many of those who answered no to one or both of the questions did so out of confusion or resentment toward the government. "The temptation to declare a 'no' 'no' position [to Questions 27 and 28] just to maintain the dependent lifestyle in the camps was very strong indeed," former Heart Mountain incarceree Carnegie Ouye said in 1981. "In such cases the issue is survival not loyalty."[6] At the time when the questionnaire was released, young Nisei men were generally classified for the draft as 4C, the category for "enemy aliens." Many could not understand why the Army would want them to serve if it considered them the enemy. If they knew their rights would be returned to them, many, such as Takashi Hoshizaki, gladly would have entered the Army to fight for their country. But they did not believe they had a country to fight for. Many young men answered yes to both questions because they believed their enemy alien status meant they would not have to actually serve in the Army. Others, however, believed a yes answer could be interpreted as volunteering, to which they objected, because they did not want to volunteer while imprisoned or while their aging parents had no one else to help them. They feared that if they answered yes, they would be drafted and their aging, non-English-speaking parents would be left alone to fend for themselves.[7] As the government tried to satisfy the incarceration's multiple stakeholders—the Western Defense Command, the War Department, the War Relocation Authority, the Japanese American Citizens League, and the incarcerees themselves—it forced Japanese Americans to make an impossible choice between their families and the country that had imprisoned them.

Question 28 posed a complicated conundrum for those asked to respond to it. Many Issei prisoners had lost everything in their forced removal and incarceration. The US government, as well as many of the states on the West Coast, was now denying them the rights to citizenship and to own land. Their children, most of them US citizens, had lost their rights, too. Given that their rights had been rescinded, these prisoners questioned the wisdom of signing away at least a chance at a normal life in Japan, even if they did not want to go there. Answering yes to question 28 might render them stateless. "Not only had our government disregarded our citizenship but put us behind barbed wire, but now it was asking these same citizens to forswear allegiance to the Emperor of Japan and to swear allegiance to the United States as if at one time all of us had sworn allegiance to the Japanese Emperor," Ben Takeshita, a former prisoner, said in 1981.[8]

Although the military and the WRA intended the questionnaire to make it easier for incarcerees to join the Army or relocate to cities across the country, its overall effect was to heighten the tensions within the camps and to bring more unwanted scrutiny from politicians who had never considered the best interests of the Japanese Americans.

Enlisting the Nisei

The campaign to persuade Nisei men to enlist was a failure, although the War Relocation Authority attempted to cast the enlistment results in the best possible light. The fact remains that only 1,208 men out of an estimated ten thousand eligible Nisei enlisted. The WRA called the enlistees the "cream of the draft-age group," though the military had originally hoped three thousand mainland Nisei would enlist.[9] Only thirty-eight out of the seven thousand men at Heart Mountain eligible to sign registration forms joined the Army, starting with Fred Yamamoto, a writer for the *Heart Mountain Sentinel*. His mother pleaded with him to wait until he was drafted and asked him if he was ready to die. "When he said that if he were killed, he knew that he would be doing the right thing for us and for his country, I gave my permission," she said.[10]

Another early enlistee was Ted Fujioka, the president of the class of 1943 at Heart Mountain High School. His large family was influential in the camp. His sister, Masa, was married to Jack Kunitomi, the sports editor of the *Heart Mountain Sentinel* and also a leader among the twenty-something Nisei.[11] "I volunteered for many reasons," Fujioka wrote to a former teacher back home. "Probably the biggest reason which prompted me to act as I did was the realization that the success or failure of the Nisei in the armed forces would greatly determine the future of all the Nisei in America after the war."[12] The JACL and other Japanese American leaders likewise believed that the community's future standing in the United States depended on how well Japanese Americans fought on the battlefield.

Yamamoto and Fujioka may have been part of the minority of Nisei men who enlisted from camp, but that was not obvious to readers of the *Sentinel*, which highlighted the good news about enlistments while minimizing the resistance to serving in the military. Much of the *Sentinel*'s coverage stuck to the JACL- and WRA-approved storylines. Editor Bill Hosokawa, an active JACL member, and the other editors believed that Japanese Americans could free themselves from suspicion only by proving they were more American than their white fellow citizens.

The attitudes of most Nisei men ranged from ambivalent to hostile. They would serve if the government demanded it, but they would not volunteer to fight for a country that had stripped them of their rights. Many Issei parents discouraged their sons from enlisting because, according to a Naval Intelligence report, "the citizen Japanese and the alien Japanese received identical treatment. This indicates, they say, the American Government does not recognize the Nisei as full citizens."[13] Many of the Heart Mountain prisoners felt this way, even if they did not protest openly.

In Hawaii, which had had no mass evacuation or incarceration of Japanese Americans, the opening of enlistment to Japanese Americans uncorked a gusher of patriotic fervor. More than ten thousand Nisei men volunteered and three thousand young men were accepted, and the two Hawaiian National Guard units that had been kept in limbo because of the post–Pearl Harbor ban on their service evolved into the Army's 100th Infantry Battalion, which would soon head to Europe and fight some of the bloodiest battles of the war in Italy.[14]

The failed enlistment campaign aimed at the Nisei and the turmoil over the questionnaires spurred outrage from the predictable quarters of Congress. Senator Albert "Happy" Chandler of Kentucky jumped in to conduct hearings into the alleged hotbeds of disloyalty in the camps. His Military Affairs Committee somehow concluded that as many as twenty thousand prisoners were loyal to Japan, not the United States, and that the camps were a failed experiment that needed to be turned over to the Army, which presumably would impose harsher discipline on the prisoners. Dillon Myer and other top WRA leaders, Chandler claimed, were "God-fearing, honest, well-meaning American citizens, but they are theorists, they are professors, they are making a social experiment of this thing." Myer appealed to Eleanor Roosevelt, and the First Lady set up a meeting between Myer and the president, who agreed to talk to other senators to persuade Chandler to accept a plan to segregate all suspected "troublemakers" into a separate camp, which would be the one located at Tule Lake in northern California near the Oregon border. Myer reluctantly agreed, as did Mike Masaoka and the JACL. Masaoka pointed to the Kibei, the US-born Japanese Americans who had been sent for schooling in Japan before they returned to the United States, as particular targets for segregation.[15] Analysts, including Lieutenant Commander K. D. Ringle of the Office of Naval Intelligence and Curtis Munson, had often singled out the Kibei as potential problems. They had the most recent and intense experience with Japan and its culture, more than the Issei, who had voluntarily left Japan for the United States, and the Nisei, who knew only the United States. But Myer and most WRA leaders also believed that singling out the Kibei for segregation solely on the basis of their time spent in Japan was a blanket accusation of guilt without any real evidence. They successfully argued that anyone removed to a segregation camp from Heart Mountain or the other camps had to be removed for just cause, such as answering no to both questions 27 and 28 of the loyalty questionnaire.[16]

Raymond Uno's Father, Clarence

Unaware of the military's deliberations about loyalty, Clarence Uno, Raymond's father, continued his work for the war effort at Heart Mountain. Despite what the government had done to him and his family, Clarence believed in his adopted country, Raymond said. He led the Selective Service unit at Heart Mountain, was a member of the registrants' advisory board, and organized United Service Organization (USO) drives for the troops. In subzero temperatures on the night of January 21, he walked from his barracks to a mess hall to attend a USO meeting and then returned home to block 27, barrack 17, apartment B, and climbed into bed. He never woke up. "I just remember him lying here," Raymond said, "and no one came to get him." Clarence Uno, the veteran of the Rainbow Division that fought the German Army to surrender in 1918 and who lobbied for seventeen more years in order to become a citizen, had died at the age of forty-eight.[17] "It was a release from confinement, against which he showed no resentment, by a government he loved and served," the *Heart Mountain Sentinel* wrote. His devastated wife, Osako, and their three children now faced a life of uncertainty. "There are born into the world a chosen few who spend their lives in service of things they love," according to the *Sentinel*, "Clarence Uno belonged to that group. His death at forty-eight cut short a life filled with service to his country."[18]

After Clarence's death, Osako tried her best to eke out a living by working in the mess hall, while Wallace, Yuki, and Raymond tried to finish school. Clarence's funeral drew hundreds of mourners, including delegations from the American Legion posts in Cody and Powell. Hansel Mieth, a German photographer, was on assignment for *Life* magazine at Heart Mountain. One of his photographs, not seen publicly until after the war, shows Clarence lying in an open casket flanked by two Nisei soldiers.[19] The widespread, heartfelt praise for Clarence was a minor balm for his family. "I had never had to face death in the family and losing someone, especially someone as close to the family as my father, it was shocking and unexpected," Raymond said.[20]

Clarence's death radicalized his niece, Amy Uno Ishii, who was also incarcerated at Heart Mountain. "That was one of the most tragic times of my life, and I wasn't even that close to my uncle," she said. "I knew him; had been to his home; knew my aunt, and I knew my cousins and all. But just the fact that he was an American citizen, an immigrant who came and gained his American citizenship. And was so very, very proud. He was so proud to wear his Veterans of Foreign Wars' uniform, put that little hat over his forehead and march in the parades and things like that. And then to see him die in the camp, it really broke me up. That's when I said, 'Where is the justice? This is my country, just as it was his country.'"[21]

Clarence had missed the turmoil that the appearance of the loyalty questionnaire would engender at Heart Mountain and the other camps with by only a couple of weeks.

Enlisting Hawaii

Daniel Inouye

Denied the opportunity to enlist after Pearl Harbor, Daniel Inouye had matriculated at the University of Hawaii in the fall of 1942 to take premed courses. When Inouye heard the announcement that he could enlist, he and several of his university classmates "literally ran from the campus to the draft board. That's a couple of miles." His parents wanted him to stay in school, but they knew he would enlist anyway.

"I was hoping you'd stay, Dan," his father told him, when he heard the news of his enlistment.

"I can't," Inouye said. "But I'll be back. I will! And I'll pick up right where I left off."

"In fact, in most homes very quietly they must have said, *shikata ga nai*"—it cannot be helped, Inouye said later. "They anticipated this. And naturally no mother or father would want to see their sons leave and possibly not return, but they sensed the mission and, I think, approved."

Like the JACL, he believed that enlisting in the Army would show the rest of the country "once and for all that we are Americans, unhyphenated Americans. So that's why over eighty-five percent of the eligible men in Hawaii volunteered." Before he could formally enter the Army, however, Inouye had to clear a new hurdle. His interest in medicine "put me in a different category, because our nation was looking for doctors because they knew that the casualties would be high." The draft board turned him down for enlistment, because he was a student at the university. When Inouye learned why, he quit school and his job, returning to the board and saying, "I'm ready now." That made him the second-to-last enlistee in the regiment, serial number 30106416 in the first batch of enlistees from Hawaii. "I got in about three days before we left," he later recalled.

Daniel Inouye, of course, did not pick up right where he left off, nor would his fellow students and most of the 2,686 Hawaiian Nisei who sailed to the mainland as part of the first group of recruits for the 442nd Regimental Combat Team. "Many never came home at all and among those who did there were those so severely wounded that a career in medicine was out of the question," Inouye wrote later. "And so it was that of all those students who had entered the university with such high hopes, and with the hopes and prayers of their parents, not a single one ever became a doctor."[22]

Hawaiian Enlistees Reckon with the Truth

The Hawaiian enlistees in the Army boarded ships to the mainland not knowing where they would land or undergo basic training. They sailed under the Golden Gate Bridge and landed in Oakland, California, where they took trains that traveled at night to their final stop at Camp Shelby in southern Mississippi. Just as with the trains that took the Japanese Americans to the ten camps, the Nisei soldiers traveled at night so that the presence of so many Japanese faces would not alarm people in the nearby towns where anti-Japanese sentiments remained strong. "If we went through a town or city and let us off at three o'clock in the afternoon and we walked out, people might stone us, they might think we're prisoners," Daniel Inouye said. Only after starting the trip from Oakland did the Hawaiian soldiers learn that their final destination was Mississippi, a place that virtually none of them had ever visited. All they knew was that Mississippians mistreated people of color, and that, the soldiers believed, included Japanese Americans. "All these scenarios became part of our imagination," Inouye said. Instead, the white Mississippians treated them well, often inviting them into their homes. About a month after their arrival, the new troops received a proclamation from the governor of Mississippi welcoming them to the state and according them honorary white-person status, which allowed them to patronize any establishment in the state that followed Jim Crow laws.

Larger tensions existed between the soldiers from Hawaii and the mainland Japanese Americans they met upon their arrival at Camp Shelby. The Hawaiians who made up the majority of the soldiers in the 442nd acted much differently from the more reserved mainlanders. They spoke pidgin, a curious stew of English, Chinese, Japanese, Hawaiian, and Portuguese that reflected the different cultures that make up Hawaii. Meanwhile, the mainlanders, who had spent their young lives trying to blend into the white-dominated culture, spoke a much more refined English and often mocked the more happy-go-lucky islanders, which angered Inouye and his fellow Hawaiians. "What are you laughing at?" Inouye said the Hawaiians responded. Fights between the soldiers broke out often, leading some of the senior officers to consider disbanding the regiment. "And so frantically they tried all these things: psychological gatherings, discussion groups, social hours," Inouye said. Nothing seemed to work, and the fights continued.

Then the unit received invitations from the two War Relocation Authority camps across the Mississippi River in Arkansas. The Hawaiians did not know the camps existed, and the poor relationship between the mainlanders meant their new comrades who might have had families in the two camps did not tell the Hawaiians. Inouye, a corporal, was in E Company, which had received an invitation from the prisoners at Rohwer. He knew only that Rohwer had a large Japanese American community, not that people had been imprisoned against their will. Inouye and his comrades showered, put on their cleanest uniforms, and grabbed their ukuleles in hopes of catching the eyes of some of the young women in Rohwer. They hopped on the buses for the long ride to Arkansas. After they crossed the Mississippi River, the bus rounded a bend, and they saw a valley that held a huge camp with rows and rows of barracks. Inouye thought it was a military camp they would pass through on the way to the town. "But no, we came up to this camp and stopped," he said. He saw the high barbed-wire fences, machine gun towers pointing inside, and fellow soldiers carrying rifles topped with bayonets. "I thought, 'What in the world is happening?' Then you look into the camp and there they were"—thousands of his fellow Japanese Americans condemned to living in the swamps of Arkansas because of their heritage. Some of the prisoners had moved out of their barracks temporarily so that the visiting Nisei soldiers could sleep there, but the soldiers refused, saying they would sleep in trucks or the mess hall instead.

The visiting soldiers tried their best to enjoy Rohwer, Inouye said, "but it's not easy realizing what's happening there." Unlike their hosts, Americans who looked just like them, the soldiers could leave. They filed back onto their buses and rode back to Camp Shelby in total silence, listening to the sound of the bus tires on the road as they rolled the miles to Mississippi. "And I can imagine what's going through their minds, and I think all of us must have asked ourselves—would we have volunteered? That's a good question." As their commanders had envisioned, the Hawaiian soldiers who visited Rohwer immediately told their friends what they had seen. That glimpse into the lives of the mainland soldiers in their ranks created an understanding and bond that fused the unit together overnight. "Next morning you had the 442nd," Inouye said.[23]

JACL Fallout and the Mineta Family

Norman Mineta's family acutely felt the tensions between the Heart Mountain factions—one that supported the government and the JACL and a second that challenged the incarceration more openly. Etsu, his sister, was seeing Mike Masaoka, the JACL's executive director.[24] A growing percentage of Heart Mountain prisoners disliked and distrusted the JACL and Masaoka particularly, because they believed he had collaborated with the military and the WRA.[25] The appearance of the loyalty questionnaire in February only heightened suspicion of the JACL. At the height of the confusion and anger surrounding the questionnaire, Etsu Mineta boarded a bus to Salt Lake City for her Valentine's Day wedding to Masaoka, an event marked in the February 13 edition of the *Heart Mountain Sentinel.* "A wedding of wide interest will be that of Etsu Mineta, daughter of Mr. and Mrs. Kunisaku Mineta, and Mike Masaoka, national JACL secretary, tomorrow, February 14, at Memory Grove, in Salt Lake City," the story said.[26] After the article appeared, a group of dissident prisoners smashed the windows of the Minetas' apartment. "People were really sore at the JACL because they thought he was the one who engineered the evacuation," Norman Mineta said. "All the windows in our barracks building unit were broken out because people threw rocks at the window to tell us the message."[27]

The Mineta family was now, by association, in a precarious position at Heart Mountain. Norman's father, Kunisaku, had already tried to secure a departure from the camp by seeking a position teaching Japanese to servicemen. He had first sought an indefinite leave clearance on December 30, 1942, and he followed up on February 13, just hours after the attack on the family apartment.[28] One stumbling block in his attempt to leave camp was a guilt-by-association memo from government investigators earlier that year naming Kunisaku as San Jose's agent for the "*Japanese-American News*, a Japanese language newspaper published in San Francisco." Of particular concern, the memo said, was that Yasuo Abiko, the son of the newspaper's owner, "has been reported to be a very dangerous Japanese and definitely pro-Japanese in his sentiments."[29]

Kunisaku's attempts to leave Heart Mountain finally paid off later that year, in April. The University of Chicago accepted him into its program to teach Japanese to the troops preparing for the Pacific. However, he could not take his family with him. So, Kunisaku went alone, in the hopes that Kane, his wife, and Norman would soon join him.[30]

Pettiness and the *Post*

The privations of wartime—the rationing of food and gasoline, along with the shortages of staples, such as sugar—strained the entire country. Those lucky enough to get some hard-to-find item drew envy and suspicion from their neighbors. Even locked away in remote pockets of the West, the Japanese Americans did not escape such suspicion. In January, Senator Robert Reynolds, a North Carolina Democrat and virulent racist, gave a speech on the Senate floor that called for an investigation of the WRA, claiming "the Japs are getting everything," including fine bathrooms, "and our people aren't getting anything."[31] That news came as a surprise to the Heart Mountain prisoners, who had to walk through the subzero cold to use the latrines with no privacy. But such was the atmosphere early in 1943 when Earl Best, an assistant project steward at Heart Mountain, was asked to resign. "He had charge of bringing in food supplies and distributing food to the various mess halls," Bill Hosokawa said.[32] Camp administrator Guy Robertson said Best was "requested to resign for inefficiency, and neglect in removing food stored temporarily in a mess hall attic when warehouse space was made available," the *Sentinel* reported.[33] Best did not take his dismissal quietly. He headed to Denver, where he found willing listeners at the *Denver Post*, then a conservative Republican newspaper deeply suspicious of President Roosevelt, the New Deal, and Japanese Americans, who believed his claims that prisoners in the camps were living lavishly. Best also went to see Wyoming's newly elected junior senator, Edward Vivian Robertson, a Republican, of Cody. Elected in an upset the previous year, Robertson had never visited the camp, but he sensed an issue he could use against the Roosevelt administration. Robertson had learned from Best that the *Post* was going to write about the alleged excesses at Heart Mountain and promised to help.

The *Post* editors sent reporter Jack Carberry to Wyoming to nail down Best's claims about prisoners' access to rationed and scarce resources. Of Carberry, Hosokawa said, "he and his editors had their minds made up. 'There are a bunch of incompetents, pampering the Japs in the camp at Heart Mountain,' and the *Denver Post* was out to expose the camp." Best had promised the *Post* a juicy scandal, said Hosokawa, who, ironically, would join the *Post* as an editor after the war. The allegation was, "They're pampering the Japs there. They're bringing tons and tons of meat that's unavailable to the people outside the camp, and these people are living off the fat of the land. They've got a three-year supply of canned goods in the warehouse.'" Carberry, Hosokawa said, "bought that story hook, line and sinker."[34]

Carberry, armed with Best's claims and Robertson's help, made a brief visit to Heart Mountain on April 19. He went straight to a warehouse where the camp stored surplus food, saw the alleged excesses claimed by Best, and then left. He spent the rest of his investigation at the Irma Hotel in Cody. The paper's series of reports made outlandish and false claims of prisoners living in relative luxury while patriotic Americans, many with sons fighting overseas, suffered. "FOOD IS HOARDED FOR JAPS IN U.S. WHILE

AMERICANS IN NIPPON ARE TORTURED," read the headline on the April 23 edition of the *Post*.[35]

Milward Simpson, an attorney in Cody who had visited the Heart Mountain camp as a leader in the American Legion, called the *Post*'s claims groundless. He knew that the camp administrators were following the rationing rules and that any extra food came from the incarcerees' work turning the dusty fields around Heart Mountain into rich farmland. Senator Robertson had no such scruples. He used the *Post*'s stories, which he had enabled, to keep up his drumbeat against the WRA, which he and other politicians believed was coddling Japanese Americans who deserved worse treatment because of the Japanese government's attack on the United States. An immigrant from Wales and a veteran of the British Army in the Boer War, Robertson wanted to deport Japanese Americans, even those born here and who possessed something Robertson would never have— native-born citizenship. "Thus, through the *Post* Senator Robertson was supplied with a political issue that rocketed the newly elected junior senator to the front page," the *Heart Mountain Sentinel* wrote in an editorial that harshly criticized Robertson and the *Post*.

Eventually, the *Post* articles were debunked as frauds, just as their source was discredited. Earl Best, it turned out, was not Earl Best at all but Gerald Earl Coull, a Canadian citizen who had twice snuck into the United States. Japanese Americans' faces betrayed where they came from, but the details about Best's background emerged only after he was arrested and jailed in Park County, Wyoming, for forging checks. Best, the *Sentinel* reported, had "unlawfully entered the country in 1941 from Canada. It was his second offense. He had previously illegally entered the United States in 1939."

The debunking of the *Post* articles did not deter Robertson, however. He had an open line to the *Post* for his ill-informed xenophobia, a "bitter gall," the *Sentinel* said, for a man born in another country and who sought to enjoy the benefits of life in the United States. "No man can be blamed for taking advantage of his opportunities but it was not until his opportunist eyes foresaw a political future did he petition for citizenship in the United States," the *Sentinel* editorialized. "This was 14 years after arriving in Park County."[36] Robertson continued to exploit the Japanese American issue until fewer and fewer people paid attention. Wyoming voters responded by ridding themselves of him at their first opportunity in 1948, replacing him by a landslide with the Democratic candidate for senator, Lester Hunt.

Alarmism and the House Un-American Activities Committee

The *Post*'s stories, though later debunked, sparked an investigation by the reliably alarmist House Un-American Activities Committee, led by Representative Martin Dies of Texas. Although the committee was originally created to investigate Nazi activities in the United States, Dies led it into more and more divisive areas that often gave a platform to racist diatribes and extremism. The committee had collected false evidence of conspiracies from a series of right-wing and anti-Asian groups working on the West Coast and used it in its own reports without any verification. In 1942, Dies claimed that evidence seized by his staff from the Transocean News Service run by the Japanese government showed that the West Coast was still under threat of Japanese attack. No such evidence existed, but Dies remained undeterred.[37] In May 1943, Dies agreed to requests from J. Parnell Thomas, a Republican from New Jersey and Irish immigrant who had changed his last name from Feeney, and John Costello, a Los Angeles Democrat and ardent baiter of Japanese Americans, to launch a deeper investigation of suspected disloyalty and corruption in the camps. The two congressmen's "investigation" led them to call for even more punitive policies. In early May, Thomas called for the end of the policy that allowed incarcerees to relocate around the country, claiming without evidence that the Japanese Americans allowed to leave included "some whose allegiance had been pledged to the Japanese government." The committee also cited the results of the loyalty questionnaire to claim that 24 percent of Nisei men between the ages of seventeen and thirty-eight "had stated . . . that they were not loyal to the United States but held their sole allegiance to the Emperor of Japan." That was a bald-faced lie; the wording of the questionnaire was so vague and misleading that thousands of people provided answers that unfairly spurred claims of disloyalty.

By June, the committee had started its hearings and visits to various camps. The final report, issued in September, contained several accusations unsupported by any evidence. The WRA, the committee claimed, lacked experts in Japanese affairs. Of course, none of the committee members had that expertise, and those who did know about the Japanese American community, such as Ringle at the Office of Naval Intelligence, had been routinely ignored. During his testimony before the committee in Washington, however, Dillon Myer demolished most of the committee's outrageous claims, including assertions that prisoners were allowed to drive cars for pleasure, received rations of five gallons of whiskey, and received cash grants for working outside the camps. The committee nevertheless doubled down on its ignorance by claiming that the presence of judo instructors meant that officials were somehow instilling suspicious Japanese cultural virtues in the prisoners. "Judo is a distinctively Japanese cultural phenomenon," the committee's report claimed. "It is more than an athletic exercise."[38]

The committee's claims angered Heart Mountain residents. "We, the people of Japanese ancestry, can look with pride at our record," wrote the *Sentinel* in a July 17 editorial. "We challenge any individual or group, including the witch hunters of the un-American Dies committee, to find another minority with a better record in two generations. Check our delinquencies, check the relief rolls for the unfortunates who received doles; check our educational records."[39]

By the time the committee concluded its report in September, it repeated some of its baseless accusations about disloyalty, although it had watered down most of its more outrageous claims. The report endorsed the segregation policy that Myer had already instituted, called for more investigation of potentially dangerous evacuees, and encouraged "a thoroughgoing program of Americanization for those Japanese who remain in the centers," as if forcing captive people to endorse the government that had forced them into prison would be effective.[40]

Through the fog of lies and propaganda circulated by the House Un-American Activities Committee report came a minority report by Representative Herman Eberharter, a Democrat from Pennsylvania, who excoriated the committee majority. "After careful consideration, I cannot avoid the conclusion that the report of the majority is prejudiced, and that most of its statements are not proven," Eberharter wrote. He agreed with the central premise of the evacuation—that there had once existed a "danger that the West Coast would be invaded by the Japanese Army"—but maintained that that danger had evaporated once the Japanese Americans were evacuated. The entire point of the relocation had been perverted into a system of prison camps for people who had committed no crime. "The whole point of the program is to help the loyal American citizens of Japanese ancestry, and the law-abiding aliens, to leave the relocation centers after investigation, and become established in normal life," he continued. "The right of citizens to live as free men are [*sic*] part of the 'four freedoms' for which we are fighting the war." Most of the committee report, Eberharter wrote, was a lie. "Life in the relocation centers is not a bed of roses," he wrote. The prisoners worked hard for little money; they lived in plain barracks and ate ordinary food. "Because of these facts I am disturbed about some of the ridiculous charges that were made early in our investigation. Stories about the Japanese people hiding food in the desert and storing contraband in holes under their houses were shown to be ridiculous when a project was visited. However, the majority's report fails to withdraw these charges."[41]

Dillon Myer managed to stave off the attacks from Congress but had to agree to the policy that would segregate the malcontents and resisters from the regular prisoners, and a congressional resolution passed in July 1943 authorized segregation and determined all problem prisoners would be exiled to the camp at Tule Lake in northern California.

Those who had answered no to questions 27 and 28 of the loyalty questionnaire were automatically shipped to Tule Lake, while the Tule Lake prisoners who were considered loyal were transferred to other camps. Heart Mountain director Guy Robertson announced in mid-July that the removal of disloyal prisoners—about 8 percent of the population—would start on September 1. The group targeted for removal included those who had sought permission for repatriation back to Japan and had not withdrawn their requests by July 1.

Questioning Loyalty:
Tule Lake and the Segregation Policy

The segregation policy for those deemed "disloyal" was foisted on the WRA in earnest in September 1943, when the first families left Heart Mountain for Tule Lake, which was designated as the new camp for Japanese Americans considered "disloyal" because its population had the largest number of incarcerees with negative answers to questions 27 and 28 on the loyalty questionnaire. Families had to choose between remaining together and being separated, with those determined to be disloyal going to Tule Lake by themselves. Either way, the segregation forced another dislocation upon an already dislocated people. The incarceration, flawed as it was, had so far at least kept families and neighbors together. Now, additional segregation blew those connections apart. Estelle Ishigo sketched and drew people huddled in front of trucks waiting to take them to the train station and off to Tule Lake. Her painting *Disloyal* shows groups of prisoners shaking hands with their departing neighbors as Heart Mountain looms in the background, partly shrouded by clouds.[42]

The segregation program that ripped a thousand people from Heart Mountain and deposited them in Tule Lake "broke apart the community of evacuees by forcing each to make a clear choice—a choice that could be made only by guesswork about a very uncertain future," the *Personal Justice Denied* report said. "It divided families and friends philosophically, emotionally and, finally, physically, as some went east to make new lives and others were taken off to the grimmer confinement of Tule Lake."[43]

As a child and young adult, I knew nothing about Tule Lake or the other camps. Through my research and experience with Heart Mountain, I learned about how deeply the segregation experience had scarred the incarcerees at Tule Lake and their children. They carry the anger from their double mistreatment by the government, first their forced evacuation and incarceration and then their placement in the worst of the ten camps.

At Tule Lake, which suddenly held all the people considered "malcontents" in what was now the largest of all camps, there was a series of protests and strikes. Unlike the prisoners at the nine other camps, those at Tule Lake were deemed disloyal and condemned to remain behind the barbed wire for the duration of the war. Their one chance to leave would come if they renounced their citizenship and sailed back to Japan. They were treated with increased suspicion by the guards, which led to continued protests and riots and which led only to further isolation. After a strike by agricultural workers, the administration replaced them with "loyal" prisoners, including one hundred from Heart Mountain who were allowed to leave even though they had previously been denied leave clearance. Myer visited in late October and early November, just in time to witness a full-blown riot among the population. As in Santa Anita, where the prisoners rioted, the military police swept through the barracks, threw incarcerees in the stockade, and clamped down on those suspected of sympathizing with Japan.

Notes in the *Sentinel* marked the wrenching apart of friends and families. "To all our Heart Mountain friends may we take this means to extend our sincerest appreciation for the generosities and kindnesses shown us during our residence here," wrote Zaishin Mukushima, a Buddhist minister from Los Angeles, and his family. Mukushima would eventually resettle in Chicago and start a Buddhist temple there after the war. "We bid you all our fondest farewell as we leave for Tule Lake."[44] Takeo Teragawa, the hardworking Issei dentist, also bid farewell; he had lost faith in the United States and wanted to be sent back to Japan, although he died of cancer before he ever got the chance. "I also wish to thank you all for the many kindnesses extended to me while residing here," Teragawa wrote.[45]

Incarceration affected my parents' families in different ways. My grand-father Saito would never have been sent to Tule Lake, because he used the skills he had developed as a merchant in San Francisco, in what would be now considered international trade, to ingratiate himself with the camp administration and settle into the white man's world. The Higuchi family, whose three oldest sons were either already in the military, in college, or in war-related industries, stuck to the rules and answered yes to the most relevant loyalty questions. For twelve-year-old Bill Higuchi, however, the subsequent segregation and transfer of "loyal" incarcerees from Tule Lake to other camps meant a "family [from Tule Lake] moved in with boys my age, and I had new friends there."[46] The Heart Mountain administration now had to welcome hundreds of new incarcerees who were facing their third upheaval in less than two years. They had first been forced from their homes and into an assembly center, then sent to Tule Lake, and finally, because the officials did not want to keep the "loyal" Tule Lake prisoners with those deemed disloyal, moved on to Heart Mountain, which welcomed them with block parties and dances. Camp director Guy Robertson, his wife, and the other camp administrators held a party in the high school auditorium for the "ex-Tuleans," including door prizes.[47] Between early August and late September, 903 Heart Mountain residents left for Tule Lake. Of these, 352 were adult aliens, 309 were US citizens, and 242 were children. Camp administrators relaxed, believing they had excised the worst elements from Heart Mountain.[48]

By mid-October, camp administrators wanted to exorcise the bad spirits caused by segregation. Only Japanese Americans deemed loyal remained at Heart Mountain, and the WRA's purpose, camp director Guy Robertson said, was to relocate Japanese Americans not just from the West Coast but from the camps and into the society as a whole. Young Nisei men and women were encouraged to relocate eastward. "One of the things I most fear," Robertson said, "is that the general public will begin to believe that the loyal young people, in particular, are not sincere. People will begin to say, 'If these young people are loyal why do they remain in the center?'"[49] Many responded; the Heart Mountain archives show that a steady stream of incarcerees left the camp throughout the rest of the war.

6

Relocation

Motivating People to the Middle

The communities of Japanese Americans that clustered on the West Coast
had long perplexed and angered Caucasians who lived there and believed
they posed an intractable racial and social problem. Despite the multiple
pieces of evidence to the contrary—Japanese American student leaders,
doctors, lawyers, and businessmen in white society—there was a widespread belief that Japanese Americans could not assimilate and become
true Americans. Within days of the signing of Executive Order 9066,
Dorothy Swaine Thomas, a sociologist at the University of California,
Berkeley, had secured grants from the Rockefeller Foundation to study the
forced evacuation's role in Americanizing young Japanese Americans for
which "the dispersal of these young people of Japanese descent is a necessity. . . . Their break with Japan will be and should be complete."[1] Dillon
Myer, the head of the War Relocation Authority, agreed. He believed the
forced removal of Japanese Americans from the West Coast gave the government the authority to disperse the community throughout the country and to force its members to assimilate in places where they would have
few Japanese Americans with whom to associate. Myer exploited the labor
shortages that affected most communities throughout the country to encourage Japanese Americans to leave the camps for jobs in the East and the
Midwest.[2] He created forty-two offices throughout the country to facili-
tate relocation by helping incarcerees find jobs and housing. The WRA's
chief employment officer said the authority was just running a series of
temporary boarding houses for West Coast Japanese Americans until they

could find jobs in other parts of the country and that Heart Mountain residents needed to step up their attempts to leave camp—prisoners in Amache, Topaz, and Minidoka were relocating faster than those from Heart Mountain.[3]

The *Sentinel* did its part. As part of its mission to motivate the camp population to move on, it published dozens of articles touting the low cost of living in midwestern cities, the availability of civil service jobs in Washington for Nisei, and the availability of help for Nisei young women who wanted to move to Chicago, one of the major hubs for Japanese American relocation. Often, the *Sentinel* more closely resembled a brochure for a midwestern chamber of commerce than a newspaper.

By the middle of 1943, the relocation arm of the War Relocation Authority found another gear. "More and more outside offers continue to flood the employment office," said an August 19, 1943, supplement of the *Heart Mountain Sentinel*.[4] Most of the available jobs were in the industrial Midwest, where the same labor shortage that empowered women in the workplace, giving rise to Rosie the Riveter, had created numerous opportunities for the Japanese Americans.

My parents' families never tried to relocate, and their WRA files show nothing to suggest that they ever considered life outside California or Heart Mountain. My father's three oldest brothers either had never been incarcerated because they were in the Army or in college or left for college soon after arriving at Heart Mountain. My mother's parents had four young children, including a newborn, so they decided to remain at Heart Mountain, wait for the end of the war, and return to San Francisco, where my grandfather Saito had stored some of the family's belongings in a church basement.

Many of the jobs for those who did relocate involved living with the new employers, another sign of the comfort many people outside the West Coast had with Japanese Americans. A farm owner in Crosby, Texas, sought a couple to work the farm. "Tenant home provided, lights and water," said the ad. "Duties to milk two cows, feeds 3 hogs and farm truck garden. Plans to share produce 50–50, field crops 50–50. Will allow family eggs, milk and weekly share of chickens; will pay $25 monthly to man and $15 to wife."[5]

This was exactly what Myer and WRA administrators wanted. Each time a prisoner left a camp for a job outside, it was another victory for those who wanted to mitigate the incarceration or, in Myer's case, promote the assimilation of Japanese Americans into mainstream American culture, an erasure of the Japanese from Japanese American. In July, the *Sentinel* reported, 352 prisoners had left, including 25 girls who traveled to Ogden, Utah, to harvest a bumper crop of apricots. Another 40 men were set to go the Ball Mason plants in South Dakota to help make jars and boxes to hold food that would be shipped overseas to US troops.[6]

Other opportunities promised potentially high salaries to men making only $16 to $19 a month in camp. An ad from Chicago sought four store managers at wages from $2,600 to $20,000 a year. Chicago, where Kunisaku Mineta had moved to teach Japanese to members of the military, had a particularly strong pull. Companies there offered jobs such as messenger boy for a steel company, which paid $100 a month, and work as a porter or an assistant baker at $80 a month. One Chicago company sought fifteen to twenty foundry men to work forty-eight-hour weeks with time and a half for overtime. Some prisoners, however, headed to Chicago solely to escape camp and find other opportunities. The *Sentinel* reported that "many evacuees are being denounced as 'six-week Japs,' inferring that they accept employment for only a short period of time in order to be given their indefinite leaves."[7]

Some of the Nisei who left to work on farms complained that working conditions were little better than those in camp. Men who left to work on a farm in Cozad, Nebraska, returned to Heart Mountain after spending weeks in a fifteen-by-fifty-foot room with twenty other men. They slept on "beds" that were little more than shelves with thin mattresses fixed as bunks. They had just four feet to walk between the bunks and little freedom to do anything outside other than work. Many of the farm's overseers were racists, often calling them Japs. When they complained, their bosses threatened to call the FBI and have them taken away. Two workers told the *Sentinel* that the WRA, in its zeal to relocate as many incarcerees as possible, "doesn't investigate the employers as well as employees." Jack Nishimoto, however, who had contracted with the Cozad farmers to find workers, responded that some of the workers expected too much from their employers and that the food and conditions were acceptable.[8] Nishimoto would surface again the next year as an FBI informant reporting on other Heart Mountain prisoners.[9]

Many of the prisoners who helped the camp function found jobs outside the exclusion zone. Bill Hosokawa left his job as editor of the *Sentinel* for a job in Des Moines with the *Register*, the city's well-regarded newspaper.

The article about his departure detailed much of Hosokawa's cooperation with the government authorities in the days immediately following Pearl Harbor, his work with the JACL, and his "steadying influence not only to Heart Mountain residents but to readers in other centers as well."[10]

Despite the proliferation of job opportunities, however, not everyone in camp found the right match. Clarence Matsumura, trained as a radio technician, initially applied for leave on February 17, 1943, shortly after the WRA teams with loyalty questionnaires came to camp. His application for leave clearance listed his top three interests as radio service work, electrical employment, and returning to college. His top three cities were Philadelphia, Chicago, and New York. While multiple opportunities existed for jobs outside camp, they were not forthcoming for Clarence. Although it was sent directly to Dillon Myer, his application for leave languished. By August 1, he was pleading with Joe Carroll, chief of the employment division at Heart Mountain, for help. "Mr. Matsumura would appreciate anything you can do to expedite his EDC clearance and also his clearance by the Provost Marshal General's Department of the War Department for work in war industries," Carroll wrote to the WRA's relocation supervisor in New York.[11] The response came on August 17 from New York: Despite his numerous pleas, a check of the Eastern Defense Command clearance list showed Clarence had not received his clearance. Once the clearance went through, a relocation supervisor wrote Carroll, "we are sure that Mr. Matsumura will encounter no difficulty in obtaining employment."[12]

But he did. When the approval for Clarence to leave finally came, on September 21, it was not for work in the radio or electronics industries or on the East Coast, as he had dreamed. Instead, he received a permit to leave Heart Mountain as part of a work crew for the Northern Pacific Railroad in Emery, Washington. He had come full circle; his father, Roy, had arrived in the United States in 1906 to work on the railroads in Wyoming. Thus, one member of the Matsumura family was back where the family had started.[13]

The Mineta Family in Chicago

Like millions of other American families, the war effort separated the Mineta family. Kunisaku moved to Chicago to teach Japanese to US troops, while his family was forced to remain at Heart Mountain. The separation seemed particularly painful and unnecessary, since the Minetas' oldest daughter, Helen, was already living in Chicago and working as an accountant. The government finally relented in late November and let Kunisaku make his family whole again. Twelve-year-old Norman and his mother, Kane, prepared to leave for Chicago in December. "The Army said, 'OK, we'll let you out,'" Norman said. The two of them walked out of camp to the road between Cody and Powell, where they boarded a Trailways bus to Billings, Montana, for the train to Chicago. "My mother got a hotel room right across the street from the train station," Norman said. It was the New Oxford Hotel, which was owned by the Japanese American Higa family. "At dinner time, we went to a little restaurant next door to the hotel, and when we got through dinner, I started stacking the dishes like I was in camp to take it over to where the dirty dishes had to be bused. And my mother said to me, 'Norman, you don't have to do that anymore.'"[14] This was Norman's first taste of freedom outside camp.

Chicago had become the unofficial capital of Japanese Americans during the war. Like most American cities with a noticeable Japanese American population, Chicago saw some vigilante violence after Pearl Harbor. Vandals attacked a Japanese-owned business, and the mayor ordered the city's twenty-five Japanese lunch houses closed. But Chicago's businesses needed workers, and Japanese Americans filled the gaps. Virtually every edition of the *Sentinel* featured a report about life in the Second City, whether focusing on the plethora of jobs available for willing workers or describing the city's open acceptance of Japanese Americans. "Chicago's strength is reflected in the healthy sign that that huge municipality recognizes its shortcomings and is ready to face them instead of burying them deeper in tenement districts, shoving them deeper and deeper into the dark recesses where the purifying light of sunshine and understanding cannot reach," the paper wrote in a February 26 editorial about race issues. "Naturally, our interests are with the minority groups since we form a growing part of Chicago's population."[15] In his new job, Kunisaku Mineta experienced the full sweep of the city. Although he taught Japanese to soldiers studying at the University of Chicago in the southside neighborhood of Hyde Park, the family lived on the more fashionable north side, in Evanston, the home of Northwestern University. Each day, Kunisaku would leave home at five in the morning, take the elevated train downtown, and transfer to another line to go to Hyde Park. Once a month, Norman would join his father at the university, and they would often stop on the way home at a Japanese grocery to buy takuan, a pickled radish that "stinks to high heaven," Norman recalls. The takuan would be placed in a wax carton that failed to hold its smell, and the Minetas would board the train for home. "People on the train start to sniff, sniff, 'What's that awful smell?' So, you look nonchalantly at the ground as though you don't know what's going on. But as soon as we got to the Foster Street station, we'd pick up that thing and run off the train."

Kunisaku urged his son to continue studying Japanese, although Norman resisted. Speaking Japanese in public was dangerous, even in relatively cosmopolitan Chicago. "I don't want to study Japanese," Norman told his father. Just study the lessons at home, Kunisaku said, and his youngest son complied.[16]

I always considered Norman Mineta an optimistic person. This was reflected in the photos I saw of him taken before he went to the camp and even during the time he was incarcerated as a child. This sunny disposition would help make him an accepted leader for the rest of his life.

To the University

By the middle of 1944, more than three thousand Nisei students had transferred to at least 550 colleges and universities around the country. Clarence Matsumura, who had left Heart Mountain in September 1943 to work on the Northern Pacific Railroad, finally got his chance to attend college in January 1944, when he joined the fifteen students who had been accepted by the University of Cincinnati. Clarence first got a job at Cincinnati's Friends Hostel, where Japanese Americans who had found work in the city started out. Then he tried to enroll in college. "Clarence is hoping to relocate now," the WRA's Cincinnati relocation officer wrote the university. "He is a citizen of the United States and any courtesy which you can show him will be greatly appreciated."[17] The WRA's letter took pains to separate Clarence from the alien Japanese who were not citizens, which the government did not do at the beginning of the war when it lumped Nisei citizens with their immigrant parents.

Clarence Matsumura's Cincinnati interlude lasted only a few months. Two months after he started his studies there, the WRA office in Cincinnati was notified that Clarence was entering the Army.[18] He passed his pre-induction physical and would go back to Heart Mountain, the camp he had worked so hard to leave, to visit his family before he entered the Army. In September, he was inducted at Camp Atterbury in central Indiana, not far from Cincinnati, and a few months later he went on to Europe as part

Clarence Matsumura stands next to a sign for the 522nd Field Artillery Battalion, the artillery component for the all-Nisei 442nd Regimental Combat Team. Matsumura's unit helped liberate Jewish prisoners on a death march from their work camp near Dachau. (Sheila Newlin)

of the 522nd Field Artillery Battalion, the artillery component of the 442nd Regimental Combat Team.[19]

Even more than one thousand miles from camp, events at Heart Mountain could cause problems for students who had left for Cincinnati. In 1944, Frank Inouye, who had been studying at the University of Cincinnati since the end of 1943, was banned from the campus by the Army provost marshal in a letter to the National Japanese American Student Relocation Council.[20] The university cited unknown security reasons somehow related to the presence of secret war-related research on campus, the *Sentinel* reported.[21]

Inouye's reputation as a potential troublemaker had preceded him, it seems. While he had answered the loyalty questionnaire to the satisfaction of the authorities, he had also started Heart Mountain's first dissident group, the Heart Mountain Congress of American Citizens, whose members later went on to form the Fair Play Committee, a dissident group with lasting influence. Despite his banishment from campus earlier that summer, Inouye wrote a column in the *Heart Mountain Sentinel* in August touting the success of the student relocation council. "When, in the not-too-distant future, the Nisei survey the fields of employment which are open to them, and find it much easier to pursue their inclinations than before the war, it will have been largely through the efforts of the national Japanese American student relocation council," he wrote. When his loyalty to the United States was later firmly established, Inouye was allowed back on campus and later graduated.[22]

7

Resistance

Perpetuating the Lies

Lieutenant General John DeWitt and his staff, specifically Colonel Karl Bendetsen, took stock of their work on the evacuation and incarceration to produce what they labeled the "Final Report." A thick 664 pages, the report assembled the same farrago of exaggerations, statistics, euphemisms, and outright lies that usually characterized the work of the Western Defense Command. So driven were DeWitt and his associates to justify their belief that the Nikkei community threatened national security that they continued to cite events, such as surreptitious radio transmissions from the mainland to Japanese ships at sea, that had long ago been debunked or were simply never supported by the evidence.[1] Before the issuance of Executive Order 9066, DeWitt and company claimed Japanese collaborators had blocked roads in Hawaii to slow down rescue crews; local Hawaiian police disproved those claims to the Tolan Committee in March 1942.[2] That did not stop DeWitt from repeating them.

DeWitt sent the report to the assistant secretary of war, John McCloy, on April 15 with a cover letter that said its contents might help with the upcoming legal challenges to the incarceration. But once McCloy received the report, he realized it had a fatal flaw. In its second chapter, the report asserted that it was "impossible to establish the identity of the loyal and the disloyal with any degree of safety" and that the military lacked the time to separate "the sheep from the goats." But McCloy knew that the Army and the WRA were in the middle of a process specifically aimed at separating the loyal from the disloyal. McCloy knew the claims about the impossibility of separating the loyal and the disloyal and the lack of time were a problem, since they were racist and contradicted earlier War Department statements.[3]

McCloy had Bendetsen and other aides track down all copies of the report and DeWitt's cover letter and destroy them. He also asked DeWitt to send him a second cover letter, dated June 5, to replace the first one. All versions of the earlier reports, notes, documents, and letters were destroyed, because they would implicate the government in an obvious lie. Meanwhile, copies of the report were being leaked to government lawyers to help them prepare for their briefs in the court challenges of the incarceration by Mitsuye Endo and Fred Korematsu, which were heading to the Supreme Court in 1944. The revised and cleaned-up report was released in January 1944, but a lone copy of the original remained deep in the file cabinets of the Justice and War departments.[4]

A year after Clarence Uno died in his sleep, his youngest son, Raymond, now thirteen, felt lost and was missing his father while his mother, Osako, worked constantly in one of the mess halls to make enough money to support the family. Osako had spent all of 1943 battling government and banking bureaucracies to retrieve whatever money Clarence had saved at the time of his death. Throughout 1944, she struggled to get the documents and other personal effects the FBI agents had taken from the Uno home when they visited shortly after the Pearl Harbor attack. On January 25, the WRA reported that it had located seven boxes and two trunks of Clarence's property at a warehouse in Los Angeles.[5] That was ten months after Osako had sent the authority a form asking it to ship the belongings to her at Heart Mountain.[6] By July, the belongings still had not arrived. A note on a July 19 form said they were being held as they waited for instructions.[7]

As his mother struggled to regain her late husband's belongings and to support herself, Raymond studied hard, feeling the competitive pressure of performing among so many strong students, including Setsuko Saito and Bill Higuchi. His family life deteriorated, because his mother, sister, and brother were never in the same place at the same time: "I remember when my mother came home, I was getting ready to go to bed." They had little to discuss other than "food, clothing, shelter." He also remembered sitting in the mess hall with his friends not long after his father died and how "I felt really alone, like I had nobody."[8]

A greater drama swirled around the extended Uno family in the United States and Japan, which Raymond knew little about. Clarence's older brother, George, had immigrated to the United States in 1905, had lived in Utah and Los Angeles, and had married and had ten children. The FBI detained George just hours after Pearl Harbor, and he spent the war years in four different FBI camps separated from most of his family, who were sent to the camp in Amache, Colorado, with the exception of his daughter, Amy Uno Ishii, who was married and had moved to Heart Mountain with her husband. Before the war, George's oldest son, Kazumaro "Buddy" Uno, had become a journalist and had landed jobs in China working for Japanese publications. By 1940, his loyalties had turned away from the United States toward Japan. When Pearl Harbor was bombed, he was stuck in Japan, and in early 1944 he was helping to run a Japanese prison camp in which the veteran American broadcaster Royal Arch Gunnison was imprisoned. Buddy interrogated Gunnison, who was soon sent back to the United States in a prisoner exchange. Upon his return, Gunnison wrote about the encounter in an article for the *Pacific Citizen*, the JACL newspaper. Gunnison quoted Buddy: "My family, my brothers, are dumb Americans. They are stupid enough to believe there is such a thing as equality for a race or creed in the United States." Three of his brothers took no chances and made sure no one, particularly those in authority, misunderstood how they felt. "We wish to inform you that the Jap officer—our brother—is a traitor to the American way of life under which he has enjoyed the benefits of education and freedom," they said in an article in the *Heart Mountain Sentinel*. "We have pledged the destruction of him and all those like him."[9]

Resistance and Fair Play

Resisting Enlistment

The Army's 1943 enlistment campaign, combined with the appearance of the loyalty questionnaire, led to the rise of opposition groups, including the Heart Mountain Congress of American Citizens, led by Frank Inouye, who had been a senior at the University of California, Los Angeles, when he was forced into the camp. He met with a small group of fellow prisoners to determine how to protest the questionnaire, an activity that led the University of Cincinnati to later ban him from campus.[10] This core group would turn into a bigger problem for the camp administrators, particularly throughout the coming year, when the military began to draft Nisei men in the camps. Three other Nisei leaders in Inouye's group would also play

119

major roles in the opposition—Kiyoshi Okamoto, Paul Nakadate, and Frank Emi. Okamoto was a fifty-five-year-old Nisei from Hawaii, forced into the camp because he lived in California in 1942. His fellow prisoners considered him an eccentric jailhouse lawyer. He was constantly talking about constitutional rights and legal theories challenging the incarceration. Sometime in the second half of 1943, he created the Fair Play Committee of One, a solitary crusade against the government that had imprisoned him.[11] "He has endeavored to thwart any effort by WRA to assist the evacuees in peaceful relocation," camp director Guy Robertson wrote to Dillon Myer.[12] Many of the Heart Mountain prisoners considered Okamoto, a bachelor, an eccentric. They could not understand him or his causes or the growing audience he would develop among the younger Nisei men. Regardless, the environment remained ripe for dissent, as the attitudes against enlistment and segregation continued to harden.

The Fair Play Committee

The all-Nisei units in the Army—the 100th Infantry Battalion and its successor, the 442nd Regimental Combat Team—had succeeded on the training ground and on the battlefield in 1943 to such an extent that the Army on January 20, 1944, suddenly changed its classification of Japanese Americans from 4C (enemy aliens) to 1A. That meant all military-age men who were physically and mentally fit were immediately eligible for the draft. That decision rekindled the ill feelings inside Heart Mountain that had arisen a year earlier with the issuance of the loyalty questionnaire and the policy of segregating all "disloyals" at the Tule Lake camp.[13]

Most Japanese Americans, including myself, never knew what happened at Heart Mountain during the winter and spring of 1944. A small group of prisoners resisted the draft, placing themselves in opposition not only to the government but also to the *Sentinel* and many of their fellow incarcerees and making them the unwanted in both the mainstream and the Japanese American communities. My family never talked about it, and it was only through my involvement with the Heart Mountain Wyoming Foundation and one of its central leaders—Takashi Hoshizaki, known as a resister—that I learned about the resistance movement and the strength and moral character Hoshizaki and others had displayed.

Kiyoshi Okamoto, the fifty-five-year-old Nisei jailhouse lawyer, had been considered an eccentric nuisance since he first arrived at Heart Mountain, but his resistance to the beginning of the military draft brought him new-found acceptance among the younger men in the camp. Okamoto and his Fair Play Committee of One attracted disciples and evolved into the Fair Play Committee, which focused on resisting the draft. Director Guy Robertson reported that camp authorities "have Mr. Okamoto under surveillance as we think he is somewhat demented and it is hard to tell what action a person of this kind might take."[14] On February 8, only four days after the arrival of the first orders for young men of military age to report for physicals, the group held its first meeting inside one of the mess halls, drawing about sixty men. The next night, hundreds more appeared in another mess hall. Interested men, who had to have professed their loyalty to the United States and expressed a willingness to serve in the Army to still be at Heart Mountain and not Tule Lake, paid $2 in dues to pay for operating expenses, including the possible hiring of an attorney to fight the anticipated court battles. Okamoto dominated the first meetings with talks about the Constitution and the right of due process, a topic about which most of the attendees were ignorant. The institution of the draft itself, Okamoto said, made it possible to fight the issue of civil rights in court. "We were fairly unsophisticated, so was everybody else," said Frank Emi, one of the group's co-leaders. "But Mr. Okamoto gave us a real fast lesson in civics and Constitutional law, and the more we understood it, the more we realized that we really had gotten shafted." Okamoto and the other Fair Play leaders knew, however, that prisoners in other camps had applied for repatriation to Japan, and they wanted to make sure no one mistook their opposition to the draft on constitutional grounds for allegiance to Japan.[15]

Takashi Hoshizaki, who had graduated from high school the previous year, attended the first meeting armed with $2 his father had given him. At Pomona, he had seen the first signs that something was terribly unfair about the incarceration: "I'd had these doubts. I remember what the older Nisei had said—that we should have protested."[16] Takashi drew from the strength his father, Keijiro, had exhibited when he predicted Japan's ultimate defeat in the days after Pearl Harbor. When the loyalty questionnaire came out in 1943, Takashi had answered a qualified yes to question 27, saying he would serve in the military only if the government restored his legal rights. His feelings had intensified the following year as he watched hundreds of prisoners who opposed the incarceration be rounded up and shipped to Tule Lake. "When this draft thing came out, I said, 'This is crazy.'" He disliked the idea of a segregated unit. "They wouldn't let the

[Nisei] go into the navy or into the air force, so I said no." He would not allow himself to be drafted from camp.[17]

Camp officials knew they faced another potential uprising, and the FBI began investigating the Fair Play Committee with the help of at least one inside informant. They soon discovered Okamoto had six key confederates: Emi, a twenty-seven-year-old grocery-store owner from Los Angeles who had invested $25,000 in his store and had to sell it for $1,500 during the evacuation; Paul Nakadate, twenty-nine, an insurance salesman from Los Angeles who taught in the camp night school; Sam Horino, also twenty-nine, a gardener from Gardena who had known Emi from a prewar judo class and who had forced the soldiers to carry him from his home during the evacuation; Guntaro Kubota, forty, the only Issei in the group; Tsutomu "Ben" Wakaye, forty-one, a former insurance salesman from San Francisco; and Minoru Tamesa, thirty-five, a poultry farmer and peach grower from Seattle who had been transferred to Heart Mountain from Tule Lake during the segregation. All opposed their incarceration, but they had not answered "no" to the key questions on the loyalty questionnaire, so they had not been exiled to Tule Lake. Also, by this time, the Army, eager for new recruits, had ruled that those who had given "yes" answers with qualifications to questions 27 and 28, as had most of the committee members still at Heart Mountain, were acceptable for induction.[18] That meant that eighteen-year-old Hoshizaki, who had said he would join the military only if his rights were restored, was considered eligible for the draft.[19]

From the beginning, the Fair Play Committee and the growing cadre of draft resisters faced opposition from all official quarters in camp, including the JACL, which had worked closely with the WRA administrators from the beginning of the forced removal. Then they collaborated on how to segregate disloyal prisoners from the loyalists. The *Heart Mountain Sentinel* also stood firmly in the camp of collaborators; its coverage skewed heavily in favor of the military as it published stories recounting the bravery of Nisei soldiers.

The Fair Play Committee's membership and influence soared shortly after its first meeting. One supporter was Satoru Tsuneishi, who hosted one of the meetings in the block in which he was the captain. He was an Issei and a pacifist whose three of four sons were nonetheless serving in the US Army at the time. One son, Paul Tsuneishi, would accept the draft and enter the Military Intelligence Service but would still support the draft resisters.[20]

On February 14, Samuel Menin, a civil rights lawyer from Denver, met with the committee members at Heart Mountain and encouraged them to keep fighting.[21] Protests continued, and the entire camp population split into factions. One faction followed the JACL's logic that the Nisei should report for induction to prove their loyalty to the United States and thereby put an end to the incarceration. Another group—the majority of prisoners—opposed drafting young men while the government denied them their rights as Americans, but most were not willing or prepared to go to prison over their views. That accounts for why seventeen young men drafted at Heart Mountain reported to Cheyenne for their physicals that February. The third group opposed the draft, believed it was unconstitutional, and worried little about going to prison—they were already imprisoned.

Members of the camp's community council, witnessing the growing tumult, scrambled to react and approved a six-member committee to study problems caused by the draft; other camps, where the government was already cracking down on protesters, had done the same. On February 23, police arrested five young men at the Amache camp in Colorado for failing to report to the Selective Service.[22] These moves put the Fair Play Committee under increased pressure, and its first circular lashed out, accusing the JACL of trying to silence the protesters. More than anything concrete, the Fair Play Committee magnified the unhappiness of the draft-eligible Nisei men, whose resolve had first been tested the year before with the loyalty questionnaire. The draft now meant that many of them could die on a battlefield in Europe if they were inducted. The committee freed a deeper passion within the prisoners, one that encouraged them to trumpet the unfairness of their imprisonment and reinforced their need to fight it by whatever means necessary. In the winter and early spring of 1944, that meant resisting the draft.

Some of the resisters bought a mimeograph machine to print out leaflets, correctly reasoning that the *Sentinel* would not cover them fairly. While the *Sentinel* was perhaps the most professionally run camp newspaper, it worked in league with the WRA and the JACL and depended on the camp's administration for its existence. While its pages frequently included stories critical of the racist politicians behind the incarceration, the paper's editors, starting with Bill Hosokawa, also believed they needed to highlight the incarcerees' patriotism to protect them against claims of disloyalty. The resisters jeopardized that mission, and so the *Sentinel* put them under a virtual news blackout unless a resister was being criticized, prosecuted, or sent to prison. For example, the *Sentinel* covered Ernest Goppert's visit to camp. Goppert was the city attorney from Cody and leader of the local draft board; he visited the camp to encourage draftees to report for their physicals. As reported avidly by the *Sentinel*, Goppert criticized the resisters, saying they were subject to the same rules as all Americans and would be arrested if they continued to resist the draft. "In wartime you can't do anything to impede the war effort, so don't go around telling people to evade the draft," Goppert said in a clear message to the Fair Play Committee. "That's sedition and there's a heavy penalty for it." He went on to explain that a white man from Park County had recently been convicted of draft resistance and sent to federal prison for four years. "This goes for anyone, regardless of race or color. I hope you will make this clear to your people."[23]

Despite the *Sentinel*'s biased coverage, Heart Mountain prisoners realized they were not hearing the entire story, so many turned to the *Rocky Shimpo*, a Japanese American publication from Denver, which they received by mail. Its editor, James Omura, had been critical of the JACL at multiple publications before the war. Omura's editorials in the *Rocky Shimpo* questioned the legality of the draft, and the paper's articles covered the Fair Play Committee far more favorably than the *Sentinel*. As an indication of just how much antidraft sentiment existed at Heart Mountain, the *Rocky Shimpo*'s circulation there grew by 20 percent once the draft resistance started.[24]

On March 3, the committee drafted a set of demands for President Roosevelt that called for, among other points, universal application of the draft, the ability to join other branches of the military besides the Army, return to the West Coast, government help to end anti-Japanese propaganda, the restoration of all civil and inalienable rights, the end of discrimination against Japanese American soldiers, and protection of the families in the camps. There is no sign Roosevelt ever saw the petition or cared about the committee's grievances. He had approved Executive Order 9066, after all, and, while he heard through his wife about the unfairness of the incarceration, he had little desire to change things until after the November election, in which he would run for an unprecedented fourth term.[25] Forces greater than the Fair Play Committee's motley band of agitators would bring about many of the changes they sought with their petition. Progress in both theaters of the war, combined with the success of the relocation, led to reduced prejudice toward and misconceptions about Japanese Americans. The committee also angered the WRA by asking a representative of the government of Spain, which was handling all requests from the Japanese government on behalf of the noncitizen Issei in camp, to intervene with the US military on behalf of Issei mothers to prevent the drafting of their sons into the Army.[26] That showed the Heart Mountain authorities they faced growing discipline problems. The passions that had led dissidents to smash the windows of the Mineta family home a year earlier, when Etsu Mineta left to marry Mike Masaoka of the JACL, had only gotten worse. The troublemakers had to go.

Heart Mountain director Guy Robertson started breaking up the committee in March. On March 18, Robertson sent a report to the War Relocation Authority that said, "Okamoto is still a member of the Fair Play Committee and he and Paul Nakadate are carrying on an active resistance to Selective Service."[27] The WRA's chief lawyer recommended that Okamoto be denied the leave clearance he had sought for more than a year and "that he be transferred to the Tule Lake Center as soon as possible." Robertson notified Okamoto and Sam Horino on March 29 that they had to leave Heart Mountain that afternoon for Tule Lake.[28] "[Horino] was picked up to go to Tule Lake just like that, plucked right out of camp without even being able to say goodbye to his family," Frank Emi said.[29]

The JACL wanted to stop the draft resisters, so it enlisted the help of the American Civil Liberties Union (ACLU), which had previously represented other critics of the forced removal and incarceration. A study of the JACL released in the 1990s indicated that the JACL had asked the ACLU to tell the draft resisters they had few legal options, leaving them to cope with law enforcement on their own.[30] The "men who have refused to accept military draft are within their rights," wrote Roger Baldwin, the national director of the ACLU, to Kiyoshi Okamoto, "but they of course must take the consequences. They doubtless have a strong moral case, but no legal case at all." The letter appeared in one of the JACL's bulletins, strong evidence of the ACLU's collusion with the JACL. It also appeared in the April 15, 1944, edition of the *Sentinel*.[31] Baldwin's legal interpretation may have been correct, but from a moral and ethical standpoint the ACLU failed to protect the resisters.

Paul Nakadate was sent to Tule Lake in mid-April. Most of the committee's leaders, Frank Emi said, had kept quiet about their work, but once the government rounded them up and shipped them to Tule Lake, they underwent a series of interviews with FBI agents and began to explain the philosophy behind the committee's creation.[32]

Family members of the resisters became collateral damage in the fight over the draft. Takashi's father, Keijiro, lost his job in the camp poultry and egg plant under mysterious circumstances. When he applied for reinstatement to his job, the camp's chief of agriculture responded in a cryptic memo on April 5 that "with respect to your termination, particularly in view of circumstances which have occurred since you left the poultry project, it appears unwise that you be reinstated for employment in this activity."[33] Keijiro protested, saying the "conclusion shows that the foreman can terminate at any time a worker who does not suit his feelings, whether the worker is earnest or not," he wrote to the community council. "I am not satisfied with such anti-democratic and autocratic procedures."[34]

The Sentinel and the Draft

Amid the tensions surrounding the draft and segregation, a shy twenty-five-year-old Army sergeant visited Heart Mountain and thrust himself in the middle of the fight. Ben Kuroki was the son of an Issei farmer in Hershey, Nebraska. Shortly after Pearl Harbor, after attending a church meeting in nearby North Platte, where JACL leader Mike Masaoka had been arrested while on a speaking tour, Ben and his brother Fred were inspired to enlist. "This is your country," their father told them. "Fight for it." After several fits and starts, Ben Kuroki was admitted to the Army Air Corps and joined the crew of a B-24 Liberator bomber piloted by Lieutenant Jake Epting, a Mississippian untroubled by Kuroki's Japanese heritage. "If there is anyone who objects to flying with Kuroki, let me know now," Epting told his crew. No one objected, and the next day the B-24 called "Red Ass" was on its way to North Africa with Kuroki as one of its machine gunners. The Red Ass flew missions over Italy, and on its final run it was supposed to end its mission at a base in England. Instead, the plane crash-landed in the desert in neutral Spanish Morocco. The crew was detained, flown to Spain, and eventually exchanged for new cars for the Spanish authorities. Back in England, they got a new B-24 and continued their missions. After thirty missions, Kuroki was given leave, which he accepted reluctantly, and was ordered home on a recruiting tour to boost the flagging enlistment rates at Heart Mountain and other camps.[35]

The April 29, 1944, edition of the *Sentinel* devoted twelve stories and almost the entire paper to Kuroki's visit. "Kuroki 'Takes' Heart Mountain" read the lead headline spread across the front page. Other headlines included "Community Celebration Features Visit of Hero," "Ben Kuroki

Average American Despite Brave Achievements," and "Service Mothers Praise Kuroki, Express Pride in Sons' Action." Bill Hosokawa said one mission of the *Sentinel* was to give camp residents a voice. This time, however, that voice was of a pro-military propagandist inveighing against the Fair Play Committee and other military resisters. "With the confidence of a man who knows the hell of war, the stark horrors of flak-filled skies and the sight of buddies plunging to a fiery death over an enemy target, Sergeant Kuroki pulled no punches to make clear the part Americans of Japanese descent must play in this war," the *Sentinel* said in an editorial. "'I happen to know how it feels to be shot at. I know what the boys in the 100th battalion are going through for you people,' he said. 'All I ask is that you do not tear down that which we are striving so hard to build up.'" Resisters, he said, "are not doing your part as Americans, as Nisei, or for that matter as human beings, in view of the conscientious absolvement of your responsibility." It did not matter, the editorial continued, that Kuroki "did not experience the bitterness of evacuation"; "he has gone through one hell after another, giving a little bit extra along the way, to prove that Americans of Japanese ancestry are as truly American as those of any other ancestry."[36]

My mother, who almost never spoke of life at Heart Mountain, *did* tell me about Kuroki's visit. Her comments were prompted by my questions after seeing a photo of Kuroki in Bill Hosokawa's *Nisei: The Quiet Americans*. Kuroki's visit made a huge impression on her, and in retrospect her memories seem tinged by the effects of the government propaganda. She remembered that Kuroki had been placed in a difficult situation because he was encouraging Japanese Americans to fight for a country that had imprisoned them. The *Sentinel*'s editorials and Kuroki's appearance did not achieve their desired effect, however. Enlistment rates at Heart Mountain remained low, certainly in comparison to those in Hawaii, where the Japanese Americans had not been incarcerated. Eighteen-year-old Stanley Hayami, a prisoner from Los Angeles who yearned to join his older brother in the Army, described the meeting in camp with Kuroki and Caucasian soldiers as tense. "A lot of people wanted to know if they could have some guarantees so that after the war was over, they wouldn't have their citizenship taken away and the lands they own taken," Hayami wrote in his diary. "They answered that we would be protected by the 14th amendment in the Constitution." One inmate said the Fourteenth Amendment was supposed to have kept the Japanese Americans out of camps and had not. Another said the Japanese Americans were going to be victimized whenever there was a war. The Army representative said the service had realized it had done something wrong, Hayami wrote, "and is now trying to help us make up for it."[37]

Takashi Hoshizaki was arrested around the time of Kuroki's visit. He knew that the FBI would come looking for him when he failed to appear for his induction physical. His mother handed him a sweater, a small spiral notebook, and a pencil as he was being arrested. The FBI interrogated him, asking for his history of activities with the Fair Play Committee. He signed a statement that the agents placed in front of him confirming the details of his interview, and then he began an odyssey through the country jails of Wyoming, landing first at the Park County jail in Cody and then the county jail in Casper. "There were so many of us that we had filled up the county jails in and around the whole area of Wyoming," he said.[38]

Roosevelt's Reticence

Despite the turmoil caused by the antidraft movement and the desire of a few thousand prisoners to be repatriated to Japan, the momentum inside Roosevelt's cabinet pressed steadily in favor of ending the exclusion and closing the camps. Roosevelt had signed a new executive order in February that put the WRA under the authority of the Interior Department and its irascible secretary, Harold Ickes, who had never supported the incarceration. Attorney General Francis Biddle, another longtime evacuation opponent, noted in April that Secretary of War Henry Stimson had "raised the question of whether it was appropriate for the War Department, at this time, to cancel the Japanese Exclusion Orders and let the Japs go home. War, Interior, and Justice had all agreed that this could be done without danger to defense considerations but doubted the wisdom of doing it at this time before the election."[39] In early June, Ickes joined in, telling Roosevelt that "the continued retention of these innocent people in the relocation centers would be a blot upon the history of this country." On June 12, Roosevelt told Ickes that he thought "it would be a mistake to do anything drastic or sudden." In other words, Roosevelt, who needed California's votes if he was going to win an unprecedented fourth term in November, did not intend to do anything as politically controversial as closing the camps until after the election.[40]

Takashi Hoshizaki and United States v. Shigeru Fujii et al.

By early June, Takashi Hoshizaki had been moved to the county jail in Cheyenne, which, he said, "was probably never really cleaned." Cleanliness is very important to the Japanese, who routinely take off their shoes before walking into homes and schools, so the defendants must have been horrified by the conditions. They volunteered to clean the jail, using rags and brushes given them by the guards. "So, for the rest of the time we had a halfway decent place to sleep. In fact, some of us were sleeping on the floor because we were just jammed in there."[41] Their trial started on June 12 in the federal courthouse in Cheyenne. Representing the government was Carl Sackett, the US attorney for Wyoming.

Samuel Menin, the Denver-based civil rights attorney who first visited the Fair Play Committee in February, represented the defendants. He wanted to make it difficult for the prosecution to identify the defendants by having all of them shave their heads, Takashi Hoshizaki said. "I thought that's not the defense we need," he said, and the idea died. Menin tried his best, Takashi said, but the outcome seemed preordained.[42]

Menin recommended that his clients opt for a trial before the judge instead of taking their chances with twelve white Wyoming jurors. The defendants agreed. Menin told his clients he would fight the draft by claiming that, since the men kept at Heart Mountain were in a prison from which they could not leave, the government was violating the law that prohibited drafting people in prison. "Frank Emi and a couple of others had tried to walk out of the camp, and the guard said, 'You can't go out,'" Takashi said. "Emi asked the guard what would happen if they did walk out, and the guard said, 'I'll have to shoot you.' That was supposed to be the evidence that, yes, we were being imprisoned. But we never got around to that."[43]

Thomas Blake Kennedy was the sole federal judge in the state of Wyoming. At first, they liked their chances. Kennedy, who had left his native Ohio for the open territory of Wyoming, had a reputation for being fair and honest. After a long career as a lawyer in Cheyenne, he had been appointed to the bench in 1921 by Republican president Warren Harding. During the 1920s, he had presided over the Teapot Dome corruption case. When the case of *United States v. Shigeru Fujii et al.* came into his court on June 12, 1944, the resisters hoped for the best. A photographer captured the resisters at the start of the trial, and Takashi maneuvered to make his face visible for the camera.

"As the photographer was getting ready to [shoot], a crazy thing flashed through my mind: Fifty years from now, this may be important," he told me. He was correct. That photo is now on exhibit in the Heart Mountain museum. "I made sure my face showed up. It's just one of these things that flashed in my mind. Get over there and show your face, because you're now a part of this group."[44]

The sixty-three defendants in the June 1944 trial of the Heart Mountain draft resisters in federal court in Cheyenne, Wyoming. (Photo courtesy of Frank Abe/Resister.com)

The group soon learned their optimism had been misplaced. "The first day, he called us 'You Jap Boys,'" Takashi said.[45]

"Oh, that S-O-B," Jack Tono, another resister, said to Takashi. "We just don't have a chance with that guy."[46]

Tono was right. The judge they had initially thought would be sympathetic or at least willing to be neutral was actually racist, anti-Semitic, and xenophobic, according to writings discovered after Kennedy's death. "Unfortunately, when we finally got in the court it was not about the civil rights," Takashi said. "The judge then threw out everything and concentrated only on the fact that we didn't show on the doorsteps of the draft board."[47] To the casual observer, however, Kennedy did not seem to favor the prosecution. At one point, he told Sackett he had to wrap up his argument in three minutes. In reality, that was because he knew how he would rule before the government had finished its case. After a six-day trial, Kennedy found all sixty-three defendants guilty and sentenced them to three years in federal prison. "If they are truly loyal Americans," Kennedy said at sentencing, "they should, at least when they have become recognized as such, embrace the opportunity to discharge the duties of citizens by offering themselves in the cause of our national defense."[48] The resisters received no solace from the *Sentinel,* which dubbed them "slackers." "Had any of the 63 held the interest of all Japanese Americans at heart they would have offered themselves, as have more than 400 other Heart Mountain youths now in the army, and relied upon proper authorities to determine their positions," the *Sentinel* editorialized. "Both the Korematsu and Endo cases now before the Supreme Court will determine the legality of evacuation but in the meantime every person of Japanese ancestry carries a personal burden of which he must at all times be conscious."[49]

Such rhetoric only reinforced the coping tools of both my parents and my entire extended family, which include perfectionism and workaholism. Naturally, Takashi's objections were not just the complaints of some slacker. As I reviewed his WRA files, I was impressed by the composure and thoughtfulness exhibited in the comments from a young man just out of high school.

Frank Emi and the Fair Play Committee on Trial

Frank Emi and the leaders of the Fair Play Committee went on trial on October 23 for inciting draft resistance. Midway through the trial, the prosecution produced a surprise witness—Jack Nishimoto, one of Emi's neighbors in camp. Nishimoto testified that he had heard Emi tell draftee Dave Kawamoto not to report for his draft physical and that the Fair Play Committee would protect him. Nishimoto also said that Emi said he would go back to Japan if he did not prevail in court. "Which was a bald-faced lie," Emi said. Then Kawamoto's mother testified and refuted Nishimoto. Emi speculated that the FBI used Nishimoto because it had no other evidence to use against Emi.[50]

Emi had worked at the Heart Mountain tofu factory and used to bring tofu home to Nishimoto after work. Perhaps Nishimoto's actions make more sense in hindsight, knowing that his credibility had been suspect since a year earlier, when he had recruited prisoners to work at a labor camp in Cozad, Nebraska, where the incarcerees complained about racism and poor working conditions. Emi later said he thought Nishimoto was an FBI spy inside Heart Mountain. Someone who would take money from employers who treated their Japanese American workers poorly would have few reservations about lying to the FBI for extra benefits.[51]

The outcome of the Fair Play leaders' trial was never in doubt, though their attorney, veteran ACLU lawyer A. L. Wirin, from Los Angeles, fought hard in court. The case before visiting Judge Eugene Rice lasted a week before going to a jury, which deliberated for a few hours before returning with a guilty verdict for all of the defendants except one, Jimmie Omura, the editor of the *Rocky Shimpo*. The jury determined that anything he published about the Fair Play Committee came from legitimate journalism. He had not conspired with anyone. Although Omura stayed free, his journalism career was essentially over. The JACL had him effectively blackballed, and he spent the rest of his working life as a landscaper.[52]

Frank Emi, Kiyoshi Okamoto, Paul Nakadate, and Sam Horino were deemed the ringleaders of the conspiracy to incite draft evasion. They received four-year sentences, to be served at the federal prison in Leavenworth, Kansas. Guntaro Kubota, Ben Wakaye, and Min Tamesa were sentenced to two years, and Wakaye's and Tamesa's sentences were made concurrent to the three-year sentences they had received earlier in the year for failing to appear for their draft physicals. During the course of the trial, however, Wirin discovered that during the case Carl Sackett, the US attorney who had prosecuted the case, had gone hunting with Judge Rice. That created a conflict of interest that none of the jurors had known about, and it also provided grounds for an appeal.[53]

Rice, Emi said, had also failed to tell the jurors that anyone "who violated law that they think is unconstitutional, sincerely, in good faith, has a right to do so." On the basis of that finding and Sackett's conflict of interest, the appeals court overruled the conviction in December 1945. "We were released later in 1946," Emi said.[54]

Imprisoned Resisters

Takashi Hoshizaki did not have an appeal. He was among the sixty-three Heart Mountain draft resisters imprisoned in the federal penitentiaries at McNeil Island, Washington, and Fort Leavenworth, Kansas. He thought he had just traded one prison for another when he was moved from Heart Mountain, and in many ways, he liked it better at McNeil Island, where he could mix with people from different races and backgrounds. "I worked in the water filtration plant and a black fellow would drive me to and from the water filtration plant every day," Takashi said. "He was in prison for hijacking semitrucks that were delivering liquor." A black fellow inmate named 609 Jackson taught him to play the piano. "It was only when I started to hear their stories at McNeil that I began to think about the situation of African Americans in this country."[55] There was a small group of college-educated inmates, many of them Quakers, in prison as conscientious objectors to the draft. "They would have seminars and I would go there and sit down, and so it became almost like a university with all these people there, and got to know a little bit more about literature and then more about political aspects going on at the time," Takashi said. One of the conscientious objectors was Gordon Hirabayashi, a Quaker who had challenged the 1942 anti-Japanese curfews in the Supreme Court.

After arriving at McNeil Island, the resisters were put in quarantine for a month to ensure they had no communicable diseases. "Since we weren't hardened criminals," Takashi said, "we were then sent out to the minimum-security area, which was the farm. There we lived in dormitories. No barbed wire."[56] The farm faced Puget Sound, giving the prisoners a brilliant view of the water. Some inmates had permission to drive the farm's truck to sit down by the water and take in the scene.

McNeil Island had operated for about seventy years before the Nisei resisters arrived. A notorious former inmate was Robert Stroud, the Birdman of Alcatraz. Reaching the prison required taking a ferry from Steilacoom, Washington, about ten miles south of Tacoma. In the prison's Big House, inmates slept in ten-man cells with no windows. The Heart Mountain inmates had an easier time of it than the resisters from the camp in Minidoka, Idaho, who for some reason had to remain in the Big House for most of their sentence while the Heart Mountain prisoners went to the farm.[57] Some of the resisters speculated that the reason was that the Minidokans had a reputation for being troublemakers. Differences between incarcerees from various camps still affect the Japanese American community today, as some Nisei consider those from Heart Mountain to have received some kind of favorable treatment from the federal government.

Takashi Hoshizaki after Incarceration

In June 1945 the Hoshizaki family returned to Los Angeles, where their neighbors, the Marshalls, had watched over their home while the Hoshizaki family was at Heart Mountain. Instead of reopening his store, Keijiro Hoshizaki started a nursery.[58] The Hoshizaki family returned minus one member—Takashi remained in the federal prison at McNeil Island, Washington. Two years in federal prison seemed little different than two years at Heart Mountain, he said, except at McNeil Island he could mix with non-Japanese Americans.[59]

Takashi finally walked out of prison on July 14, 1946, two years after Judge T. Blake Kennedy convicted him and sixty-two other Heart

Mountain draft resisters. Their accumulated "good time" had cut their sentences from three years to two. If not for Dillon Myer, the WRA director, they would have been released earlier. But Myer had asked prison officials to deny parole to the resisters, because if they had gotten out of prison earlier it would have caused problems for the military and the WRA. "If we came back after one year, the guys would say, 'Hell, instead of serving how long in the military, we serve two or three years [in prison] and be out in one year,' which would present a chaotic situation for the authorities," Takashi said.[60]

Takashi and his fellow inmates got their free suits and $25 and headed to the train station for home. It was his first trip alone; he had gone to Pomona and Heart Mountain with his family and to McNeil Island with his fellow convicts. He boarded a southbound train to Los Angeles carrying only what he could take with him and a criminal record. "I'm traveling completely by myself, so it was kind of a mixed feeling," he said, "but it was nice to be out."[61] When he arrived at Union Station in Los Angeles, Takashi thought "I would just walk the three miles home. But to my surprise, my dad was there with my youngest sister. It was the first time I saw the LA smog."[62]

For the resisters, the joy of getting out of prison was darkened by the sudden death of one of their own—Fred Iriye. An electrician, he was showing his replacement how to do his job when he touched a switch he thought was turned off and was electrocuted. The Los Angeles resisters soon gathered again for a memorial service for Iriye. It was, as the historian Eric Muller wrote, the last time they would meet as a group.[63]

Fighting Incarceration in the Courts: Hirabayashi, Yasui, Korematsu, and Endo

Some Japanese Americans, such as my uncle James's wife, had fled the West Coast for arranged marriages, schools, and jobs outside the exclusion area to avoid incarceration. Others, such as my uncle Takeru, avoided incarceration entirely; he was studying at the University of Wisconsin when the war started. Others took their fight to the legal system. In Seattle, University of Washington student Gordon Hirabayashi started violating the curfew for Japanese Americans shortly after it was declared on May 4, 1942. Less than two weeks later, he went to the Seattle FBI office to inform them he would not comply with the exclusion order and was promptly jailed. He languished in jail until October, when an all-male jury, after ten minutes of deliberation, found him guilty of violating the curfew and sentenced him to two concurrent ninety-day sentences.

Portland lawyer Minoru Yasui, a Nisei, was arrested when the curfew started there on March 28, 1942. After his release, Yasui ignored the evacuation order for Portland and drove to his family home in Hood River, Oregon, where military policeman found him and drove him back to the Portland Assembly Center, which held prisoners bound for the Minidoka, Idaho, camp. Yasui reached out to the American Civil Liberties Union and the Japanese American Citizens League, whose executive director Mike Masaoka had called Yasui and other dissenters "self-styled martyrs who are willing to be jailed in order that they might fight for the rights of citizenship."[64] Yasui was convicted, sentenced to a year in jail, and sent to Minidoka. Both Hirabayashi and Yasui appealed their convictions.[65]

In California, two Nisei—Fred Korematsu and Mitsuye Endo—protested the evacuation, too. Korematsu was a shipyard welder in Oakland, where his family owned a plant nursery. He lost his job following Pearl Harbor. On May 9, 1942, Korematsu's father and three brothers reported to the assembly center at the Tanforan race track south of San Francisco, but Fred refused to go, staying instead with his Italian American girlfriend.[66] So determined was he to avoid the evacuation that he underwent plastic surgery to make him look less Japanese, and he pretended to be of mixed Hawaiian and Spanish descent. That did not work, and police arrested him on May 30. The American Civil Liberties Union of Northern California agreed to handle his legal challenge. Korematsu spent more than two months in jail before he was convicted in federal court on September 8 on a charge of violating curfew. Authorities promptly shipped him to Topaz, Utah, the prison camp for most Bay Area Japanese Americans. The ACLU filed an appeal for Korematsu, who was shunned at Topaz by most of the camp's JACL members, who considered Korematsu a troublemaker.

Endo, who worked in Sacramento for the California Department of Motor Vehicles, received help from the JACL, especially lawyer Saburo Kido. Endo had lost her job with the state shortly after Pearl Harbor, but Kido was sent to Poston, Arizona. Before he left, he asked James Purcell, another lawyer in San Francisco, to fight the firings. By then, Endo had been shipped to the camp at Tule Lake, California, so Purcell never met his client in person. Her case was argued before a judge in July, and Endo had to stay in the camp for a year as she waited for her ruling.[67]

Appealing to the Supreme Court

After they were convicted at their criminal trials in 1942, Minoru Yasui and Gordon Hirabayashi appealed to the US Supreme Court. Infighting among their legal teams and the American Civil Liberties Union hampered their cases, but they found ample support inside the camps, especially Heart Mountain, where the blocks raised a total of $1,261.97 for Hirabayashi's defense fund.[68] However, their cases never had a real chance of success in the high court. The government continued to cite false information in its arguments in favor of the curfew order that Hirabayashi had violated and to justify Yasui's loss of his job and citizenship, which the government tied to his former employment at the Japanese consulate in Chicago. It was also true that Hirabayashi had openly violated the curfew and that Yasui had virtually begged to be arrested. Both had violated the law of the time, unfair as it may have been.

The JACL, which should have aided both men, was oddly hostile to Yasui, whom Masaoka called a "propaganda agent" for the Japanese government. Masaoka also worried about arousing resentment among white Americans in response to their complaints, writing that "it might have been better either to have lost or not have attempted a contest." The national JACL headquarters, Masaoka wrote in a press release, "is unalterably opposed to test cases to determine the constitutionality of military regulations at this time."[69]

The Court ruled unanimously against Hirabayashi and Yasui on June 21, 1943. Yasui was sent to the concentration camp in Minidoka, Idaho, while Hirabayashi made a circuitous route to a federal prison in Tucson, Arizona, before he refused the draft and ended up in another prison.

Two other internment cases remained: Fred Korematsu's challenge to the entire system and Mitsuye Endo's case, which challenged the policy of incarcerating US citizens who were determined to be loyal. Of the two, Endo's proved the most problematic for the US government, especially given the government's use of the loyalty questionnaire to determine who could join the military, leave the camps for employment elsewhere, or be sent to the segregation camp at Tule Lake. By showing it had the ability, however flawed, to distinguish loyal Japanese Americans from the rest, the government weakened the chance of success for claims that it could not determine who was dangerous and who was not and therefore had to keep everyone detained and away from the West Coast.[70]

On October 11, 1944, the Supreme Court heard arguments in Fred Korematsu's fight against the exclusion and Mitsuye Endo's case against the incarceration of loyal Japanese Americans. Although Gordon Hirabayashi and Minoru Yasui had lost their cases the year before, both Korematsu and Endo and their attorneys believed they had a good chance of winning before the Court, which was dominated by such Roosevelt-appointed liberals as William O. Douglas and Hugo Black, two noted civil libertarians. The plaintiffs, however, did not realize that government lawyers had rigged the case against them by failing to introduce evidence that showed that no proof existed of Japanese American collusion with the Japanese government or of sabotage in the weeks leading to the signing of Executive Order 9066.[71] As evidence in the cases against Hirabayashi, Korematsu, and Yasui, the government relied on the final report about the incarceration approved by Lieutenant General John DeWitt, the former leader of the Western Defense Command, who had led the demands for the exclusion order. Even so, government lawyers preparing the defense against the plaintiffs realized that many of the claims about so-called fifth-column support among Japanese Americans for the Japanese military were false. A series of memoranda between the attorneys and the solicitor general who argued the case showed that they knew the government had relied on false information to justify the incarceration. Nevertheless, two Justice Department attorneys signed off on the government's brief in the *Korematsu* case out of loyalty to the government, even though they knew it contained "facts" that were incorrect. The government went on to argue in court that the wholesale evacuation and detention of 120,000 people was justified.[72]

Inside Heart Mountain, the mood among those tracking the case was one of cautious optimism. Although they had watched Minoru Yasui and Gordon Hirabayashi take their cases to the Supreme Court and lose, they read coverage from the *Sentinel*'s Washington reporter, John Kitasako, who had left camp for a job in Washington and who also attended the hearings. He sent back dispatches that revealed his contradictory emotions— optimism, realism, and despair. He noted the number of Nisei spectators in the crowd inside the court and the stirrings among the Japanese American and Caucasian spectators in response to some of the pointed questions from the justices in both cases.

Korematsu's and Endo's attorneys, Kitasako noted, emphasized the words "imprisonment" and "imprisoned" when referring to the evacuation, mincing no words in describing the bleak and dehumanizing conditions of the assembly centers and camps. "The term 'concentration camp' was used liberally," he wrote. The "graphic description [by Endo's attorney, James Purcell] of the stench and filth of the Tanforan assembly center stable barracks, south of San Francisco, must have hit the justices and audience hard and deep."

"Our strictly non-legal impression, judging from the questions and comments of the justices during the hearings, was that the Endo case stands a better chance of a favorable decision than the Korematsu case," Kitasako wrote in the October 21 *Sentinel*. Kitasako had reached that conclusion by watching Justice Felix Frankfurter, a founder of the ACLU, a former Harvard Law School professor, and a Roosevelt appointee, question Purcell about how Endo had been determined to be loyal to the United States.

"By whom was she declared loyal?" Frankfurter asked.

"By the US government," Purcell said.

"Then if she were considered loyal, she shouldn't have been evacuated and detained," Frankfurter said. "She should have been released right there."

"Right there!" Purcell said.[73]

That Endo and the tens of thousands of other Japanese Americans who had been determined by the loyalty questionnaire to be loyal to the United States and yet were segregated in detention camps was acknowledged as a mark against the government, and the tide seemed on the verge of turning, however late it might have been.

Roosevelt *and* Korematsu v. United States

On December 17, 1944, President Roosevelt authorized the end of the exclusion of Japanese Americans from the West Coast, a move that was pushed by the belief that the Supreme Court would force the administration to change its policy. Opponents of the incarceration thought the Court would strike down the legal reasoning behind Executive Order 9066, dismantle the WRA, and allow the more than seventy thousand prisoners to return to their homes. Instead, they received a very rude surprise when the Court's ruling in *Korematsu* appeared on December 18. In a 6–3 decision, the Court ruled that the government had acted legally when it announced the evacuation and incarceration of Japanese Americans living on the West Coast.[74]

Black wrote the Court's opinion. "Korematsu was not excluded from the military area because of hostility to him or his race," Black wrote. "He was excluded because we are at war with the Japanese Empire," and "because they decided that the military urgency of the situation demanded that all citizens of Japanese ancestry be segregated from the West Coast temporarily."[75] So, the military's lies about a nonexistent national security threat posed by Japanese Americans, which was conjured up by fear and ignorance, were enough to justify the wholesale removal of people from their homes and livelihoods. Just as the cooler heads in the Roosevelt administration had buckled under the military's pressure and the anti-Japanese hysteria in early 1942, the Supreme Court had given constitutional protection to the military's wartime claims. What had been obvious in the run-up to Executive Order 9066—that military demands would supersede civil liberties in wartime—had now been sealed into legal precedent by some of the most liberal members of the Supreme Court.

Black's opinion brought angry dissents from the three justices in the minority. Frank Murphy, a former attorney general, governor of Michigan, and mayor of Detroit, called the majority opinion an outright "legislation of racism." Japanese Americans had been consigned to camps solely on the basis of racial origin and had been denied any individual hearings to determine their loyalties or whether they endangered the safety of the United States. "Racial discrimination in any form and in any degree has no justifiable part whatever in our democratic way of life." Robert Jackson, another former attorney general on the court, wrote that the *Korematsu* decision "for all time has validated the principle of racial discrimination in criminal procedure and of transplanting American citizens." Owen Roberts, who led the commission that investigated the Pearl Harbor attack and gave initial credibility to the idea of possible fifth-column collaboration, called the decision what it was—a validation of racism that failed to account for an individual's loyalty or potential threat.[76]

As the Pearl Harbor attack lives in infamy, so too does the decision in *Korematsu v. United States.* Subsequent courts and legal scholars have attacked its reasoning; those who cite it as a precedent are denounced as racists. In a 2014 speech, Justice Antonin Scalia called it one of the worst decisions in the court's history and warned that the hysteria that had caused it could happen again. "But you are kidding yourself if you think the same thing will not happen again," Scalia said. He cited a Latin expression— "*Inter arma enim silent leges* . . . In times of war, the laws fall silent"—to explain why. "That's what was going on—the panic about the war and the invasion of the Pacific and whatnot," Scalia said. "That's what happens. It was wrong, but I would not be surprised to see it happen again—in time of war. It's no justification but it is the reality."[77]

In virtually the same breath in which it announced its *Korematsu* decision, the Court ruled 9–0 in favor of Mitsuye Endo. John Kitasako had predicted the outcome of both cases from his monitoring of both arguments. Douglas, who was known as one of the court's great liberals but who ruled against Korematsu, switched teams in his opinion in the *Endo* case: "We are of the view that Mitsuye Endo should be given her liberty," Douglas wrote. "In reaching that conclusion we do not come to the underlying constitutional issues which have been argued. For we conclude that, whatever power the War Relocation Authority may have to detail other classes of citizens, it has no authority to subject citizens who are concededly loyal to its leave procedure." In other words, all prisoners in camp, except for those sent to Tule Lake because of questions about their loyalty, were free to leave.[78]

That meant that, in some way, the wrenching dislocation caused by the loyalty questionnaire and followed by segregation had some meaning. It somehow proved the loyalty of the Japanese Americans who remained in camp after 1943, which gave the government little reason to detain them. Government lawyers had told Endo's legal team they realized they had little ground to stand on. Nevertheless, Solicitor General Charles Fahy pressed on, using the false evidence from DeWitt's "Final Report" in his argument. "In light of Fahy's knowledge of the FBI and FCC reports that refuted these espionage allegations, their inclusion in the outline seems inexplicable," scholar Peter Irons wrote.[79]

This mixed bag of reasoning—the justification of a racist roundup of one people but the rejection of a blanket assumption of disloyalty—has confounded legal scholars for decades. Along with Roosevelt's proclamation ending the exclusion, it meant that the Japanese Americans remaining in the camps could now return home, if they had homes to which to return. While the incarcerees rejoiced that they no longer were compelled to remain in prison, they were scared and uncertain about where they would go and unsure of what to expect.

8

The Nisei Units
Uncommon Courage

◇◇

In Italy, the two Nisei units, the 100th Infantry and the new 442nd Regimental Combat Team, fought their way north. The first Heart Mountain combat deaths came in early July, when Lieutenant Kei Tanahashi and Corporal Yoshiharu Aoyama were killed in Italy. Tanahashi, from Los Angeles, had been among the first group of prisoners to arrive at the Heart Mountain camp in August 1942. A graduate of UCLA, he had been the bookkeeper for the family's cleaning plant in Pomona. Tanahashi was imprisoned at Heart Mountain for barely a month; he was among the first students picked by the National Japanese American Student Relocation Council and left to work toward his master's degree at the University of Nebraska. Aoyama, also from Los Angeles and a UCLA student, joined the Army in March 1942. Both had been members of the famous Los Angeles Boy Scout Troop 379 that was presented to President Roosevelt during the 1935 scout jamboree. Tanahashi left for Europe in May 1944.[1]

Aoyama was awarded a posthumous Silver Star for his heroism on July 6. During a firefight with German troops, mortar and artillery shells dropped all around the members of the 442nd as they pressed forward. A forward artillery observer for Aoyama's unit fell after being wounded by shrapnel, and Aoyama ran ahead to help him. While Aoyama was giving first aid, a German artillery shell fell on him, blowing his legs off below the knee. Aoyama treated his own wounds as best as he could, and when he was brought back to a field hospital, he directed doctors to treat others before him. "I'm all right," Aoyama said. "The others need help more than I do. Treat them first." Only when medics actually inspected Aoyama's wounds did they realize the extent of his injuries. By then it was too late to do anything. He died the next day.[2]

By July, the month Tanahashi and Aoyama died, American commanders were routinely praising the Nisei units for their extraordinary courage. Lieutenant General Mark Clark, the commander of the Fifth Army in Italy, singled out the 100th Infantry Battalion, whose members had received more than one thousand Purple Hearts, forty-one Silver Stars, almost thirty Bronze Stars, three Legions of Honor, eleven Distinguished Service Crosses, and fifteen field promotions. Inside Heart Mountain, the *Sentinel* provided ample publicity for the success of the Nisei units, while the struggles of the draft resisters went unmentioned.[3] In August, twenty-eight draftees left camp for induction into the Army at Fort Logan, Colorado. Before they left, agricultural supervisor and block manager chairman Eiichi Sakauye honored them by saying "the opportunity which awaits you is the chance of a lifetime to expose as loathsome lies, the pratings and charges of the West Coast race baiters that we, because of our face and blood alone, are not as good as any other American and cannot be trusted to stand by our country in her hour of trial." Sakauye cited the deaths of Tanahashi and Aoyama as examples of how "Japanese Americans in uniform are willing to make the supreme sacrifice in order to help make a greater and better America."[4] Tanahashi and Aoyama would not be the last Nisei soldiers from Heart Mountain to die in combat; each soldier's sacrifice was used to justify military service as the best way to demonstrate the commitment of Japanese Americans to the United States.

Daniel Inouye and the 442nd

Daniel Inouye deployed with the 442nd in Italy as it fought its way north from Sicily to Naples and on to the horrendous battle to capture the monastery atop Monte Cassino, which commanded the heights between Naples and Rome. Allied commanders believed the monastery had to be taken to prevent the Germans from controlling the high ground, but it had negligible strategic value. The fight for Monte Cassino cost thousands of troops, many of them from the all-Nisei unit, whose heroism and sacrifice were shared with Heart Mountain residents by the *Sentinel*, which featured frequent stories about the battles. One involved Ted Fujioka, one of the camp's golden boys. In a July letter to the *Sentinel*, he expressed frustration with the elements in camp who were not supporting the war strongly enough. "Too many Americans aren't doing their part, aren't sacrificing enough, are prolonging the war. But regardless, we won't let anyone down."[5]

In 1944, in one sixty-day period, Inouye led seventy-two combat patrols up to and through enemy lines. During one battle, he was shot in the chest by a German bullet, his life saved only by the two silver dollars he carried for luck. By the end of the year, the nineteen-year-old sergeant Inouye had received a battlefield commission as a first lieutenant and slogged through most of the 442nd's battles, but he had missed two critical fights: the struggle to cross Italy's Arno River and the fight in the last week of October to rescue the so-called Lost Battalion in the Vosges Mountains in northeastern France. He missed the first campaign because of severely ingrown toenails and the second because his unit's command surgeon had determined that Inouye had lost too much weight to allow him to accept his officer's commission. By the time Inouye rejoined the unit, the fight for the Lost Battalion was over. He would later ruminate that this delay might have saved his life.[6]

The Lost Battalion was never lost. Its commanders knew exactly where it was. The 1st battalion of the 141st Infantry, a unit from Texas, had been cut off by the Germans in the mountains. The soldiers could not escape and attempts to reach them had failed. The divisional commander, Major General John Dahlquist, then ordered the 442nd to rescue them. Over one week, the 442nd fought its way into the woods to reach the Texans. "The bombardment from the German defenders was unbelievable; endless rounds of artillery and mortar shells, and at every roadblock a withering hail of rifle and machine gun fire," Inouye remembered.[7]

On three days during the fighting for the Lost Battalion, Corporal James Okubo, a medic whose family was incarcerated at Heart Mountain, crawled more than 150 yards through enemy fire to rescue members of his unit. Okubo's path to France highlighted the twisting journey of many prisoners. Originally from Bellingham, Washington, he was in his third year of premed studies at Western Washington College when the war started. He and his family were sent first to Tule Lake and then on to Heart Mountain during the segregation of suspected disloyal Japanese Americans. Okubo was inducted in 1944, and on October 28 and 29 he rescued twenty-five members of the 442nd while under machine gun, mortar, and artillery fire. Five days later, he ran seventy-five yards, again dodging machine gun fire, to rescue a seriously wounded comrade from a burning tank. Such heroism would normally have merited consideration for a Medal of Honor, but Okubo's Caucasian commander thought he could receive only a Silver Star, so that was all he submitted Okubo's name for.[8] Chester Tanaka, one of Okubo's comrades, never forgot what he saw Okubo and the other medics do. "No matter if fire was pouring in from all directions and mortar rounds were dropping all over the place, when a guy was hit those crazy medics would run out and drag him out of there," Tanaka said.[9]

Military historians have rated the battle for the Lost Battalion as one of the Army's ten most demanding. As much as anything, it cemented the 442nd's reputation as a group of tireless fighters in the face of tremendous odds. Some of the unit's members from Heart Mountain would receive commendations for extraordinary bravery, while others lived on as memories in the minds of their families and friends. A memorial now stands at Heart Mountain that honors the fifteen soldiers who fought and died during the war.

By the time Inouye returned to his unit, it had spent twenty-five out of twenty-seven days in major combat. Dahlquist called the 442nd to a retreat parade to thank them personally and was irked that so few members were there. "Colonel, I asked that the entire regiment be present for this occasion," Inouye reported Dahlquist saying. "Where are the rest of your men?"

"Sir, you are looking at the entire regiment," the unit's commander said. "Except for the two men on guard duty at each company, this is all that is left of the 442nd Combat Team."[10]

Of Inouye's E Company, only 40 soldiers out of 197 remained to march to the parade ground. One of the Nisei who had fallen during the battle for the Lost Battalion was Fred Yamamoto, the former *Sentinel* reporter who was the first camp prisoner to enlist in early 1943. He was twenty-six. In July 1945, the Army presented a Silver Star to his mother, an award noted in the final edition of the paper for which he once worked. Yamamoto and the other Heart Mountain soldiers who died fighting for the Lost Battalion "probably were more cognizant of the reasons behind their fighting and dying than most of America's youth who are dying from the same painful wounds and on the same unfriendly foreign soil," the *Sentinel* wrote. "One must be many times braver after having been cast out like a stranger to fight and die for principles that have been denied, to prove that he believed in them, even though denied. That is the lot of our boys who are fighting and dying."[11]

Yamamoto's friends and family held two funeral services for him, one in Detroit and another in Chicago. In Detroit, a friend called Yamamoto "a fellow who always gave his services unstintingly in the hope that by his action others might benefit." Bill Hosokawa dedicated his "On the Out-Side" column in the *Sentinel* to him, calling Yamamoto "the farthest thing imaginable from the soldier type, but he was a thorough workman who learned his lessons well." Perhaps, Hosokawa wrote, the mainland Nisei would finally realize that the war had a cost from which they had been spared until recently. "Too many of them, it seems, have lost their sense of values in the evacuation," he continued. Americans of all races and ethnicity were dying in the war, he concluded, and those who survived would make the world a better place. He concluded, "This, if I could, is what I would like to write today to Fred Yamamoto."[12]

Another young Nisei to die in that fight in France was Ted Fujioka, who left behind a large and devastated family. His death, which they were told came during a special assignment, would cast a shadow over all of them for the following seventy years. Even his relatives who were not born until after the war feel his presence, including his nephew Darrell Kunitomi, a Heart Mountain board member. His comrades who saw him killed or saw his lifeless body immediately afterward were also deeply affected. Among them were Ernest Uno, one of Raymond Uno's cousins who served in the 442nd, and Ted's cousin, William Fujioka, who would remain forever scarred by his wartime experiences.[13] When I spoke to Darrell about his uncle Ted, I heard of an all-American boy who embodied patriotism; the war had made Ted even more militant. He sent word back to his family that if he died in combat while they were still imprisoned, he did not want his body returned home. He is buried in a military cemetery in Epinal, France.[14]

Many of the Issei mothers and fathers at Heart Mountain often felt helpless in the face of the government authorities that had forced them from their homes and into the camps. Confronted with the loss of their sons in the war, they often withdrew further. For the Fujioka and Kunitomi families, the death of Ted Fujioka in France left a hole in their souls that remains to this day.

442nd Regimental Combat Team and the Forgotten Front

In Europe, Russian forces closed in on Germany from the east, while Allied troops pushed toward Berlin from the West. After the collapse of the final German offensive in the West over the winter of 1944–45, Germany

145

effectively gave up on the Western front. Exhausted German soldiers began to surrender to Allied forces, but German soldiers continued to put up fierce resistance in Italy, and, as usual, the 442nd Regimental Combat Team was found at most of the action. What war correspondents had dubbed the "Forgotten Front" heated up again in the final weeks of the war. On April 21, Lieutenant Daniel Inouye and his soldiers attacked a German unit dug in along a ridge near San Terenzo along the Gothic Line in northern Tuscany, where German soldiers had massacred villagers several months earlier in retaliation for an ambush by Italian partisans. Atop the ridge, three German machine guns fired at Inouye's unit, cutting down many of its thirty men, including Inouye, who caught a bullet in the stomach as he looked for cover. Inouye ignored the wound as much as he could and destroyed the first machine gun with hand grenades and his submachine gun. A medic told him how badly he was wounded, but Inouye would not stop fighting. "I was shot through the guts," he said. "And the messenger walking behind me said, 'Hey, you're bleeding.' I thought some rocket hit me or something like that. And then all hell broke loose." Inouye led an attack with the second machine gun, which they destroyed before Inouye collapsed from loss of blood. He managed to crawl toward the third machine gun while his men distracted the crew. Ten yards away, Inouye stood up and readied his arm to throw another grenade. Just then a German soldier shot his right elbow with a rocket propelled grenade, almost ripping his arm completely off. The grenade, however, remained tightly "clenched in a fist that suddenly didn't belong to me anymore," Inouye said. His troops tried to rush to help him, but Inouye ordered them to stay back, worried he might drop the grenade, causing it to explode and wound them. As the German inside the bunker paused to reload his rifle, Inouye pried the grenade from his right hand with his left and threw the grenade into the bunker, destroying it. He rose again, fired his submachine gun, and killed the remaining German soldiers. Another shot hit him in the leg. "And now my limb is just hanging with shreds and it's flapping and the blood is just shooting out and you got to be crazy for me to pick up my tommy gun and move forward and fire," he said. Inouye then fell down and rolled unconscious to the bottom of the ridge. When he awakened, he told his troops to get back to their positions. "You might say that's heroics, but if I had to think about it today, you don't think I'd be charging in there like that. The first injury I would say, 'Goodbye, I'm going.' But at that time, I was young, and the mission was very important."[15]

Medics carried Inouye, his right arm barely attached, to the closest field hospital. There, medics amputated the right arm without anesthesia; Inouye had received a great deal of morphine at an aid station, and doctors worried that anesthesia might lower his blood pressure and kill him. His commanding officer recommended Inouye for a Congressional Medal of Honor, but instead he received a Distinguished Service Cross, the Army's second-highest decoration. "I guess they only give [the Medal of Honor] to you when you're dead, which is, maybe, the way it should be," Inouye wrote later. "I was proud of them all, of course—and am now—but somehow they didn't seem terribly important at the time."[16] Fifty-five years later, Congress and President Bill Clinton would correct that injustice; racism, not Inouye's survival, had kept him from receiving the Medal of Honor.

Lost Lives and the 442nd

The fighting that wounded Inouye claimed the lives of two soldiers tied to Heart Mountain—the sensitive, artistic Stanley Hayami, who recorded his time in camp in a vivid diary, and Joe Hayashi from Pasadena, California, who enlisted in May 1941.

Private Hayashi's unit of the 442nd moved against German forces near the Tuscan town of Tendola on April 20. That day, Hayashi, the temporary squad leader, led his squad to within seventy-five yards of a German position before they came under heavy machine gun fire. Hayashi ordered his outnumbered squad to fall back, but he stayed back to help a wounded comrade to safety. He directed mortar fire that wiped out three German machine gun nests. A day later, he singlehandedly killed five German soldiers and wiped out two machine gun nests before he was shot and killed by a Nazi wielding a machine pistol. For his bravery, Hayashi was awarded the Distinguished Service Cross. His sister, Kiyo Hayashi, was a prisoner at Heart Mountain when her brother died.[17]

Two days after Inouye was wounded, his unit made another assault on San Terenzo, which was still heavily fortified by German soldiers. Within moments, German machine gun fire cut down the squad leader. Five other soldiers in the 442nd died during that fight, the last of the Italian campaign. One was Private Hayami, who had rushed from cover under sniper and machine gun fire to give first aid to a wounded soldier. He went to help another wounded soldier before he was killed by sniper fire. He would receive the Bronze Star for his bravery in the same battle that wounded his brother, Frank.[18]

Stanley Hayami, whose artistic diaries would captivate future generations studying life during the incarceration, would never have the chance to demonstrate his talents in life. In his final diary entry, on August 21, 1944, he wondered about his friends and the future. "I wonder what sort of future scientists and artists they'll make," he wrote.[19] Like so many others before him, he never had the chance to find out; he died fighting for the country that had incarcerated him and his family. Hayami's story lives on at the Japanese American National Museum in Los Angeles and has been the subject of a documentary about Heart Mountain.

Throughout Germany and in parts of Eastern Europe, the Nazis had built a series of labor camps near their extermination facilities. The labor camps sustained the German war machine for much of the conflict, making weapons, ammunition, and aircraft. A series of these centers known as the Kaufering concentration camp complex was clustered around the small Bavarian town of Landsberg am Lach, the site of Dachau. Kaufering's prisoners built underground factories for fighter aircraft. By late April, Nazi commanders feared they would be overrun by the Allied troops moving in from the west. They forced the thousands of prisoners to march south toward the Alps.[20]

Members of the 522nd Field Artillery Battalion discovered some of the Kaufering camps soon after the Germans fled. What Clarence Matsumura and his comrades witnessed horrified them. "We saw piles of dead bodies all over the place," he said. The unit continued on the road toward Munich, where they saw a group of skeletal figures stumbling down the road through snow from a surprise spring storm. They wore the striped prisoner uniforms that marked them as Jews from Dachau or the Kaufering complex. One of them was Solly Ganor, a young Lithuanian Jew who had spent the war as a slave laborer. Ganor and his fellow prisoners walked without overcoats and often without shoes. Some of the few remaining Nazi guards shot their prisoners and left them dead in the roadside snow, then fled. Ganor himself trudged on and then found a dead horse from whose belly he cut some strips of meat to make a crude soup. He was in a daze from eating until he heard a noise.

"Below me, on the road, a tank appeared," Ganor wrote later. "Then what looked like a jeep. I closed my eyes, waiting for a bullet to put me out of my misery." What Ganor feared were Nazis returning were instead elements of the 522nd Field Artillery Battalion. Ganor stared at them, not fathoming how Asian soldiers could be in Germany. One of them gave Ganor a chocolate bar, for which Ganor thanked him in halting English. "My name is Clarence," the Japanese American soldier said to him. It was Clarence Matsumura.[21] The gaunt Jewish prisoners were so physically destroyed that they could not swallow food. "We were trying to feed them from the start," Clarence said. "I was trying to feed them biscuits and Hershey bars, and then trying to get it out of their throats."[22]

Clarence took Ganor and his fellow prisoners to his unit's camp, where the soldiers gently fed them what they could tolerate. More survivors streamed in seeking food and shelter. "Toward evening Clarence appeared again and knelt down at my side," Ganor wrote. "'We have to go now,' he said, clasping both my hands in his. 'Thank you, thank you,' I whispered, clinging to his hands. Then he was gone."[23]

Solly Ganor did not realize that until recently his rescuer had also been a prisoner. While Heart Mountain never resembled the gruesome extermination factory of Dachau, it nevertheless held more than ten thousand Japanese Americans prisoner. Clarence had found his way out of camp by working on the railroad, then going back to college before he was drafted. Clarence knew plenty about prisoners and cruel treatment, but Solly Ganor would know nothing about that for another thirty-six years. This chance encounter saved Ganor's life; Clarence would remain haunted for the rest of his life by the scenes he had witnessed at Dachau.[24]

Daniel Inouye:
Zigzagging Home

Daniel Inouye's journey home zigzagged through a series of military hospitals across Italy. The first hospital belonged to the all-black 92nd Division, where Inouye received seventeen pints of blood from another group of Americans victimized by racial discrimination. When he was able, he finagled a pass out of the hospital and made his way to Milan, where he watched a mob hang three fascists upside down and beat their dead bodies to a pulp. He turned away, feeling sick, but did not leave. "I wanted to feel the cries of that mob in my bones. I wanted to know, beyond any possibility of ever forgetting, that the tides of war are violent tides, indeed, not alone for soldiers, but for every human being swept into their tug and haul, tormented beyond endurances by war's cruel and impersonal use of them," he wrote.[25]

Next, it was on to hospitals in Leghorn and Naples, where doctors sewed up the flap over the stump of his amputated right arm; on to a troop ship from Morocco to Miami; and then to a recuperation hospital in Atlantic City, New Jersey. There, he met a fellow Hawaiian Nisei, Sakae Takahashi, whose frustration with the prewar racial discrimination in Hawaii would also influence Inouye. Takahashi, who had left the Army as a captain, said: "What I'm interested in is tomorrow. I want my kids to have every break. I demand it!"[26]

The Medal of Honor

As recognized as the 442nd Regimental Combat Team was for its bravery, its members had thus far been denied, on racist grounds, the highest military commendation—the Congressional Medal of Honor. Many military leaders did not submit the names of Nisei soldiers for the Medal of Honor, instead giving them consideration for the Distinguished Service Cross, a significant accomplishment but in this case a consolation prize from the white commanders, who had often used the Nisei as cannon fodder.[27] In 1996, Senator Daniel Akaka of Hawaii inserted an amendment into that year's annual defense bill that called for a review of the 104 Distinguished Service Cross commendations given to Asian American members of the military during World War II to determine whether they deserved an upgrade to the Medal of Honor. One of the soldiers reviewed was Joe Hayashi, who received a posthumous service cross after his heroics in fight for the Po River valley in April 1945. The case of another soldier, medic James Okubo, was examined under another provision of the law, because Okubo received the Silver Star after his actions during the fight for the Lost Battalion in France in October 1944.[28]

Only one Nisei soldier received the Medal of Honor near the time of his heroism—Sadao Munemori, a native of Los Angeles who enlisted in the Army in February 1942 despite the general prohibition on accepting Japanese Americans into the military. During fighting near Seravezza, Italy, on April 5, 1945, Munemori knocked out a German machine gun nest with grenades. Then a grenade bounced off his helmet and into the foxhole he shared with two fellow soldiers. Without regard for his safety, Munemori jumped on top of the grenade, smothering it before it exploded and killed him instantly. His quick reactions and heroism saved the lives of his comrades. For that, Munemori received the Distinguished Service Cross posthumously. Only the intervention of Mike Masaoka helped Munemori receive a Medal of Honor. Masaoka appealed on Munemori's behalf to Senator Elbert Thomas, a Utah Democrat, a longtime Japanophile, and Masaoka's chief political patron. Thomas engineered the awarding of the Medal of Honor in 1946 to Munemori's family members, who had been incarcerated at Manzanar.[29]

The results of the military review Akaka had pushed for came back in 2000. Twenty-one Asian American veterans, including Inouye, the review concluded, deserved an upgrade to the Medal of Honor. On June 21, the seven surviving veterans—Daniel Inouye, Barney Hajiro, Shizuya Hayashi, Yeiki Kobashigawa, Yukio Okutsu, and George Sakato—gathered in a pavilion on the south lawn of the White House, where President Bill Clinton draped the medals around their necks. Seven others, who had all died before 2000, had had family members incarcerated at the time of their heroics, including Okubo, who rescued several comrades during the intense fighting for the Lost Battalion. A dentist after the war, he died in a car accident in 1967 in Detroit.[30]

It was a ceremony drenched in emotion. "In early 1945 a young Japanese-American of the 442d Regimental Combat Team lay dead on a hill in southern France, the casualty of fierce fighting with the Germans," Clinton said. "A chaplain went up to pray over him, to bless him, to bring him back down. As the chaplain later said, 'I found a letter in his pocket. The soldier had just learned that some vandals in California had burned down his father's home and barn in the name of patriotism. And yet, this young man had volunteered for every patrol he could go on.'"

Clinton's remarks summed up the ironies surrounding the men who served despite the racism directed at them by their fellow countrymen, some of them relatives of the men with whom they served in Europe. "Rarely has a nation been so well served by a people it had so ill-treated," the president said. "For their numbers and length of service, the Japanese-Americans of the 442d Regimental Combat Team, including the 100th Infantry Battalion, became the most decorated unit for its size in American military history. By the end of the war, America's military leaders in Europe all wanted these men under their command. Their motto was 'Go for Broke.' They risked it all to win it all."

The president acknowledged Inouye, saying, "Senator Inouye, you wrote that your father told you, as you left at age eighteen to join the Army and fight a war, that the Inouyes owe an unrepayable debt to America. If I may say so, sir, more than half a century later, America owes an unrepayable debt to you and your colleagues." He nodded to Inouye, Norman

Mineta, Spark Matsunaga, and Robert Matsui, who had led the push for the redress movement that finally led the nation to call "internment an injustice, based on 'race prejudice, war hysteria, and a failure of political leadership.' It prescribed several steps for redress, one of which was an apology from the Congress and the President."

The nation needed, Clinton said, to acknowledge that "it is long past time to break the silence about their courage, to put faces and names with the courage, and to honor it by name: Davila, Hajiro, Hayashi, Inouye, Kobashigawa, Okutsu, Sakato, Hasemoto, Hayashi, Kuroda, Moto, Muranaga, Nakae, Nakamine, Nakamura, Nishimoto, Ohata, Okubo, Ono, Otani, Tanouye, Wai. These American soldiers, with names we at long last recognize as American names, made an impact that soars beyond the force of any battle. They left a lasting imprint on the meaning of America. They didn't give up on our country, even when too many of their countrymen and women had given up on them. They deserve, at the least, the most we can give—the Medal of Honor."[31]

9

Ending the Exclusion Order

◇◇◇

After the 1944 election, Roosevelt and his cabinet decided they would end the exclusion order that had forced the Japanese Americans from their homes on the West Coast. They knew the Supreme Court was close to issuing opinions in the *Korematsu* and *Endo* cases and preferred to act on their own rather than possibly have their hand forced by court order. Attorney General Francis Biddle wrote Roosevelt on November 20 to tell him that rumors were building inside the camps and within the Japanese American diaspora around the country that the exclusion order would be lifted and that people would soon be allowed to return to the West Coast. Roosevelt told reporters the next day that he did not know whether the dangers to the military bases on the West Coast still existed, but it was clear that virtually all of the decision makers in his administration believed it no longer existed, if it ever had.[1]

The Army made the end of the exclusion official on December 17 with Public Proclamation No. 21. It had ominous news for those prisoners whom authorities had judged as disloyal, those who had answered no to questions 27 and 28 on the loyalty questionnaire, and virtually everyone whom the WRA had sent to Tule Lake. It stated that "persons of Japanese ancestry whose records have stood the test of Army scrutiny during the past two years will be permitted the same freedom of movement throughout the United States as other loyal citizens and law-abiding aliens."[2] The proclamation continued, saying that the decision to revoke the exclusion orders had been "prompted by military consideration," at best a shading of the truth. In fact, key members of the military had known before the promulgation of Executive Order 9066 that there was little military justification for the incarceration of so many people. So had the politicians and members of the War Department. The proclamation also repeated the fiction that no one could determine which Japanese Americans were loyal and which were not. "Mass treatment of all Japanese Americans, therefore, was a necessary military precaution," it continued. "Since that time, persons of Japanese Ancestry who were evacuated from the coastal area have been thoroughly investigated from the standpoint of loyalty probably more thoroughly than any other segment of our population."

It would take decades for the government to acknowledge what it knew and when it knew it. At the time of the proclamation, however, the 8,789 prisoners at Heart Mountain knew nothing about the government's deceptions. They cared only that they had only days, weeks, or months to remain in camp. Their freedom, however, would prove difficult, because many of them had no homes to which to return.[3]

At Heart Mountain, the remaining prisoners were jubilant. "X-Day—the end of exclusion of American citizens of Japanese ancestry and their law-abiding parents from the Western Defense Command—brought to more than 100,000 persons Sunday their greatest Christmas gift: freedom to trod the streets and fields of the nation with the same rights and privileges of others," the *Sentinel* wrote in its December 23 edition, the first since the end of the exclusion. "Thus after two years and seven months of confinement in hastily constructed camps in six states, American citizens and their alien parents had the opportunity to return to the flowing stream of life."[4]

Within hours, the mechanisms of the War Relocation Authority shifted to move the prisoners from their camps and back to their former homes or wherever else they wanted to go. Camp director Guy Robertson quickly appointed Joe Carroll, the jobs director, to coordinate the relocation of the prisoners and the eventual closing of the camp. "All developments, as they are announced from Washington, will be transmitted and circulated to Heart Mountain residents as quickly as they are received," the *Sentinel* said in a rare extra edition. Block committee leaders joined with the camp administration to work with the families to arrange their departures. Many of the families, such as the Higuchis, had long thought about where they would go and what they would do. Others, such as the Unos, viewed the announcement with trepidation. They had left their lives in Utah and relocated to California to be with Clarence, a skilled Japanese community organizer. His death at Heart Mountain, however, left them with no natural place to go.[5]

In California, some of the politicians responsible for removing the Japanese Americans claimed to welcome them back. Governor Earl Warren, the former attorney general who had fed fears of thousands of potential saboteurs, urged "cheerful compliance" with the military's decision. "I am sure that all Americans will join in protecting the constitutional rights of the individuals involved and will maintain an attitude that will discourage friction and prevent civil disorder."[6]

President Franklin Roosevelt's decision to end the exclusion and allow Japanese Americans to return home meant that Heart Mountain and the other camps would close during 1945. The camp in Jerome, Arkansas, had closed in 1944, and at least four hundred of its prisoners had gone to Heart Mountain, where the seven thousand remaining incarcerees faced the challenge of arranging new jobs and places to live. Most of those who had the ability to leave had already done so, building Japanese American communities in cities such as Cincinnati, Cleveland, and Chicago. More than three thousand Nisei, such as my uncle Kiyoshi, studied in universities in colleges outside the exclusion zone. The Higuchi family's three oldest sons were either in the military, working on their graduate degrees, or working in military industries in the Midwest. Now, thousands of others would be free to either follow them east or return to the West Coast.

My paternal grandfather's health suffered in the months after the end of the exclusion, because he realized he had lost his farm in San Jose and would have to replace it. He had never wanted to cooperate with the forced sale of the 14.25 acres in San Jose, and the stress caused by thinking about replacing it was immense.

What Next?

At Heart Mountain, administrators and prisoners alike scrambled to close the camp and return home. Many incarcerees feared what would greet them at their former homes in California, Oregon, or Washington. They knew the long-standing racism in the area had not disappeared. While some of the early returnees sent reports of favorable welcomes and neighbors who had watched their homes and businesses, others faced vandalism and violence. Readers of the *Sentinel* became familiar with the case of the Doi family, which returned to the family farm in Auburn, California, after more than two years in the camp in Amache, Colorado. The family was harassed by local white men, including two soldiers. Four people were indicted and later acquitted on charges that they had planned to burn and dynamite the

Dois' home and farm. The *Sentinel*'s coverage no doubt heightened the concerns of the prisoners preparing to return to California.[7]

The War Relocation Authority, charged with the task of moving the prisoners out of the camps, teamed with the *Sentinel* to counter the negative reports and set the prisoners' minds at ease. Dillon Myer said he did not anticipate problems for the returning evacuees and expected that they would not encounter difficulty from returning soldiers who "are familiar with the exploits of the 442nd Regimental Combat Team in Italy. And too many of them are familiar with the work being done by Japanese Americans with our forces in the Pacific right now."[8] All of that may have been true, but many of the people at Heart Mountain and the other camps remained concerned about what they would find in their former homes. Many had experienced racism before they left, and those who lived in the cities, such as Los Angeles and San Francisco, knew the attitudes there remained bitter toward Japanese Americans.

In February 1945, the *Sentinel* regularly trumpeted jobs opening throughout the country as the nation tried to end the war by year's end.[9] In New England, reports said, Japanese Americans could find work in agriculture or service industries. One Heart Mountain prisoner, Samuel Nagata, traveled to Boston for three days to investigate job options and told the *Sentinel* about how impressed he had been by the opportunities there.[10] For the farmer from the Yakima Valley, an advertisement in the *Sentinel* touted 150 acres of rich farmland featuring "Deep rich soil, lots of water" to anyone willing to rent it.[11] In San Jose, to which former Heart Mountain agriculture chief Eiichi Sakauye had returned, he reported there were plenty of jobs paying $1.25 an hour to those who could do them. "We are now pretty well settled in our once evacuation-torn home, enjoying the very comfort and normality of everyday rural living," Sakauye said. He added the almost obligatory note of optimism to encourage the returning prisoners. "So far we have been treated very well. We have experienced no feeling of prejudice."[12] One San Jose family, however, had a much different experience. The Takedas, who had moved inland to Fresno, California, before their incarceration and then been sent to the Gila River concentration camp in Arizona, returned to their farm. In March 1945, an arsonist doused their home with gasoline and set it afire. When the family ran outside to put out the fire, someone drove by and shot at them.[13] Even those who had left camp for comfortable lives in other cities, such as Cincinnati, knew they were being "spoon fed" propaganda by the WRA, said Sumi Kiba, a former prisoner who had moved to Cincinnati and been elected as the Parent Teachers Association publicity chief at her children's school. "Cincinnati is not wonderful; it is just normal," she told the *Sentinel*. Acceptance in the rest of the United States, she said, "depends on the individual no matter where he goes."[14]

Limited Options

By early summer 1945, the WRA had increased its efforts to persuade the remaining prisoners to leave. Too many, however, had very limited options. Three years of incarceration had paralyzed many of the Issei, so the authorities prepared what the *Sentinel* described as "relocation assistance for those families who have no place to go, no reserve funds to make their resettlement easier and no employable members to provide even day to day earnings."[15] Incarcerees who did not leave now, officials argued, might lose their chance at government help. Camp facilities would close, Guy Robertson warned, leaving the stragglers without "food and other comforts." Already, the hospital had stopped providing dental care except in emergencies. Administrators added extra trains to California and the East Coast to accommodate the rush of people leaving Heart Mountain and considered adding trains to Spokane, Portland, and Seattle.[16]

In the San Francisco area, the Federal Housing Authority teamed with the JACL to locate homes, because the lack of housing was keeping many incarcerees from returning to the cities where they had lived before the war. They released questionnaires to Heart Mountain residents to see what types of homes they wanted. Temporary hostels were opening in cities around the country to accommodate departing prisoners. In Pittsburgh, a hostel said it would have room for twelve to eighteen families, while three hostels opened in Seattle. All this happened while the WRA tried to fix problems that affected the trains taking people back to the West Coast or elsewhere. Some of the train cars ran out of drinking water, while others lacked functioning bathrooms.[17]

Messages posted in the *Sentinel* showed just how widely the prisoners had scattered. "We wish to express our sincere gratitude to friends and neighbors for the many courtesies accorded us during our stay in the center. We have relocated to Oklahoma," wrote Mr. and Mrs. Keiichi Kobuchi and family, who were originally from San Francisco. Tokichi Hashimoto, of 25-18-E, thanked friends and neighbors "for the many courtesies accorded my wife, Haruko, and son, Toshio, during their stay in the center."

His wife had moved to Cleveland, while his son was in the Army. Kazuo Mihara and family moved to Buffalo, New York. Tadao Toyoshima and his family returned to their former home in Los Angeles.[18] These messages showed that Heart Mountain was a community, not just a prison camp. Proof of this comes from the frequent reunions of former incarcerees and their pilgrimages back to Heart Mountain each year.

Some families that had lost businesses, homes, or both felt they could not return to the West Coast. Bacon Sakatani's family, which had farmed land in Southern California's San Gabriel Valley, moved to Idaho, where Takami Sakatani had found work on a farm. The primitive conditions they encountered on arrival in Idaho took Bacon's breath away. A coal-burning stove provided the only heat for the small house, which used running water from a cistern and an irrigation ditch. "That water was coming from the river, so that water from the ditch was going into the cistern," he said. Other families from Heart Mountain also settled in Idaho, and their children attended the same school as Bacon. When the potato harvest ended, so did the jobs, so the Sakatanis packed up and headed back to California.[19]

The Mihara family, which had lived in San Francisco near the Saitos before the war, had different reasons for its move to Utah, where many Japanese Americans had fled to avoid incarceration. Before the war, Tokinobu Mihara had worked as a newspaper editor in San Francisco, but the dust at Heart Mountain had stolen his sight. His father, Tsunegoro, had died from colon cancer aggravated by malpractice by the Heart Mountain doctors. In poor health and worried about the remaining racism back in San Francisco, Tokinobu moved the family to Salt Lake City, where he opened a Japanese-language bookstore. "He had to get into a new business because he went blind in the camp," said Sam Mihara, Tokinobu's son.[20]

The first year after the end of the war saw millions of Americans returning home, either from their wartime posts or, in the case of the Japanese Americans, from their exile. White Americans tried to cope with their dramatic reentry into society, while Japanese Americans returned to communities that often resented their presence. Transitions were difficult. The years families spent in camps might have provided a respite from the pressures of tending to a farm or business; however, most Issei had either lost or sold such properties at a steep discount when they went to the camps. Now they had to start from scratch to provide for their families, rebuild their savings, and prepare for their retirements. Family problems that had started before the war had festered and grown into larger disputes as years of enforced idleness gave many the time to nurse their grievances, real or imagined. These conditions exacerbated the expected problems associated with reentry to regular society as well as whatever mental health issues existed, which remained undiagnosed and untreated.

The Higuchis

The Higuchis had lost everything and had sold their farm in San Jose for pennies on the dollar in April 1942, just days before they took the train to Santa Anita. They spent the first half of 1945 worrying about their future. Their two children who remained with them at Heart Mountain—my father, Bill, and his sister Emily—were fourteen and eight. My grandparents now needed to find work and put a roof over their heads, a difficult challenge for farmers in a nation still at war.

On May 9, my grandfather Iyekichi wrote the relocation office to seek permission to allow my father to leave camp for Akron, Ohio, where his brother Takeru, who was married with a young child, was working alone as a scientist in a military rubber factory. The family's future was still uncertain, but the family was "talking about going east to relocate and thinks during the summer they will leave this center," a camp official noted in my father's WRA file, which also had the inappropriate notation that "he is a sturdy, well-built boy, unusually good looking."[21] I believe my father was torn, because his parents were ready to let him leave for Ohio and a better life, while he wanted to keep his family together.

Later that month, however, my grandfather Iyekichi was eating in the mess hall when he felt a tightness in his chest and numbness in his arms. He was having a heart attack. The medical staff rushed him to the camp hospital, where his condition stabilized. But the event stopped Bill's plans to leave for Akron. The Higuchis had to pause and determine what to do once Iyekichi recovered.[22] The illness was most likely Iyekichi's subconscious way of expressing his desire that his remaining son not leave.

By early June, three hundred people were leaving Heart Mountain each week, a pace that no other camp had reached so quickly. Each departing prisoner received a train or bus ticket to his or her final destination and $25 once it had been determined where the person was going. Dillon Myer congratulated camp director Guy Robertson, who said the departures represented "the desires of the progressive and loyal residents of the center. The part played by the administration is simply one of assistance—we are the means to the residents accomplishing their desires."[23]

Iyekichi had recovered enough by early July to start planning his trip to Santa Clara County to look for a new home. He paid for his travels with the unemployment benefits he had received while recuperating from his heart attack.[24] Robertson signed Iyekichi's permission slip to leave camp for Cupertino, California, to "investigate relocation possibilities" via the "usually traveled bus and train route"; he was to depart on July 30 and return by August 28.[25] It was a trip into the unknown. Upon reviewing my family's files, I was heartbroken to see that a camp administrator had noted the family's huge financial loss in the hurried sale of their farm and commented that "the family hasn't a house yet, and is having a hard time." But on August 8, Heart Mountain's relocation officer, Joe Carroll, reported to Robertson that Iyekichi had arranged to rent a farm to which he would take my grandmother, father, and Emily on August 17. They had another member of their party—sixty-two-year-old Juntaro Iwori, an Issei widower they had known in camp and who had nowhere to go. In keeping with the way that my grandfather had allowed the Briones family to live for free on the family farm before the war, Iyekichi was looking out for others. Iwori, Carroll wrote, "will work for Mr. Higuchi as a farm laborer. Their departure will complete the family relocation."[26]

Iwori, my father remembered, "was a friend from the previous days. He was a bachelor. I remember him not being able to go elsewhere. He stayed with our family for quite a while after we came back to California," Bill said.[27] Throughout my life, I always considered Iyekichi to be gruff and distant, but my research into his experience showed that he was someone who gave whenever he had the chance, whether he had the money or not.

For Iyekichi and Chiye Higuchi, anti-Japanese discrimination was less of a concern than the challenges of finding a suitable home and promising land to farm. After staying with another Japanese American family, they moved to a small cabin in Los Altos owned by George Cummings, a San Francisco businessman. Their new home in Los Altos had been vacant for years and lacked plumbing and heat. In exchange for staying there rent-free, Chiye did housework for the larger Cummings estate and covered the cabin's dirty walls with newspaper, and Iyekichi and my father installed plumbing. It was not much, but it was a home outside barbed wire, and it gave them a chance to rebuild.[28]

For Bill, the thought of starting at a new school in Mountain View made him more nervous or upset than going to Heart Mountain had. As stressful as camp life had been for the Issei who knew what they had lost, being released from camp posed a similar challenge to children and adolescents. Life inside camp was controlled and predictable. The prisoners lived in a community consisting only of Japanese Americans. Life in California, in contrast, meant adjusting to a new school, new classmates, and the reality of helping the family get reestablished. Bill knew the family had a lot to do to get back to where their lives had been before the war, but he felt as if he were not helping enough. "I couldn't be sitting around," he said. "I felt I had to help my father."[29]

Iyekichi worked as a gardener for various landowners around the county, and my father accompanied him on the weekends, trying his best to help but wondering if he was actually more of a hindrance. The Higuchis felt pressure to make and save enough money to buy another farm of their own. Meanwhile, family tensions made life more difficult. Their three oldest sons had grown up and moved elsewhere, except for James, the eldest, who had returned to San Jose to start a medical practice. Even before the war, James had had a strained and alienated relationship with Iyekichi. "I felt that he didn't trust me; that I was sure to go astray," James said. Matters worsened when they all returned to San Jose, James from the war and the rest from Heart Mountain. For some reason, James noted, Iyekichi had an "unreasonable, malevolent, almost insane hatred" of James's mother-in-law, Tsuchiye Iwagaki, who sometimes "irritated and angered" James, too.[30] Perhaps at this point the stress of losing everything, including his sons, had affected my grandfather strongly and caused him to act this way. I do not completely understand the friction that characterized this relationship, but I can only imagine that my grandfather had hoped his sons would stay closer to the farm and help him rebuild his business. Perhaps the marriage between Amy and James compromised those plans.

As James coped with the stress of building a medical practice, Iyekichi worked to raise enough money to buy a new farm—twenty acres in south San Jose. After seeing patients all day, most of them drawn from the returning Japanese American community, James often drove to the new farm to help his father and younger brother. Just as often, however, James had to stay at work to care for his growing practice, which hurt his relationship with his father, who "thought that I was getting rich and that I should be helping him more money-wise."[31]

My father, who before the war had spoken more Spanish than Japanese, became more focused on his new Japanese American friends at his new school. Now fifteen, he did not feel any overt discrimination from the white students. "I was left alone but if I wanted to participate I could," he said. He joined the high school track team, where he ran and threw the shot put. The team won the county championship, which gave Bill bragging rights and a dose of confidence. When the summer of 1946 rolled around, he found work on the farm of a returning Nisei veteran and the older brother of a friend from school. He irrigated the land and picked tomatoes. "It was inspirational," Bill said, adding that he gained confidence and a sense of the future. "It really felt like I was breaking out into the open."[32]

The Saitos

Fourteen-year-old Setsuko Saito also dreamed of a new home. Her father, Yoshio, was preparing a trip to San Francisco to look for work and a place to live for him, his wife, and their four children, ages two to sixteen. In the mail to the family home at Block 2, Barrack 14, Apartment B, my mother received a book by George Nelson and Henry Wright, a consultant and managing editor for the magazine *Architectural Forum*, that she had sent away for. *Tomorrow's House* presented advice to homeowners seeking to plan a new home or to remodel their current home and to "make the best use of the latest materials, equipment, and appliances." *Tomorrow's House* heralded the postwar construction boom that would dramatically reshape America. It gave advice about efficient kitchen planning, windows, and even solar heating, decades before that became in vogue.[33] Around the same time, Setsuko also received a pamphlet she had requested from the Timken-Detroit Axle Company of Detroit featuring "home hints for post-war planners."[34] The book and pamphlet signaled at an early age what would evolve into Setsuko's long infatuation with real estate and acquiring the best home ever. By the time she died, in 2005, she had obtained her real estate license and had bought, renovated, and sold more than twenty homes.

My grandfather Saito arrived in a San Francisco dramatically different from the one he had left. Much of the city's Japantown, which had spread over seventy-four blocks, had been taken over by wartime migrants, many of them African Americans from the South. The Saitos had to adapt to the changing San Francisco while also reclaiming a semblance of their former lives. By early August, Yoshio still had not found a new home, and he asked the WRA for an extension. Shortly afterward, he found a home in a residential hotel called Yoshimoro's. My uncle Al Saito remembered his father's return and the journey from Heart Mountain at the end of August. "By train we went north up to Billings, and the train stopped there for several hours, so we got off the train and walked up this hill, and we saw this restaurant, and we had this dinner. It was a steak dinner, and it was wonderful. We hadn't had tender steaks in I don't know how long, and it really created an impression."

The train went on to Salt Lake City and finally to Oakland, where the Saitos took a ferry to San Francisco. "My father took a limousine and took us to Japantown," Al said. The family—Yoshio, my grandmother Fumi, my uncles Al and Hiroshi, my aunt Kathleen, and my mother, Setsuko—stuffed themselves into a small apartment.[35]

The family may have had a place to live, but it had virtually nothing else. What Yoshio had stored in the church basement in San Francisco had been lost or stolen. Yoshio haggled with the remaining WRA officials back at Heart Mountain, where he had worked in the warehouse, where he had stored whatever possessions the family had acquired while at Heart Mountain. On September 30, he wrote Harvey Burnett, the camp's property officer, asking him to keep the family's belongings in storage. In his typically ingratiating fashion, Yoshio expressed "sincere appreciation of gratitude for everything that you did for me while I was in Heart Mt., especially your kind attention and courtesies extended to me in regard to my properties and other matters upon my departure from the camp." His children, Yoshio reported, were now in junior high and high school. "I'm so grateful that we came back to San Francisco just in time for school opening and we didn't miss a day," he wrote. Yoshio had a temporary job in the WRA warehouse in San Francisco as he sought a more permanent home than the residential hotel. "As to my housing problem, it's still my biggest headache, up to this time I'm still unable to find my permanent living quarter, although I have one in mind on Sutter St., near Buchanan St. which house is owned by a friend of mine. The tenant is still occupying the premises despite of the fact that they received an eviction notice some time ago and we are unable to move in yet."[36] After they returned to San Francisco, my mother, Setsuko, and her brother Al entered the city's Lowell High School. This began a four-year period that tested Setsuko's resolve; during this time she bore increasing burdens to help the family, including working as a hotel maid to raise money to pay college tuition for Al and then her younger brother, Hiroshi. This period had a huge impact on her life, and she brought it up periodically throughout my life. These years in the paternalistic world of her father increased her already strong desire to secure her own home and destiny. I think she was torn between her desire to be independent and a highly functioning professional and the pressure on her to assume the traditional woman's role, which required putting men first, with her father, then her brothers, and, finally, my father. She underestimated her value, perhaps because she had no female role models to show her what she could be.

Her father had found a home, but much of what he considered his property still remained in a warehouse at Heart Mountain. There he had stored thirty-one boxes that he hoped to have shipped to his new home, but warehouse workers and WRA officials had opened the boxes and found material that "could definitely be identified as having been pilfered" from the warehouse.[37]

In a letter on February 6, 1946, my grandfather was told he would receive only twenty-four of the thirty-one boxes in the warehouse because "your boxes contained considerable government property, all of which was removed." Throughout his time in camp, Yoshio had cultivated the Caucasian administrators, ingratiating himself as best he could, but clearly he still remained under scrutiny. The WRA Internal Security Office had monitored Yoshio, property officer Harvey Burnett wrote, because "you had been under suspicion. . . . I sincerely regret that after the confidence bestowed upon you, that so much evidence of deliberate theft was obtained from your shipment."[38] Neither Burnett nor the government ever detailed what they claimed my grandfather had tried to steal, but since the government had already started to give away the camp's building and equipment, how valuable could it have been? Was it worth more than the store that Yoshio Saito had lost when he was imprisoned without trial? I often wondered what was in those boxes, theorizing it was most likely toilet paper and canned goods. There is no sign that anyone besides Yoshio knew about this, because the information in the WRA files was a revelation to me and to my aunt Kathleen, the only surviving member of the family.

The Minetas

In Chicago, the end of war meant there was little demand for Kunisaku Mineta to continue teaching Japanese at the University of Chicago.

The Minetas returned home to San Jose in October with a truck filled with crates, trunks, and boxes of belongings. Their friends had watched their home during the war, and they found their house intact but in disarray. "The trees in the garden grew so tall, and the garden is in awful condition," Kunisaku wrote a friend in Chicago. "The house was so dirty so [it] kept us so busy every day, actually we did not know what to do first. But we worked so hard and so long hours and [it's] getting little better." But in San Jose the air "is so nice," and the fall rains had started, turning the surrounding hills and valley green.[39]

Kunisaku Mineta resumed his insurance business, but many of the farmers and businessmen who had once relied on insurance from the Minetas no longer had businesses or homes to insure. Norman returned to school and tried to pick up where he had left off in 1942, when his classmates had walked from school to see him off at the freight yards. He remembered his parents trying to tamp down anti-Japanese sentiment in the community and how the *San Jose Mercury News* spoke out against discrimination against the returning Japanese Americans. Just as he had made friends at Heart Mountain with Alan Simpson from the Boy Scout troop from Cody, Norman formed friendships back home that spanned the ethnic diversity of the area. Even though Filipino Americans bore resentment against the Japanese for their invasion and occupation of the Philippines, Norman's best friend in school was a Filipino. Norman's parents, he said, "were trying hard to tamp down any animosity between the majority of the community and especially the Japanese Americans."[40] San Jose, like the rest of the country, had changed. Ethnic communities, even the Japanese Americans, could no longer remain as isolated as they had been before, which the Minetas and other forward-thinking Japanese Americans realized had made it easier for Caucasians to see them as rivals and to imprison them. The Minetas realized they had to integrate into the larger society after the war, emulating one of their business associates, the influential Issei farmer I. K. Ishimatsu, who urged the area's Nikkei community to become more politically active.[41]

The Unos

At least the Minetas had a home to which to return. For months, Raymond Uno's family did not. Raymond, his mother, Osako, and his sister, Yuki, could not go back to El Monte, California. The house they had left there no longer belonged to them. Clarence Uno's death had stripped them of their breadwinner and anchor. Osako had struggled for more than a year just to get some of Clarence's possessions shipped to her at Heart Mountain. Her oldest son, Wallace, had left Heart Mountain in 1944 to finish high school in Ogden, Utah. In February, Osako looked for a home for her and her two children who remained with her, Yuki and Raymond. She asked her niece, Amy Tanaka, who was at the camp in Amache, Colorado, whether the family could live with her family, but "Mrs. Tanaka has two small children of her own and did not wish to assume responsibility for Mrs. Uno's children," said a memo from the Heart Mountain welfare section. Amy Tanaka thought that the Unos' home in El Monte, California, belonged to the family, when in fact it was actually owned by the San Gabriel Valley Japanese Association. Osako wanted to either go back to California or move to Ogden to rejoin Wallace, who had moved there in November 1944.[42]

In July, Osako visited her aunt in Ogden and found a job and an apartment at Esther Hall, a women-only Methodist home, where her sons could not live with her. The three remaining Unos prepared to leave on August 17 with $163.20 in cash Osako had received from the government to get her started.[43] In Ogden, Raymond said, Osako had "just a bedroom, a kitchen and a front room and she and my sister stayed there," while he and Wallace moved in with another family. Even outside the camp, the Unos remained separated.

Separated from his mother and sister, fifteen-year-old Raymond Uno essentially cared for himself in the months after his return from Heart Mountain. His older brother, Wallace, turned eighteen while they lived together and then joined the Army in June 1946, leaving Raymond essentially alone and virtually broke. He channeled his energies into sports, playing football and wrestling well enough to become Utah champion in his weight class.

"We had no more contact with California" and their prewar life there, Raymond said. "My mother had an aunt in Ogden," so the family moved there. "We got $25 and a bus ticket. We left the way we arrived with what we could carry."[44]

Daniel Inouye

Daniel Inouye remained in the rehabilitation hospital in Atlantic City until the middle of 1946, and he took every training class he could, "because I was incapable of allowing anyone's sympathy to make things easier for me." He used everything the military gave him except for the artificial arm he had been fitted with, because he "hated it from the instant it touched me." For the rest of his life, Inouye would be known for the empty sleeve that hung from his suit jackets.

After Atlantic City, Inouye moved to the Percy Jones Army Hospital in Battle Creek, Michigan, for another nine months of training. He again witnessed the discrimination that had existed before and during the war and began to exercise the powers of persuasion and stubbornness that would mark his political career. He had the impression that too many of the patients at the new hospital had begun to divide up by ethnic groups— Irish soldiers would hang out with other Irish patients, while Italians would associate with other Italians. "I suppose it reminded me of the kinds of discrimination I'd come up against," he wrote. All of the groups, however, welcomed Inouye, most likely because he was the only Japanese American there. Gradually, he began to pull all the various groups together. If the Irish veterans were going out as a group with Inouye, he would insist on bringing others or he would stay home. "It wasn't very hard; there were only thirty in our barracks and I can be very persistent," he said.[45]

While in Battle Creek, Inouye became acquainted with two other wounded soldiers with whom he would serve in Congress—Philip Hart of Michigan and Bob Dole of Kansas. Hart had been wounded in 1944 during the landing on the beaches in Normandy, France, while Dole had been shot in April 1945 by German machine gun fire in Italy's Apennine Mountains, not far from where Inouye had suffered his wounds. All three men's wounds required lengthy recoveries, and their joint service tied them together despite their partisan differences. The Percy Jones hospital closed in 1953, but the entire federal complex in Battle Creek is now named the Hart-Dole-Inouye Federal Center, after its three most famous patients.[46]

After his discharge from Percy Jones, Inouye had one experience that more than anything cemented his feelings about the common prejudices inflicted on Japanese Americans, including and especially those who had served honorably and had lost limbs in the service of their country. He was traveling back to Hawaii for good and had stopped in a barber shop outside San Francisco, wearing his crisply cleaned and pressed uniform.

"Are you Chinese?" a man at the door of the barbershop said.

Inouye looked into the shop and saw three empty chairs.

"I'm an American," he said.

"Are you Chinese?" the man asked again.

"I think what you want to know is where my father was born," Inouye answered. "My father was born in Japan. I'm an American."

"Don't give me that American stuff," the barber said. "You're a Jap and we don't cut Jap hair." Inouye wanted to hit him but held back. "I'm sorry," he said finally. "I'm sorry for you and the likes of you." Then he left, soon to board his ship and return home. He would never forget what had happened, and the story would become a central part of the Inouye legend that most Japanese Americans would learn about and feel, as if it were a part of their own story.[47]

Clarence Matsumura

Clarence Matsumura returned home scarred by what he and his comrades had found at Dachau and by the sheer scope of the inhumanity of the Nazis. He did not know the names of the young Jewish men they had rescued on the side of the road or what had happened to them. After the war, he gravitated to Minneapolis, Minnesota, as did his parents, who had nowhere else to go after their release from the camp. He had served in the Army for little more than a year, but the experience had scarred him more than the time he spent in camp. Once back stateside, he had few people with whom he could share his experiences, so he said nothing about what he had seen, what he had felt. "How could anyone understand who didn't see it?" he asked later. "You can't really explain how it is, when you've got all of these people, so many of them, and you're trying to help them and they're dying, right there in your hands?"[48]

Clarence had elements of what psychologists now call posttraumatic stress disorder, as did many other veterans. He rarely talked about the trauma that would affect his life and relationships for the next forty years. He bottled up his experience at Heart Mountain and what he had seen in Dachau and on the roads where the Jewish prisoners were sent on their death march. "Just like many other things, that story was hidden for many, many years," said his niece, Sheila Newlin.[49]

Takashi Hoshizaki and the Antidraft Activists

After he returned home, Takashi went to college, just as millions of other young men returning from the war did. At Los Angeles City College, the ex-convict and draft resister sat among returning combat veterans. Tak kept quiet and studied botany, the subject in which he would eventually earn his PhD. On his first day at Los Angeles City College, he met Barbara Joe, a fellow botanist whom he would marry in 1952. Barbara was Chinese American, and her parents recoiled at their daughter being involved with a Japanese American. "I had to be very careful step-wise to introduce Barbara to my parents and then go and get to meet her parents," Takashi said seventy-two years after they met. "At the wedding we sorta make a joke of it. I said, 'Yeah, we had my family sitting on the left side of the church, her family sat on the right side, and all the Caucasian friends sat in between.'"[50]

Many of the other antidraft activists returned to far more unsettled lives. Frank Emi went back to his family in Los Angeles. He had lost his grocery business when he went to Heart Mountain, so he found a job working for the US Postal Service.[51] Back in Los Angeles, Kiyoshi Okamoto tried to write a book about his experiences. "Yes, you may have a book in the material you outlined in your letter," an agent wrote Okamoto from New York. "If you ever finish a few chapters, I should be very glad to look at them."[52] Min Tamesa returned to Washington State and worked in a foundry.[53] Ben Wakaye could find work only as a janitor after he returned home; he died too young, at thirty-nine, in 1952.[54] Guntaro Kubota, a graduate of a Japanese university, became a landscaper.[55] Paul Nakadate opened a produce stand after he returned to Los Angeles.[56]

Meanwhile, the Nisei veterans received hero's welcomes. Most Americans knew nothing about the incarceration, but they knew about the Go for Broke! boys of the 442nd Regimental Combat Team. Mike Masaoka and the leaders of the JACL had counted on the bravery of the Nisei soldiers to win acceptance for the larger Japanese American community, a belief that seemed to be validated when President Harry Truman hosted a contingent of the 442nd at the White House on July 15, 1946. "You fought for the free nations of the world along with the rest of us. I congratulate you on that," Truman said, "and I can't tell you how very much I appreciate the privilege of being able to show you just how much the United States of America thinks of what you have done."[57] Truman also understood that the resisters had received unfair treatment from the government, which had imprisoned them unfairly and then tried to force them into the Army. He pardoned the draft resisters on December 24, 1947.[58]

The Korean War

On June 25, 1950, North Korean troops rushed across the 48th Parallel into South Korea in a frantic attempt to unify the two countries under the banner of Communism. The United States, which had demobilized much of its military after World War II, had to rebuild its forces again to fight the invasion along with a contingent of troops from the United Nations. Troops rushed to Korea from occupied Japan, and Americans who had been kept in camps during the last war were now being drafted into the Army to serve in Korea. Among them were former Heart Mountain prisoners Raymond Uno, Norman Mineta, Takashi Hoshizaki, and Clarence Matsumura. Meanwhile, my uncle Kiyoshi Higuchi had moved to Maryland to work in one of the military's most secret bases, the Army's biological and chemical warfare center at Fort Detrick.

All of these men, once deemed enemy aliens, served in multiple capacities during the Korean War. Raymond became a member of the Military Intelligence Service focused on finding potential security threats in Japan. He served with the 441st Counterintelligence Corps, which worked near the Imperial Palace in Tokyo. At one point, Raymond asked for a transfer, because he resented how some of the Caucasian officers treated the Nisei soldiers. It was only through a coincidence that he did not get shipped to Korea with the rest of his unit. While on leave, he encountered a former instructor in the train station of the old city of Kyoto. Raymond asked what the instructor was doing, and he said the entire unit had been sent to Korea. When Raymond asked to join his unit in Korea, his commanders told him his Japanese language skills made him too valuable. "We've got too much invested in you," they said.[59] Those late nights studying in the Fort Ord latrines had helped spare him from combat.

Takashi, who had entered college after returning from prison, was drafted in 1953, at the tail end of the war. Unlike in 1944, he reported for induction, went through basic training, and became a medic. He was one of six Heart Mountain draft resisters who were drafted and served during the Korean War—proof, he said, that his resistance had more to do with fighting injustice than any cowardice on his own part. He and his fellow resisters had meant it when they said they shared the same patriotism as the soldiers in the all-Nisei units. Takashi, who was studying for his doctorate in botany, also went to Fort Detrick in Maryland to conduct secret research. Although he had spent two years in federal prison, he had also spent two years in the Army as a medic, and that made him eligible for the GI Bill, which paid for him to get his PhD from UCLA. With that, he said, "all kinds of doors opened up."[60] In a small way, he believed the government had paid him back for some of the four years he had spent in confinement.

Norman Mineta was a lieutenant based in Fort Lewis, Washington, when his commander called. His whole unit was set to deploy to Korea. The commander asked Norman how well he could speak Japanese, and Norman hedged, saying it was good enough. They changed his orders and rushed him to Vancouver, British Columbia, from where he took a Canadian Pacific flight to Tokyo. There, the Army asked him to take another test, this time of his understanding of Japanese, the language he had grudgingly learned at his father's insistence. He could neither read nor write Japanese, but, luckily for Norman, the test included only conversational Japanese. Kunisaku Mineta's home lessons gradually came back to Norman well enough for him to pass the test, and he joined a Japan-based intelligence unit, where he interrogated prisoners. Both Norman and Raymond likely would have spent the war fighting the waves of Chinese soldiers swarming over a rocky and meaningless hill in Korea if not for their basic understanding of the language they had once resisted learning.

While in Japan, Norman visited the family members his father had left behind when he moved to the United States almost fifty years earlier. When they welcomed him into their homes, he spoke in his home-schooled Japanese, which made them giggle behind their hands. Kunisaku's lessons had taught Norman enough Japanese to keep him off the battlefield in Korea, but it was hopelessly out of date. "We haven't used those words since 1902," his relatives said.[61]

10

Moving Forward

The Higuchis

It has always amazed me that my grandfather Higuchi saved enough money to buy a new twenty-acre farm in San Jose in just one year after he left Heart Mountain. By 1948, the raspberries he planted on that farm had begun to flourish. All of my family members told me my grandmother was critical to the farm's success. She sorted the berries into baskets that would be stored in crates. "My mother would be working late into the night to make sure that they got taken care of," Bill said. The farm cleared $20,000 that year, enough to provide some security. Bill liked working with his father on the farm and thought about staying, but he also shared his older brothers' interest in science. The farm was doing well enough that Iyekichi could make do without him. After he graduated from high school in 1948, he went to San Jose State, where his older brothers had gone before him, and worked on the farm after class. Santa Clara County was at the beginning of an economic revolution triggered by wartime spending and new technology, which was turning the county's future away from agriculture, an idea that Takeru Higuchi impressed upon his younger brother. "You can never be sure of farming," Takeru had told Bill, so "I did less and less on the farm," Bill said.[1]

My mother spoke often about how Bill felt conflicted about leaving his father and the farm. I told her how glad I was that his brothers had talked him out of being a farmer, since I loved the university life that my parents had created for me growing up in Ann Arbor. I used to get anxious when my mother talked about farm life, which seemed hopelessly spartan and unsophisticated to me. In private conversations with my mother when no one else was around, it was obvious to me how proud my mother was of my father. It was clear that she believed he would be successful at anything he did. I remember sometimes thinking that I was glad the incarceration had happened, because without it my parents would have never met and I would not be here.

After ten years working at their farm in San Jose, which they had bought in 1946, Iyekichi and Chiye Higuchi could afford to retire. They sold the farm and knew they could now move back to Japan, which they had contemplated for years. Moving to the United States had always been a financial decision for them, and, while they were loyal residents, they had long kept their affinity for their native country. In 1956, my aunt Emily said, they made the leap. Emily, a student at Berkeley at the time, remembered seeing them off at the port in San Francisco. So did Fumi Saito, the mother of their new daughter-in-law. "We didn't know when we would see them again," Emily said.[2]

The Japan they encountered upon their arrival had largely rebuilt itself after the war through sheer determination and American aid. Iyekichi and Chiye enjoyed being back in their home country, in which they could speak Japanese and not worry about navigating American society. But then the winter came, and they realized what so many longtime Californians already knew: they missed the weather. They booked passage on another ship back to what was now their home—San Jose—and bought a home in the city, where they lived together until 1963, when Iyekichi died from lung cancer at age seventy-seven. This driven man who left Japan twice to find his fortune, ending up first in the harsh fields of Peru and then in the United States, had ultimately prospered in the country that had tried to deny him the chance to succeed.[3]

Raymond Uno

In Ogden, Utah, Osako Uno awoke at four each morning, went to work at the Methodist home, and then went to her second job, at the Bamboo Noodle Parlor downtown. "She used to put in eighteen, twenty hours a day every day, seven days a week almost, because she had those two jobs to make ends meet," her son Raymond said. "She'd start doing the cooking and taking care of things upstairs and then she would work all the way through till six and then from six to one cutting vegetables." Raymond had to fend for himself. He first worked in a local cannery, and then the father of a friend fixed it so the underage Raymond could get a job on the railroad.

Raymond matured quickly on the railroad, where he worked with whites, Native Americans, blacks, and Mexicans, many of whom were in their forties and fifties, with families to support. They roamed all over Nevada, laying track. "My hands, fingers were like I had arthritis, but finally I got used to it and found what hard work was really like," he said. "You don't rest." At work, he never experienced any anti-Japanese discrimination. For the two and a half months in the summer of 1946, Raymond traveled and slept in boxcars that had baked in the sun all day. "When I first got there, I thought, 'Gosh, I wish I were home,'" he said. The work was often as dangerous as it was primitive. One day a rock bounced up from the tracks and hit Raymond in the head. Blood went "streaming down my face. Everyone thought I got shot in the head."

In 1947, Raymond worked another summer on the railroads before returning for his senior year in high school. After graduation, Raymond enlisted in the Army, eager to leave Utah. He deeply felt what he had lost in the incarceration, starting with his father's death. If his father had not died in camp, "I would still be in California," where he had a greater sense of community. "I wouldn't be in Utah. I'd be among a lot of Japanese in California. Our family would have been closer together."

The Army sent Raymond to Fort Ord, California, for basic training and then to language school. His commanding officers, who were all white, assumed that he knew Japanese. "I told my mother I would try to learn, but I never picked it up," he said. "I had no idea how hard the language was." Now, he *had* to learn it. Raymond knew that if he was going to pass the language test, he needed to study more than anyone else. The only place he could study at night without having the lights wake up his fellow soldiers was the latrine, so he studied there. "I was sitting on the potty for hours and hours studying," he said.[4]

Clarence Matsumura

Clarence Matsumura was one of the one million veterans called back to serve during Korea in the early years of the war. He returned to California, where he met Lily Yuri Oki, who had also been incarcerated at Heart Mountain with her family. They married in 1952. Their engagement and wedding photos show them happily opening a wedding present, a gleaming chrome toaster, and looking hopefully into the camera. However, Clarence held deeper troubles inside that his new marriage could not calm.

During the rest of the 1950s, Clarence combined work for the military with jobs in commercial communications and television. Lily said he often left home for days with little notice, leaving little money for her and their young daughter, Darice. Lily believed the charming, handsome man who looked so good in his Army uniform had been broken by his wartime experiences and untreated posttraumatic stress disorder. "After I left home to live with him, he'd do things, and then he'd get upset and he'd leave house," Lily said. "And I don't know if he's ever going to come home." Once Lily was by her baby's crib and realized that she did not know when or if Clarence would return home. "I've got to get a job," she said. "How am I going to pay the rent?"

At one time, Clarence told Lily he had a job in Alaska helping to build a series of radar stations and that the job would pay enough money for them to buy a house, but this did not happen. "He came back after a while," Lily said, and then "he took all the bank book, the car keys, things he said all belonged to him which is true, I wasn't working. And it was his but I had nothing." Lily called her mother, who brought over a bag of rice to feed her and Darice, who was traumatized by the events at home. "I took her to school and she hung onto my legs saying, 'Mommy, mommy,' and I cried, too," Lily said. "And he'd come back and stay for a while, and then take off."[5] They eventually divorced, and Clarence drifted out of their lives.

Setsuko Saito

Setsuko Saito graduated from Lowell High School in San Francisco in June 1948. My mother's high school yearbook shows a radiant young woman ready to take on the world, a look that belied the challenges with which she was already struggling. Ambitious, she continued to read about new homes and how to build them. She helped my grandmother around the home and worked as a hotel maid after school to earn money to help pay for her brother Al's tuition at the Massachusetts Institute of Technology. The family spent most of its time in the years after the war trying to make enough money to pay for housing and education so it could claw its way back and replace what it had lost during the war, said John Higuchi, my youngest brother, in whom Setsuko and Al confided during the last twenty years of their lives.[6] John was essentially an only child, since he was six years younger than Robert, the next youngest. When my family lived in Utah, John was the only one of the children still at home, while the rest of us had moved away, married, and started families.

In early 1950, Setsuko's parents sent her on an unlikely mission. Her mother, Fumi, had steadily sent packages of food and clothing to her family, the Hattoris, in Japan. One of Fumi's sisters had adopted a son, who now needed a wife. Perhaps Setsuko, who had never been to Japan, could help the family by marrying the young man. "You have to understand that the whole culture was different," said my aunt, Kathleen (Kathy) Saito Yuille, Setsuko's younger sister, who was born at Heart Mountain. "Transportation was outrageous, so they hadn't seen each other since my mother left Japan. It was a big deal for them to have a telephone conversation." Yet this was the world to which Setsuko's parents were willing to send her as a wife for a distant, adopted cousin. She was a tool with which they could satisfy their own needs and those of their extended family, all the while not seeming to care what my mother needed or wanted.

A tiny black-and-white photograph shows Setsuko standing on the dock in San Francisco with my grandfather and my aunt Kathleen the day she left for Japan. She looked as she always did—poised and immaculate—wearing a crisp white cotton blouse and a light-colored double-breasted suit. After weeks aboard the ship, Setsuko arrived in Tokyo, which was still devastated from the war, and met her potential match, who was, Kathleen said, "mesmerized by Sets. She was tall, slim, well dressed." But just as her father twenty-six years earlier had rejected the match arranged with my grandmother's sister, Setsuko declined the match her parents had arranged for her. She stayed in Japan for a few weeks, met many family members her parents had not seen for at least twenty years, and returned home determined to set her own course.[7] She wanted to go to college on her own and stop working to pay for her brothers' educations. The young woman who had rejected her parents' arranged marriage to a man in Japan wanted to test her own ambitions, even as the postwar society tried to define her role for her. My aunt Kathleen said her parents were not bothered by Setsuko's turning down the arranged marriage, and I believe her. They simply moved on.

Shortly after returning to San Francisco, Setsuko started college at the University of California, Berkeley, and studied education. She wanted to be a teacher, a desire that stayed with her for most of her life. Even after

Setsuko Saito at the docks in San Francisco before she sailed for Tokyo for an arranged marriage that she rejected. From left to right are Yoshio, Hiroshi, Setsuko, and Kathleen Saito. (Higuchi family collection)

she had four children, Setsuko would return to college at Eastern Michigan University to get her master's degree in education.

Setsuko and Bill

One day in 1954, Bill Higuchi hurried across the Berkeley campus near the tennis courts and looked up just in time to avoid bumping into a young woman walking in the other direction. Her face looked familiar, so he slowed and realized it was Setsuko Saito, whom he had first met in seventh grade in the Heart Mountain prison camp school. "I remembered her as a nice-looking person but when we met, I thought maybe we could do something," he said. "I had a lot of courage to say we should get together."[8]

By this time, Setsuko had worked as a hotel maid, traveled to Japan and rejected an arranged marriage, and then finally attended Berkeley on her own. She often told me how challenging it was to attend college given the family pressures she faced. She agreed to have dinner with Bill, who wanted to get married after the first date—a story that my brothers and I joke about to this day. They had a two-year relationship in which they double-dated with Bill's longtime friend Ed Kawahara, a fellow Heart Mountain prisoner, and his wife, Kay. They camped together in the Sierra Nevadas and ate dinners in Chinatown, often with members of Sets's family. "Sets's family was a very family-oriented family," Bill said. "They did a lot of things together."[9] When I think about this comment, I think that this closeness must have kept the family together in camp.

They were married in 1956. My mother told me when I was growing up that her father had turned her wedding into a business function—he had invited all of his work associates. Once again, my mother was a commodity. As I reflect on this part of my mother's life, I wonder if the circumstances surrounding her wedding were the reasons she seemed so disengaged about my wedding almost thirty years later.

My father inherited much of his father's focus. He put Heart Mountain in the rearview mirror and strove to carve his own niche in the world of pharmaceutical sciences. After he finished school, he and my mother moved to Wisconsin, where his older brother, Takeru, had established himself as a professor and scientist. My father completed his postdoctoral studies there. In 1957, he and Setsuko welcomed the birth of their first child, a son they named Kenneth, a popular Anglo name among Japanese Americans. They later moved to California, where Bill worked for Chevron and I was born in 1959.[10] By 1962, we were in Ann Arbor, Michigan, where my father had joined the University of Michigan faculty.

My parents had never felt compelled to remain in the California Japanese American community. Neither had their siblings. Only my Uncle James, the oldest Higuchi son, returned to San Jose after his honorable service as a doctor in the Army. Takeru had moved to Wisconsin and then Kansas, and Kiyoshi worked in the military's biological and chemical warfare unit at Fort Detrick, Maryland. The youngest, Emily, moved to Washington, DC, where she worked for the Environmental Protection Agency. Fumio "Al" Saito finished school at MIT and remained on the East Coast; he married and moved to Florida. Hiroshi, my mother's younger brother, moved to Washington, DC, and Kathleen, who was born at Heart Mountain, moved to the Midwest at my mother's urging.

For whatever reason, be it personal ambition or a subconscious desire to assimilate, the Higuchi and Saito children embodied the War Relocation Authority's social engineering, which sought to integrate Japanese Americans into mainstream white American society. In some ways, I grew up thinking there was something foreign about the Japanese Americans who remained back in California, because they seemed so different from me and from my life in Ann Arbor, where all of my friends were either black or white. The California Japanese Americans seemed to me to lack the gumption necessary to escape their cocoon. My mother, and Kathleen to this day, said the Saito children made a concerted effort to leave the West Coast because they felt there was a somewhat unhealthy environment in the Japanese American community, where there was a lot of backroom gossip and criticism between families. Now that I am embedded in the community through Heart Mountain, I have periodically experienced the same kind of cliquishness and criticism. I have been told I am too direct at times, and perhaps it is the same criticism my mother had of me growing up: that I am not demure and ladylike enough.

Like his older brothers, my father found his life in science. Research fascinated him, particularly how drugs are delivered into the body and then find the health problems they are meant to fix. That passion for discovery energized his professional life, and my mother, even as a young wife and mother, recognized her need to help him succeed. From the outset of their marriage, Setsuko ran the house, taking care of virtually everything having to do with the home and family, while he spent most of his time in the laboratory. Periodically, out of the blue, she would announce to me that we were picking dad up for work. I never knew how he got there. I would have to sit in the car in the parking lot while she went in to get him. My father never wrote a check or paid a bill or went shopping. She did everything and organized his social life to build the connections he needed outside the lab.

Norman Mineta

Norman Mineta returned to California after serving in the Army. He graduated from Berkeley and joined his father's insurance business. By then, the community's attitudes toward Japanese Americans had turned from distrust to benign acceptance. Norm became active in the family's Methodist church and the JACL, which still bore the imprint of his brother-in-law, Mike Masaoka. Through the church, he worked with the Santa Clara County Council of Churches. A family business associate, I. K. Ishimatsu, had encouraged Japanese Americans in Santa Clara County to engage in politics. Ishimatsu, an Issei, had collected a dollar here and two dollars there from various Japanese American businessmen in the county, and he pooled that money to buy "two tickets to the Lincoln Day Dinner of the Republicans and two tickets and the Jackson Day Dinner of the Democrats, and sent two young Japanese Americans to those functions, because he wanted their visibility to be known and to then make some connection to the political leaders of the two parties in our area," Norman said. During the 1960 presidential election contest between Richard Nixon, the Republican vice president, and Democratic senator John Kennedy of Massachusetts, Norman was the beneficiary of one of the tickets to the Democrats' Jackson Day dinner in San Jose. At the time, Norman was a Republican, but the enthusiasm surrounding Kennedy converted him.[11]

Norman's father told him, "I always wanted you children to be active in the community, but I never expected anyone to be in political office." He passed on an old Japanese adage: "If you're in politics, you're going to be like a nail sticking out in a board. You know what happens to that nail, it always gets hammered." Later in his career, Norman looked back at that saying and realized, "Papa, you were so right about being hammered if you're in politics." But he also realized then that the Mineta family and 120,000 people like them had been sent to prison camps because they had no political power to stop it. Few white politicians at the time knew any Japanese Americans, making it easier to demonize them. Norman knew this could not stand. He moved from community organizations to government in 1962, when he was chosen to replace San Jose's human relations commissioner, who had been appointed a judge. Norman Mineta was now a politician.[12]

Daniel Inouye

After his recuperation, Daniel Inouye returned to the University of Hawaii and told his former mentor that he could no longer be a doctor. Advised that he could be an internist, Inouye declined. He wanted to be a surgeon or nothing, and without a right arm, even though he had taught himself to use his left arm for everything, he could not be surgeon. Inouye had noticed the consistent discrimination against Japanese Americans in Hawaii, so he became active in politics in the hopes of wresting control of Hawaii from the Republican Party, which had controlled it dating back to when it had first become a US territory. While studying at the University of Hawaii, he met John Burns, a former police officer and activist in the slowly building Democratic Party.[13] Burns was one of the few Caucasians who understood the yearning of the Hawaiian Japanese Americans to be seen as equal citizens.

Inouye finished school, met and married Margaret Awamura, and the couple moved across the Pacific and across the entire United States so that Daniel could attend law school at George Washington University in Washington, DC. While in law school, he worked in local Democratic politics and returned to Hawaii eager to build the territory's party. The day after he passed the Hawaii bar exam, Honolulu's mayor, a Democrat, appointed Inouye an assistant prosecutor for the city and county of Honolulu. By 1954, when he was thirty, Inouye had collaborated with Burns to promote a slate of Democratic candidates that included Spark Matsunaga, a fellow 442nd veteran who would eventually join Inouye in Congress, and other veterans. They managed to upset the ruling Republicans and take control of the territorial legislature for the first time, an event for which Inouye and his fellow Democrats were not prepared. Floundering, he reached out to Sam Rayburn, the Texas Democrat who was the US Speaker of the House, who "took sympathetic notice" of Inouye and gave him advice.

Meanwhile, Burns had been elected Hawaii's lone delegate to Congress in 1956. He pushed hard for statehood, which Congress approved in early 1959. Inouye ran to succeed Burns as Hawaii's one member of the House of Representatives in 1959. He won, was elected to the Senate in 1962, and remained there for the rest of his life.[14]

Raymond Uno

Raymond Uno never forgot about being placed in the B group of students at Heart Mountain; he always felt the pressure to keep up with the smartest kids in his class. That attitude remained when he returned to Utah after the Korean War. At first, he tried to get jobs that would place him in positions in which he would have to interact with white people. Some potential employers told him they could not afford to have customers seeing a Japanese face at the door and would not hire him. That inspired a renewed sense of activism, reviving what had started at Heart Mountain. Like his older cousins in California, Edison Uno and Amy Uno Ishii, he became active in the JACL, which was moving from the cooperative organization that had acquiesced to the incarceration to becoming a more aggressive advocate of civil rights. He entered the University of Utah to study political science and graduated in 1954. Then he got a teaching certificate, began teaching English, and entered law school. Raymond, who had studied Japanese in the base latrine while in military language school, never stopped studying. When he applied for a job as a state social worker, he received the highest grades on the state test. "That surprised me, because I was not that smart," he said.[15]

Raymond started working as a social worker and attended the university to get his master's degree in social work. For two years, he worked half-time and attended school the other half. He worked as a probation officer and then a family caseworker. After years of working his way through law school and the government, Raymond became an assistant county attorney in Salt Lake City.

Takashi Hoshizaki

After serving in the Army, Takashi returned to UCLA, finished his master's and doctoral degrees in botany, and drew the attention of the military and the nascent space program. The government believed Takashi's research could help people who worked overnight or who traveled in space to handle the rapid shifts between day and night or life in constant darkness. In the late 1950s and early 1960s, he participated in the Navy Antarctic research mission called Operation Deep Freeze.[16] His work with his UCLA colleagues at the McMurdo Bay station in Antarctica showed that life at the South Pole had no noticeable effect on the inner metabolic rhythms of bean plants, hamsters, fungi, and fruit flies. One experiment involved keeping hamsters in a darkened cage and monitoring them throughout the day to determine the effect of the darkness and the reduced effect of the earth's rotation, which is less marked at the poles, on their life cycles.

Takashi said the researchers focused on hamsters, which one could put "in a complete dark cage, give him water and food, and then within one minute of that 24-hour period that hamster would get up and run on an exercise wheel." The result, he said, was that animals still maintained their biological rhythms despite what the scientists had done to them.[17] To me, it seemed an experiment taken directly from Takashi's experience as a prisoner at both Heart Mountain and McNeil Island. He always maintained his biological rhythms in spite of everything around him.

11

Creating a Memorial

◇◇◇

The Blackburns:
Farming the Legacy

Within months of when the last train of prisoners left Heart Mountain in November 1945, the camp itself started to disappear. The government sold the barracks to anyone with $1 and the ability to haul them away. The War Relocation Authority had chosen the camp's location because of its proximity to water and the railroad, and the improved irrigation channel completed by the incarcerees in 1943 made the land more valuable. The Reclamation Act had first opened the Bighorn Basin for homesteading in the early 1900s, and the government opened it again with a lottery for veterans willing to test their fortunes on the often-unforgiving soil between Cody and Powell. They faced daunting odds; most of the post–World War I homesteaders in the 1920s had left because the conditions made farming too difficult.

Chester Blackburn, a veteran from Cottonwood Falls, Kansas, was willing to take the chance. Before the war, he worked on crews in the hard prairie country of central Kansas, and then he served as an engineer in Hawaii and the Pacific island of Saipan before returning home to his wife, Mary, his son, and his two daughters. Chester knew that he, like most returning veterans, had limited opportunities at home in a changing economy. He and Mary applied for a homestead after seeing an advertisement in the October 19, 1946, edition of *Capper's Weekly* for the lottery to be held on February 7, 1947.[1] "Then we had sort of forgotten about them and one Saturday morning we got up and there was a Bureau of Reclamation car in front of the house and the man came in and he congratulated us on our name being drawn in the drawing," Mary Blackburn said. Theirs was the fiftieth application drawn out of what would be 217 chosen over the next three years. The agent told Chester and Mary that they needed to go to Wyoming to pick their homestead after the first forty-nine applicants had selected theirs. When they arrived, they had no idea what had existed on the land just months earlier.[2] "Mother and Daddy had always talked about coming to the mountains," said their daughter, Ruth Blackburn Pfaff. "I mean, in Kansas we didn't hear about the Heart Mountain Relocation Center; we didn't know about that!"[3]

Many of the new homesteaders had never been to Wyoming and were shocked by what they found. Irrigation lines did not reach all of the land, which made farming it difficult, if not impossible. Of the Blackburns' 135 acres, only 88 could be irrigated. The desolate conditions only reaffirmed how great the accomplishment of the Japanese American farmers had been. The first homesteaders might have known little or nothing about the Heart Mountain camp, but they lived in the few barracks that remained in Block 23. Although the barracks now included kitchens, they still lacked running water, which homesteaders had to fetch outside. The Blackburns' barrack lacked heat and electricity, but that did not faze Chet and Mary Blackburn. Their homes in rural Kansas had lacked indoor plumbing; northwestern Wyoming did not throw anything at them they could not handle.[4] The life was not for everyone.

Larry Jones, a longtime neighbor of the Blackburns, reached the breaking point after a sinkhole threatened to swallow his family home. "We're going back to Denver," his wife told him.[5] The Blackburns themselves mark their family history by the elements, such as the time in 1950 when the Heart Mountain canal broke and Chester Blackburn and his fellow homesteaders rushed to fix it, earning Chester a commendation from the local water authorities. During the war, the Japanese American farmers in camp had mastered the science of matching crops with the soil and the available fertilizer, knowledge that many of the new homesteaders lacked. The newcomers who could not succeed by growing barley or hay on the relatively small plots soon sold their land to other homesteaders and moved on. "Some of the homesteaders didn't get the good land and they generally didn't last very long, sold out and left," said LaDonna Zall.[6] The Blackburns, however, remained.

Gradually, the newcomers realized who had farmed their land only just months before their arrival, often by discovering artifacts of the former camp. Farmhands on Verne and Dolly Solberg's homestead ran a plow into something buried underground. When they stopped the tractor and started digging, they uncovered a large rock covered with Japanese characters. The Solbergs found a translator, who told them the inscription said: "A mountain peak at my shoulder, 1,000 barracks under an autumn moon."[7] Known as the Haiku Rock, it is now one of the most popular artifacts at the Heart Mountain Interpretive Center.

Other new farmers in the area knew exactly what had been on their land, because they had farmed it as prisoners. Kazuo Uriu, who was originally from Los Angeles, spent the war in camp and then stayed in Wyoming, moving about eighty-five miles east to Worland, where he "really scratched the farm out of the sagebrush," said his daughter, Barbara Uriu, who grew up there and became one of the first leaders of the Heart Mountain Wyoming Foundation. Uriu brought barley farming to the Bighorn Basin and served on the Wyoming Board of Agriculture.[8] Another Japanese American, Tak Ogawa, entered the homesteader lottery after returning from military service. A native of Idaho Falls, Idaho, who was never incarcerated, Ogawa would later help preserve a slice of camp life by donating a former Heart Mountain barrack to the Japanese American National Museum. He farmed on his homestead until 2019 and was a frequent visitor to the annual Heart Mountain pilgrimages.[9]

Led by the Blackburns, homesteaders started the work of preserving the memory of Heart Mountain. They had all benefited from what the Japanese Americans—led by Eiichi Sakauye, Jim Ito, and Kazuo Uriu—had done to improve the area's soil. It had helped them stay in business. They would soon learn how much the Japanese Americans appreciated their efforts, too.

Making a New Legacy

For most of the Nisei, the 1950s and 1960s were decades filled with school, work, and raising families. They stuffed away thoughts of their incarceration and tried to make it in American society, often by trying to appear more American than their white neighbors. Daniel Inouye made it in politics. So too did Norman Mineta. Takashi Hoshizaki became a scientist for the space program, which by the early 1960s epitomized American ambition and achievement. Raymond Uno mastered the law and fought for civil rights. Even Clarence Matsumura, the most scarred by his wartime experiences, held steady jobs and made a living. Setsuko Saito and Bill Higuchi left for the Midwest, where few Japanese Americans lived. Most of the Japanese Americans who had relocated to the Midwest during the war had by then returned to the West Coast. If they thought about the incarceration, they did not talk about it. The incarceration, for most Americans, was a silent scandal that could have faded away without a trace.

Former prisoners might not have said much, if anything, about life in camp, but that did not mean they had forgotten. Around 1960, Wyoming homesteader Chester Blackburn said he started seeing the occasional car filled with Japanese Americans driving around the former campsite looking for remnants of what had been their home for three years.[10] By that time, virtually every building had been sold and hauled away. The only remaining structures were the former hospital, the chimney for the power plant, and the administration building, where members of the Homesteaders Extension Club would gather. Women who made quilts together in the club building, which looked downhill to Alternate US Route 14, which ran between Cody and Powell, often saw cars pull off the road and drive up the hill to the former campsite and the old honor roll dedicated to the men who served in the military from Heart Mountain. Throughout the 1960s, as the Sansei generation came of age and became more active and the Nisei began to talk more, the number of cars driving around the camp increased. Some of the homesteaders and local residents began to think they needed to do more to make the site recognizable. Local residents wanted to have a more permanent marker instead of the one placed there by the local American Legion and Veterans of Foreign Wars posts, which implied that the camp had been created for the safety of the people imprisoned there.[11] This was the beginning of the restoration efforts at the Heart Mountain site, the seeds of building a world-class museum and the foundation that I now lead.

In June 1973, the homesteaders voted to have the hospital's chimney preserved as a landmark, and they began to plan for something bigger and more enduring. "We felt something should be done to preserve the Honor Roll and show them that the people here cared about the center," Mary Blackburn wrote in 1984.[12]

The local effort to erect a plaque on the site of the Heart Mountain camp culminated in a ceremony on July 2, 1978, which featured Bill Hosokawa, the informal historian of the Nisei in America. His appearance at the dedication drew national attention to the Blackburns, who said they had thought their work was done. "Up to this point all of the project was only from state and local organizations," Chet Blackburn wrote in 1989.[13]

But momentum for something larger at Heart Mountain was starting to build.

The Blackburn family's continued efforts to place Heart Mountain on the National Register of Historic Places had an ally in Senator Alan Simpson, owing to his long history with the camp. Simpson continued to press the US Interior Department and the National Park Service to make the camp a national historic site.[14] But the Blackburns and their allies could not determine which part of the camp deserved the status. They initially wanted to include the entire site, but the farmers who owned most of the land resisted. Finally, the decision was made to designate only the land atop the hill looking down on the main road between Cody and Powell, which included the flagpole, the old honor roll, the hospital, and the chimney.

On June 21, 1986, about three hundred people—former incarcerees, their families, and local leaders—gathered to unveil a memorial to the men from Heart Mountain who had died in World War II. They were joined by Minoru Yasui, who had been one of the defendants in the test cases against the incarceration, Norman Mineta, Alan Simpson, and Bill Hosokawa.

The crowd sang "America the Beautiful," a bugler played taps, and military riflemen fired off a salute. Norman summed up what many of the former prisoners felt, even forty years after leaving camp. "Like everyone else who passed through this camp, virtually everything about my life has been affected by my stay in this bleak, desolate place," he said. "And now, more than forty years later, here we are again. Back at a hot, mountainous, windswept plain, which, but for an aberration of history, we probably would have never seen; which would have been forever nondescript and forgettable."

In the audience was Chiye Watanabe, whose brother Joe Hayashi had joined the Army from Heart Mountain and died a hero fighting the Nazis in Italy. When the family tried to bury Hayashi in Forest Lawn cemetery in Los Angeles, administrators refused, saying they did not take Japanese soldiers. Norm continued: "I believe that if Sgt. Hayashi and his companions could speak to us today, they would say just what it says on the plaque: 'May the injustices of the removal and incarceration of 120,000 persons of Japanese ancestry during World War II, two-thirds of whom were American citizens, never be repeated.'"

On that first day of the summer of 1986, Norman Mineta, deep into a fight to get Congress to redress the wrongs done to the victims of the incarceration, closed with a message of hope. "Let me close by saying that I was not pleased to be here, but I am proud of what we did here," he said. "I am proud of the friends I made. I am proud of our loyalty to each other and our nation. Everyone here has the right to share in this pride."[15]

The Heart Mountain Foundation

For fifteen years, the Blackburns and their fellow homesteaders dominated the local efforts to preserve what remained of Heart Mountain. Then, in late 1988, the Powell Centennial Committee, which was dedicated to marking the one hundredth anniversary of Wyoming statehood, made restoring the Heart Mountain site its centennial project. A group of Powell activists, including banker David Reetz and businessman John Collins, turned the centennial committee's work into the Heart Mountain Japanese-American Memorial Association Foundation, and Bacon Sakatani joined their advisory board.[16] The Powell Valley Chamber of Commerce met in September 1991 with local residents interested in the camp, including the Cody and Powell American Legion and VFW posts, which had placed a marker at the campsite in 1963 that had enraged Japanese Americans because it presented the incarceration as a benevolent act. Reetz suggested that the various groups unite to build an interpretive trail, a topographical scale model of the site, an authentic guard tower and fence, a restored barracks, a library, and an audiovisual presentation.[17]

The Blackburns had more modest ambitions for Heart Mountain, believing a simple memorial and the honor roll would be enough for returning incarcerees and their families. Reetz and the Powell group had bigger dreams and viewed Heart Mountain as a way to attract visitors and tourists to Powell and the surrounding area. In October 1991, Collins proposed combining the two groups into a new organization that would essentially be dominated by the Powell group. Unsurprisingly, the Blackburns declined. Feelings grew raw between the two groups.

Finally, on August 31, 1994, the two groups met to resolve the conflicts that had stalled their efforts and limited their work to preserving the chimney, placing markers in the memorial area, and developing a walking tour. By the end of the meeting, the two groups had agreed to create a new organization with a new name. Its board of directors would rely on an advisory board of former Heart Mountain incarcerees—Bacon Sakatani and Paul Tsuneishi, the Los Angeles–based activist who had attended the meeting—and would also include representatives of the larger Nikkei community. Nancy Araki of the Japanese American National Museum in Los Angeles, which was moving an old Heart Mountain barrack from Wyoming to the museum, and Sue Kunitomi Embrey of the Manzanar Committee agreed to join the advisory board. By November, the reorganization was complete.[18]

The new Heart Mountain Wyoming Foundation was finally incorporated in March 1996. It had three board members—Tsuneishi; Barbara Uriu, the daughter of incarceree and farmer Kazuo Uriu; and Ken George, the son of a homesteader and a friend of the Blackburns. Reetz, the Powell banker, incorporated the new foundation and was now in charge. Chet Blackburn died a month later, estranged from the cause that he had pioneered.[19]

Much of this local drama inside the workings of two small foundations was unknown to most of the former prisoners of Heart Mountain, even those interested in the former camp. The creation of the Heart Mountain Wyoming Foundation involved hard feelings and small-town intrigue that would hinder the group's ability to meet its goals and almost caused it to implode. The new foundation leaders, primarily David Reetz, Patricia Wolfe, and John Collins, knew they wanted to create something durable at the site. They worked tirelessly for years to raise money, develop a board of directors, and reach out to the local community to build an organization that people would support. But they had limitations that they did not always see, said Takashi Hoshizaki, who likened them to a "small-town bridge club" that did not draw in outsiders who could help them.[20]

Growing Pains at the Foundation

Dave Reetz aggressively courted local businesspeople and activists in Wyoming, academics interested in Japanese issues, and a growing list of Japanese Americans who had either been imprisoned at Heart Mountain or were connected to it through family or professional ties. Particularly active in the early years was a group of Los Angeles–based former incarcerees that included Marjorie Matsushita Sperling. In 1998, both of my parents joined the foundation's advisory board with their friends Raymond Uno and Jeannette Misaka from Salt Lake City, both of whom had actively supported the redress movement. My father concentrated mostly on his profession, working hard and allowing my mother to invest their savings at Heart Mountain. She focused on building something that would last on the site of the old camp.[21]

From the beginning, many of the Japanese Americans wondered how much influence they actually had with the local Wyoming residents leading the foundation. Many, such as Sperling, felt that they only provided a convenient cover for the Caucasians running the foundation, while Japanese Americans' actual concerns and interests were often dismissed. She urged the foundation to buy the land near the camp's site, which would give them a place to build a museum, which was also my mother's dream. Sperling said she and Reetz fought often about the foundation's future. In March 1999, Sperling was demanding that the board come up with a coherent master plan for what it wanted to do.[22] "She had become a public enemy," Doug Nelson said of Sperling and her complaints about Reetz. "She complained about them, and that split the LA group" of board members.[23]

Sue Kunitomi Embrey also felt frozen out. At a meeting in Los Angeles in November 2002, she said Reetz snubbed her multiple times. She noted that Sperling had resigned from the foundation's Southern California advisory group after Reetz accused Sperling of "being out of control" at a meeting in San Jose.[24]

While even members of her own family found Embrey difficult, she had credibility within the Japanese American community that Heart Mountain could not deny. She had helped turn Manzanar into a National Park Service site and knew most of the key people on the West Coast. Alienating her was symbolic of what a growing number of Japanese Americans had experienced with Reetz and some of the local Wyoming board members. It was just a matter of time before something broke.

Progress on All Fronts

Inside Washington and the Heart Mountain Wyoming Foundation, the year 2000 was filled with progress. In early February, Vice President Al Gore announced that the Clinton administration would ask for $4.8 million for grants to preserve what remained of the former camps and to build museums to commemorate them. Gore was running to succeed Clinton in the White House, so putting him at the head of this effort seemed aimed at courting the votes of Japanese Americans. Leaders of the foundation hoped this was the break they needed. "Is this good news for HMWF?" Carolyn Takeshita asked in a fax to Pat Wolfe.[25] Although the federal money for the foundation had not been approved, the foundation's organizers continued to plan for a museum. LaDonna Zall led the work collecting artifacts for the museum in part to help answer many of the questions about Heart Mountain that had bothered her since she, her father, and her sister had watched the last train filled with prisoners pull away in November

1945.[26] In April, the foundation received a small package from Los Angeles that was a vote of confidence. It contained the boots young Toshi Nagamori had worn when she reported to camp. The package contained a note:

> At long last, I have come to parting with my cherished "security boots." Hope it will be of interest in an exhibit as to what was worn at Heart Mountain, Wyoming Internment Camp.
>
> Executive Order 9066 caused my father, Seiichiro Nagamori to surmise we would be incarcerated in a bleak cold area. He sent my mother and me to purchase boots to take with us. How wise he proved to be. Heart Mountain, Wyoming, where we were eventually sent, had winters with snow and temperatures that would go below zero some days.
>
> These boots have been in my closet wherever I have lived since being incarcerated in 1942. They are wear worn. The heels need reheeling, they have been half soled, and the lining has split away. It has become a symbol of my father's love; that there was a caring, loving parent. It has been my "security boots" for half a century plus eight years.
>
> It is time to part with my boots to tell a story of walking and standing in line in the dust of a prairie land, and of the snows and mud. Perhaps, it will be of interest in an exhibit of what was worn in the Heart Mountain, Wyoming Concentration Camp to keep one pair of feet protected and warm.[27]

The foundation and its efforts to build a museum were gaining momentum. Federal money had pushed the foundation closer to buying the land for what my mother and others hoped would be the eventual museum, or interpretive center, as the foundation called it. By early 2001, they had raised $265,000, boosted by an anonymous donation of $50,000, which came from my mother.[28]

12

Acknowledging Wrongs

◇◇◇

The Financial Toll

The government had ignored the Tolan Committee's 1942 recommendation that it do something to protect the assets of the Japanese Americans during their incarceration. Three and a half years in camp cost the Issei millions of dollars worth of property and revenue that they never got back. My grandparents managed to regain their financial footing after they sold their fourteen-and-a-quarter-acre San Jose farm for a pittance, but they were far behind where they would have been if they had not been forced to leave. "I think we lost the best years of our lives," said Eiichi Sakauye, their fellow San Jose farmer and Heart Mountain prisoner.[1] Younger Nisei, such as my mother and father, returned to lives that were poorer financially than their lives before the war and that were also marred by the psychological toll and the shame resulting from the incarceration. They deserved some form of reparation for their losses.

President Truman agreed and wrote public letters to congressional leaders asking them to authorize redress payments to the incarcerees, but California Democrats killed the bill in Congress. They thought they would lose seats in the 1946 midterm elections if they supported paying Japanese Americans.[2] The Democrats lost anyway, and Republicans took control of both houses of Congress.

But the hostile Congress that faced President Truman actually seemed receptive to passing a new bill to redress the grievances of the formerly incarcerated Japanese Americans. Truman's staff teamed with Mike Masaoka and the JACL to whip up support. The cause was also bolstered by the

October release of a comprehensive report by Truman's commission on civil rights in America. The report—*To Secure These Rights*—mostly focused on discrimination against African Americans, but several passages highlighted the unfair treatment of Japanese Americans. "It should be noted that hundreds of evacuees suffered serious property and business losses because of government action and through no fault of their own," the commission wrote, adding that it had been more than a year since the War Relocation Authority had recommended redress payments. Truman signed the Japanese-American Claims Act on July 2, and it was the signature civil rights legislation of his tenure.[3]

Truman won a shocking reelection upset that November, buoyed by a win in California, where the anti-Japanese sentiment had started to subside. The new law gave Estelle and Arthur Ishigo, the conspicuous mixed-race couple at Heart Mountain, a chance to recoup some of their losses. They had endured life after the war in a rundown trailer park outside Los Angeles. They asked for $506.50, but the government would pay only about a quarter of that, arguing that Estelle, as a Caucasian, could have avoided many of the couple's losses if she had let her Japanese American husband go to camp alone. They would have been just another couple separated by the demands of war. If only it had been that simple. Estelle had lost her job immediately after Pearl Harbor just for being married to a Japanese American. Estelle did not give up. She bombarded her member of Congress, the Justice Department, and even Truman himself with letters seeking help. The law, she wrote Representative Cecil King on March 30, 1952, "has distinguished us by ancestry & disregards loss of the family as a unit creating a barrier of discrimination & a loss of faith & confidence in justice here in the country for which we stand."[4] In 1953, she received her final rejection from the new head of the Justice Department's civil rights division, a lawyer from Minnesota named Warren Burger, who in 1969 would succeed Earl Warren as chief justice of the Supreme Court. "The enforced separation of husband and wife . . . is a normal consequence of war and, although very hard, was the lot of many," Burger wrote.[5] The rejection stung Estelle and fueled her rage for the rest of her life. My research eventually revealed that this was not the last time Burger would demonstrate his animus toward Japanese Americans.

The new law did not automatically pay incarcerees for their losses. They had to apply to the Justice Department for benefits, and then it was up to Justice officials to separate which claims they considered legitimate from those that were not. Hundreds of former Heart Mountain prisoners filed claims for compensation. Their case files at the National Archives show what the Justice Department approved and the often-arcane reasons used to reject others. My grandparents, Iyekichi and Chiye Higuchi, used the money they received from their claim to help buy their new farm. No family records exist to show their claim and what they received, but, given the records of other claimants, they most likely did not receive what they had sought. For example, Kiyoji Murai, a gardener and rooming house operator from Los Angeles, sought $1,121 in 1949 to compensate him for the loss of his household possessions and a 1927 Ford pickup truck. More than a year later, he received a settlement for $352.50.[6] Nizo Okano of Los Angeles claimed $619.23 for losses suffered because of the rapid sale of his furniture and car, in addition to the loss of multiple boxes of canned food that disappeared. For that, the Justice Department judged he was owed $438.36.[7]

By 1965, when the government paid its final claim, it had paid only $38 million out of a total of $131,949,186 sought by the incarcerees.[8] Some former prisoners paid more in legal fees than they ever received from the government. For the Ishigos and thousands of others, the payments did not come close to making them whole and compensating them fully for what they had lost when the government forced them into prison. But later in the 1960s, stimulated by the rise of black Americans demanding their full civil rights, a new drive for redress would start.

Redress and Social Change

In the mid-1960s, two sweeping social movements—the civil rights movement and the protests against the war in Vietnam—triggered a reaction from the Sansei. Now on college campuses roiled by social change, the Nisei generation's children were learning more about the incarceration than they had heard from their parents and grandparents. They began to agitate for something, even if only symbolic, to be done to address the injustice. This agitation began to ruffle the carefully composed lives of the Nisei, who had strived to put the incarceration behind them. In my own immediate family, my father was a successful professor at a Big Ten university, and his three older brothers were a physician, a professor, and a scientist working on secret military projects. One of my mother's brothers was an engineer, while the other was a lawyer. Whatever suffering they had endured as younger people was not apparent to the Sansei. The few times they spoke of "camp," it seemed as if they meant a summer camp. Many

Nisei had no desire to jump into the social ferment of the 1960s. They believed they would succeed by burying the bad memories of the incarceration and working as hard as they could.

Not all Nisei kept quiet, however. Raymond Uno's cousin Edison Uno burned with a fervor to correct the injustice. His branch of the Uno family had been ripped apart by the incarceration. As an adolescent, Edison had lived in multiple FBI detention centers with his father, George, who was arrested shortly after Pearl Harbor. The Justice Department freed them from the camp in Crystal City, Texas, in 1947, almost two years after the war ended. The government had kept George Uno in Crystal City after the war ended because of his son Buddy's work during the war for the Japanese government, and Edison had refused to leave his father alone in prison. When Edison left Crystal City, when he was almost eighteen, he was told that he had spent 1,647 days in prison and that he was the last US citizen to be released.[9] In the 1960s, he championed an effort to get Earl Warren, then the liberal chief justice of the Supreme Court, to apologize for his role in the incarceration. Warren never apologized publicly, although the memoirs published after his death include an apology that Jim Newton, a Warren biographer, believed was added by the book's editor to make Warren look better. "Warren's regret somehow deepened only after he died," Newton wrote.[10] Edison Uno also led the successful effort to repeal Title II of the Internal Security Act, while his sister, Amy Uno Ishii, worked in Los Angeles with other activists, including Warren Furutani, a UCLA student inspired by the movements for civil rights and against the war.[11]

Furutani's parents had been imprisoned at the camp in Rohwer, Arkansas, which Daniel Inouye had visited from Camp Shelby, Mississippi, as a young soldier. While Furutani had a friend in the campus Black Power movement, he realized there was little that explained what had happened to his parents and 120,000 other Japanese Americans. When he learned that the camp at Manzanar, California, was just a few hours north of Los Angeles in the Owens Valley, he drove there with a friend to see what remained, finding only an old auditorium and a memorial left by the prisoners.[12] Meanwhile, Sue Kunitomi Embrey, a forty-six-year-old mother and budding activist, had learned of the growing interest in Manzanar. She and her family had been incarcerated there, although her older brother Jack and his wife, Masa, had been sent to Heart Mountain with Masa's family, the Fujiokas.[13]

Furutani, Embrey, and a small group of former prisoners and their families took the initiative and organized the first informal pilgrimage to

Manzanar, in December 1969. This was the first of many pilgrimages to Manzanar and the nine other camps to feature former prisoners, their families, and events aimed at memorializing all or parts of detainees' incarceration experience. The Manzanar organizers picked December for the pilgrimage so that they would come to know how the incarcerees, most of them from Los Angeles, had felt during their first winter behind the barbed wire. Manzanar, which began as an assembly center, was the closest camp to the major population centers on the West Coast, which made it the logical site for the first pilgrimage. But the local white residents who had the camp in their backyard wanted little to do with the newfound activism of the Japanese Americans "With Manzanar, you had a lot of competing interests—the city of Los Angeles, the feds, the locals, the forest service, the Indian tribes," who all had some claim to the land of the former camp, said Darrell Kunitomi, Sue Embrey's nephew.[14]

The following year, the pilgrimage organizers formed the Manzanar Committee, which channeled the energy generated by the pilgrimage into making the Manzanar site a state and then a federal historic landmark. Manzanar was a natural starting place for the budding movement to remember the camps and to demand they not be repeated. It was also close enough to the major cities in California for the former prisoners and their families to visit.

Sue Embrey was too edgy even for the combative Kunitomis, who "were always fighting. They had hot tempers," her niece Kerry Cababa said. "People in the family would say, 'Sue's a radical,'" Cababa said.[15] Embrey, however, used her energy to work not only for Manzanar but also for a variety of causes. In 1975, she created EO 9066 Inc. with, among others, Amy Uno Ishii and Paul Tsuneishi. Tsuneishi was a Los Angeles insurance man, a former Heart Mountain prisoner, and an Army veteran who had served in the occupation force in Japan. The new group's mission was to promote redress for the losses suffered during the war. It also brought together some of the most doggedly committed members of the Japanese American community to work together not just on redress but also on a range of civil rights issues. As a sign of the continuing tensions in the community, Tsuneishi recommended that the new group remain independent of the JACL, which was also promoting redress, because he feared the JACL connection would deter some Japanese Americans from joining.[16]

As his cousins Edison and Amy worked alongside Sue Embrey on the West Coast to rally Japanese Americans to demand redress, Raymond Uno established himself in Utah as a leader in the JACL during twenty years as a social worker and lawyer working to help minority and other communities. He and his group of friends were active in the Salt Lake City chapter of the JACL, and they encouraged him to run for the national presidency at the 1970 national convention in Chicago. It was at that convention that the JACL took its first stand in favor of seeking a national apology for the incarceration as well as redress for the losses the Japanese Americans from the West Coast had suffered during the war.[17] Floyd Mori, a future JACL president and California legislator, said some members resisted the proposal, saying it would "rock the boat" and endanger the gains Japanese Americans had made in the thirty years since the war. Mike Masaoka, who had advocated for the 1948 law that paid some claims, criticized the new initiative, saying the idea of asking for money to compensate Japanese Americans for "a sacrifice we accepted in a time of war" was unseemly. Masaoka had apparently forgotten that the idea of necessary sacrifice was mostly in his mind; the majority of Japanese Americans in 1942 had not shared his opinion.[18]

The 1970 debate over whether to support asking for reparations was the first in a series of debates inside the Japanese American community. The JACL itself was becoming a more vocal and aggressive civil rights organization. It formally created the National Committee for Redress in 1974, the same year the first redress bill was introduced in Congress, although it failed to get out of committee.[19] In 1976, the National Committee for Redress helped persuade President Gerald Ford to officially abolish Executive Order 9066.[20] In January 1977, Ford granted a pardon to Iva Rose Toguri D'Aquino, the young Japanese American woman who was caught in Japan at the outbreak of World War II and forced to make English-language propaganda broadcasts targeted at US troops. Known as Tokyo Rose, she was arrested after the war and convicted of treason in 1949. Japanese Americans did not support D'Aquino at the time of her arrest, acting JACL director Don Hayashi said in 1977, "because most Japanese-Americans after the war were so anxious to become part of American society, they were flag-waving Americans almost to the point of subservience."[21]

In 1976, JACL members led the fight to support Wendy Yoshimura, a California artist who had been born in Manzanar. She had fallen in with members of a radical group known as the Symbionese Liberation Army, which went on a cross-country spree that included kidnapping newspaper heiress Patricia Hearst, whose grandfather's newspaper had heartily endorsed the evacuation and incarceration of Japanese Americans. Hearst and

Yoshimura went on the lam with some of the remaining SLA members but were arrested in early 1976. Yoshimura was eventually convicted of illegal possession of a machine gun and explosives, but Japanese Americans defended her, saying they believed she was being railroaded as D'Aquino had been.[22]

All of this activism culminated in a one-sentence resolution passed at the JACL's July 1978 convention calling for legislation that would compensate the Japanese Americans incarcerated during the war and demanding a formal apology from the government. The JACL's National Committee for Redress proposed a $25,000 payment from the government for each incarceree plus a $100 million fund for Japanese American organizations. The plan drew opposition almost immediately. Senator S. I. Hayakawa, a California Republican, attacked the idea of a payment as "absurd and ridiculous" and "not Japanese."[23]

Working Together, Making It Work

At the start of 1979, fresh out of Boston College's law school, Carolyn Sugiyama joined the staff of Senator Daniel Inouye as his sole civil rights staffer. Her mother was Inouye's wife's cousin, and her father, Francis, was one of the few Hawaiians incarcerated during the war.[24] Soon after she started working for him, Inouye brought her to a meeting called by John Tateishi, the leader of the JACL's redress campaign. Tateishi wanted to know how Inouye and the three other Japanese American Democrats in Congress—Norman Mineta, Spark Matsunaga of Hawaii, and newly elected Representative Robert Matsui of California—viewed the JACL's redress proposal.

Hayakawa, a Japanese American by way of Canada, opposed redress, because he believed the evacuation had actually protected Japanese Americans. Without Hayakawa's support, Inouye knew they could not pass a straight bill appropriating money to pay Japanese Americans for their losses during the war. Too few Americans even knew about the incarceration, let alone wanted to pay for it. However, Inouye believed he could get Congress to create a commission that would investigate the incarceration, call witnesses, and educate the American people about what had happened. If she wanted to make that happen, Inouye told Sugiyama, the new staffer would have to get the bill through Congress.[25]

Tateishi and the JACL leaders, including the author and researcher Grant Ujifusa, who had grown up outside the exclusion zone in Worland,

Wyoming, wanted to put reparations into an existing appropriations bill. Tateishi already knew they faced an uphill fight. He had talked to other civil rights leaders, who had told him that few people understood the incarceration and that "those who do think you guys are guilty anyway." They all told Tateishi he should seek a commission to study the issue. Going into the meeting with the legislators, Tateishi fought the commission route, which he knew "would be long and . . . difficult and . . . wouldn't be popular at all" within the Japanese American community."[26]

Inouye said little at first. Tateishi and the other JACL members proposed their two ideas, and then Matsui and Matsunaga dominated the debate. They were also skeptical of their chances; they understood that the undercurrents of racism that ran through the country were reflected in the House. Few members, they said, would support a bill that called for paying off members of a specific ethnic group, regardless of the offense committed against them.

Then Inouye stepped in and, of course, proposed creating a commission, saying those that had studied the assassination of President John Kennedy and the fatal shootings of four students at Ohio's Kent State University in May 1970 had produced bestselling books that highlighted their findings. Only after more people knew the truth about the incarceration would they create enough momentum to support redress. Because Inouye had also served on the 1973 Senate committee that investigated the Watergate scandal, he knew that committee's hearings had not only built the case against Nixon but also increased Inouye's national profile. Mineta jumped in, saying a commission would help create a consensus in Congress in favor of redress. Tateishi and the JACL redress committee were convinced that if they were going to get anywhere, they had to support a commission and then hope for the best.[27]

Norman Mineta and Glenn Roberts, his legislative director, reworked an existing Matsunaga bill about Native American claims to call for a commission, "the Commission on Wartime Relocation and Internment of Civilians," Norman said. He and his team started lobbying fellow House members, realizing they faced some significant challenges. Japanese Americans did not make up a large enough percentage of the population in any congressional district to give them sway over any particular legislator. Aside from the Hawaiian senators, few members represented any districts with many Japanese Americans; Mineta's and Matsui's districts were majority white. "You're talking about a community of a few hundred thousand people scattered around the country," Roberts said. Some House members believed the war had justified the incarceration. "Members of Congress were saying, 'After all, we were at war with Japan and we couldn't trust you folks,'" Tateishi said.[28] But enough members were swayed that the House passed the bill 297–109 on July 21, 1980, giving the Japanese Americans a rare win in a Congress that had approved the legislation that imprisoned them.

Sugiyama started out frustrated. She needed fellow staffers on the Judiciary Committee to schedule a hearing on the bill to create the commission, but none would cooperate. She went to Inouye, who asked which senator was in charge. Henry "Scoop" Jackson of Washington, she said. "Oh, he owes me one," Inouye responded. He called Jackson, who scheduled the hearing, and the bill breezed through the committee and then through the Senate.[29] New in the Senate that year was Alan Simpson, Norman Mineta's old friend from Heart Mountain. Simpson knew what he had seen during his visits to Heart Mountain and that the treatment of the Japanese Americans was racist.

On July 31, Inouye, Mineta, and the other supporters of the bill creating the commission gathered in the White House to watch President Jimmy Carter sign the bill into law. It was another step toward having the government officially acknowledge what it had done during the war. Over the next eighteen months, Carter said, the commission would examine "one of the disappointing and sometimes embarrassing occurrences in the history of our nation." While the government claimed military necessity, "no German American citizens or aliens were incarcerated and no Italian Americans were interned either. The only ones who were interned in these camps were the Japanese Americans," Carter said.[30] Carter had tipped his hand about where he stood, but he would have little to do with the commission other than to lend moral support. Polls showed Carter in close to a dead heat in his race for reelection with Republican Ronald Reagan, the former California governor. That November, Reagan beat Carter easily, putting someone less sympathetic to the redress movement and its goals in the White House.

Catharsis and Redress

The nine members of the commission started work in early 1981 and hired a staff led by the Washington lawyer Angus Macbeth. He was aided by Aiko Herzig-Yoshinaga, a former prisoner at three camps during the war—Manzanar, Jerome, and Rohwer. After the war, she had moved to New York with her young child and her mother and joined a group of Asian American activists. She married Jack Herzig, a fellow progressive, and moved to Washington in 1978, when she read Michi Weglyn's *Years of Infamy* and immersed herself in the history of the incarceration. She became an indefatigable investigator who developed critical leads for the commission. Most of the commissioners had backgrounds that made them sympathetic to the Japanese Americans imprisoned in the camps, although some, like the young Republican congressman Dan Lungren of California, were skeptical of paying the incarcerees for their losses during the war. One commissioner, however, Pennsylvania judge William Marutani, had been an incarceree at Tule Lake until he left for college in South Dakota.[31]

Over twenty days from July to December 1981, more than seven hundred people testified in what became group catharsis. For many, it was the first time in almost forty years that they had opened up about what had happened to them and their families. They told how their families had lost everything when they were rounded up, the shame many had felt in the years since then, and the scarring effect of government-sanctioned racism.[32] On August 6 in Los Angeles, a panel of mental health professionals including Amy Iwasaki Mass testified about what the incarceration had done to the psyches of the incarcerees and their families. "We lost our dignity and self-respect when we were imprisoned based on our race and ancestry," she wrote. "The imprisonment experience had a repressive, oppressive impact on the psychological well-being of Japanese Americans."[33]

A majority of the commission and the hearing's audience obviously believed in some kind of compensation, so skeptics faced hostile audiences. Senator S. I. Hayakawa of California called the incarceration a "three-year vacation." While Hayakawa had voted for the bill to create the commission, that was the end of his commitment to redress.[34] An elderly John McCloy, the former assistant secretary of war who had been instrumental in the evacuation, was jeered when he said that the war "caused disruption in all our lives. It isn't feasible for us now, forty years after the fact, to redistribute the damages."

McCloy, a reluctant enabler of the incarceration, appeared to have rationalized what his decisions had done to the Japanese Americans. "The deconcentration of the Japanese population and its redistribution throughout the country resulted in their finding a healthier and more advantageous environment than they would have had on the West Coast following the

Pearl Harbor attack and the reports of Japanese atrocities in the Philip-pines," McCloy testified. Some Japanese Americans on the West Coast did suffer from retaliation and bigotry after Pearl Harbor, but, while the anti-Japanese sentiments were real, the claims of serial retaliation were ginned up by politicians. McCloy also characterized the conditions in the camps as "very pleasant," which drew hoots of derision from the audience. Maru-tani challenged McCloy's claims that Japanese Americans were not "un-duly subjected to the distress of the war."

"What other Americans, Mr. McCloy, fought for this country while their parents, brothers and sisters were incarcerated?" asked Marutani.

"I don't like the word 'incarcerated,'" McCloy said.

"Well, all right, behind barbed wire fences," Marutani countered.[35]

The commission also heard from Karl Bendetsen, the Army colonel who made the evacuation and incarceration a reality. In a June 21 letter to the commission, Bendetsen presented himself as an innocent bystander in the months following Pearl Harbor, as Lieutenant General John DeWitt, the head of the Western Defense Command, and assistant attorneys general James Rowe and Tom Clark and others organized the incarceration.

Bendetsen glossed over how Rowe had been one of his most vocal an-tagonists in the tense weeks leading up to the issuance of Executive Order 9066. Bendetsen, not Rowe, had pushed the hardest for the evacuation and incarceration, and Clark had played only a minor role. Bendetsen's statement contained multiple falsehoods, including his claim that few Japa-nese Americans were exploited financially during the rapid evacuation and forced to sell their properties at a serious loss. In Bendetsen's world, "ex-traordinary measures were taken to preserve their properties." That would come as a surprise to those whose families lost most, if not all, of their belongings, such as the Saitos, Unos, and Higuchis, who either sold their homes at a loss or had their stored belongings lost or stolen during the war. Finally, Bendetsen denied that he had promoted the evacuation that he had bragged about in his speech to his staff in November 1942. "It had not occurred to me that there would be an evacuation or that I would be as-signed to General DeWitt's command with duties related to an evacuation of persons of Japanese ancestry from the West Coast," Bendetsen said.[36]

Luckily for the witnesses, commission counsel Angus Macbeth and re-searcher Aiko Herzig-Yoshinaga had conducted extensive primary research from the National Archives and other repositories. She found the only re-maining copy of the original version of DeWitt's error-filled and inflam-matory "Final Report," which acknowledged that the military planned to keep the Japanese Americans in camps for the duration of the war and had no firm evidence to support any of the claims of potential sabotage. That discovery unmasked the government's lie. "When I saw it," Herzig-Yoshinaga said, "I just about hit the ceiling. I had operated for the past few years under the assumption that there were no more of these copies, so it was like finding a gold nugget."[37]

Personal Justice Denied

On February 24, 1983, the Commission on Wartime Relocation and Internment of Civilians released its report about the incarceration. *Personal Justice Denied* validated the testimony from the more than seven hundred former prisoners who told the commission about their forced removal from their homes and their imprisonment. Aiko Herzig-Yoshinaga's research had exposed Karl Bendetsen as a liar. No evidence had supported the incarceration, the report said, adding that "Executive Order 9066 was not justified by military necessity, and the decisions that followed it—exclusion, detention, the ending of detention and the ending of exclusion—were not founded on military considerations. The broad historical causes that shaped these decisions were race prejudice, war hysteria and the failure of political leadership."[38]

Four months later, the commission released five recommendations to right the wrongs caused by the incarceration. It called for another national social movement, which this time would seek a joint resolution by Congress that apologized for the incarceration; pardons for previous incarceration-related convictions; liberal rulings for redress; a fund to pay for research into the social issues that had led to the incarceration; and $20,000 for every surviving prisoner. At the time, there were about sixty thousand former prisoners still alive, a number that dwindled daily as the aging Issei died off. Commissioner William Marutani, a former prisoner, renounced any claim to redress payments so that no one could accuse him of trying to benefit financially from his vote.[39]

Daniel Inouye was right again. He had said a commission backed by hearings and a compelling report would generate publicity to help the redress movement. Redress advocates could now wield *Personal Justice Denied* as proof of what had been unfairly done to 120,000 people. But proof, no matter how compellingly presented, did not guarantee justice, as Inouye, Norman Mineta, and their allies would learn.

A Midlife Awakening

The commission hearings helped draw the former incarcerees together, and they decided to conduct the first Heart Mountain reunion in 1982. One of the organizers reached out to Bacon Sakatani, who was then a fifty-three-year-old computer programmer living in West Covina, California, not far from where his father had farmed before and after the war. He remembered camp, how his family struggled afterward in Idaho, and how they had lived in a tent back in California. He knew nothing about the larger history of the incarceration, which Sakatani thought he needed to know if he was going to help lead the reunion. He started his research at the local library by reading *Heart Mountain: The History of an American Concentration Camp* by Doug Nelson. What Sakatani learned turned him into someone his fellow incarcerees call "Mister Heart Mountain." "I found out how much the government lied when it sent us to camp, how much they cheated us out of our land, and it really pissed me off," he said. Sakatani, who had once rescued Raymond Uno from a fight in elementary school, now channeled his energies into becoming a scholar of the incarceration. Not only did he organize the first Heart Mountain reunion; he also revived interest in the Heart Mountain draft resisters and located an impoverished Estelle Ishigo. Eventually Sakatani would help the efforts in Cody and Powell to create the Heart Mountain Wyoming Foundation and to build a museum on the grounds of the former camp. "Since that reunion I would say I have not stopped working on Heart Mountain," he said.[40]

Sakatani learned about what Chester and Mary Blackburn were doing to honor the incarcerees in Wyoming when he met them at the reunion. They shared slides and memories of the camp and the homesteaders. Sakatani climbed Heart Mountain for the first time that year, making the ascent with Chet Blackburn, who had recently had open-heart surgery.[41] Each started giving presentations to interested groups about the governmental order that had created the incarceration and about life inside the barbed wire at Heart Mountain. Chet Blackburn had spent the war fighting the Japanese in the Pacific; now he numbered some of his closest friends among Japanese Americans. "My folks had more Japanese friends," said Ruth Blackburn Pfaff, his daughter. "I mean, when they go to Arizona, they visit with Japanese; when they went to California, they visited with Japanese. The Japanese would come here and visit with them. They had Christmas cards, all of that."[42]

Part of that bond, Darrell Kunitomi said, reflected the people who were imprisoned at Heart Mountain. They had a different outlook than was common among prisoners from Tule Lake or Manzanar, the toughest camps with the most difficult prisoners. "Heart Mountain was known as a good camp," he said. "They always had a big reunion. You'd think, 'Do these people really want to remember those times?'"[43]

Holding Space for Draft Resisters

Bacon Sakatani put together a slideshow about the incarceration, spurred by his research for the 1982 Heart Mountain reunion, and took it to schools and other groups around California and the West. By 1983, it included the protest by the draft resisters, and, at an event that year at California State University at Fullerton, in Orange County, he invited Frank Emi, a leader of the antidraft Fair Play Committee, to participate. That, Emi said, was the first time he had thought about the draft resistance since leaving Fort Leavenworth for Los Angeles, where he worked for the US Postal Service. The resisters, long shunned by many in their community, were being seen in a new light, especially by the Sansei. CSU Fullerton was one of the leaders in studying the incarceration and the Japanese American experience. After the speech and the question-and-answer session, students clustered around Emi, telling him they had never heard of the resisters. "They thought that everybody had just remained quiet and hadn't made any fuss," Emi said, "but they seemed very pleased to know that there had been resistance in the camps."[44]

By 1983, only Emi and Sam Horino remained of the Fair Play Committee leaders. The rest—Kiyoshi Okamoto, Minoru Tamesa, Ben Wakaye, Guntaro Kubota, and Paul Nakadate—had all died by 1974. Only Okamoto, the committee's rabble-rousing founder, lived to anything close to a ripe old age. The others were dead by the age of sixty-four; Wakaye had died at thirty-nine. President Truman may have pardoned them in 1947, but the rest of the Japanese American community had not. They were often shunned by their community and forced to work in jobs for which they were overqualified, which likely contributed to their early deaths.

Some of the Fullerton students belonged to the National Coalition for Redress and Reparations. The students' involvement helped fuse the causes of those seeking redress and the resisters, men about whom many Sansei and even some former prisoners knew little. Emi met with them and "saw how dedicated they were to this redress movement, even though they themselves wouldn't be its beneficiaries." Before then, Emi had thought little about the draft resistance, because "it just didn't occur to me that it was anything significant. We had just felt that it was such an injustice that we fought against it."[45] Now, spurred by Sakatani, the resisters started to make themselves heard. This second fight for legitimacy and recognition would take longer than the incarceration itself and the prison terms the resisters had endured.

Healing Community

In the mid-1980s, two movements to heal the Japanese American community of the wounds suffered during World War II began to converge. The efforts of Japanese American politicians—including Daniel Inouye, Spark Matsunaga, Robert Matsui, and Norman Mineta—to extract an apology from the federal government and financial compensation for some of the losses suffered during the incarceration gained momentum. So, too, did the efforts to get the JACL, still the nation's dominant Nikkei group, to apologize for its treatment of the prisoners who resisted the draft during the war. Inspired by the civil rights movement of the 1960s, many Sansei began to both aggressively support redress for the incarceration and to view the draft resisters as principled heroes, not the cowards that many Nisei had believed them to be.

The emotionally draining hearings and then the release of *Personal Justice Denied* gave the supporters of redress hope that they could get a bill through Congress. They soon learned otherwise. Norman Mineta introduced a bill shortly after the commission's report, and he hit a roadblock almost immediately when he met with Thomas Kindness, the top Republican on the Judiciary subcommittee that would conduct hearings on the bill. Kindness, a polite Ohioan whose demeanor matched his name, said he would ask a friend for guidance. Unfortunately, that friend was Karl Bendetsen.

"Don't you know Bendetsen?" Norman asked Glenn Roberts, his chief aide. "He was the general [*sic*] who put us in the camps, the son of a bitch."[46] When Bendetsen testified before the Judiciary Committee's Subcommittee on Administrative Law, he claimed that top-secret cables from the Japanese government showed they had planned to recruit Japanese Americans to spy for them. That was a lie. The reports by Lieutenant Commander K. D. Ringle of the Office of Naval Intelligence showed the opposite.

Representative Dan Lungren, a member of the Commission on the Wartime Relocation and Internment of Civilians, also opposed payments, arguing that an apology should be enough and that other groups that had suffered at the hands of the government, such as slaves and Native Americans, would also want money if the Japanese Americans were to receive compensation. Most important, however, was the opposition to the bill from the subcommittee chairman, Sam Hall, a conservative Democrat from Texas. Without Hall's support, the bill would go nowhere.

Then one of those serendipitous events in politics occurred through no effort by the Japanese American members of Congress. After winning election to the Senate in 1984, Senator Phil Gramm of Texas, a Democrat turned Republican, wanted to hasten his state's realignment from Democratic to Republican. He persuaded President Ronald Reagan, who had just won a landslide victory to a second term, to appoint Hall a federal judge in order to create a vacancy in Hall's House seat that could be won by a Republican. That plan got Hall out of the way, but Gramm's plan backfired when a Democrat narrowly won the special election. But the bill still remained stalled in committee through 1986. It was only after the 1986 midterm elections that conditions changed, as Democrats regained control of the Senate and Representative Barney Frank, a liberal Democrat, gained control of the Judiciary subcommittee that had authority over the redress bill.

Now the supporters of redress had a more favorable playing field. The lobbying effort in the House involved Norman Mineta, Matsui of Sacramento, and activists like John Tateishi and Grant Ujifusa of the JACL. As with earlier attempts to pass the bill, they faced some House members who believed that the Japanese Americans at the time were possibly spies, despite the evidence to the contrary, or that paying reparations would grant the Nikkei a privilege that other oppressed minority groups, such as blacks and Native Americans, had been denied despite their suffering.

Frank's rise was a supreme stroke of good luck for redress, because he believed the Japanese Americans had suffered a great injustice. "I think as a country, we need this bill more than the victims," Frank said.[47] He told Ujifusa they needed the support of the subcommittee's ranking Republican, the very conservative Pat Swindall of Georgia. Ujifusa said he thought Swindall would be difficult to sway, but he sought the help of Mike Masaoka, who recommended they get the support of the Anti-Defamation League, which had taken Swindall and other evangelical Christian representatives to Israel.

Over his years working the halls of Congress, Masaoka had built an unparalleled perspective about how to make Washington work. Evangelical Christians, Masaoka knew, were just developing an affinity for Israel that would reshape US-Israeli relations over the next thirty years, and that Swindall's passion for Israel came from his biblical scholarship. David Brodie, the chief lobbyist of the Anti-Defamation League, arranged a meeting with Swindall, who agreed to back the bill, which moved out of the full committee and to the House.[48]

Norman Mineta, Matsui, and the other supporters in the House also received an unexpected boost when it was revealed that the Reagan administration had been working on a plan to monitor and perhaps deport Muslim Americans and immigrants because of concerns over possible ties to terrorism. Once more, national security was being used to justify racial and ethnic discrimination.

"I believe it is vital to bring to the subcommittee's attention that in recent months, a Department of Justice task force has proposed as legal and appropriate the mass round-up and incarceration of certain nationalities for vague national security reasons," Norman told Frank's subcommittee. "So, this bill is not just about the past. It is about today and the future as well."[49]

With Swindall's help, Frank's support, and Mineta's testimony, the bill passed the subcommittee, then the full committee, and then the full House by a 243–141 vote. Matsui brought along two conservative members from his House class of 1978: Newt Gingrich of Georgia, a future House speaker, and Dick Cheney of Wyoming, Gerald Ford's former chief of staff and a future vice president.[50]

In the Senate, Daniel Inouye's help had always been essential, but it was Spark Matsunaga who collected the votes. The diminutive Matsunaga, known by his colleagues as Sparky, was beloved by members of both parties as a warm and friendly colleague who was always true to his word. At first, he had twenty-five cosponsors, most of them fellow liberal Democrats, but when he was done, more than seventy senators, Democrats and Republicans, had signed on. The Senate passed the bill. "That great and gentle man should not be someone forgotten among us nor among scholars and students of redress to come," Ujifusa said about Matsunaga.[51] One small speed bump came from an unexpected source—Alan Simpson. Norman Mineta's longtime friend did not like the costs associated with the bill; he believed the people unjustly incarcerated deserved an apology, but he worried that the payments would set a precedent that would lead to payments of claims brought by other groups. Simpson had supported an amendment that would have stripped the payments from the bill. The incarceration was "the gravest of injustices," Simpson said, but "I have trouble with the money." While Simpson finally said he would vote for the bill, which ultimately passed 69–27, the payments left "a strange feeling in my craw."[52]

Redress supporters had reached a point they once thought impossible. But they still had to persuade one of the most conservative presidents of the twentieth century to sign the bill without violating his principles. Two years earlier, one of Reagan's Justice Department advisers, John Bolton, had said the president would veto the bill, because the government had already paid reparations. Reagan's Office of Management and Budget also recommended a veto, saying the payments would exacerbate a rising federal budget deficit crisis. Redress supporters pulled every lever they had with the White House to persuade Reagan.[53]

First, they tweaked the bill in Congress to extend the time period over which the payments to former prisoners would be made. That placated some of the deficit hawks. The new version passed both houses. Ujifusa lobbied the education secretary, William Bennett, a Harvard classmate, and domestic adviser Gary Bauer, a staunch religious conservative. Both agreed to urge Reagan to sign the bill. Rose Ochi, a former incarceree, sent Reagan a newspaper article from 1945 about a meeting Reagan had attended with General Joseph Stilwell, the leader of US troops in China during World War II. A cemetery in Santa Ana, California, had refused to accept the body of Kazuo Masuda, a member of the 442nd who had been killed in combat and awarded the Distinguished Service Cross. Stilwell, with the young actor Ronald Reagan in tow, had gone to Masuda's family to present the medal in person. The article quoted Reagan this way: "Blood that has soaked into the sands of a beach is all of one color. America stands unique in the world: the only country not founded on race but in a way, an ideal. Not in spite of but because of our polyglot background, we have had all the strength in the world. That is the American way." Reagan remembered; his staff said he was inclined to sign the bill.[54]

Reagan lived up to his word on August 10, 1988, in a ceremony attended by more than one hundred Japanese Americans and supporters in Congress. Flanked by Mineta, Inouye, Matsunaga, Matsui, Republican representative Patricia Saiki of Hawaii, Republican senator Ted Stevens of Alaska (a close friend of Inouye's), and Barney Frank, Reagan had one of the greatest moments of his presidency. "We gathered here to right a grave wrong," he said. Reagan cited Norman Mineta and his family's experience at Santa

Anita, where they showered in horse paddocks, and then at Heart Mountain. With the stroke of his pen, Reagan officially apologized for the incarceration and authorized the redress payments to the surviving incarcerees. "Yet no payment can make up for those lost years," he said. The packed room of Japanese Americans clapped in appreciation. "Thank you all again and God bless you all," Reagan said. "I think this is a fine day."[55]

The JACL and Coming to Terms
with Draft Resisters

By persuading Congress to pass the Civil Liberties Act that apologized to Japanese Americans for the incarceration and paid them each $20,000, the JACL had achieved its greatest victory. But it had not yet acknowledged its harsh treatment of the young men who resisted the draft, including Takashi Hoshizaki, and the path toward an apology was twisted and blocked by dissension. The discord between the JACL and the Heart Mountain resisters lasted for decades, long past the deaths of most of the leaders of the Fair Play Committee. Many accusations against Mike Masaoka and the group's leadership were exaggerated or invented, but some rang true for the victims of the JACL's actions, such as the support for the segregation of loyal and allegedly disloyal prisoners into different camps and the targeting of the Kibei as potential subversives. The JACL craved the acceptance of white America so much that it had traded away the rights of its own people. When that acceptance did not come, it continued to placate the government in the blind hope something would change. After the war, however, the JACL led the fight to eliminate alien land laws, grant citizenship to immigrants, pay some form of redress, and wipe out parts of the Internal Security Act. Following the passage of the Civil Liberties Act, driven in large part by Masaoka and JACL lobbying, its leadership became more open to admitting error. In 1989, the leadership commissioned Deborah Lim, a professor at the University of California, San Francisco, to dig into the group's archives and determine what really happened.[56]

Lim spent the next six months at work, interviewing scholars and activists and combing through documents at the National Archives. She gave the JACL select committee a 95-page report at the end of 1989 and then finished a more detailed 154-page report by the spring of 1990. Her report supported the claims that the JACL had collaborated with the military and WRA officials and that it had held down dissidents, such as the draft resisters.

Her report was devastating to the JACL.

The JACL leadership now faced a dilemma: whether to release Lim's work or to hide it. "I decided to just set the stage and let the historical material speak for itself," Lim told the historian Frank Abe, adding that the extent of the JACL's collaboration with intelligence agencies had surprised her. "The whole notion of informing on people where there wasn't any basis to . . . there was a lot more of that activity than I was expecting to find."

The JACL, she found, had, among other things, colluded with the American Civil Liberties Union to deny legal help to the Heart Mountain draft resisters. The group had also sent Minoru Yasui, one of the defendants in the test cases challenging the curfew, to the Cheyenne County jail with Joe Grant Masaoka, Mike Masaoka's older brother, to try and convince the resisters not to challenge the draft. "At a recent forum on the Heart Mountain Draft Resisters, the irony of what Min Yasui was attempting to do did not go unaddressed," Lim wrote. "'It was all right for Min Yasui to challenge the government and to fight for his constitutional rights, but it was wrong for us to do so.'"[57]

Inside JACL, Paul Tsuneishi agitated for the apology. While Tsuneishi had accepted the draft himself, he respected the resisters' courage. His father, Satoru, had also supported the resisters and the Fair Play Committee despite having three of his four sons in the Army. After entering the Army, Tsuneishi had served with the occupation forces in Japan and then returned to Southern California, where he ran an insurance agency whose clients included Takashi Hoshizaki. His interest in the resisters had started with his father's statement before the Commission on Wartime Relocation and Internment of Civilians in 1981, in which Satoru Tsuneishi said his study of the American Revolution made him understand why Japanese Americans would not want to serve in the military while their families were incarcerated.[58] Tsuneishi was committed to helping preserve what remained at Heart Mountain. In 1994, he and Sakatani helped bring a barrack from Heart Mountain to the grounds of the Japanese American National Museum in Los Angeles.[59] They also helped create the Heart Mountain Wyoming Foundation. A year later, Tsuneishi was in such full rebellion against the JACL that he argued that the group "must reclaim its civil rights roots if it wants to do anything further in a number of areas of concern for Japanese Americans. What we need, really, is a change in the mentality of the JACL leadership at its top level."[60]

Draft Resisters at Heart Mountain

Before I joined the Heart Mountain board, I knew very little about the draft resisters and their struggle to gain some understanding and acceptance for their actions inside the Japanese American community. I also knew next to nothing about the former incarcerees and their families who fought the draft and then pushed to have the foundation acknowledge their efforts. That was because I had been indoctrinated by my mother into the JACL perspective on the incarceration and the Japanese American community. I relied on Bill Hosokawa's book, *Nisei: The Quiet Americans*, for most of my information about the incarceration, not realizing the schism between the JACL faction, which included Hosokawa, and the resisters. People like Paul Tsuneishi meant nothing to me until I discovered two thick files in the Heart Mountain archives that included his letters to and from other members of the foundation and leaders in the community. Then it became obvious to me that Tsuneishi had made the Heart Mountain Wyoming Foundation a leader in the effort to recognize the struggle of the draft resisters and bring them into the larger Japanese American community. Even more than fifty years after the camps closed and the draft resisters left prison, the schism that separated the resisters, veterans, and JACL supporters divided the Heart Mountain board. Although many Issei and Nisei considered the resisters to be troublemakers, the political center of gravity in the Japanese American community, influenced by the Sansei, had shifted toward the resisters. Lance Ito told me once that he was pressured not to play with the children of the resisters in his neighborhood in Los Angeles while he was growing up. The Sansei, while they valued the valor demonstrated by the members of the 100th and the 442nd, also believed that the resisters deserved credit for opposing an unjust system. More journalists and historians had discovered the resisters, and Heart Mountain board members wanted to promote that research.

Tsuneishi brought Takashi Hoshizaki back to Heart Mountain. By the early 1990s, after Takashi retired following a career as a scientist in the space program, he became more active in the effort to commemorate Heart Mountain. He received an award in 1993 from the Los Angeles Japanese American Bar Association to honor his "courage and strength of conviction in demanding 'fair play' by refusing to serve as US soldiers during World War II while your families were incarcerated solely on the basis of race in violation of their constitutional rights."[61] During a series of meetings in

Wyoming around 1994, Tsuneishi took Tak out for coffee and donuts and brought him into the group.[62]

The pro-resister faction worked tirelessly to win over every Japanese American organization. By the mid-1990s, Tsuneishi had assembled a formidable group that included Michi Weglyn, the author of the powerful 1976 incarceration history *Years of Infamy*, and Ernest Uno, a 442nd veteran and the brother of Edison Uno and Amy Uno Ishii and cousin of Raymond Uno. "It is very clear that [the resisters] are not publicly honored or respected within the J-A community by *any* organized group today," Tsuneishi wrote the Heart Mountain board on July 5, 1998.[63] He and his group pressed on. They first got the Hawaii chapter of the Japanese American Veterans Association to urge "all other Japanese American veterans to extend their hands of friendship and goodwill to members of the Fair Play Committee, their families and supporters, in recognition of their unswerving vigilance in upholding the laws of the land under the Constitution of the United States."[64] Several local JACL chapters agreed. "We did it!" Ernest Uno wrote Weglyn on August 4, 1998. "It took a long time coming, but the stage is set to get the other veterans' organizations such as Club 100, MIS, and any of the Nisei VFW and American Legion posts, to pass similar resolutions."[65] Frank Emi agreed. "Better late than never," he wrote Uno. "Coming from such a prestigious organization, it is bound to cause beneficial ripples in the future and help lead to a genuine movement for understanding and recognition with other organizations."[66]

Outsiders also took notice. The filmmaker Frank Abe from Seattle began working on a documentary called *Conscience and the Constitution*, while the University of North Carolina law school professor Eric Muller was researching and writing a history that would be called *Free to Die for Their Country*. Tsuneishi had shared oral history interviews of some of the surviving resisters with Muller, Abe, and other scholars.[67] By 1999, as the Heart Mountain Foundation began promoting itself more around Wyoming and inside the Japanese American community, Tsuneishi chafed at what he considered the patronizing attitude of David Reetz, Pat Wolfe, and John Collins toward him and other supporters of the resisters.[68]

In January 1999, Ann Noble, a Heart Mountain board member and historian, proposed showing at the upcoming board meeting parts of two documentaries in progress—Abe's *Conscience and the Constitution* and *Honor Bound* by Wendy Hanamura, a film about her father, Sergeant Howard Hanamura, and his experience in the 442nd. Abe had specialized in work about civil rights and the inherent unfairness of the incarceration. He was not in the *shikata ga nai* camp. Tsuneishi hoped the preview would help Abe's work in progress.

After some encouraging signs from the board leadership, Reetz, the foundation president, declined to show the excerpts because he did not want to create the perception that the board supported a film that could turn out to be controversial, particularly given the foundation's need to raise money. While the resisters had stirred the interest of the Sansei and academics, the real clout and money inside the community remained with the veterans and their supporters. Angering them meant losing money needed to build an enduring memorial at the campsite.

Tsuneishi urged Reetz and the board to reconsider, but they declined. Tsuneishi didn't give up. "I really regret that you disagreed so strongly with my philosophy that you hung up the phone on me," Reetz wrote Tsuneishi on February 17, 1999.[69] Tsuneishi, livid, suspected that political motives lurked behind the board's decision. "I do not accept the stated reason that I was given: that a board policy is (now) in place wherein a decision cannot be made on a work in progress, as it might be biased or might embarrass Norman Mineta. . . . I also understand that there was concern over some negative comments made by one or more Japanese Americans here in LA."

Finally, Tsuneishi resigned from the board.[70]

The next month, the board wrote Abe that it was sorry it could not show his film and that Tsuneishi had resigned. "While we believe that ultimately the right decision was made for the right reasons, we regret the process that got us there," the letter said. "Our hasty action resulted in hurt feelings that we can only hope time will heal. We have learned a hard lesson."[71]

They had more lessons to learn. Tsuneishi remained just as active off the board as he had been as a member. Tensions flared again at a September 19, 1999, board meeting that focused on a debate over whether to support a school program featuring the resisters. Predictably, the board and its advisers split, as if the debate were being held in 1944, not 1999. Hosokawa, whose *Heart Mountain Sentinel* had never supported the resisters, called the issue too volatile and asserted that it was bound to hurt the foundation. Tsuneishi had for years argued that such a claim was overblown and no longer valid. Board adviser Nancy Araki, a leader at the Japanese American National Museum, agreed with Hosokawa, saying they should wait for the foundation to develop a stronger sense of identity. Alan Kumamoto, a board adviser, wanted to know who was behind the request for this. "Do we have to do this?" he asked. But Carolyn Takeshita, an educator who had been incarcerated in Poston, Arizona, argued that the foundation needed to acknowledge the resisters while a significant number of them were still alive. Hosokawa finally came around, saying that people would be upset regardless of what side the forum took.

For Hosokawa, it was a significant step, but it was not one he took lightly. At eighty-four, he was one of the oldest members of the foundation and the one most steeped in knowledge. He had been a part of the first group of prisoners at Heart Mountain, arriving early so he could launch the *Sentinel* after working with the government and JACL to identify possible security risks inside the Japanese American community. The *Sentinel* under his editorship had followed the line promoted by the War Relocation Authority, the military, and the JACL. After the war, his book, *Nisei, the Quiet Americans* set the standard for informing most Americans about Japanese Americans and the incarceration, but it also promoted the same themes he had espoused during the war: the need for Japanese Americans to prove they were more patriotic than white Americans and a fierce devotion to the spirit embodied by the 442nd Regimental Combat Team. His embrace of the resisters' forum, even so tentatively arrived at, showed that the issue had come of age and that the Heart Mountain Wyoming Foundation was willing to take a stand.[72] It was a vindication for Tsuneishi and for Hoshizaki, whose involvement, backed by donations financed by his income from working as a scientist for the Jet Propulsion Laboratory and as a consultant, had grown in scope and enthusiasm. As much as anyone, he pushed the foundation to take a stronger stance.

Tsuneishi found a Cheyenne, Wyoming, high school willing to do a school theater production of the resisters' trial and told Barbara Uriu that resisters Frank Emi, one of the leaders of the Fair Play Committee, and Yosh Kuromiya, a resister, would be willing to provide background information about the trial to the school.[73] They organized a wider forum on the resisters around the production of the play. The organizers of the Cheyenne forum invited Floyd Mori, the president of the JACL from 2000 to 2004. A relatively young Nisei, Mori was born in Utah, and his family had not been incarcerated. He was also heavily influenced by Mike Masaoka. But Mori had moved after college to California, where he was active in the JACL redress efforts along with Edison Uno. He also served as a Democrat in the state assembly. By the time he attended the Cheyenne conference, he had a deep appreciation of the divisions within the Japanese American community. What Mori learned, however, touched him in ways he did not anticipate. "I got to know some of the resisters and their stories and what they had gone through," Mori said. "My heart went out to them."

Mori's awakening spurred a final debate about apologizing to the resisters inside the JACL. Some of the hardline veterans in the organization fought the apology; they still considered the resisters cowards. "There were some veterans who walked out of the session," Mori said. Eventually, he said, the veterans in the JACL meetings began to listen and understand more about the resisters.[74] It also helped that Senator Daniel Inouye, a certified war hero, had praised the resisters for their courage. In 2002, Mori issued a formal apology from the JACL to the resisters at a ceremony in San Francisco, and Frank Emi accepted it. The apology represented a change in the attitudes that had divided the two groups and a sign that the wounds from this enduring battle were starting to heal.[75]

Finding Community

My mother's metamorphosis from a hardcore Japanese American assimilationist began when my parents moved from Ann Arbor to Salt Lake City in 1982. She went from living in a city with few Japanese Americans to one with a small but thriving community led by Raymond Uno. She now had friends with whom she could discuss shared experiences of the incarceration and the anti-Japanese discrimination that persisted after the war. Raymond Uno and Jeannette Mitarai Misaka had also been her classmates at Heart Mountain. They had all been gripped by the redress hearings, which motivated a group of former Heart Mountain inmates to organize a reunion. Setsuko joined them.

Even as Setsuko grew more interested in her experience at Heart Mountain, she continued to champion my father after they moved to Salt Lake, where he became the chairman of the pharmaceutics department at the University of Utah, which was encouraging its faculty to develop start-up companies that advanced research and built the local economy. Bill knew he now had the chance to emulate the work of his older brother Takeru, who had built a towering reputation in the field at the universities of Wisconsin and Kansas, where a building had been named after him. Bill Higuchi was building a similar reputation in the science of drug delivery. All that time he'd spent in the laboratory when we were children was paying off. Dinesh Patel, one of his brilliant graduate students from Michigan, followed him to Utah. By 1985 they had started TheraTech, a company that developed time-released medicines, particularly through absorption through the skin. *Newsweek* magazine, in a 1987 cover story, featured the testosterone patch they invented. His financial success, coupled with Setsuko's work in real estate, helped finance her growing interest in Heart Mountain and creating an enduring legacy there.[76] Setsuko "just became more involved [with Heart Mountain] as she was living here," my brother John Higuchi reports of Salt Lake City. "It turned her from being an assimilationist to someone more sensitive to the real importance of the incarceration. There was a synergy involving her moving here and the increased activity for the redress."[77]

Out of the first reunion grew a desire among my parents' generation to do more at Heart Mountain than put up a sign or monument. "We need to build a museum," my mother said. Always the builder and decorator of homes, she envisioned something more permanent and educational at Heart Mountain, but neither she nor her fellow incarcerees knew what that should be. Neither did the Blackburns. The Japanese Americans who had lived at Heart Mountain involuntarily, along with their Sansei children, would have to determine what that would be.

13

Preservation under Duress

Narrating the History:
Doug Nelson

Doug Nelson graduated from the University of Illinois with a degree in history in 1968 and faced a choice. A fervent antiwar activist and newly married, he sought out opportunities to delay entry into the military, which was drafting young men in record numbers to feed the demands of the Vietnam War. Almost accidentally, he learned of a graduate school program at the University of Wyoming that would offer him a part-time teaching position combined with the chance to get a master's degree in history. Accepting the Wyoming invitation allowed him to gain a draft deferment for teaching, and Doug grabbed it, even though it meant moving to a place he knew nothing about. He and his young wife, Linda, packed their car and drove to Laramie, where he met Roger Daniels, the member of the history department who would become his thesis adviser. Daniels was a leader in the tiny group of academics studying Asian immigration to the United States and the Japanese American incarceration. Nelson had not focused on Asian American history, but he was interested in the World War II treatment of Japanese Americans and had a vague awareness of the "relocation camp" at Heart Mountain. When Daniels advised him that there had been little formal history written on any of the camps, he jumped at the chance to learn and write about Heart Mountain.[1]

Initially, Nelson found little to work with. The site of the camp itself, located between Cody and Powell, had been scoured of virtually all its barracks and other facilities. There were also surprisingly few people to interview. The Japanese American prisoners had moved far away from Wyoming, and Nelson had no convenient way of locating, let alone interviewing, them. And to his surprise, many of the local people in Cody and Powell who remembered the camp were reluctant to talk about the incarceration, and more than a few seemed irked that he wanted to explore what they considered a best-forgotten chapter of local history. A few older folks told him about the "No Japs allowed" signs on the windows of Cody businesses, and others described the fear and suspicion locals had felt when they first learned that more than ten thousand Japanese, allegedly too dangerous to remain on the West Coast, were being deposited just miles from their homes. Nelson remembers that the Park County people he eventually got to know generally acknowledged that the incarceration was probably wrong, but, as one older woman told him, "We were much more worried about our boys in service than these people we knew nothing about." Nelson remembers, "The overall sense I had about my year of researching the Heart Mountain camp in 1970 was that there weren't many local people enthusiastic about the prospect of a history being written about what had actually happened there."[2]

Dave Bonner, the young editor of the *Powell Tribune*, was an exception. He gave Nelson one of his first breaks by opening up the weekly newspaper's entire World War II–era archives for his research. There Nelson found extensive reporting on events that touched on the camp, which had been a place of great interest to Powell residents, since it was just eight miles down the road. Even before incarcerees arrived, the *Tribune* had reported on the local employment and other economic benefits of providing services to what would become the third largest community in the state. In contrast to the *Cody Enterprise*, the Powell paper looked for the positives. The *Tribune*, as an example, gave significant coverage to the role Heart Mountain prisoners had played in saving the local bean and sugar beet harvests for the region's labor-short farms during the war years. By 1943, the paper took uncomplaining note of the growing number of "cleared" camp residents who were receiving passes to go into Powell to shop or do other errands. The *Tribune*'s editors even came to the defense of the Japanese American incarcerees and the WRA administrators when the *Denver Post* and other papers published inflammatory claims that Heart Mountain was a place where dangerous "foreigners" were being coddled and treated better than "Americans." Nelson noted that the *Tribune* "never failed to stress the economic benefits that Powell's new neighbors brought to local farmers and businessmen."[3]

The *Tribune* archives also held a complete archive of the camp paper, the *Heart Mountain Sentinel,* which gave Nelson a window into life, conditions, and controversies inside the camp as they were reported by talented incarceree journalists. While the *Sentinel* reflected the controversial JACL perspective on the importance of projecting an attitude of cooperation and loyalty, it also gave voice to the incarcerees' acute awareness and critiques of the racism and unfairness that had led to their incarceration and continued to perpetuate it. In the pages of the *Sentinel,* Nelson discovered the existence of the Fair Play Committee and the breadth of the well-organized, articulate, and influential draft resistance movement at Heart Mountain. Through his research, Nelson brought the long-shrouded story of Heart Mountain's significant resistance to a wider public audience.

Nelson expanded his research well beyond Wyoming to mine the abundant government, court, and university collections pertaining to Heart Mountain that were scattered in several government and West Coast university archives. He was often the first person to open record boxes that had been packed and shipped off shortly after the camps closed in 1945. His research concluded in a thesis, submitted in May 1970, that provided the most comprehensive overview of an individual camp and the first to extensively and sympathetically describe the presence of significant protest and resistance at Heart Mountain. He remembered the process of learning about what had happened to the fourteen thousand people forced to live at Heart Mountain as a pivotal life experience. And he was haunted by the fact that there was nothing built or remaining at the site to tell the world what had happened there. He remembers telling his wife on their final visit to Heart Mountain before heading to Wisconsin: "You know, someday somebody important ought to put something here that tells the real story of this place." He never imagined that decades later that he would be one of the people who would make that happen.[4]

During his time at Wisconsin, one of Nelson's professors read his thesis and submitted it for publication to the Wisconsin State Historical Society. The resulting book, carrying what was the then controversial title *Heart Mountain: The History of an American Concentration Camp,* was published in 1975 and provided one of the clearest pictures yet of what happened during the incarceration and inside the camps. "The Constitution was not the principal victim of relocation; the Japanese Americans were," he wrote. "Although there were no gas chambers, ovens, or S.S. at Heart Mountain, it was nonetheless a concentration camp. Its establishment and operation involved a thoroughgoing repudiation not only of legal guarantees, but also of the traditional Western values of liberty, privacy, individuality, and human dignity."[5] Nelson had helped give a voice to the Issei and Nisei who had only just started telling their stories. Perhaps he did not realize it at the time, but Nelson had embarked on a path that he would follow for the next four decades.[6]

His book, which earned a nomination for the Pulitzer Prize in 1976, became one of the foundational pieces of incarceration literature. Joining it in 1976 was *Years of Infamy*, a searing history by Michi Nishiura Weglyn, who was incarcerated in the Gila River, Arizona, camp. She left for Mount Holyoke College in 1944 and became a fashion designer and then a historian. Her book ripped apart the flimsy government rationale that military necessity had required the evacuation and incarceration of Japanese Americans. She used the newly available Freedom of Information Act to find documents that showed there was no evidence of sabotage or espionage that warranted the wholesale movement and imprisonment of 120,000 people. "They who say that it can never happen again are probably wrong," she wrote. The *New York Times* said, "Michi Weglyn, herself one of the teenage inmates, in *Years of Infamy* gives an appalling view of the privation, neglect and even brutality that the bewildered Japanese Americans underwent in the camps. Her account, based largely on government documents, is decidedly grimmer than most earlier books on this disgraceful subject."[7]

The world of incarceration history, bolstered by Nelson and Weglyn, would not only influence future historians but also educate some of the Nisei who had been too young to understand the events that their parents never wanted to discuss or try to explain.

Narrating the History:
Eric Saul

Eric Saul was a young historian when he became the curator of the small museum at the Presidio, the old fort overlooking the Pacific Ocean in San Francisco where DeWitt, Bendetsen, and the rest of the Western Defense Command oversaw the genesis of the forced removal and incarceration. In 1981, Saul wanted to create an exhibit about the Nisei soldiers from World War II, primarily the 100th Infantry, the 442nd Regimental Combat Team, and the 522nd Field Artillery Battalion. He knew there was a bigger story to tell about what the Nisei soldiers had done, and he had the support of the base commander to tell that story even if the ties between the Presidio and the incarceration were embarrassing.[8]

While the exploits of the 100th, the 442nd, and the 522nd had received plenty of daily press coverage during the war, particularly in newspapers like the *Sentinel*, Saul quickly learned there was little other information available. The Army, Pentagon, and National Archives contained some sketchy details, but none of the major war historians had studied the Nisei soldiers. It looked like they might have to do their exhibit about something else. Then one day, Henry Oyasato, a former colonel who had commanded the 442nd's F Company, was visiting the museum. He asked Saul why the museum did not have an exhibit about the Nisei soldiers.

"You must be reading our mail," Saul said. "That's just what we're trying to plan now!"[9]

Saul was soon overwhelmed by the help of Oyasato, Chester Tanaka, and other veterans who eagerly supplied him with memories and mementos from their service. Soon Saul had more than enough material for the exhibit, which opened to great fanfare on March 7, 1981. Senators Daniel Inouye and Spark Matsunaga of Hawaii attended the opening ceremonies, as did Mike Masaoka, who had agitated for the unit's creation. Masaoka made the self-justifying comment that the exhibit showed that the United States, which had stained its record with the incarceration, remained the one country capable of admitting and correcting its mistakes. San Francisco mayor Dianne Feinstein, who would later serve in the Senate with Inouye, said, "To forget such things is to make it possible for them to happen again."[10]

Soon after the exhibit opened, a Nisei man in his late fifties—Clarence Matsumura—approached Saul. Clarence had been through a lot in the thirty-six years after the war. He had married a fellow inmate from Heart Mountain, served during the Korean War, held several jobs, had a child, and then divorced. He was estranged from most of his family, suffered from untreated posttraumatic stress disorder, and was unable to process what he had seen during the spring of 1945 in Dachau. He told Saul that he enjoyed the exhibit but that Saul had missed something. Did he know that the 522nd had liberated Dachau? As a Jew with a keen interest in the Holocaust, Saul said he had never heard that. "I didn't believe him, to be honest with you," Saul said. "Wait here," said Clarence, who went to his car and pulled out a box containing photographs and other memorabilia from the war. Together they began reviewing Clarence's experience, and memories erupted from him like lava from a long-dormant volcano. Saul realized the drama of Clarence's story and how it tied together the Holocaust and the Japanese American incarceration. Not even the National Archives contained records of what the 522nd had done, and few of the surviving veterans had ever wanted to talk about it. "In my lifetime I have never seen anything more terrible," one veteran said. "I tried to put away all those thoughts."[11]

So had Clarence, whose revelation to Saul began a friendship that lasted the remaining fourteen years of his life and gave him renewed purpose. He no longer bottled up his memories, including those of Heart Mountain, his work on the Northern Pacific Railroad, and his escape to the University of Cincinnati before joining the Army. He shared those memories liberally with Saul.

Some of Clarence's comrades from the 522nd were irked by his newfound activism. Most of them were Hawaiians who had spent the years after the war far removed from the mainland veterans. Katsugo Miho, who became a state legislator, had actually told the story of the Dachau rescue to a reporter from the *Honolulu Star-Bulletin* in 1968, but no one on the mainland had noticed. "Why did he keep quiet all these years," Miho asked in 1993. "At one point he [Matsumura] even wrote to us asking about Dachau, and the next thing we hear is reports of what he has experienced."[12] This is seemingly an example of how Japanese Americans fight among themselves to validate their accomplishments.

A More Perfect Union

Eric Saul's museum exhibit about Japanese American soldiers that drew Clarence Matsumura from the shadows in 1981 had an enduring effect inside the Japanese American community. It became a point of pride for the veterans, who were finally receiving just recognition for their valor, and it also fit in with the larger efforts at redress and reconciliation. Soon after it appeared, General William Peers, one of the leaders of the Presidio, asked Saul if he thought the exhibit could be mounted at the Smithsonian Institution in Washington, DC. Saul said he did not think the Smithsonian accepted outside exhibits. But Peers, who had fought in Burma during World War II with the secret Office of Special Services, did not give up so easily. After all, he had led the military's investigations into Vietnam war crimes, such as the 1968 My Lai massacre. Peers also had a friend and former comrade at the Smithsonian, S. Dillon Ripley, who had been attached to the Japanese American unit that fought with OSS Detachment 101 in

Burma. Peers wrote Ripley, who replied immediately, saying he wanted to add the exhibit for the Smithsonian's commemoration of the two hundredth anniversary of the Constitution. Ripley assigned the project to Roger Kennedy, the director of the Museum of American History.[13]

Kennedy and curators Tom Crouch and Jennifer Locke Jones used new oral history techniques and videotaped interviews with former incarcerees to examine the issues created by Executive Order 9066 and the incarceration. The Smithsonian team knew before the exhibit opened on October 1, 1987, that it would attract controversy. "Hate letters are already coming in to the Smithsonian because we are treating people of Asian extraction like other Americans, as if that were a strange thing to do," Kennedy told the *Washington Post* in March 1987, seven months before the exhibit was set to open. "We've gotten letters from folks saying, 'My dad was on the Bataan death march' and 'Don't you realize that Manzanar wasn't Dachau?'" Crouch said.[14]

One obstacle to the exhibition, Saul said, was retired Supreme Court Chief Justice Warren Burger, the chancellor of the Smithsonian. He objected to the exhibit's size and message and pushed to reduce its impact. To me, that was a continuation of Burger's animus toward Japanese Americans and their incarceration, which he had exhibited as a young lawyer with the Justice Department by rejecting redress claims from Estelle Ishigo and other former prisoners.

When it was finished, however, the exhibit, called *A More Perfect Union*, was a searing account of the incarceration, and it drew millions of visitors over the course of its run at the museum. Just as Saul's initial Presidio exhibit had inspired Clarence Matsumura to tell his story of the Dachau rescue, *A More Perfect Union* heightened the awareness of the redress campaign and encouraged its supporters.

"One of the things that we recognized is that many members of Congress came down to see the exhibition," Locke Jones said.[15] The exhibition remained on view for seventeen years and then was spun off into an online exhibit that remains on the Smithsonian website. Eric Saul, who first inspired Clarence Matsumura, helped educate a nation when it most needed the lesson.

Collecting and Preserving

Shortly after the camps opened, the art historian and collector Allen Eaton, a longtime friend of Dillon Myer from the Agriculture Department, asked

Myer whether he could organize an exhibit of art created by the prisoners for display around the country. "The Japanese, more than any people I knew, had a genius for making something out of nothing, so scarcity of materials need not be considered a deterrent," Eaton wrote.[16] Myer said the WRA did not have the resources, but he would support an exhibit if Eaton found another way to pay for it. Eaton approached his employer, the New York–based Russell Sage Foundation, which also pleaded poverty. Eaton shelved the idea but stayed in touch with individual prisoners and updated them on his interest. Eventually, packages started to arrive at Eaton's office, starting with a set of pebbles from the camp located in Jerome, Arkansas, that, Eaton wrote later, had been polished into "perfect spheres, so that figures, colors and veinings revealed unexpected beauties as the pieces were turned in the light." By 1945, Eaton had accumulated enough vacation time to allow him to visit Heart Mountain and four other camps. He saw the birds carved out of whatever wood the artists could scavenge in a camp with few trees. He saw the rudimentary furniture incarcerees had made from scrap and the beautiful watercolors painted by Estelle Ishigo, with whom he struck up a friendship. Eventually she became Eaton's art adviser at Heart Mountain and a regular correspondent, as he depended on her to identify pieces for his hoped-for nationwide exhibit.[17]

Before he joined the Russell Sage Foundation, Eaton had already had a full career as a politician in Oregon and as a writer, art curator, and folk-art expert. He believed the Japanese American prisoners had created a unique brand of folk art that needed to be seen around the nation and world. An exhibit of Issei and Nisei painters, some of them former detainees, drew eighty thousand visitors to a Boston art museum in June 1945. Eaton avidly cultivated Estelle's eye and relied on her often. "I am glad to tell you that on the whole the record is going very well, and yet I feel I ought to say that there is nothing more interesting in all the places I have been than the work of the artists and craftsmen which you have uncovered for me," Eaton wrote Estelle on October 1, 1945.[18]

One of the paintings Estelle sent to Eaton showed Heart Mountain prisoners scavenging for coal dumped in the snow as the wind and snow whipped around them. Heart Mountain, Eaton observed, was perhaps "the least prepared for winter of any of the ten camps." Along with Estelle's art, Eaton remarked favorably upon the notes she sent him from Heart Mountain, which were, "in point of form, the most unusual from any of the War Relocation Centers. The typing of these reports was excellent in both

Heart Mountain prisoners rush to gather coal to warm their barracks. Artist Estelle Ishigo captured such scenes of ordinary life in her artwork. (Okumoto Collection / Heart Mountain Wyoming Foundation)

composition and impression; but it was the illustrations, the sketches by Japanese members of the staff, and often a full-page watercolor by Mrs. Ishigo, which gave them special distinction."[19]

Estelle, in turn, hoped Eaton could help her and Arthur regain their footing. They had no jobs to which to return and nowhere to live. Arthur Ishigo had started looking for work almost immediately after President Roosevelt lifted the exclusion order, writing his former employer Paramount Pictures to see if the company would rehire him. He had no luck. Estelle's letters to Eaton betray a rising desperation, as she tried to serve his needs while also trying to answer her nagging questions about an uncertain future. Eaton responded by saying he had checked with associates in New York about possible jobs but had found none so far. Camp life had helped Estelle create the art that built her reputation, and she might be completely unknown if not for the experience. But camp ripped open her soul, weakened her sense of right and wrong, and cast her life into disarray. She and Arthur had lost their jobs and home, their savings and direction. With nowhere else to go, they stayed in camp as long as they could before the last train to Los Angeles took them away.[20]

Preserving a Legacy

Watching that last train was a young LaDonna Zall, who had grown up in dozens of towns across the west while her father worked laying pipe. In November 1945, her father had picked up a hitchhiking soldier, who told them, "I'm not supposed to say this or tell you this, but the last train leaves from camp tomorrow morning." Her father took LaDonna and her sister out of school and drove down the highway toward Heart Mountain. It was bitterly cold, and the winds blew the snow horizontally. As they watched, the remaining prisoners "bundled tightly in drab clothing, streamed down over the hill in a seemingly endless line," she would write later. "They came by threes and guards were spaced among them. The line looked like a giant, dark caterpillar." LaDonna wondered why the soldiers stood with their bayonets still fixed to their rifles. "I couldn't figure it out because the war had been over for two months," she said. On their cheeks, the two girls felt the cold air from the November wind mixed with warm tears. "I had a big lump in my throat," LaDonna wrote, "It was one of the most-sad moments I had experienced."[21] That experience of empathy led her to be one of the first members of the group that was trying to build a museum at the site of the Heart Mountain camp. As the foundation built our museum, LaDonna found and recorded many of the artifacts that were donated by the former prisoners.

Finding Estelle Ishigo

Bacon Sakatani's newfound advocacy on behalf of resisters made him the man to see about Heart Mountain. In 1984 came a new request: The Bureau of Reclamation office in Montana wanted to use one of Estelle Ishigo's drawings for a plaque at the site of the Heart Mountain camp. Could Bacon find her?

"So, I asked around Los Angeles and I found Estelle," Sakatani said. Her husband, Arthur, had died more than twenty-five years earlier. Estelle now lived alone in a basement apartment in Los Angeles, her spirits and her health shattered. Both of her legs had been amputated below the knee because of gangrene. "She was in a wheelchair, she was penniless," Sakatani said. Estelle had one hot meal a day and used a hot plate to cook cans of Campbell's soup, which she stacked around her small apartment. At the end of their first meeting, Sakatani said he gave her a $20 bill, which

Estelle took, held in her hand, and looked at as if "she'd never seen money before."

After meeting Estelle, whom he remembered as the striking blonde Caucasian artist from camp he had seen as a teenager, Sakatani called Bill Hosokawa at the *Denver Post*. Hosokawa sent Sakatani another $20 and asked that he give it to Estelle but not tell her where it was from. Estelle clearly needed help.[22]

The rediscovery of the aging and ailing Estelle Ishigo in her sad Los Angeles apartment helped revive interest in her life and art. "She had this book called *Lone Heart Mountain* that she published, I don't know, some years earlier and was out of print, so she kept pestering me about getting her book republished and, 'We got to tell this story to the whole world of what we went through,' and she was so, her feeling was so strong about the injustices of the camp and she was, she was just like a Japanese," Sakatani said. He gathered members from Heart Mountain class of 1947, and "we raised the money to republish her book, and then we put on a fundraiser for her." That was in the spring of 1986, and their activity drew the attention of the filmmaker Steven Okazaki, a Japanese American who had previously made documentaries about the survivors of the atomic bombs at Hiroshima and Nagasaki and the test cases that challenged the incarceration.

Estelle had multiple drawings of camp in her dingy apartment "next to this broken window where rain could come through," Sakatani said. "I told Estelle, 'Hey, let me hold these drawings,'" and she gave them to him. Okazaki knew Estelle's life would make a great story. She was heavily medicated but able to understand him. "I've been waiting for someone to tell my story to," Estelle said. "Then I can die."[23]

The hardships Estelle had experienced through most of her life—the abandonment by her family, the racism surrounding her marriage, the incarceration and years in a trailer park—had hardened her and made her often difficult to work with. "She went from one convalescent home to another," Sakatani said. "I guess she couldn't get along with the nurses and so forth." The last time he saw Estelle, she did not recognize him. He recalled, "And the next day, I think, she passed away." That was in March 1990, five months before *Days of Waiting* first aired on PBS, on August 15, 1990. The film used archival photos and footage from life in camp and Estelle's own artwork to tell the story of how Estelle, ignored by her parents, found comfort in the Japanese American community while most of white America shunned her for marrying a Japanese American man. Sakatani did not understand at the time why anyone would want to tell her story, but he soon realized that Okazaki had crafted a gem from her experiences.[24] Estelle never saw this moving portrayal of her life and work, which won an Academy Award for best documentary the following March.

In 1999, Sakatani took Estelle's ashes to Heart Mountain on one of his frequent trips back, fulfilling a request she had made years earlier. Dozens of former incarcerees and supporters hiked to top of the mountain, where Sakatani opened the urn containing Estelle's remains and watched them mix into the dirt and float in the air around them. It was a fitting coda to the life of a rare woman who had gone behind the barbed wire for love.

Estelle Ishigo's Legacy

Estelle Ishigo and her luminous, evocative artwork is fused with the history of Heart Mountain. No study of the years the camp existed can be complete without an understanding of Estelle and the art she created while incarcerated there. It all starts with the fact that, as a white woman, she had a choice of whether she wanted to be there. She went to Heart Mountain voluntarily because she loved her husband, Arthur; she found solidarity with the Japanese American community in Los Angeles and later at Heart Mountain.

Estelle's art flourished on the scrubby plains of northwestern Wyoming. Commissioned by the War Relocation Authority to chronicle the lives of the incarcerees through her sketches and paintings, she brought a keen and sympathetic eye to the conditions inside the barbed wire. These are not idealized paintings of happy children or industrious Asians who put the best face possible on their plight. No, her art bristled with the daily indignities of life at Heart Mountain, such as going to the toilet exposed to everyone else in the latrine building. Freezing residents endure the wind, snow, and subzero temperatures to collect coal to heat their tarpaper barracks without insulation. Families huddle around their wood stoves inside the barracks to eat and share stories. Boys with a kite climb part of the barbed wire to play. These watercolors are as vivid as they would have been if they were painted with the most expensive oil paints.

When Estelle and Arthur—and thousands of other Heart Mountain incarcerees—were sent home after the war, they really had nowhere to go. Their jobs and homes had been lost, and they prepared to leave the camp with no real idea of where they were going next. The Ishigos landed in a trailer park on the outskirts of Los Angeles, where Estelle continued to paint and struggle for work. Arthur died in 1957, and Estelle drifted into the shadows, forgotten by both the white community and the Japanese Americans whose lives she had so lovingly captured in her art until, prompted by the Bureau of Reclamation, Bacon Sakatani found her.

Not for Sale

It was in part because of the value of Estelle's work and the outsize importance it has among the Nisei and the incarceree community that I was particularly incensed to read a March 2015 article in the *New York Times* about a collection of about 450 Japanese American artifacts coming up for public auction.[25] I was reminded of the suffering of my parents and grandparents when they were unjustly forced from their homes on the West Coast and wrongly incarcerated in isolated areas during World War II. The artifacts had been procured by the arts and crafts expert and collector Allen Hendershott Eaton, and from the article, it appeared to me that the current owner's family and the Rago auction house of New Jersey did not fully appreciate the personal, emotional, and even spiritual meaning these objects had for many in the Japanese American community. When Japanese American families were torn from their homes and forced into camps in desolate parts of the country, many turned to arts and crafts to pass the time and to cope with their significant loss of livelihood and freedom. Estelle was part of that; she taught art to hundreds of people in the camp while also drawing and painting their stories. With the closing of the camps, incarcerees were given $25 and a train ticket to any location in the United States. Having arrived in camp with only what they could carry, many were focused on rebuilding their lives from scratch and were in no position to preserve their artwork. They entrusted their work to Eaton because they believed he did not intend to sell it and would instead do what they could not—preserve and exhibit their work for the education and interest of the public good.

Eaton did exactly that. His 1952 book, *Beauty behind Barbed Wire: The Arts of the Japanese in Our War Relocation Camps*, was a beautiful and heartfelt account of the relocation and the art created by the people imprisoned at the camps. It featured eighty-one sets of photos of Japanese American artists, all who were incarcerated, and their art. He wanted to tell "the story of the arts of the Japanese in our War Relocation Camps, a story without parallel in our country and one of the most remarkable chapters in the long history of the human arts."[26] Eaton had initially planned to exhibit the art nationally, but he had to put off his plans because of lack of funding. At the end of the war, he visited five camps to collect art from the prisoners who were heading home or to whatever remained of home. Many of the items in the collection were given, not sold, to Eaton for the book; he also used photographs from the camp that he had commissioned during the war. In his book, Eaton wrote that the Japanese Americans who had given their artwork to him did not want to sell it. He wanted to "preserve as much as possible of [Heart Mountain]" because of the impression it had made upon him. Eaton's book helped prod the conscience of the nation that had backed the internment. As the critic Lyman Bryson wrote in *The Saturday Review*, the book "may even suggest to us, now that we are beginning to substitute a condescending kindness for the hatred of wartime in our attitude toward all of Japanese culture, that we can learn lessons of great value for our own development."[27] Eaton was not a man who wanted people to profit from the sale of art made in captivity.

Reading the *New York Times* article about the art auction made me think about our moral and ethical obligation to advocate, resist, and fight for what we believe in. In this case, it means recognizing the significance of a public sale of camp artifacts crafted out of the talent, suffering, and hope of a population that was wrongly incarcerated during World War II. At first, however, the divisiveness that plagued the Japanese American community stood in our way. Activists like Nancy Ukai began a Facebook campaign called Not for Sale to publicize the unfairness of the auction, but they did not get support from institutions.[28] The actor George Takei of *Star Trek* fame, who was incarcerated as a child in Tule Lake and Rohwer, joined in and gave us vital public support, but the sale seemed destined to go on.[29]

The Heart Mountain Wyoming Foundation's dedicated leadership went to work to stop the sale by joining with other Japanese American organizations to agree on where these artifacts would most appropriately be preserved, housed, and exhibited. Through the auction house we reached out to the seller, whom we knew only as John Doe, to prevent the items' sale at auction, but that failed. I called my father to raise $50,000 to buy the art for Heart Mountain, which was far above the $26,900 estimated value that Rago had placed on the collection. My father asked me why I was making an offer that was far more than the estimated value. I said I wanted to make an offer that they could not refuse, and if they did refuse,

I would be able to show their bad faith as part of a larger strategy. My father and the other Nisei on our board agreed. The seller, whose ownership of the art always seemed suspicious to us, indeed refused to sell. So, we hired a New Jersey law firm to file an injunction on the basis of the legal theory that the Japanese Americans had entrusted their work to Eaton for public interest purposes and not for private gain. We and our supporters reached out to key Japanese American organizations to best serve the interest of the public. The poet Janice Mirikitani issued a powerful statement in which she said, "I was shocked and appalled, to say the least, in seeing my cousin, Jimmy Tsutomo Mirikitani's photo up for sale in the auction. Jimmy has endured more adversity than most human beings could imagine, not only with the injustice of our incarceration in American concentration camps, but also his struggle for validation as an American citizen."[30] The Not For Sale Facebook page quickly gained more than 7,700 followers. It worked. Eventually, the owner of the collection, John Ryan of Connecticut, surfaced and canceled the auction. "We have tried to be good stewards of this material and protect it over the years," Ryan told the *Times*. "We weren't trying to extort money from anyone."[31] We were not sure if that was true. After all, the *Times* had reported on the curious way the art came into Ryan's possession. Eaton's daughter, Martha, had inherited the pieces when her father died. She "sold some of them to Thomas Ryan, John Ryan's father, a Yonkers contractor who repaired Ms. Eaton's house after a fire," the *Times* reported. "When she died in 1990, Thomas Ryan served as the executor of her estate and received her property, including the rest of the camp artifacts." That was challenged in court by some of Martha Eaton's friends and relatives, but a judge ruled in Thomas Ryan's favor. Ryan then passed the art to his son when he died, in 2008. So, the legitimacy of Ryan's ownership always seemed like an open question to us, and, as I told the *Los Angeles Times*, "The only thing that stopped them was the threat of an injunction."[32] Ryan then sold the art to the Japanese American National Museum (JANM). We started working with the museum and the families of their items' creators to find the best ways to share these artifacts, such as Estelle Ishigo's art, with the sites and institutions where they would have the most positive meaning and impact.

Estelle's work was prominently featured in the New Jersey auction lots, and it is the crown jewel of the Heart Mountain art. It speaks to the sadness and desperation of life there, and of its ironies. We wanted her art to return to Heart Mountain, where it was created and whose spirit it so beautifully shows. We believe that her artwork, along with other artifacts in the collection, should be returned, wherever practical, to the appropriate confinement sites of origin—to the sacred and significant places where they were created. Just as there has been a movement to repatriate Native American cultural artifacts, there needs to be a conversation about the appropriate treatment of items created in the camps. Furthermore, the Japanese American Confinement Sites (JACS) grant program was passed by Congress to help confinement site groups build their capacity to protect the memory, tell the stories, and preserve the artifacts and history made at the World War II confinement sites. We were certain that returning Estelle Ishigo's artwork to Heart Mountain would not only strengthen our museum immensely but also ensure that her memory and the experiences of the almost fourteen thousand people who were unjustly imprisoned at Heart Mountain during the war would not be forgotten by future generations of Americans.

Estelle Ishigo's drawings and paintings from the Eaton Collection came home in May 2018, courtesy of the foundation's growing relationship with the Japanese American National Museum. The artwork lined the walls of the exhibit space in the Heart Mountain interpretive center, the result of our successful fight to save it from an auction that might have scattered it around the world. I know that if Estelle Ishigo were still alive, she would want her artwork to be displayed at Heart Mountain, the place where she wanted her ashes spread after her death.

Generational Trauma and the Model Minority

Lingering Trauma

Behind the glass in the cabinet doors of my kitchen pantry is a black-and-white photograph of my parents, my older brother Ken, my younger brother Robert, and me, taken sometime in 1962. My father is wearing a dark jacket with a narrow bow tie, while my mother looks like a Japanese American June Cleaver, in a sleeveless dress with a string of pearls. Ken wears a striped sport jacket; I wear a plaid jumper over a white blouse. Robert wears a baby sailor outfit with a little fish on it; I distinctly remember that outfit as red, white and blue. If you were to put white faces on the bodies in the photo, we would have looked like any other American family photographed at a studio anywhere in the country. It represents the ideal that I remember my mother sought during my childhood, a constant striving to have our family blend into the white American mainstream. However, she displayed subtle hints of her Japanese background, most frequently demonstrated by the food she prepared, the art she displayed, and her choices in design, such as the Japanese-influenced double doors on the last home that she designed and built in Ann Arbor. As a child in the Midwest during the 1960s, I knew few Japanese Americans outside my immediate family. My grandfather Saito and his second wife, Ryoko, lived in San Francisco; we saw them infrequently. My grandmother Higuchi had moved to Washington, DC, where she lived with my aunt Emily in a home my grandmother had bought in the northwest part of the city. My uncles from

The Higuchi family in 1962. From left to right are Ken, Shirley Ann, Bill, and Setsuko. Robert is sitting on his mother's lap. (Higuchi family collection)

my mother and father's families lived all over the country. In Ann Arbor, however, if there were Japanese Americans, we did not know them. And that, it seemed to me, was fine with my mother.

She did not get attached to new people or material goods, which may have been an effect of her incarceration. Most of her attention was focused on my father's professional connections, particularly his colleagues and graduate students, and a few neighbors. She lived as if she could pick up and move at a moment's notice and not worry about what she left behind. When she moved from her home of twenty years in Michigan to Utah, she was excited by the prospect of a new opportunity. She had little use for sentiment and threw out everything that she did not need. Unlike my father, who saved his Heart Mountain High School yearbooks and copies of the camp newspaper, she left no evidence of ever having been there, as if it was an insignificant event that had occurred in her life.

Setsuko Saito Higuchi burned with the desire to assimilate into white American society. It showed, my brother Robert recalled, not in anything Setsuko said but rather in how she acted. We never spoke about the incarceration, he said, because "we didn't dwell on unpleasant things."[1] She

simply brushed off any question she did not want to answer and changed the subject. If she thought someone was too closely associated with anything troublesome, such as unemployment or peculiar extended families or bumptious ethnic communities, she cautioned us against spending too much time with that person. This helped control our lives and shape our environment in a way that her parents had been unable to do for her in 1942.

She wanted to be ahead of the Joneses, not just keep up with them. In our neighborhood, we had the first color television, bought the first microwave, and were the first to eat frozen TV dinners. When I was eight years old, my father came home from work and casually asked, "Is anything new?" In a matter of fact tone, Setsuko said, "I bought a house." Even then, I realized most families were not like mine. This became the first of the houses she bought and flipped during her lifetime.

Setsuko had urged her younger sister Kathleen to leave San Francisco for Michigan, where our family had settled. She knew that Kathleen had already spent six years caring for their father, Yoshio, after their mother died, and Setsuko also knew she had to escape San Francisco and Japantown and make it into the white mainstream society. When Kathleen met David Yuille, a medical student, Setsuko "was very happy that Kathy had found someone who was established. That seemed important to her," my youngest brother, John, said. "That Kathy married a white person was favorable, in my mom's view. She married up, so to speak."[2] In Setsuko's mind, David checked all of the boxes that indicated a successful life: he was a white medical doctor, and the fact that he was a graduate of the University of Michigan was the cherry on top of the sundae for her.

Setsuko applied the same standard in picking which friends her children associated with. She did not approve of John associating with Asians who were not assimilated into the community, as they did not represent mainstream American society. She was overly focused on credentials from what she considered the top US institutions. We had a dentist who seemed to routinely claim we had cavities so that he could bill the insurance company for my father's generous University of Michigan benefits. My brother and I recalled that he used to say, "John, you've been a bad boy today," and announce he had three cavities that needed to be drilled and filled. I complained about him to my mother, who responded, "But he has a degree from the University of Michigan," as if that inoculated him from being a crook. Another doctor gave me a breast exam as a teenager, and I could tell from his breath that he had been drinking. When I told her after the

Although they were born twelve years apart, Setsuko (*right*) and Kathleen (*left*) were close throughout their lives. (Higuchi family collection)

appointment, her response again was, "But he has a degree from the University of Michigan," as if this meant he could not be an alcoholic. Her reaction was another example of this lacquer box that looked pretty on the outside but contained hidden problems.

Many Japanese Americans had this urge to assimilate stamped into their psyches before and during the war, and the incarceration only exacerbated it. When you are imprisoned for what you are instead of what you did, you do not want to be what you are. Setsuko did not speak at all about the incarceration or what motivated her, but something clearly drove her to put her stamp on everything in our lives. Experts in multigenerational trauma say victims display their trauma in three ways—perfectionism, caretaking, and workaholism, in efforts to obsess, care, and work their way through their problems. That fit my mother. Our home was generally perfect, beautiful, expansive with upscale furniture. She meticulously maintained our home's landscaping and cared about its curb appeal. Any messy part of the home remained behind closed doors. She shunned friends or neighbors who did not meet her standards, just as she did not visit or discuss relatives with inconvenient lives. Setsuko hovered over my father and her children, often driving my father to work even though he had a car of his own. That may have been a way for her to make sure that Dad came home from work, where he seemed to spend all of his waking hours teaching, advising graduate students, or working in the laboratory. We rarely saw him, and when we did, he was working.

When it was announced that I would give the convocation at my 1977 high school graduation and that I had been named Miss Huron High School for academic and civic achievement, my mother was happier than I had ever seen her. It was validation for her that her children could succeed in mainstream America, that our assimilation had succeeded. The society that had shunned her in 1942 and sent her to a camp had validated her daughter, which Setsuko took as a reflection on her.

The Model Minority and the Sansei Effect

Setsuko and, to a lesser extent, my father displayed the classic symptoms experienced by incarceration survivors. Amy Iwasaki Mass, who was at Heart Mountain as a child, said she had once believed that her time in camp had not really affected her. Only after going through therapy in her thirties did she scrape away the callouses that covered her emotions: "I cried and cried as I remembered and re-experienced painful feelings of fear, rejection, and shame that I had experienced as a child."[3] Mass at least had forced herself through therapy. Most Nisei did not, and their children, certainly those in my family, were never sure of the reasons behind the rules we had to follow. We did not know what the incarceration had done to my parents' generation and how it created the various rules, spoken and unspoken. For my older brother Ken, that confusion manifested itself in sporadic outbursts of anger—he once flipped over a six-person round table in the family room for reasons I cannot recall—and a manic desire to live up to the expectations he believed our parents had for him.

For Darrell Kunitomi, who grew up in Los Angeles as the fourth of five children of two camp prisoners, that meant keeping quiet and living up to the memory of his dead uncle, Ted Fujioka, the former Heart Mountain High School class president who had died fighting with the 442nd Regimental Combat Team in France in 1944. "He was seen as a hero who sacrificed for the cause," Darrell said, "Ultimately, the best son ever." "We still have that shame factor in our JA subculture," Darrell said. "Look how well behaved everybody is. Everyone is very accommodating. For those that are achievers in the JA family, they follow the rules, they do what's expected of them, and the rewards are great."[4] Those who follow the rules are rewarded with prestigious careers, financial stability, and higher status in the community.

Psychologists have developed entire practices studying the effects of the incarceration on Japanese Americans. Therapists such as Amy Iwasaki Mass; Satsuki Ina, who was incarcerated at Tule Lake and the FBI camp at Crystal City, Texas; Donna Nagata, of the University of Michigan; and Nobu Miyoshi have shown the disabling and durable impact of the incarceration on the Sansei, detailing how younger Japanese Americans are crippled by a trauma they did not experience personally. Much of that, Mass wrote, comes from how the Nisei handled their own trauma. "I came to realize that we lulled ourselves into believing the propaganda of the 1940s so we could maintain the comforting image of a benevolent Uncle Sam," she wrote. "The insult, the pain, the trauma, and the stress of being imprisoned were so overwhelming, we used the psychological defense mechanism of repression, denial, and rationalization to keep from facing the truth."[5]

Many Sansei feel lost, in part because they do not understand the events that shaped their parents and grandparents and that directed their behavior. They do not know why their parents were obsessed with propriety, worked all of the time, or carried an unspoken shame. Miyoshi said, however, that the Sansei could eventually determine their identity needs "through open dialogue between themselves and their Nisei parents. The process by which such a goal is achieved in family therapy sessions requires mutual striving, giving, and trusting."[6] My family never considered that; it never came up. My mother was warm and loving in some ways, especially when it came to worrying about whether we had enough to eat or whether we were wearing the right clothes. She nurtured us that way, not through hugs or by saying she loved us. In some ways, that created an emotional vacuum in which I operated and of which I am only now making sense. Kunitomi and Kerry Cababa, whose parents, Masa and Jack Kunitomi, were incarcerated at Heart Mountain, know the same experience. All of the members of their large extended family had been incarcerated, but they never talked about it. Darrell Kunitomi said he drove his silent father around their native Los

Angeles for twenty years. "We used to call him 'Old Stone Face,'" Darrell said.[7]

The Kunitomis practiced a familiar form of coping similar to ours. The evacuation and camp experiences had disturbed them so much that they, like tens of thousands of other Japanese Americans, rarely discussed them. They participated in Japanese American events in Los Angeles, such as the Nisei festivals in Little Tokyo, but they said little about the central shame of the Nikkei experience on the West Coast. For Kerry, there was one sign of trauma. Her mother refused to watch *Go for Broke!*, the 1951 movie about the 442nd Regimental Combat Team, because her younger brother Ted had been killed fighting with the unit. They spent most of their family time with their mother's family, the Fujiokas, who were more fun and happier than the Kunitomis, particularly Jack's younger sister Sue Kunitomi Embrey, who carried her anger more openly. It was only after Masa Kunitomi died from cancer in 1985 and her children started having kids of their own that Jack Kunitomi begin to tell his own stories. "We thought our father never talked," Kerry Cababa said, "but once my mother died, he started talking and he never stopped."[8]

In our family, however, no one exposed us to the unpleasant aspects of the incarceration. Our parents never mentioned it; neither did our aunts and uncles on either side of the family when we saw them, which was not often, other than my uncle Al and my aunt Kathleen, who remembered nothing about Heart Mountain despite being born there. Kathleen's daughter Vanessa realized her mother had been born in camp only when she asked why her mother's records said she had been born in Wyoming when all Vanessa knew was that her mother's family was from San Francisco. Kathleen had wanted to assimilate into mainstream society as much as my mother. The only real contact we had at home with the larger Japanese American community was through the biweekly copies of the *Pacific Citizen*, the newspaper of the JACL, which featured a legal column by Raymond Uno called "Uno Bar." I knew about neither the controversies surrounding the JACL and the incarceration nor the larger divisions within the community. I got only one side of the story reading the *Pacific Citizen*, and I have spent the last fifteen years learning the other side.

Sansei Effect Tragedy

On September 16, 1986, I had a scheduled Caesarean section delivery of my son, Bill. I was working as an attorney for a Washington law firm, billing ten hours a day, and feeling overworked. My first real vacation was my seven-day stay in the hospital after giving birth. I had worked so hard before childbirth that I never watched television, so spending time recuperating allowed me to watch as much television as I wanted while eating Jello and sandwiches with white bread. After I was discharged, I woke up in the middle of the night repeating over and over the names of my three brothers—Ken, Bob, John, Ken, Bob, John. While I did not know the particulars, my subconscious was telling me something was wrong.

On the Tuesday after I returned home, my mother called. Ken's fiancée in San Diego, Khanh, told her that Ken was acting very strange and claiming he was being chased. My mother asked me to try to reach him; she always wanted me to handle emotionally complex situations. It was as if I had the ability to reach an audience that she could not. I called Ken but got his answering machine. My mother called me again, screaming that Ken had died. That was September 28, 1986.

The brief report in the next day's *Los Angeles Times* left many unanswered questions beyond that Ken had died in a single-car accident in National City, California, not far from where he worked in San Diego for General Atomics, a defense contractor. Ken was an engineer, another in the family's long line of scientists. He had somehow driven his car into a Jersey barrier under an overpass of Interstate 5, the main north-south highway on the West Coast. According to the *Times*, Ken was driving "the wrong way on the northbound access road from 18th Street to Harbor Drive when he hit the wall, on the southern side of the westbound lanes of West 18th Street. He was dead at the scene. The cause of the accident is being investigated."[9]

At the time of Ken's death, I knew something had to be wrong and that he had been under a lot of pressure at work. His death was more than just a simple car accident; it was the result of the Sansei Effect. Members of our generation whose parents were incarcerated carried the burden of having to live up to not only their parents' expectations but also those of the entire community. Our parents' generation, who never spoke of their time behind barbed wire, had accomplished much in the forty years since the war. They were doctors, dentists, scientists, inventors, and entrepreneurs. Most, especially those who lived away from the West Coast, had assimilated deeply into American society. As the so-called model minority, they set a high standard to uphold. Ken felt he had never lived up to society's expectations.

Within days, I had left my infant son in the care of my mother in Salt Lake City and flew to San Diego with my dad to investigate my brother's life and mysterious death. I discovered a life that I knew nothing about. There was a suggestion that this was a twenty-nine-year-old man who might have used cocaine to cope with the pressures of work and personal life. One of Ken's colleagues told me that some of the stress Ken felt came from knowing our mother did not approve of Khanh, Ken's divorced Vietnamese fiancée. At work, Ken's boss, a domineering Iranian immigrant, was driving him and the rest of their team to meet arbitrary and unrealistic deadlines for a project building a nuclear reactor. My investigation supported that claim. General Atomics was in trouble. By the time I had finished, I had interviewed at least fifty people who had known or worked with my brother. I consulted Doctor Thomas Noguchi, the respected Japanese American Los Angeles County coroner, for advice. The legendary creator and producer of *60 Minutes*, Don Hewitt, took my call and discussed whether there was a story in Ken's death. In the end, the local coroner could not determine whether Ken had died from an accident, suicide, or homicide, so he asked me how I would rule. It was at that moment that I realized I had the ability to make very difficult decisions. My family learned that Ken had had a one-way airline ticket to San Francisco the day he died and that he had checked in for that flight earlier that day. One of Ken's neighbors told us that he had heard people fighting and furniture being thrown around in Ken's apartment. I did not think Ken had committed suicide, and while I had suspicions about foul play, I told the coroner I thought his death was an accident. As a result, my parents were able to collect on a $100,000 work life-insurance policy.

While I believe Ken's death was probably an accident, I also know his work-related stress exacted a serious toll. He carried such a self-directed burden to work hard, succeed, and endure—the *gaman* spirit—that he never asked for outside help. He was the first son in his family and the first grandson of my mother's parents. Many, if not most, people in his situation would have spoken to someone or seen a therapist, but not Ken. He most likely self-medicated through alcohol and drugs. Instead of reaching out to his family, he borrowed $10,000 from a friend that my mother had to pay off after Ken died. I learned recently from Carl Rivkin, Ken's friend and college roommate, that Ken had borrowed the money to pay for a home for him and Khanh.

For the twenty-nine years of his life, I believe Ken felt the societal pressures associated with being an eldest Japanese American son. I do not remember my parents overtly pressuring him. The Japanese American experience of incarceration set a very high bar for anyone to reach or justify, which is something that my Heart Mountain colleague Darrell Kunitomi and I discuss often. My mother, however, had expectations that caused tension whether she intended it or not. "Ken felt he had to work harder to feel he was important in society," my brother John said more than thirty years later.[10] My mother believed in assimilating, and his fiancée, Khanh, and her heavily accented English did not present that image.

Rivkin confirmed that Ken burned at a higher temperature than most people, whether that was the result of an unspoken trauma or self-imposed pressure driven by family and its experience. He received two degrees, in chemistry and chemical engineering, "in the time it took me to get one degree," Rivkin said. He had a demanding job and was getting his master's degree in electrical engineering in his spare time. When Ken learned to play blackjack, he went all in and eventually became so good that casinos kicked him out for counting cards. Ken had learned to sail and spent many of his weekends on the water. "Ken just wanted to be an ordinary guy who could go sailing and not feel guilty that he was having fun," Rivkin said. Finally, Ken felt pressured by Khanh, because he knew she had left her husband, a former Vietnamese fighter pilot, for him. "Getting married was her idea," Rivkin said, adding that Ken knew he could not fail her.[11]

My mother gave me signed blank checks to pay for what I needed to finish the investigation. I activated the Japanese American network in Congress, writing and talking to the staffs of Norman Mineta and Robert Matsui, who had been incarcerated at Heart Mountain and Tule Lake. In my correspondence with them, however, I did not reveal that I knew about the painful history we all shared. Matsui pushed our case to the Justice Department, asking its congressional liaison, John Bolton, who later became President Donald Trump's national security adviser, if there was evidence of any potential federal crimes involving General Atomics. Bolton said their office did not believe any evidence of a crime existed.[12]

Ken's death gutted my mother, who refused to talk to Khanh, despite the aggrieved letters she sent us trying to explain my brother's feelings, her love for Ken, and her great sadness and shock about his death. It was the first time I saw my father cry. I was on maternity leave with my parents in Salt Lake City with my infant son, and when I went downstairs to get something from the kitchen, I saw my father on the landing in the dark. I was holding my son and continued walking downstairs. I always regretted the moment and wished I had stopped and let him hold my son. I wish I had told him everything would be OK, even though I was not sure it would be. My brother Robert observed that my father later began to open up more about life in camp and what the experience had meant to him, but Robert did not know whether that was caused by Ken's death, a new exhibit at the Smithsonian Institution in Washington, or the rising calls for redress from inside the Japanese American community. "I think the death of my older brother affected him a great deal," he said.[13]

My research into Ken's death revealed an unhealthy workplace at General Atomics, where Ken's colleagues felt besieged by their boss. I believed the company's top management was ignorant of the true dimensions of the problem, so I asked to meet with them to share my findings. My father and I brought the results of our investigation to the meeting, which featured us and a sea of middle-aged white men in suits. They did not admit any wrongdoing, but they offered to create a memorial in his name. We declined. My father told them, "You need to be able to walk down the street and look people in the eye and know who you are." In other words, what my father was saying was that you need to know who you are and make sure you are doing the right thing. This was coming from a man who knew what it was like to be unfairly persecuted by his own country. They listened politely and seemed interested, but our correspondence with the company showed they feared we would sue them. I do not know what happened after we finished our investigation, although I still have those files today. Only recently, when looking through court files, I found letters that indicated General Atomics had relieved Ken's supervisor of his position the next year because of my research, which showed wrongdoing. That led the supervisor to sue the company for wrongful termination, a lawsuit that court files show was later dismissed.[14]

For Ken and myself, the episode demonstrated multiple signs of the Sansei Effect. Ken would never share his anxiety with anyone, certainly not his parents. Living up to the unspoken expectations of society meant bearing the burden alone. On my part, I learned that a crisis can send me into overdrive. I dug into the circumstances of his death and life at General Atomics with a vengeance, as if I did not want to leave any lead left unexplored. It also showed that I am not good at taking care of myself while caring for others. One night at my parents' home, I tried to wake up and move, but I felt paralyzed, so my mother called an ambulance to take me to the hospital. After the Caesarean delivery of my son, followed by the extensive research into Ken's death, I had stretched myself too thin. I knew there was nothing significantly wrong with me, and I thought my mother's reaction, as it often was, was overkill. It all seemed like a distraction to take my mother's mind off the death of her oldest son.

When I sat down to write about this part of my life, I knew I risked hurting my family members by bringing up events that had happened more than thirty years ago. I never wanted to hurt anyone and hope I have not, but my research into the incarceration and related traumas has shown me I am not alone. As a community, we need to address our traumas, not sweep them away.

Life after Incarceration

Daniel Inouye

When I was a child, Daniel Inouye was the one person outside our family who made me proud to be a Japanese American. By 1968, he had established himself as an up-and-coming leader in Washington. He had the favor of President Lyndon Johnson, who had known and supported Inouye from the time he came to Washington, just after Hawaii's statehood. Just months earlier, Inouye had published his memoir, *Journey to Washington*, which introduced him to a national audience. Inouye had also endorsed Vice President Hubert Humphrey's campaign for the presidency shortly after Johnson said he would not seek reelection. For all of those reasons, Johnson selected Inouye to give the keynote speech at the Democratic National Convention in Chicago.[15]

The forty-three-year-old war hero who voted for the landmark civil rights law in 1964 presented an image of diversity to the rest of the country as he stood on the riser inside the convention hall. "This is my country," Inouye said. "Many of us have fought hard for the right to say that. Many are now struggling today from Harlem to Da Nang that they may say this with conviction. This is our country." He was the first person of color to give a national convention's keynote speech, and he made the most of it.[16]

Inouye's introduction to the nation was overshadowed within hours by the violence that swept the streets of Chicago. Police clashed with student protesters amid clouds of tear gas as the students chanted, "The world is watching."[17] Three days after Inouye's speech, with the clouds of tear gas still hovering over the streets of Chicago, Johnson called Humphrey, then the Democratic nominee, to tell him to name Inouye as his running mate. Inouye, Johnson said, had "cold, clear courage," and he had never known Inouye to make a mistake. Inouye's amputated right arm, virtually blown off in combat, would give Democrats political capital to use in the fall campaign against the Republican nominee, Richard Nixon. "He answers Vietnam with that empty sleeve," Johnson said. "He answers your problems with Nixon with that empty sleeve." Inouye's military record would help Humphrey in the South, Johnson said, and "he would appeal to every other minority because he is one."

Humphrey was not sold. He said "yes" a few times while Johnson spoke, but Johnson sensed his reluctance.

"Inouye doesn't appeal to you?" Johnson asked.

"Well, I just don't believe so. He does, Mr. President, but I guess maybe it just takes me a little bit too far, too fast. Old conservative Humphrey."[18]

Humphrey picked Senator Edmund Muskie of Maine as his running mate, and they narrowly lost to Nixon that November.

Inouye remained in the Senate and gained influence. In 1969, he joined the effort to repeal Title II of the 1950 Internal Security Act, which authorized the use of detention camps for suspected subversives. President Truman had vetoed the bill when it was originally passed, and Congress had overridden his veto. Although Title II had remained unfunded since 1957, its mere existence posed the threat of another incarceration. Activists led by Edison Uno, Raymond Uno's cousin, began calling for its repeal in 1967, making it the first push by Japanese Americans for a larger social movement since the war. Representative Spark Matsunaga, a Hawaii Democrat and a veteran of the 442nd Regimental Combat Team, proposed a similar measure in the House. During Senate debate, Inouye said the government's arrest powers frightened Americans "who are by birth or choice not 'in tune' or 'in line' with the rest of the country." This first effort at repeal failed. Advocates tried again in 1971 with the help of Representative Chet Holifield, a California Democrat and a longtime critic of the incarceration. This time, when Matsunaga called Title II a remnant from a time many Americans would like to forget, House Speaker Carl Albert agreed. The bill to repeal passed overwhelmingly in the House and by voice vote in the Senate, and Nixon signed it into the law. Japanese Americans now had confidence they could chip away the laws that had imprisoned them during the war and were a bit closer to a government apology. It would take seventeen more years to get there, but Inouye was part of each step.[19]

Inouye and Nixon would cross paths again in 1973 during the tumultuous Watergate scandal that forced Nixon from office. Inouye became one of the seven members of a special Senate committee created to examine the campaign tactics used by the Nixon campaign, along with other questionable White House activities.[20] Televised hearings during the summer of 1973 transfixed the nation, and Inouye earned a reputation for his thoughtful and probing questions, but not everyone appreciated Inouye's persistence. John Wilson, the lawyer for former White House chief of staff H. R. Haldeman, derisively called Inouye the "little Jap." Senators from both parties rallied to his defense. "There is no man who is more loyal or dedicated to his country," said Senator Howard Baker of Tennessee, the committee's top Republican.[21]

Norman Mineta and Alan Simpson

In San Jose, Norman Mineta had moved from advisory commissions to elected office. In 1967, he was appointed to the San Jose City Council, making him its first nonwhite member. Four years later, he was elected mayor of San Jose. The news appeared in an Associated Press story in Wyoming, which prompted an old friend to reach out. "Alan [Simpson] was practicing law in Cody, and next thing I get is, 'Dear Norm, congratulations on being elected mayor of San Jose. I have been wondering what the heck you have been up to all these years,'" Norman said.[22] In 1974, after Nixon resigned, Norman was elected as part of the Democratic wave that swept into Congress. Four years later, the friendship between Norman and Alan Simpson would resume where it left off when Alan was elected to the Senate from Wyoming.

Raymond Uno

In Salt Lake City, Raymond Uno built his legal practice by representing civil rights cases and minorities in one of the whitest and most religiously monolithic states in the country. He had a small group of friends, many of them Japanese Americans who had experienced time in the camps, who encouraged him to enter politics. He demurred. Then, in 1968, a local Democratic Party activist asked him to run for the state senate seat representing a district in the heart of Salt Lake City that was held by an experienced and popular Republican. The Democrats had no challenger for him, and without one they risked losing votes for other races in that area. Raymond agreed to run if another candidate did not materialize, and he prepared his papers and waited at the election office. When it became clear no other Democrat planned to run, he turned in his papers ten minutes before the deadline. While he had the support of his friends from the local JACL chapter, there was not a big enough bloc of Japanese American voters to make a difference. So, he and his team had to expand their base, and they contacted every potential Democratic voter they could find, knocking on doors and canvassing neighborhoods. "We went door to door in fifty of the fifty-eight precincts," Raymond said. Even in a Republican-dominated district, they sensed their growing momentum. Raymond went to bed on election night with a narrow lead, but when he awoke the lead was gone. The precincts with the well-to-do Republican voters had come in late, and that was enough to tip the race to the incumbent. He lost by 150 votes out of 20,000 cast. He would never lose another election, winning every one he ran in as he sought various judicial seats in Utah.[23]

Clarence Matsumura and Solly Ganor

One day in April 1992, former Dachau prisoner Solly Ganor received a telephone call at his home in Herzliya, Israel.

"May I speak to Solly Ganor?" an American voice at the other end of the line asked. It was Eric Saul, the curator of the Presidio museum.

Ganor identified himself.

"I am here with a group of Japanese American veterans who were among the liberators of Dachau in 1945," Saul said. "I was told that you were among the survivors of the Death March from Dachau."

Ganor knew the call would stir up unpleasant memories that he had tried to bury. Saul asked whether he remembered the name of the town in which he had been rescued and whether his rescuers were Japanese Americans.

"Yes, I remember the Japanese Americans," Ganor answered. "I remember them well. As a matter of fact, they were the first American soldiers I saw. They were my liberators."

Saul was gleeful he had found someone who had been in Dachau and then liberated by the Nisei soldiers. He told Ganor that he had come to Israel with a group of soldiers who had rescued the Jews who had been kept in Dachau. Would he meet with them in Jerusalem?

Before the trip, Saul had placed an ad in several Israeli papers asking for leads on former Dachau prisoners who were still alive and living in Israel. Someone had passed Ganor's name to him.

Ganor, who had moved to Israel after World War II and changed his name, had spent the forty-seven years since the end of the war trying to forget his imprisonment and slave labor. Still, he told Saul he would meet his group the next day in Jerusalem. He drove there from Herzliya and entered the hotel, where he found the tall, genial Saul surrounded by smaller Japanese American men in their seventies. "I looked into their faces to see if the particular man who lifted me from the snow so many years ago was among them," Ganor wrote later. "I was sure that even after all this time I would know him. But I felt no jolt of recollection."

Ganor and the veterans went into a meeting room, where he began to read an account of the Death March and rescue that he had written earlier. As he was reading, he noticed a small, slim man in his seventies with graying hair and glasses who was standing next to Saul and watching Ganor. "I looked up again and met the eyes of the newcomer," he wrote. "They were filled with tears."

Solly Ganor, a man in his sixties who was among the handful of Lithuanian Jews to survive the Holocaust, burst into tears. He had not allowed himself to cry since the war, not even when he fought in Israel's bitter war for independence. A psychiatrist had once told him that the Holocaust had dried his tears, but the day's events, under the watchful eyes of the Nisei veterans, had tapped a new emotional well. The tears gushed forth. Saul stepped forward and held his hands.

"Don't be embarrassed by your tears," he told Ganor. "You are among friends here."

Saul then pulled Ganor aside and brought the mysterious man toward him.

"Solly, this is Clarence Matsumura. We think he is the man who saved you."

The two men, rivers of trauma and sadness flowing between them, reached out and hugged each other, sobbing. The forty-seven years since that day in Waakirchen, Germany, when Ganor was hours away of dying from starvation, melted away.

Their reunion complete, Ganor and the veterans of the 522nd Field Artillery Battalion listened to the stories about the end of the war and the Dachau rescue. Some of the men from Charlie Battery told about how they had taken chickens from a German farm to make soup for the liberated prisoners. The next day, they all gathered for a news conference to talk about their reunion. Ganor, who had dreaded the idea of speaking in public about his ordeal, enjoyed it. He also realized, as did Clarence and Saul, that their story was something that captivated the world and shed new light on both the incarceration and the Holocaust. That an American soldier whose family was behind barbed wire in an American concentration camp could free a young man and the few other survivors from a Nazi concentration camp proved to be an irresistible story. After their first meeting that April in Jerusalem, Ganor and the veterans met again in Israel, Germany, and the United States.

In 1995, Ganor would finish and publish his memoir, *Light One Candle*, which became one of the few books about the Holocaust to become required reading in German schools.[24]

The last fourteen years of Clarence Matsumura's life brought him more fulfillment than any of the years that had preceded them. From the moment he met Eric Saul at the Presidio museum in 1981, Clarence became a walking expert on the similarities between the German death camps and the Japanese American concentration camps. Few reports on the 522nd or on the connections between the Japanese American experience and the Nazi concentration camps did not mention Clarence in this period. He had moved from the troubled silent vet to one of the most voluble and visible. His meeting with Solly Ganor in April 1992 gave Clarence renewed purpose. He and Ganor, along with the other vets, made multiple appearances together around the world, and Clarence became one of the most sought-after veterans of the war and the incarceration.

By the spring of 1995, however, Clarence's slight body was wracked by cancer, and he died that May. He had remarried, but he and his wife, Joon, remained estranged from most of the Matsumura family. His niece, Sheila Newlin, was one of the closest members of the family to Clarence, and she learned of his death after his funeral.

Joon took Clarence's ashes to Wyoming, Sheila Newlin said, and spread his ashes there. If she had known, Newlin said, she would have taken the ashes "either to Granger, or buried them in Cody or Powell, or somewhere near Heart Mountain."[25]

Clarence Matsumura, who struggled to leave Heart Mountain and who bottled up the story of the rescue at Dachau for thirty-six years, finally was released from his torment. Even if he did not receive a hero's burial or a commemoration at the site of the former camp, his memory endures at Heart Mountain. His great-niece, Aura Newlin, is a member of the board of the Heart Mountain Wyoming Foundation. Not a moment goes by at the site in which Clarence's memory does not linger. One of the exhibits at the interpretive center features a restored apartment in which a University of Cincinnati pennant, a souvenir from the university where Clarence studied before he entered the Army, hangs on the wall.

Norman Mineta Goes Back to Washington

One month after President Clinton corrected the injustice done to the Nisei heroes, he achieved another first. Commerce Secretary Bill Daley had resigned in June 2000 to join Vice President Al Gore's presidential campaign. To succeed him, Clinton nominated Norman Yoshio Mineta, the son of Kunisaku and Kane Mineta, former Heart Mountain prisoner, and twenty-year member of the House of Representatives, to be the first Asian American cabinet member. Norman had left Congress in early 1995, after the Democrats lost control of the House in the 1994 elections, to join the defense contractor Lockheed Martin. His nomination inspired a series of profiles, including one by an author whose name was familiar to students of the incarceration—Ken Ringle of the *Washington Post*, the son of Office of Naval Intelligence Commander K. D. Ringle, whose analyses in 1941 and 1942 determined that the Japanese Americans posed little threat to national security.

Ringle's profile gave Norman a chance to examine the incarceration that had shaped his life and forged his passion for public service. It also provided, as did Clinton's awarding of the Medal of Honor to twenty-one Japanese American vets, some posthumously, another rare chance for the nation to examine its history with Japanese Americans. "Somewhere in some corner of Norm Mineta's quiet, outwardly tranquil soul, the searchlight of internment is obviously still sweeping, back and forth, back and forth," Ringle wrote. "Even a Cabinet post can't blanket it completely." Indeed, it could not. Norm had not forgotten how his family was hustled from San Jose to Santa Anita and then to Heart Mountain, how the nation he now represented "couldn't make a distinction between people piloting the Zeroes that bombed Pearl Harbor and those Americans who by accident of birth were Japanese Americans. . . . General DeWitt said, 'A Jap is a Jap.'"

Norman's confirmation hearing was remarkable for one conducted by a Senate controlled by the opposition party. Senator John McCain, the Arizona Republican and a former prisoner of war in North Vietnam, rushed the nomination through the Senate in only two days. His old friend Alan Simpson from Cody, Wyoming, just four years removed from three terms in the Senate, said that Mineta "really does love this country. He came through all that with the camps by just rising above any kind of resentment or bitterness. He's like Nelson Mandela that way. There's some sadness, certainly, and there's regret. . . . But you look at the way he's handled it and how hard he's worked since and you say, 'There's a person of depth.'"[26]

Norman Mineta's bright outlook and ability to work with people from both parties made him the only Democrat to serve in the cabinet of the new Republican president, George W. Bush. After the Supreme Court resolved an election standoff in Bush's favor, the new president-elect named Norman his secretary of transportation.[27]

On the beautiful, clear, and crisp late-summer day of September 11, 2001, Mineta sat in his office meeting with his counterpart from the European Union, Isabelle Durant, and Federal Aviation Administration chief Jane Garvey. An aide hurriedly entered his office and whispered in his ear that an American Airlines 767 had just crashed into the north tower of New York City's World Trade Center. Norman excused himself from the meeting. He came back a few minutes later, and shortly afterward the aide returned to tell him that another plane, a United Airlines 767, had crashed into the south tower of the World Trade Center. "I said to Mrs. Durant, 'I don't know what is going on in New York, but I know I have to attend to it, and, Jane, you've got to get back to your operation center at FAA,'" Norman said. "And by the time I came back into the office, we had a call from the White House, saying, 'Get over here right away!' So, I grabbed some manuals and some papers, went down to the car, and we sped over to the White House. As we are going up West Executive Drive people were coming out of the White House; people were coming out of the Executive Office Building. And I said to my driver and security guy, 'Is there something wrong with this picture? We're driving in and everybody else is running away.'"

They soon met in the emergency operations center under the White House with Vice President Dick Cheney. They realized that another flight had dropped off the radar and that it had crashed into the Pentagon. By then, Norman had determined the crashes were no accident but part of a plan. He quickly ordered all the flights over the country and on their way to be grounded. Norman did not want a pilot somewhere over the middle of the country deciding he wanted to fly to Los Angeles so he could sleep at home. "I wanted to get all of the planes down, so we can start putting all of the pieces together," he said.[28]

Within hours, every flight over the United States and those en route from overseas had landed. Travelers around the country were stranded for days as they searched for ways to get home from wherever their flights had ended up. Thousands of flyers were stuck in the remote Canadian town of Gander, Newfoundland, after their flights from Europe were diverted there.[29]

During a meeting at the White House two days later, Norman would learn how much his incarceration experience would influence future policy. Democratic representative David Bonior, whose Michigan district included thousands of Muslims, said they worried they could be rounded up in the postattack hysteria against Muslims. After all, the Reagan administration had contemplated something similar in 1986 and 1987 before Norman and others exposed and killed the plan. Bush wasted little time. "David, you're absolutely correct," the president said. "We're equally concerned about all that rhetoric." Bush nodded at Norman, adding, "We don't want to have happen today what happened to Norm in 1942."[30] That statement by the president of the United States knocked Norman's socks off.

15

Uncovering Setsuko's Secret

◇◇

Setsuko's Activism

The first time I saw my mother engaged in anything related to the incarceration was at the 2002 Heart Mountain reunion in Salt Lake City. She coordinated the hotels, meeting halls, and restaurants and decided who would attend and who would speak. Collaborating with Raymond Uno and Jeannette Misaka, she drew three hundred former prisoners to the city she had called home for twenty years. I flew west to attend the event not knowing what to expect and found Setsuko in her element, the queen bee in control as she had controlled our family's social life. Everything was just so, and everything was immaculate, a mirror image of her photo at the beginning of ninth grade in the Heart Mountain school. "That reunion," Raymond said, "I heard from a lot of people, we did a lot of things that other reunions didn't. Considering all the things that took place, that was one of the most successful reunions that Heart Mountain has ever put on."[1]

Setsuko's activism was also fueled by the presence of her older brother, Fumio "Al" Saito, who had moved to Salt Lake City in the early 1990s. He was one Nisei who was not afraid to talk about the incarceration, particularly after he had suffered some career and personal setbacks. "He was a realist, as opposed to an assimilationist," John Higuchi said. "He was bitter. He alluded to the fact there was a lot of anger and resentment toward Japanese Americans. He talked about it a lot."[2]

The Salt Lake City reunion gave me my first experience with the Heart Mountain prisoners and their cause. My mother asked me to speak for her on a panel of Nisei women who had been incarcerated. Perhaps she thought she would not be able to comfortably convey the pain that she experienced. In the same way that she wanted me to reach out to my brother Ken at the end of his life, perhaps she thought that I would be able to reach out to the audience and express her feelings, about which I knew nothing. Although she presented herself as poised and glamorous, just as she had in her ninth-grade class photograph at Heart Mountain, she preferred to work behind the scenes and not expose her emotions to the public.

Around the time of the Salt Lake City reunion, Setsuko had also engineered the purchase of my current home in Washington, DC. Armed with the proceeds from the sales of various homes she had flipped in California and Utah, as well as some of the money from my father's stock in TheraTech, she bought a new home in the wealthy neighborhood near the National Cathedral in Washington. She intended this to be where she and my father would retire. Until they moved to Washington, she made it clear that I would live in this new home with my two children, Bill and Adele. By the time they were ready to move, she thought, I would be remarried and living somewhere else.

I loved Washington's Tenleytown neighborhood where I lived, but I could not argue that the new home was not grander, more impressive, and in a more prestigious neighborhood. It was also across the street from where my children were going to school. It was, and still is, all of those things. It was not, however, my choice. Instead, it reflected the obsession with real estate my mother had fed since her time at Heart Mountain, when she had brochures and books about modern homes mailed to her family's barrack in camp. Later, she bought and sold homes with abandon, including two condominiums in Salt Lake City after she learned she was dying of cancer and would never live in them. My kids and I moved into the home knowing it was an extravagant place to live and that it was a conditional gesture. Sometime later, there would be a price to pay, although I did not know what it would be.

I believe my mother was influenced by her family's forced removal from their home in San Francisco, their imprisonment, and the experience she knew my father's family had had losing their home in San Jose. Home means so many things to people, and her reaction to that trauma in childhood was to acquire and exchange as many homes as possible, perhaps never becoming too attached to anything and always having a backup in case events forced her to react. She and my father owned multiple houses and condominiums in Salt Lake City. She also bought an estate in Los Altos, California, where my parents never lived but which was in the middle of Santa Clara County. I think in some odd way she wanted to show she could buy a home in the vicinity of where my father had lived in a shack with his family after the war.

Then one day in 2003, everything changed. Setsuko's hairdresser noticed her eyes were yellow and recommended she go straight to the emergency room. Her skin tone had also started to change. When she went to the hospital, the attending physician conducted a series of tests and told her she had six months left to live. My mother had pancreatic cancer, an almost certain death sentence. She called my brother John, crying, and told him that she was going to die. Setsuko knew her remaining time was limited, making it difficult for her to accomplish her dream for Heart Mountain, because her total focus in her remaining days was on her family and her dreams for us.

When my mother realized she had pancreatic cancer, my brothers in the science industry knew the odds against her surviving were great. Still, she fought hard, going first to Johns Hopkins in Baltimore to undergo what is known as the "Whipple procedure," named for its inventor, and then going back to Salt Lake City for follow-up treatment. I shuttled between Salt Lake and Washington to help my father care for her, all the while raising my two children, working full time, and serving as the DC Bar president.

I knew she realized she was going to die when we were shopping at a local clothing store in Washington—Saks Jandel—that was known for sales on high-priced, high-end designer clothing. My mother, who was known to buy me two or three items of the same clothing but in different colors when she thought she was getting a bargain, saw an intricate leather designer jacket, a silk cream-colored blouse, and black corduroy slacks. Since these items were not on sale, I knew Setsuko would not buy them. But without hesitation, she turned to the saleswoman and said she would buy all three pieces for me. I was stunned, and I immediately started to cry, because I knew at that moment that she knew she was going to die, too. At her home in Salt Lake City, she started stocking up on staples to spare my father from having to go to the store. She bought multiple boxes of laundry and dishwashing detergent. To this day, I still find unused boxes stored in the cabinets.

Setsuko became steadily weaker. Although she was in constant pain, no one wanted to keep living more than she did. She never accepted the fact she was dying. My father wanted her to hold on, knowing how much his life would change without her. Setsuko had organized every part of his life outside the laboratory, and she had made their home a showcase. He loved her more than anyone else, and life without her seemed impossible.

On April 21, 2005, when my father was at a dental appointment, my mother turned to me and asked for the white powder the hospice nurse had left for her. There was no white powder. She was in fact talking about the painkillers she had been prescribed. From the makeshift hospital bed set up next to her tall California king-size bed in her spacious master bedroom, she said, "There's somebody in the room standing next to us." Then she looked at me, smiled, and said, "But there's nobody here, right?" I believed there was someone in the room and said, "Mom, I don't know if there's somebody here or not." But I knew she was talking about my brother Ken, who had died in 1986. She then started to talk about the intricate design of the armoire in her room. Ken's ashes, it turned out, were in the armoire. I frantically looked for them after my mother passed, wanting those ashes to be with my mom's when hers were handed to me.

Even though she was in a hospital gurney, she asked me if I could help her go to the bathroom to take a bowel movement. I tried to lift her, and she felt so heavy. I realized how dangerous it was for me to try to lift her—I could have dropped her. That was a foreshadowing for me that I was not as physically strong as I thought I was. I was no superhero.

Alone with me, she told me that she wanted to die and that I had to deliver that message to my father. She could not bear to tell my father that she needed to leave him.

My father came home and was especially peppy. He was trying to put on a good face. He came into her room and asked us how things were going. My mother looked at me and said, "Shirley, tell him what I told you." Once again, my mother was asking me to communicate emotionally difficult information.

I looked at him and said, "Mom wants to die."

Without missing a beat, my father said, "But I don't want you to die, because you make me so happy."

Setsuko gave him sort of a blank stare and then quickly looked at me. I quickly added, "But Mom's not happy."

"OK," he sighed with a deep resignation. His tone conveyed sadness and loss. This man who had survived three years behind barbed wire as a child and built three start-up companies did not know how he would face the future alone in a giant house overlooking Salt Lake City. If I had not worked with psychologists for so many years, I doubt I could have handled it, but I had worked on so many issues with them and learned how best to communicate under difficult situations.

He and I went into the kitchen. He had been giving my mom the minimum exact dosage of painkillers, which was not enough to eliminate the pain and allow her to sleep. She had told us earlier that she was concerned she would become an addict if she took the full dosage. I told her then, "Do you think that's what you need to worry about now?" We put the painkillers in her mouth, and I held her up, and we gave her water so she could swallow them. Then she fell asleep. I called her sister Kathleen on the telephone and held it by Setsuko's head so she could hear her voice a final time.

"Sets, I'll see you in heaven," Kathleen said in her loud and clear voice over the phone. I knew that while my mother could not see or move, she could still hear her voice.

Then I tried to call my brother John, who lived in Salt Lake, but he did not answer.

Several hours later, at 8 p.m., he arrived. "John, she's been waiting for you," I said.

John went into the master bedroom, shut the doors, and tuned the television to her favorite show, *The Apprentice* with Donald Trump. I still joke to people to this day that the last voice she heard was Donald Trump's.

About twenty minutes later, John walked out and, without emotion, said, "I think Mom's dead."

I immediately felt a thump, and all of the power in the house went out. I looked out the window and saw a sea of lights downhill in Salt Lake. I called the power company, and they said there were no other outages and no explanation for why the power went out. I know Setsuko's spirit took that power with her when she left.

Discovering Setsuko's Legacy

Soon after Setsuko died, my family received a call from Pat Wolfe, the board member from the Heart Mountain Wyoming Foundation. She had contacted my father earlier and said they were naming a walking tour in Setsuko's memory. My brothers and I had just absorbed the news that our mother wanted to have her *koden* sent to the foundation, which we discovered she had supported financially for years. Pat asked if we would come to Wyoming for the dedication. I had many reservations about going, but since this total stranger wanted to honor my mother, I agreed to go. I knew nothing about the foundation, the people who ran it, their motives or plans for the future. Since my mother had told us nothing about this, I thought someone was trying to capitalize on her death.

Neither my father nor my brothers wanted to attend, so I agreed to go. I really did not want to go alone, which I told my son, Bill, who was named after my father. My son had always been close to my mother. Without hesitating, he said, "I'll go with you." We flew together from Washington to Salt Lake City to Cody, Wyoming, and then drove to the site.

The walking tour followed a circular path adjacent to the flagpole and honor roll atop the hill looking down on Alternate US 14, which ran between Cody and Powell. It had a stand with a marker honoring Setsuko and places that designated various landmarks, including the high school, hospital, and the swimming hole. Only a few buildings from the hospital complex remained, along with the hospital's boiler chimney.

Standing onstage with the stalwarts of Heart Mountain—Norman Mineta, Alan Simpson, and Bill Hosokawa—I spoke of how shocked Setsuko would be "to know we were standing here recognizing her." It was my first time at Heart Mountain, and I was overwhelmed. I started to cry. My son came up next to me and put his arm around my shoulder, giving me the strength to finish my remarks.

Dave Reetz and Art Reese, the Wyoming director of cultural resources, joined my son, Norman Mineta, Alan Simpson, Bill Hosokawa, and me as we cut the ribbon around the walking trail. Hosokawa told the crowd about the Heart Mountain camp, describing it as a "devastated place filled with heat, dust, confusion and more dust." He did not, however, say anything about my mother. Then, as often happens during the summer in Wyoming, a massive thunderstorm developed over the mountains to the west and rolled over Heart Mountain itself. The rain pounded down on the trail and the chairs set up near the honor roll.

After my mother was cremated, my family held a memorial service for her in Salt Lake City. My aunt Kathleen organized the program, and Raymond Uno gave the eulogy. As he had been throughout my parents' lives since 1942, he was there again, providing the solace we needed to move on after her passing.

It was Raymond who had brought my parents into the Heart Mountain Wyoming Foundation, and it was he who, along with Jeannette Misaka, had encouraged my mother to speak more about the incarceration and what it meant for her. During his eulogy, Raymond said he, my mother, and father shared a bond that grew out of spending three years together in the Heart Mountain school and the terrible injustice of being imprisoned as children, without due process, because of their race. He reflected on how he was able to connect with my parents again in 1982 when they moved to Salt Lake City. He knew that Setsuko's work to build something on the camp's site would succeed.

The stress of my mother's death in addition to all my other responsibilities left me exhausted. I may have helped my family cope with their grief, but I had not handled mine. Because I was Setsuko's only daughter, we had a special bond, a connection that meant she always wanted me to help her through difficult tasks, and when she died, I felt I had failed her. When she was dying, the imagery I had was of holding her hand at the edge of a cliff and letting her go. I saw various health care professionals in Washington, but the physicians were not able to detect what was wrong with me. One day, when I was at the University of Utah hospital waiting for my mother to complete her treatment, I made an appointment with a specialist in respiratory diseases. After the examination, the doctor said, "Your immune system is shot. You have a really bad sinus infection, and your body is not able to ward off infections."

After I returned to Washington, I went to bed one night and fell into a really deep sleep. I dreamed that I felt a lump in my breast, but I ignored it. I awoke crying. A few weeks later I was in the kitchen with my children.

"I think I have a lump in my breast," I said, and they touched it. They confirmed my suspicions.

I went to see physicians, who determined I had breast cancer. They scheduled surgery and removed the tumor. I needed another surgery to get anything that had been left behind, followed by chemotherapy and radiation. My doctors eventually gave me a clean bill of health. The cancer was gone, but I knew the stress of Setsuko's death had weakened my entire system and that I had to take better care of myself, so I changed my diet, stopped eating red meat and poultry, and switched to organic products. I started practicing yoga. I realized that in order to be here for my family and to fulfill my mother's dream, I had to be healthy.

Taking on Heart Mountain Leadership

The Japanese Americans who went to Heart Mountain in 1942 spent three years of their lives being controlled by a government dominated by the white community. The incarcerees who rocked the boat were segregated and banished to the even more isolated camp at Tule Lake, California. Sometimes the leadership of the Heart Mountain Wyoming Foundation seemed no different in structure. Dave Reetz and the local Wyoming residents who controlled the foundation had their own vision of what they wanted, and they tried to dictate that vision to the Japanese Americans on the board. They marginalized those who objected, often leading them to quit. My mother could be outspoken; she vocally supported building a museum. But she got along with all of the board's factions, donated tens of thousands of much-needed dollars, and was never considered a threat. "I never remember anyone saying anything bad" about Setsuko, Doug Nelson told me. "She wasn't seen as a pet," like some of the other Japanese Americans affiliated with the foundation.[3] Knowing my mother, I believe she liked Dave and Pat, and since she did not live on the West Coast, she was insulated from that drama. My mother felt very comfortable around the white community, and, if anything, she did not get sucked into the cliquishness of the life she was exposed to as a child. She was very good at keeping a distance. Perhaps those who asked me to succeed Setsuko on the board thought I would follow her lead. This is where my mother and I were different. She would not get drawn into gossip, but as a lawyer, I was going to scrutinize everything that passed before me, including the gossip. I am not as polite as my mother.

I found that fault lines that had developed in the foundation's leadership and goals over the past half of the 1990s had widened. While Reetz worked very hard to make the foundation into something worthy of attracting government grants and the support of local elected officials, he also maintained too much control over a piece of history that needed to be narrated by the Japanese Americans who had experienced it. Throughout much of its short history, the foundation had lacked the voices of activists such as Sue Kunitomi Embrey, who often felt ignored by Reetz.[4] I knew none of this when I joined the board, but it did not take long for me to realize we had some serious relationship issues.

Nevertheless, we started raising money to build the museum my mother always wanted. If I did anything important during this period, it was putting my faith in Doug Nelson, who is a master fundraiser and navigator of the complicated politics of nonprofit foundations. After fielding a variety of off-the-wall pitches from various architects—one design looked like a pagoda—we settled on a design suggested by Pat Wolfe that captured the essence of the incarceration: three main wings that looked like the tarpaper barracks in which everyone had lived. Doug Nelson started attracting major donors from the world of nonprofit foundations, and Irene Hirano Inouye, the senator's wife and the head of the US-Japan Council, relayed to me when I met with her about writing this book that Nelson had changed the face of philanthropy for Japanese American organizations like Heart Mountain. My father also donated more money. Combined with the federal grant we had received, that pushed us closer to completion. Members of the foundation, the former prisoners, and their families donated. I formed a close relationship with Margot Walk, whose foundation gave a generous donation to the campaign to build the center. I later learned that her father, Maurice Walk, had resigned from his position with the War Relocation Authority because he believed the incarceration was unconstitutional. Our program committee, led by Eric Muller, a historian and law professor, and Carolyn Takeshita, an educator and a former incarceree, used contributions to create world-class exhibits for our new museum. Margot was particularly touched by my parents' story and continues to be a major financial supporter of our foundation. LaDonna Zall, too, had already done a tremendous job in collecting mementos and artifacts of the incarceration.

I believed, as did Nelson and the majority of the board, that the interpretive center should accurately tell the story of the incarceration and its effect on the Japanese American community. Reetz and Wolfe, however, feared the center would cast the local Wyoming residents during the war as callous, unfeeling racists. They worried that Muller and later Nelson, combined with the sometimes-angry rhetoric from Bacon Sakatani, would create an interpretive center that projected a message of strident liberalism that would not be welcomed by the conservative northwestern Wyoming area and that would alienate the local community. At some local events with activists such as Sakatani, audience members, particularly students, felt as if they had been blamed for the acts of their grandparents' generation. Likewise, "there were Japanese Americans who didn't trust white people with their story or deciding what to do," Nelson said. "They resented the expropriation of their story by local folks who may or may not have been well intentioned. Dave and Pat wanted to control the organization and keep out anything controversial."[5]

My mother did not have those issues; she had spent her life buying into the assimilationist world portrayed by Bill Hosokawa, Mike Masaoka, and the JACL. She identified more with mainstream thinking than with many of her fellow incarcerees.

We needed a full-time executive director, not a volunteer board chairman who also filled in as a part-time executive director, because the job of running the foundation was becoming too complicated. Nelson and I believed Reetz should be the executive director and resign as board chairman. He resisted, because he thought Pat Wolfe should have the job. Finally, in early 2010, the board met to discuss our progress toward completing the interpretive center. Reetz's term as board chairman was ending, and Nelson proposed replacing him with me.

That suggestion blew up everything.

Reetz quit the board, and Wolfe left with him, one month before the 2010 pilgrimage. We had lost the local leadership we needed to finish the museum, which was already under construction. Nelson rushed from the East Coast to Wyoming to meet with local leaders, starting with Alan Simpson, to demonstrate that we remained on schedule and deserved their continued support. They agreed, but we had no time to waste. My aunt Kathleen used the master list of Heart Mountain members to assure them that our 2011 grand opening pilgrimage was on track and to make sure they would remain active with the foundation. The architect responsible for the design of the interpretive center agreed to replace Reetz as the project manager, which gave us the oversight we needed to complete the project. We had to show our membership and the local community that we still expected to meet our goal of opening the center in August 2011.

Dedicating the Space

On August 20, 2011, as I looked into the crowd of hundreds of visitors under a massive tent next to our new interpretive center, my mother's dream, I saw the different threads of people connected to the camp coming together in a complex weave. My father, Bill Higuchi, who had kept quiet about his experiences at camp while I was growing up, had pushed to build the museum we were now dedicating. Raymond Uno, such a stalwart in helping change the direction of the JACL and in leading the cause of civil rights in Utah and around the country, was there with members of his family. Sheila Newlin and Aura Newlin, the niece and grandniece of Clarence Matsumura, brought his spirit back to the land he had so desperately tried to escape. Takashi Hoshizaki, whose draft resistance had taken him from Heart Mountain to a federal courthouse in Cheyenne and then to federal prison, looked on. Beside me stood Norman Mineta, whose memories of the incarceration informed his handling of transportation

Shirley Ann Higuchi, center, leads the Pledge of Allegiance on August 20, 2011, the grand opening of the Heart Mountain Interpretive Center. From left to right are Dr. Melba Vasquez, Irene Hirano Inouye, Judge Lance Ito, Doug Nelson, Shirley Ann Higuchi, Steve Leger, Senator Daniel Inouye, Secretary Norman Mineta, and Senator Alan Simpson. (Don Tanguilig / Heart Mountain Wyoming Foundation)

issues during the 9/11 crisis. Alan Simpson, whom Norman had met as a Boy Scout at Heart Mountain, joined us. Judge Lance Ito, whose parents were both incarcerated at Heart Mountain, stood near me, too. On my other side was my personal hero, Senator Daniel Inouye, whom I introduced as the man who "inspired me, as a young Japanese American child, to go to law school." I told the story of how Inouye, wearing his Army uniform with his decorations and the empty right sleeve, had been denied a haircut. Welling up with emotion, I remembered how he introduced me as the president-elect of the DC Bar in 2002.

The senator stepped forward to the lectern as we leaned forward to hear him. At eighty-seven, he had slowed down, but his baritone voice still carried. Inouye said he remembered the day in 1943 when the 442nd Regimental Combat Team marched to the docks in Honolulu to steam to the mainland, where most of them had never been. "And this was a time some saw their parents for the last time, some parents saw their sons for the last time. Instead of a glorious march to the ship, we had to carry our duffel

Shirley Ann Higuchi, Norman Mineta, Takashi Hoshizaki, LaDonna Zall, Bacon Sakatani, Alan Simpson, and Daniel Inouye cut the symbolic stand of barbed wire to open the Heart Mountain Interpretive Center on August 20, 2011. (Don Tanguilig / Heart Mountain Wyoming Foundation)

bags, and keep in mind we were in the service for just a few weeks, not in condition, clothes didn't fit well, dragging ourselves about a mile walking, and along the way thousands of family members, parents, brothers and sisters. And I can still remember that plaintive voice 'Takeshi.' This woman was calling her son. Then I saw a woman rush out, an elderly woman, to try to embrace her son. MP came in and said, 'Get the hell out!'"

He told of the day members of his unit left Camp Shelby, Mississippi, to visit the concentration camp in Rohwer, Arkansas. "We knew something was wrong," Inouye said of the day that ended the squabbling between the unit's Hawaiians and mainlanders. If he had been in that camp, would he have volunteered to fight for the country that had imprisoned him and his family? "It was a question that I've asked myself many, many times, and I honestly cannot tell you what it would be," Inouye said. "As a result, in Heart Mountain, for example, there was a group of men called 'no-no people' that resisted the draft. And I don't blame them. It took a lot of guts to come out and do something that the majority did not agree with. It takes a lot of courage. But these men stood their ground, and they got their views across. Many were condemned, some spent time in prison—well, that's what it is."

Inouye's embrace, coming from a certified hero of the Second World War, bound the draft resisters, the veterans, and the other factions of the Heart Mountain community together. Inouye's approval meant the resisters no longer remained in the shadows. In that moment under the tent outside our new museum, liberal Democrats like Inouye and Mineta stood arm in arm with a Republican, Simpson, to acknowledge the wounds we had suffered as a nation and the healing we had all embarked on together. "Was it worth it?" asked Inouye, this small man but a giant icon of our community. "Yes, I think so."

Despite his optimism and the unity on the stage behind him, Inouye gave us a warning that still remains valid: "Well, but the work is just starting. This center will play an important role in reminding people that it did happen in this great nation. And if we don't watch ourselves it could happen again. So, it's very important as to what you're doing at this moment. Helping to keep this going. Helping to advertise it. Learning, so it won't happen again. I want to thank all of you for inviting me to share some of my thoughts. It wasn't easy to come here, but I wanted to be here."[6]

We needed him to be there. No other Japanese American had done more for his community than Daniel Inouye. Aside from my parents, no other Japanese American had influenced my life more. Even growing up so isolated from the rest of the Japanese American community, I knew he was the best example of what we could achieve in this country through dedication and hard work. Inouye had honored me by introducing me as president of the DC Bar nine years earlier, and he had blessed our interpretive center at Heart Mountain. His presence, along with those of Norman, Alan, and the author and journalist Tom Brokaw, gave us the national recognition we needed to show that we had a message that had to be heard. Brokaw told the audience there were four lessons from Heart Mountain: the fundamental values that founded this country should not be compromised; the strength of America comes from the dignity and determination of citizens who have been wronged; we are an immigrant nation; and "great challenges require common cause."[7]

Not only did the opening of the center provide a tremendous relief to the foundation board, which had fretted about its ability to have everything ready; it was also a catharsis for many of the visitors, some whom had never yet returned to Wyoming after they were freed. Amy Iwasaki Mass worried that it would rekindle painful memories that she had once bottled up.

The Heart Mountain Interpretive Center. The old smokestack for the camp's boiler room and the buildings for the camp hospital are on the hill in the background. (Don Tanguilig/ Heart Mountain Wyoming Foundation)

Instead, she was pleasantly surprised by the warm welcome from the local residents. "There were no hostile faces or tense encounters," she said. "The townspeople who participated in the event were friendly, welcoming, and seemed happy to have us."[8] Psychologist Satsuki Ina said, "Pilgrimage is a powerful process for healing from the trauma of the incarceration."[9] For the incarcerees' children and grandchildren, the pilgrimage gave them a chance to ask questions they had kept to themselves.

Pilgrims at the grand opening also climbed to the summit of Heart Mountain. Bacon Sakatani, who was eighty-two, made his eighth climb. To prepare, he had spent the previous month hiking around his California neighborhood wearing a backpack filled with ten pounds of rocks. Some of the pilgrims older than Sakatani had to be carried to the summit or on the way down.[10]

Right after the grand opening, I received a call at work from Sam Mihara, who said he was going to be in Washington and wanted to meet with me. He had been at the grand opening, and he wanted to figure out how he could help the foundation. I had never met Sam before, did not know he had been a neighbor of my mother's family in San Francisco or that he,

Setsuko, and her younger brother Hiroshi had spent time together on the University of California, Berkeley campus. Likewise, Sam did not know that I was related to Setsuko at all. He had seen me at the grand opening as Shirley Higuchi, with my father's surname.

Despite his reluctance to set foot back in Wyoming after his time in camp, Sam burned with a desire to spread the word about the incarceration and to help the foundation. It was not long before he was traveling the country giving talks and presenting slide shows to interested audiences. I soon asked him to be a member of our advisory board and later accelerated him to the board of directors. It was one of the best moves I have made as board chair, because no one works harder than Sam to tell people about the injustice that befell 120,000 Japanese Americans, including his grandfather, who died in the camp, and his father, who went blind there. Sam is another example of how the Heart Mountain experience helped me learn more about my mother than I knew when she was alive. He knew about her life after the war and when she was struggling to break free from her father's plan and to make her own life.

Honoring Bill

On February 19, 2012, seventy years to the day after President Franklin Roosevelt signed the order that sent my father and his family to a concentration camp, my father stood in the ballroom of the Grand America in Salt Lake City to receive the Japanese government's Order of the Rising Sun Gold Ray with Neck Ribbon. As a scientist and researcher at the universities of Michigan and Utah, my father worked with dozens of Japanese graduate students to develop the drug delivery industry in Japan. They went on to careers in Japanese academia and industry. He traveled to Japan often to teach and lecture at Japanese laboratories and universities. His support for the Heart Mountain Wyoming Foundation, which commemorated the sacrifices of his fellow incarcerees, was of great interest to the Japanese government. Throughout it all, my mother encouraged him, courted his business associates, hosted dinners for his students, and coordinated his social life. She had two dreams: building a museum at the site of Heart Mountain and seeing my father receive this award. She lived to see neither.

Gathered with us was the whole range of the surviving members of the Higuchi and Saito families. There was Al Saito, my mother's older brother, whose outspoken criticism of the incarceration had galvanized her spirit to build a museum at Heart Mountain. Her younger sister, Kathleen Saito Yuille, came from Milwaukee with her husband, David, and two children, Kevin and Vanessa, who was developing a career as a filmmaker documenting human rights challenges such as the incarceration. My father's younger sister, Emily, who was five when the family went to Heart Mountain, was there, as were two of his sisters-in-law: Amy Iwagaki Higuchi, who escaped the incarceration by marrying his now deceased brother James, and Thelma Higuchi, wife of his late brother Kiyoshi. Takeru Higuchi, who managed to evade incarceration entirely, died in 1987, but three of his children—Kenji, Chiye, and Junji—and their children represented him. It was a gathering that represented how the past seventy years had spread the Japanese American community around the country and how much that community had changed. The group of people that white Americans had said would never assimilate had done so to the extent that only 58 percent of Japanese Americans were of pure ancestry, according to the 2010 Census.[11] My father's three older brothers had married Japanese American women, but their children had not married Japanese American spouses. The Yonsei, or fourth generation, looked much like all of America—a mixture of races. My cousins Mary Ann, Jimmy, and Paul, three of the four children of James and Amy, had all married Caucasians. So had Takeru's children. My cousin Annette, adopted as a baby by Kiyoshi and Thelma, had married a white man. So had I; my son, Bill, was there, too. Together we represented the strength of the Japanese American community and what it had contributed to both the land of our ancestors and the United States. My cousin Kenji was a world leader in developing dental implants. His brother Junji was a noted pulmonologist. Both were in attendance. Their father, Takeru, had helped both my father and Kiyoshi establish their careers as scientists.

My father was one of three members of the Heart Mountain class of 1948 to receive the award, which is presented by the Japanese government in the name of the emperor. His Heart Mountain classmates Raymond Uno and Jeanette Misaka also received a version of the Order of the Rising Sun. Raymond received his Order of the Rising Sun, Gold Rays with Rosette, in 2014, while Jeanette received her Order of the Rising Sun, Gold and Silver Rays, in 2016. They received their awards for their work preserving Japanese American history in Utah and elsewhere and for their activism in the JACL. "The three of us were given the Japanese Foreign Minister's Commendation, and the three of us were given the Order of Rising Sun," Raymond said. "That's three of us in the same class, in Salt Lake City.

I don't think that's happened in any other camp."[12] Norman Mineta, who was in the class of 1949, received the Order of the Rising Sun, Grand Cordon, the highest level, in 2007.

The years following my mother's death brought my father and me closer together, as we tried to fulfill her dream at Heart Mountain. It gave us something more to discuss than just engaging in small talk, which he does not do. In the first few months after Setsuko died, I was talking to him about something mundane, and he cut me off, saying, "You told me about that last week." Now our conversations matter more. He dotes on his grandchildren and great-grandchildren, of course, but he also focuses on what we need to do with the foundation. "I consider that a very great thing to be able to work with Shirley and help with Heart Mountain, and it's a major spinoff of the things I've done over the years," my father has said. "It was a dream of Sets's."[13]

Saying Goodbye

Daniel Inouye, who had cheated death on that Italian hillside in April 1945, remained in the Senate for slightly more than a year after he spoke at Heart Mountain. One of his final public appearances was at the Capitol for the memorial service for his former colleague Republican senator Warren Rudman of New Hampshire, who had been the ranking member on the Republican side of the Senate committee that Inouye chaired as it investigated the Iran-Contra scandal in 1987. "We're both infantry people," Inouye said of Rudman. "Infantry people don't BS each other."[14] One month later, on December 17, 2012, he passed away. My daughter Adele and I joined hundreds of dignitaries in Washington who gathered at the National Cathedral for his memorial service, including President Barack Obama. Afterward, Inouye's body lay in state in the Capitol rotunda, where former senator Robert Dole, the Kansas Republican who first met Inouye when they were both recuperating in Battle Creek, Michigan, paid his respects. Dole, who was eighty-nine and mostly confined to a wheelchair, rose from the chair to stand as he approached the casket, because "I wouldn't want Danny to see me in a wheelchair."[15]

Full Circle

My relationship with Raymond Uno has come full circle: I remember my mother talking about him when I was growing up in Ann Arbor, Michigan, and feeling protective of my dad when she would talk about their "crush." The impact that he had on my mother's awakening as an activist and her dream that "something" could be built at Heart Mountain has left me forever indebted to him, not only for what he has done for my family but also for the entire Japanese American community and for our country. He was there when my parents were incarcerated as children in 1942, and he mentored my mom as a leader in the Heart Mountain community when she moved to Salt Lake in 1982. When she died from cancer, he was there in 2005 to speak at her memorial to remind us of what had happened in 1942. He was there at the center's grand opening and at many pilgrimages, and in 2015 he officiated at the wedding of my parents' only grandson and my only son, Bill. Raymond is still with me today, still supporting the cause. How lucky I am to know him. How blessed I am to have learned from him.

This is not a coincidence; many of the relationships formed through my involvement with Heart Mountain, including those with Norman Mineta and Alan Simpson, were meant to be. Without the chance encounters that followed from my mother's family's being diverted to Heart Mountain or that the accidental meeting of my parents at Berkeley many years later, I would not be here to tell this American story. I have learned more about my mother by working side by side with the people who knew her as a child, like Sam Mihara and Raymond. To be able to get closer to your mother when a dramatic event like the incarceration had previously kept her distant (because she never talked about it) is a gift; I have been able to get to know her in a different way since she left, a way that transcends her role as the protective mother who orchestrated our family dynamics. She was and is a beautiful, smart, and loyal daughter, mother, wife, sister, and friend to many. She could have been a brilliant lawyer or had her own career, but the family demands of supporting first her father's dreams and then the dreams of my father and me kept her too busy to see to her own dreams. The only sadness I feel from time to time is that she is not here to see what we accomplished at Heart Mountain. Yes, Setsuko, your dreams came true: we built "something there." You truly put others before you. You were someone that we could count on, and for my dad you were the force behind his career and success. The incarceration scarred you as it scarred many, but it also made you who you became. As my dad once said, he considered the incarceration part of his life's story. Maybe that is why you and many others showed no bitterness and gave so much.

Not every former camp has a group of alumni as well connected and as motivated to act as does Heart Mountain. The local residents of Cody and Powell have long supported the efforts to commemorate what happened in their backyards, and a good number of the former prisoners and their families live close enough to travel there. Not all of the other camps are as lucky. But only by acting together can the remaining Japanese American population and those who care about civil liberties mark this part of history and prevent it from happening again. A key part of doing that is the Japanese American Confinement Sites (JACS) Consortium, a collection of the various groups affiliated with each of the ten former concentration camps. Not only do we try to support the efforts of all former camps and FBI detention centers, but also we have joined together to maintain the federal JACS program that provides grants for development at all incarceration-related sites.

Taking Note:
The Legacy of Racism

The 2016 election that made Donald Trump president divided the country but never threatened the unity of the Heart Mountain Wyoming Foundation, even though the campsite and the interpretive center are deep in the heart of Trump Country. Seventy percent of voters in Park County, Wyoming, chose Trump over the Democratic nominee, Hillary Clinton, and the Japanese American leaders of the foundation have long understood the diplomacy involved in pursuing our interests while recognizing that the residents of the county in which we work may not share them. But since Trump's election, his administration has taken many steps that evoke painful and difficult memories of the hysteria that caused the incarceration of Japanese Americans and made the Heart Mountain Wyoming Foundation possible and necessary. These threats to civil liberties and human decency started almost immediately after Trump's election and have continued unabated.

During the campaign, Trump proposed banning the entry of Muslims into the United States until the government determined "what was going on" with the terrorism threat they allegedly posed. That talk turned after the election to the creation of a "registry" of Muslims in the country, a divisive proposal that had disturbing echoes of the incarceration and the use of census records to determine the locale of allegedly subversive Japanese

Americans. The Heart Mountain Wyoming Foundation had taken an early stand on the issue with a 2012 exhibit called "Esse Quam Videri: Muslim Self-Portraits," which showed how Muslims and Japanese Americans had common cause.[16] One Trump supporter, Carl Higbie, cited the incarceration as a precedent, which set off alarms in our community as well as among millions of other Americans. "We did it during World War II with Japanese, which, you know, call it what you will," Higbie said, adding that he was not calling for putting people back in camps. Ominously, however, he added this: "There is precedent for it." I wrote a column for *USA TODAY* that referred to the suffering the incarceration had caused my family and for 120,000 other Japanese Americans and said it should never happen again to members of any racial, ethnic, or religious group. I also encouraged the president-elect to visit Heart Mountain or the site of any of the other nine camps, which, other than in California and Colorado, were located in states that elected Trump. "Trump, whose campaign comments alarmed so many Americans, would be well served by a visit to Heart Mountain to see firsthand the consequences of unchecked fear," I wrote.[17]

Two months after the opening of the Estelle Ishigo exhibit, we held our largest pilgrimage yet in Cody and at the center. Norman Mineta and Alan Simpson led the way, along with Raymond Uno and Takashi Hoshizaki, who had inspected a tract of land for sale next to the interpretive center that held the remnants of the camp's old swimming hole.

The pilgrims and speakers reflected on the various current threats that echo those of the 1940s, including increasing racism from government officials, the travel ban on majority-Muslim countries, the debate about the national-origin question planned for the 2020 Census forms, and the anti-immigrant policies that have separated families at the border and called for a series of for-profit detention centers around the country—including one in Uinta County, Wyoming. Since 1942, Americans who have assessed the sins of the incarceration have called for us to remember what occurred and to make sure it does not happen again. Those warnings seem more real now than ever, as white nationalist racism is on the rise in an increasingly diverse nation. This bigotry can be a recipe for disaster that Japanese Americans, mindful of our history, cannot let go unchallenged.

Epilogue
Back to Where It Started

◇◇

When I touched down in Tokyo after fourteen hours flying across countless time zones in November 2019, I had gotten little rest. On my first night there, I slipped into a deep, deep slumber, and my mother appeared in my dreams, in the very city from which her father, Yoshio Saito, had left in 1918 for life in the United States. In that dream, several people milled in the hallway of a large rooming house that I saw in the sepia tones of an old black-and-white movie. One of the faceless women I was traveling with turned to me and said, "Is your mother coming?" Since I was now in a new part of the Heart Mountain experience in which my mother never participated, I was convinced she did not want to come, but I chose to walk down the long hallway toward her room to see for sure. I thought for a split second that I should approach the room gingerly, but since my nature was to always annoy her, I thought, "What the hell. I'll just walk into the room." It was almost as if my push and knock on the door were simultaneous. To my surprise, she was getting dressed and leaning over, pulling up her nylons. She turned to me and smiled and said: "I'm coming with you." Then I woke up.

My mother had not visited me in my dreams for many years. Shortly after she died, she often appeared in multiple, vivid dreams. In the first, I was sitting in my daughter's bedroom and the telephone rang. I quickly picked up, and I could hear her voice on the other end of the line, clearly calling out my name: "Shirley, Shirley, are you there?" Another dream took place in the public area of the garage underneath my home, in which I ran into her, knowing that we were extremely late for an event. She was carefree, light, and unaffected, while I was agitated and yelling at her that she was making us late and that she should get into the car. She lightly flitted around; she wore a flowing summer dress, smiled, and chided me for being so stressed out. In that dream, I believed, I saw my mother as she could have been if the incarceration had not made her unable to relax, and that was the person I wanted to be.

During this time of grieving after her death, I recall my excitement at hearing her voice again and, when I awoke, the feeling of dread—the reality that she was gone forever.

My work with Heart Mountain had brought me to Japan. The Japanese Ministry of Foreign Affairs had invited me and three other Japanese American scholars to participate in their Japan Up Close program about the incarceration, which featured meetings with government officials and presentations to school groups. My parents had tried to stay in touch with our relatives in Japan, but during my childhood I felt disconnected from them, just as many young Japanese have lost connections with the Japanese American community. For example, I discovered that they knew virtually nothing about the incarceration during World War II or even much about the war itself.

The trip helped bring me closer to my heritage and my ancestral home. World War II and the subsequent shame of many Japanese Americans, knowing that our parents and grandparents had been imprisoned because of their ancestral ties to Japan, had blocked me from a deeper experience. Part of the US government's plan had been to force Japanese Americans to assimilate into white mainstream society, and for me the plan worked. During my two previous trips to Japan—once as a high school student in the 1970s and again in 2012, as my father took our family there as his doctoral students and colleagues honored him for being awarded the Order of the Rising Sun—I was a bystander. Those trips were more about my parents. This time, however, the trip was about me; it enabled me to be openly present and to investigate my family's history.

Part of my exploration and my work to connect with Japan involved meeting with some of my father's former graduate students from the universities of Michigan and Utah. They looked up to my father as their professor, who mentored them not only in pharmaceutical sciences but, along with my mother, about life in the United States. I wanted to meet with them to make sure they understood the part of my parents' life that took place during the war. Growing up, I was annoyed by all of the comings and goings of these foreign doctoral students who visited often, but those relationships had led those Japanese students to nominate him for the Order of the Rising Sun, which was one of the dreams my mother had had for my father. I felt that they needed to know how my father's experiences had informed his ability to support them in their success in life. Both of my parents had supported them, and in some odd way they benefited from my parents' incarceration, because of my father's desire to make work a priority and my mother's need to make a home large enough to entertain in.

The trip's final stage brought me to Saga prefecture, which my paternal grandparents, Iyekichi and Chiye Higuchi, had left in 1915 for their journey to the United States, which led them eventually to San Jose. The Japanese government had located Sumiko Aikawa, my grandmother's beloved niece, and also provided me with a superb interpreter, personal driver, and assistant to help me connect with Sumiko at the assisted-living home in Takeo City where she lived.

When I first arrived, I had few expectations. I was tired after our flight from Tokyo to Saga and felt dehydrated, still recovering from the

Sumiko Aikawa, shown here embraced by Shirley Ann Higuchi, learned about the hardships of Heart Mountain from her aunt, Chiye Higuchi, when Chiye returned to Japan in the 1950s. (Ray Locker / Higuchi family collection)

fourteen-hour flight to Tokyo days earlier. Once we arrived at Sumiko's residence, I excused myself to go to the bathroom, which, to my surprise, featured a squat toilet. The bathroom smelled like a tired old hospital, and I wondered if I could squat and how quickly I could pay my respects and leave.

I stayed for more than two hours.

I had brought ten laminated photos of my family and Heart Mountain with me, and I showed them to Sumiko, who seemed quiet but alert. Her son, Fumitake, who runs a car rental agency in nearby Fukuoka, was there with her, but he spoke no English and remembered nothing about Chiye or the family in the United States. The photos, however, triggered deep memories in Sumiko, which also opened my eyes. First, as she looked at a photo of the assembly center at Santa Anita, I told her about how my aunt Emily had gotten lost on the family's first day there in May 1942. At just five years old, Emily, who had never seen so many Japanese Americans before, wandered away after going to the latrines. My grandmother Chiye, my father said, was delirious with worry, which was the first sign I had seen that she could fall apart like the rest of us.

Sumiko looked at the photo of the Heart Mountain museum when it first opened in 2011. Suddenly her memories flooded out, which brought forth her tears and mine. Chiye, Sumiko told me, had returned to Saga in 1957, when Sumiko was a young woman. Chiye visited her brother, Sadai-chi, and engaged in a night-long conversation with Sumiko about life in the United States, including the time inside Heart Mountain's barbed wire. Chiye and Iyekichi spent eight months in Japan during that visit, which they had originally planned to be their final return to the country. "Chiye visited me in Saga," Sumiko said, crying. "She told me a lot about her life in the United States and the hardships. All of the harvests from the farm and all her tools were taken away. In California, they worked so hard, and then the war came and everything was taken from them. When it was over, they had to start over, and it was so hard."

As she held me close, Sumiko told me that she could feel my grand-mother's presence through me. The war, Sumiko continued, had cost so many people so many things. She and Chiye had spoken all night about it and cried together, and now I was crying with her.

I had spent my entire life believing that grandmother Chiye was a rock, someone composed who had few needs. She never expressed much emo-tion other than the love I felt emanating from her during my childhood.

Like all of my relatives, I thought the incarceration experience for her, as well as for the rest of Japanese Americans, was just a blip on the screen. I never realized the extent of my grandmother's anguish during the war and the years afterward. I had never heard about how she panicked when Emily got lost at Santa Anita, how her husband collapsed the moment they entered Heart Mountain, and I knew nothing about Sumiko. I certainly never knew how Sumiko and Chiye had bonded when she returned to Japan. My grandmother had ventured to an unknown country as an eighteen-year-old bride and had hidden her experiences behind a veneer of dignity and love. I had to investigate my life and the Japanese American experience, which in turn had sparked the Japanese government's invitation, to meet the remaining relative who could draw me even closer to my family's past.

I should not have had to travel to Saga to learn something that someone in the United States could have told me. No one in my family had ever cried and held me like Sumiko; I wish that my mother or my other relatives could have held me in their arms and showed their emotions the way Sumiko did. As a mother and grandmother in my own right, sitting in the reception area of an assisted-living center in a remote part of Japan, I learned something that I should have known decades earlier. The Japanese American incarceration and the war itself had fractured our families and also our ability to connect with our heritage, which the Nisei, the quiet Americans, locked away with their memories of the incarceration. While we strove to be the best Americans, we were taught to be ashamed of being Japanese, too. It has taken me a lifetime to realize that I am not alone; there are other Sansei daughters like me.

It also reminded me of what a colleague once told me: "Shirley, if you were on the top floor of a home and had to leave, you would take the longest way out."

Well, at least I am finally home.

Afterword

Irene Hirano Inouye

◇◇

Through my work within the Japanese American community, I have had the privilege over the years of getting to know so many of our community's leaders. Through my work and through personal friendships I have learned much about the searing experiences of the incarceration of 120,000 people during World War II. Much of that experience is at the core of the museum I cofounded in Los Angeles—the Japanese American National Museum—and what I have devoted my life to sharing with the rest of the world. With my late husband, Senator Daniel K. Inouye, I participated in the grand opening of the interpretive center on the former site of the concentration camp at Heart Mountain, Wyoming. But as I read Shirley Ann Higuchi's *Setsuko's Secret*, I realized how much more there is to the story.

The Japanese American experience is one of hope, struggle, shame, resilience, and triumph, and it has left a lasting imprint on what it means to be Japanese American. Higuchi shows all of that here, weaving the personal stories of those connected to Heart Mountain into the wider experience of an entire community.

I have known Judge Ray Uno for years through our work in the community, but through Higuchi's book I learned so much more about how the incarceration changed his life, forcing him and his family from their home in California to Wyoming, where his father, a World War I veteran, died as a prisoner, and then, after the war, to Utah, where he remains today. His story of dislocation and loss was followed by triumph, as he became Utah's first minority judge.

Alan Simpson served in the US Senate for eighteen years with my husband and grew up fourteen miles down the road from the Heart Mountain camp. I knew of his childhood friendship as a Boy Scout with Norman Mineta and their later bond as members of Congress. I did not know, however, that Alan's father, Milward, had achieved a bond of his own with Ray Uno's father, Clarence, when the Cody, Wyoming, leaders of the American Legion visited the camp in September 1942 to welcome the Japanese American veterans there.

The Japanese American National Museum is now home to the masterful art created at Heart Mountain by Estelle Ishigo, a Caucasian woman who went to camp rather than be separated from her Japanese American husband. In *Setsuko's Secret*, I learned just how much the Heart Mountain Wyoming Foundation did to keep that art from being dispersed around the world through an illegitimate auction. It again shows the universal and powerful theme of what can happen if people work together.

There is much for all Americans to learn in *Setsuko's Secret* about the forced incarceration of Japanese Americans in ten prison camps and Department of Justice camps stretching from California to Arkansas during World War II. It was a policy based on a lie, something we have become all too familiar with over the past seventy-five years.

It was also a policy based on racism and fear, two impulses our nation has had to fight almost from the time of its creation.

And yet, despite those impulses, the US government has the capacity, rare as it may be, to examine its actions and apologize for them. This book expertly shows how community leaders led the push for the government to provide redress to Japanese Americans unjustly imprisoned during the war and how Norman Mineta, Spark Matsunaga, Bob Matsui, my late husband, and so many others in the community worked to make redress a reality.

It was the successful passage of the 1988 Civil Liberties Act that led Japanese Americans of my generation, the Sansei, to believe that the impulses that had led to the incarceration had been curbed, only to hear demands from some politicians to round up Arab Americans and Muslims after the 9/11 attacks. Americans were fortunate that Norman Mineta was part of our national leadership then, unlike in the 1940s, and the diversity at our highest levels of government shaped a more tolerant government response.

The success of the Japanese American community since World War II and its status as a so-called model minority has whitewashed much of what the people had to endure. This book sands away that whitewash to expose the financial hardships, political influences, and psychological effects of the incarceration that have had a lasting impact on our society.

With the increasing attacks on immigrants today and the building of tent cities in military bases to house those who cross the border seeking asylum, we're seeing a repeat of the xenophobia that befell my ancestors shortly after Pearl Harbor. This time, however, there are more people who know of the lessons of the incarceration and are determined to speak out and fight injustice.

The Japanese American community is also so much more diverse now, with more mixed-heritage members who may feel disconnected from the Japanese American community because their families were not incarcerated. When younger people learn about the incarceration through books like *Setsuko's Secret*, they can gain a better understanding of our shared community history and its relevance for all Americans.

Most of the 120,000 Japanese Americans who lived in the camps are no longer with us. Many of them were so impacted by their experiences that they did not share their stories with their children or grandchildren. Those memories were lost to history. Through *Setsuko's Secret*, however, Shirley Ann Higuchi is bringing back those memories and exploring the pain and shame that caused many of them to be hidden for years.

We need those memories now more than ever.

Acknowledgments

Setsuko's Secret attests to the value of genuine friendships and the importance of strong familial relationships. This book wouldn't exist without my close friends and family.

My personal friend Ray Locker is also a great friend to the Japanese American community and is committed to telling this American story. Ray is a talented journalist and published author and helped carry this book to the finish line. I couldn't have completed this task without him.

Doug Nelson, my mentor and vice chair of the Heart Mountain Wyoming Foundation (HMWF), believed in what I could do before I believed in myself. He trusted me to help oversee a foundation that has great meaning to him and his own legacy, and I am grateful for his guidance, patience, and wisdom.

I send much love and appreciation to all my Heart Mountain board members and advisers. Special recognition goes to the Nisei who spent their childhood at Heart Mountain and have shared their experiences with me for this book: Takashi Hoshizaki, Toshi Nagamori Ito, Sam Mihara, Jeanette Misaka, Bacon Sakatani, Prentiss Uchida, Raymond Uno, Shig Yabu, and my aunt, Kathleen Saito Yuille, who was born at Heart Mountain. Other legacies of the incarceration include Darrell Kunitomi, who was helpful in sharing his memories as a Sansei son, Kris Horiuchi, Julia Ishiyama, Lia Nitake, Dana Ono, and Hanako Wakatsuki. The other board members represent greater Wyoming: Aura Newlin, Pete Simpson, Claudia Wade, and LaDonna Zall.

I am also grateful for the dedicated support of HMWF executive director Dakota Russell and his talented staff, including the executive assistants who have helped me keep the HMWF wheels moving. This position has been filled by Hana Maruyama, Helen Yoshida, and now Julie Abo, each of whom had family behind barbed wire and contributed to this book. A special thanks to Julie, who is always around to watch my back.

My personal heroes, Norman Mineta and Alan Simpson, have always supported me every step of the way. I am honored to be among these giants who, no matter how difficult times are, always find a way to laugh. I also thank their beautiful and committed partners, Deni and Ann.

Most of all, I thank my family who helped knit together my memories and cheered me on throughout my life. My father, William, has done so much for the Higuchi/Saito family and has supported HMWF since its inception. In addition, over the years Dad has funded the executive assistant position at HMWF to support me as chair, freeing up my time to write this book and focus on my other professional demands. My mother, Setsuko, introduced me to HMWF, which has become a passion for me as it was for her. She met my father while they were both incarcerated at Heart Mountain as children. She made immense sacrifices for her children and without her this book would not have happened. She inspires me to work harder to tell this story. Other family support and contributions came from my brothers Kenneth, Robert, and John Higuchi; my sister-in-law, Rebecca Schmitt, for her research and insights; my cousin Vanessa Saito Yuille, for her commitment to tell our family history; Vanessa's father, Uncle David Yuille; Uncle Al Saito; Aunt Emily (Higuchi) Filling; Aunt Thelma (Uncle Kiyoshi) Higuchi; and Aunt Amy (Uncle James) Higuchi.

Other people I have met through HMWF have also contributed to my experiences and to this book. I was able to travel to Japan through the Up Close program of the Japanese Ministry of Foreign Affairs thanks to Minister Kenichiro and Mrs. Midori Mukai. That allowed me to connect with my grandmother's niece, Sumiko Aikawa, who gave me the inspiration to finish this book. Ambassador and Mrs. Shinsuke J. Sugiyama visited our Heart Mountain pilgrimage and have spread the word of our mission to the Japanese people. Their work in the United States is making a difference. Special thanks to Sheila Newlin, Eric Saul, Solly Ganor, Tom Brokaw, Irene Hirano Inouye, Senator Daniel K. Inouye, David Ono, and Jeff MacIntyre. And if you believe in angels, meet Erika Stevens, the editorial consultant brought in by Dennis Lloyd, director of the University of Wisconsin Press. I thank them and the entire press team for making this book a priority and transforming the manuscript from good to great.

Finally, I've saved the most important part of my life for last. One of the best things I've done over the years was become a mother—twice. I thank my son, William Collier, and his caring wife, Angeline, for all they have done for our family, including bringing two beautiful children into the world, Amelia and little William. And to my only daughter, Adele Setsuko, named in part for my mother, I hope that you, your brother, and those you care for will be surrounded by as much love and positive energy as you have given me.

Glossary

Issei 一世 — The first generation of Japanese immigrants to the United States; this generation was born in Japan.

Kibei 帰米 — Nisei, second-generation Japanese Americans, whose parents sent them to Japan as young children for education and upbringing and who returned to the United States as young adults.

koden 香典 — Often translated as "condolence money," a Japanese tradition of giving money to the family of the deceased. This money traditionally covered the costs of the funeral, but in Setsuko Saito Higuchi's case, she asked for it to be donated to the Heart Mountain Wyoming Foundation.

Nikkei ニッケイ — Japanese emigrants and their descendants who have created communities throughout the world.

Nisei 二世 — The second generation of Japanese in the United States, the offspring of the first generation. This generation was born in the United States.

omiai お見合 — Arranged marriage, as was the custom in Japan. There are still some arranged marriages in Japan today, but they are not as common as they once were.

Sansei 三世 — The third generation of people of Japanese ancestry in the United States. This generation is the offspring of the Nisei and was born in the United States.

shi kata ga nai 仕方がない — A Japanese expression meaning "it cannot be helped"; being resigned to one's destiny.

takuan たくあん — Pickled daikon radish that can have a very strong vinegar odor; a common Japanese condiment.

Yonsei 四世 — The fourth generation of Japanese Americans. They are the sons and daughters of the Sansei.

◆

100th Infantry Battalion—Also known as the "One Pukka Pukka," this was the first Japanese American unit to fight in World War II in the European theater. It eventually merged with the 442nd Regimental Combat Team.

442nd Regimental Combat Team—Formed in 1943, this unit fought in France and Italy and was the most decorated unit in US military history for its size and length of service.

522nd Field Artillery Battalion—An artillery unit of the 442nd Regimental Combat Team that was known as "one of the fastest units in Europe." It rescued some of the prisoners in forced-labor camps around the Dachau concentration camp in Germany.

Assembly Center—Any of fifteen temporary detention centers, some of which were horse racetracks where incarcerees were housed in dirty horse stalls; run by the Civil Affairs Division and the Wartime Civil Control Administration.

California Alien Land Law of 1913—Legislation that mandated Japanese immigrants could not own land, so many families, such as the Higuchis, put their land in their children's names.

Chinese Exclusion Act of 1882—This law restricted Chinese immigration to the United States, which opened the way for greater Japanese immigration.

Civil Liberties Act of 1988—Law signed by President Ronald Reagan after multiple attempts. It apologized for the incarceration and paid $20,000 to each surviving prisoner.

Commission on Wartime Relocation and Internment of Civilians—Nine-member commission created by Congress in 1980 and signed into law by President Jimmy Carter. It conducted twenty days of hearings that exposed the suffering of Japanese Americans during the incarceration.

Dies Committee—Common name for the House Un-American Activities Committee, headed by Representative Martin Dies, Jr. It investigated the WRA camps in 1943.

Emergency Detention Act—Passed as the Emergency Detention Act, Title II of the Internal Security Act of 1950, and based on the incarceration. It was repealed in 1971.

Executive Order 9066—Signed on February 19, 1942, by President Franklin Roosevelt; authorized the evacuation of Japanese Americans from the West Coast.

Ex parte Endo—Successful challenge to the incarceration of loyal citizens by Mitsuye Endo, a California state employee; led to the closing of the concentration camps. The Supreme Court ruled 9–0 in her favor in December 1944.

Final Report—Report by General John DeWitt of the Western Defense Command. Issued in 1942, it contained false information about the alleged justification for the incarceration. Assistant Secretary of War John McCloy ordered the first erroneous copies of the report destroyed, but researcher Aiko Herzig-Yoshinaga found a copy of the report during her research in the 1980s.

General Information Bulletin—Printed bulletin that publicized various announcements and information for the incarcerees. Preceded the *Heart Mountain Sentinel*.

Gentlemen's Agreement of 1907—Informal agreement between Japan and the United States that slowed the flow of Japanese immigrants in exchange for the desegregation of San Francisco schools. One provision allowed the immigration of picture brides.

haole—Hawaiian term for nonnatives, especially whites.

Heart Mountain Fair Play Committee (also known as Resisters)—Led by Kiyoshi Okamoto, Frank Emi, Paul Nakadate, and Sam Horino, the Fair Play Committee led the resistance to the military draft at Heart Mountain.

Heart Mountain Sentinel—Newspaper edited by Bill Hosokawa at the Heart Mountain camp. It was published by the local newspaper in Cody, Wyoming.

Hirabayashi v. United States—Lawsuit filed by Gordon Hirabayashi, a student at the University of Washington, that challenged the legitimacy of curfews targeting Japanese Americans. The Supreme Court ruled against him 9–0.

Immigration Act of 1924—Prohibited Japanese immigrants from gaining citizenship. This prohibition was lifted by the Immigration and Nationality Act of 1952.

internment/relocation/incarceration/concentration center or camp—Any of ten semipermanent "internment camps," now called incarceration centers, concentration camps, or confinement sites run by the War Relocation Authority.

Japanese American Citizens League (JACL)—Largest Japanese American organization, formed in 1929 by the merger of three organizations. Its leaders supported the removal as part of a shared "sacrifice" by Japanese Americans during the war. Many Japanese Americans resented what they considered the group's presumption to speak for the entire community.

Korematsu v. United States—One of the four major cases that challenged the Japanese American incarceration. The Supreme Court ruled 6–3 in December 1944 that the incarceration of Japanese Americans was justified. Dissenters, such as Justice Frank Murphy, said it institutionalized racism.

Lim Report—Report, prepared by university professor Deborah Lim, that determined the Japanese American Citizens League unfairly punished members of the draft resister movement.

loyalty questionnaire—Formally called the "Statement of United States Citizen of Japanese Ancestry" or "Selective Service Form 304A," a questionnaire devised by the military and the War Relocation Authority. It was designed to test the loyalty of Japanese Americans in concentration camps to determine who could join the military or relocate elsewhere in the country. The forms created great resentment and led to the segregation of "disloyal" prisoners at the camp in Tule Lake, California.

"A More Perfect Union: Japanese Americans and the US Constitution"—An exhibit that showcased the Japanese American experience in the United States with a special focus on the incarceration at the Smithsonian's National Museum of American History on display from 1987 to 2004.

National Coalition for Redress and Reparations—Organization formed to push for redress for Japanese Americans who were incarcerated. It succeeded when, in 1988, Congress passed and President Ronald Reagan signed the Civil Liberties Act.

National Council for Japanese American Redress—Group, formed out of the Seattle JACL, that sought a legislative solution for redress for Japanese American World War II incarcerees. It brought an ultimately unsuccessful class action lawsuit against the United States.

No No Boy—Term for Japanese Americans who answered no to both questions 27 and 28 on the 1943 loyalty questionnaire.

Nye-Lea Act of 1935—Law that allowed Asian immigrant veterans of World War I to become naturalized citizens, which benefited Clarence Uno and about five hundred others.

Reclamation Act of 1902—Act that created a system of water irrigation projects intended to make the West suitable for farming and development.

Sansei Effect—Shirley Ann Higuchi's term for the effects of the Japanese American incarceration on the second and third generations. Dr. Satsuki Ina, a psychotherapist and professor emeritus at California State University, has an extensive body of research on this topic.

Tolan Committee—Formally called the House Select Committee Investigating National Defense Migration, the Tolan Committee, led by California representative John Tolan, featured false claims about Japanese American sabotage.

War Relocation Authority (WRA)—Federal agency created in 1942 to care for the 120,000 Japanese Americans removed from the West Coast. Its mission was also to relocate Japanese Americans to other parts of the country where they could live freely.

Wartime Civil Control Administration (WCCA)—The government agency, led by Colonel Karl Bendetsen, that carried out the forced removal and incarceration of 120,000 Japanese Americans.

Western Defense Command (WDC)—Led by General John L. DeWitt and charged with defending the Western region of the United States, the body that coordinated the forced removal of 120,000 Japanese Americans from the West Coast.

Yasui v. United States—Case brought by Minoru Yasui that tested the constitutionality of curfews. Yasui lost in a 9–0 ruling in the US Supreme Court in 1943.

Cast of Characters

Higuchi

Amy Iwagaki Higuchi—The daughter of a neighboring family in San Jose, she married James in an arranged marriage after she rode alone from California to Arkansas.

Chiye Higuchi—Iyekichi's wife, William's mother, and Shirley's grandmother. She was vital to the success of the family farms.

Emily Higuchi Filling—The youngest child and only daughter of Iyekichi and Chiye Higuchi. She went to Heart Mountain when she was five years old.

Iyekichi Harada Higuchi—The father of William Higuchi and the grandfather of Shirley Ann Higuchi. He emigrated to the United States after having emigrated to Peru and then returned to Japan. He owned a 14.25-acre farm in San Jose, California, before he was incarcerated at Heart Mountain.

James Higuchi—The oldest son of Iyekichi and Chiye, he was a doctor in the US Army when he had to sign over his family's farm in 1942. He became a family practitioner in San Jose.

John Higuchi—The third and youngest son of Setsuko Saito Higuchi and William Higuchi.

Kenneth Higuchi—The oldest son of Setsuko Saito Higuchi and William Higuchi, he died in a 1986 car accident in San Diego. He is representative of the Sansei Effect, which influences the behavior of descendants of the incarceration experience.

Kiyoshi Higuchi—Iyekichi and Chiye's second son, he suffered from pleurisy as a teenager. After camp, he became a scientist in the military's secret chemical and biological weapons program.

Robert Higuchi—The second son of Setsuko Saito Higuchi and William Higuchi.

Shirley Ann Higuchi—The daughter of Setsuko Saito Higuchi and William Higuchi is an attorney in Washington and chair of the Heart Mountain Wyoming Foundation. She is the author of this book and has two children, Bill, named after her father, and her daughter, Adele Setsuko Collier.

Takeru Higuchi—The third son of Iyekichi and Chiye, he missed the incarceration entirely, because he was studying pharmaceutical sciences at the University of Wisconsin in Madison. He later became a leader in the field and has a building named after him on the campus of the University of Kansas.

William Higuchi—The fourth son of Iyekichi and Chiye Higuchi, he was incarcerated as a child at Heart Mountain, where he met Setsuko Saito in seventh grade. After camp, he became a distinguished professor of pharmaceutical sciences at the University of Michigan and rose to chairman of the pharmaceutics department at the University of Utah. He is an entrepreneur who helped start three pharmaceutical companies.

Saito

Fumi Saito—Yoshio's wife, Setsuko's mother, and Shirley Ann's grandmother. She married Yoshio after he rejected a match with her older sister.

Fumio "Al" Saito—Setsuko's older brother, he was one of the few members of the family who spoke openly about the injustice of the incarceration.

Hiroshi "Taisho" Saito—Yoshio and Fumi's youngest son. He was an attorney for the federal government when he died in a car accident near Washington, DC, in 1968.

Kathleen Saito Yuille—The youngest child of Yoshio and Fumi, she was born in August 1943 at Heart Mountain. She is an active member of the board of the Heart Mountain Wyoming Foundation and chaired the 2011 grand opening of the museum.

Setsuko Saito Higuchi—The daughter of Yoshio and Fumi, she was forever influenced by the three years she spent at Heart Mountain. She bought, renovated, and sold multiple homes throughout her life and vowed to have something built at the site of Heart Mountain.

Yoshio Saito—He was the father of Setsuko Saito Higuchi and grandfather of Shirley Ann Higuchi. He emigrated from Japan and lived with his older brother in San Francisco's Japantown. In the United States, he managed stores that sold goods to the area's Japanese community.

Yoshiro Saito—The oldest son of Yoshio and Fumi, he died of a mysterious infection in 1940.

Hoshizaki

Keijiro Hoshizaki—He graduated from college in Japan and worked in Manchuria before he left for the United States, where he operated a market in Los Angeles.

Shortly after Pearl Harbor, he told his family that Japan would not win the war despite its early victories.

Takashi Hoshizaki—The son of Keijiro, he went to federal prison in 1944 for resisting the draft and then served in the Army during the Korean War. A botanist, he worked for the space program and went on research missions in Antarctica. He is a member of the Heart Mountain Wyoming Foundation board.

Inouye

Daniel Inouye—The first Japanese American elected to the House and the Senate, he led the way in Congress for most civil rights legislation that helped Asian Americans. He received the Congressional Medal of Honor in 2000 for his bravery during World War II. He was the president pro tempore of the Senate when he died in 2012.

Irene Hirano Inouye—The widow of Senator Daniel Inouye, she was a leader in the creation of the Japanese American National Museum and was head of the US-Japan Council. She died in April 2020.

Mineta

Etsu Mineta—A daughter of Kunisaku and Kane, she married Mike Masaoka, the executive director of the Japanese American Citizens League.

Kane Mineta—Norman Mineta's mother, she came to the United States as a picture bride.

Kunisaku Mineta—He immigrated to the United States as a teenager and eventually ran his own insurance business. He encouraged his son, Norman, to become active in politics and government.

Norman Mineta—He went to Heart Mountain as a child and after his release was elected the first Japanese American mayor of a major US city, San Jose, California. He later served in the House of Representatives, as commerce secretary for President Bill Clinton, a Democrat, and as transportation secretary for George W. Bush, a Republican. He is an adviser to the Heart Mountain Wyoming Foundation.

Matsumura

Clarence Matsumura—A graduate of UCLA, he was rounded up and incarcerated at Heart Mountain. He left to work on the railroad and then attended the University of Cincinnati before entering the 522nd Field Artillery. He helped rescue prisoners from the Dachau death camp.

Rokuzaem "Roy" Matsumura—He immigrated to the United States to work on the railroad in Wyoming and moved his family to Los Angeles for better schools. That move led to the family's incarceration.

Sheila Newlin—A niece of Clarence Matsumura, she is currently an active member of Heart Mountain. Her daughter, Aura Newlin, is currently the secretary of the board of directors for the Heart Mountain Wyoming Foundation.

Uno

Amy Uno Ishii—A daughter of George Uno, she became a leading activist for redress. She remembered watching her Uncle Clarence's funeral at Heart Mountain.

Buddy Uno—The oldest son of George Uno, he spent the war years in Japan and helped run a Japanese prison camp that held US prisoners. Some of his younger brothers vowed to kill him during the war.

Clarence Uno—He followed his older brother to the United States, served with the Army's Rainbow Division in World War I, received his citizenship in 1935, and worked to help his fellow Japanese immigrants. He died at Heart Mountain in his sleep at the age of forty-eight on January 21, 1943.

Edison Uno—Another son of George Uno, he led the fight to get redress for Japanese Americans for their losses suffered during the incarceration.

Ernest Uno—Another son of George Uno, he helped the Heart Mountain draft resisters gain acceptance from the JACL and veterans' groups.

George Kumemaro Uno—Clarence's older brother, he spent the war in a series of FBI detention centers and fought being sent back to Japan.

Osako Uno—She came to Ogden, Utah, to visit a sister and met Clarence Uno, whom she married. She was the mother of Raymond Uno.

Raymond Uno—Incarcerated as a seventh grader, he was in the same class at the Heart Mountain school as Setsuko Saito and William Higuchi. He became the first minority judge in Utah.

Incarcerees

Sue Kunitomi Embrey—The younger sister of Heart Mountain prisoner Jack Kunitomi, she was the leader of the Manzanar Committee, which led the effort to have the camp at Manzanar, California, recognized as a historic site.

Frank Emi—A leader of the antidraft Fair Play Committee, he owned a grocery store in Los Angeles before camp. After the war, he worked for the US Postal Service.

Ted Fujioka—The president of the first graduating class at Heart Mountain High School, he was one of the first men in camp to enlist in the Army. He was killed fighting in France in October 1944.

Bill Hosokawa—The first editor of the *Heart Mountain Sentinel*, he arrived in camp after working closely with the Japanese American Citizens League. He later became a high-ranking editor at the *Denver Post* and a chronicler of the Japanese American experience.

Satsuki Ina—A psychologist who was incarcerated in Tule Lake as a child, she is a leading expert on the incarceration's effect on the Japanese American community.

Arthur Ishigo—The Japanese American husband of the artist Estelle Ishigo. He was fired from his movie job immediately after Pearl Harbor.

Estelle Ishigo—An artist and a Caucasian, she went to Heart Mountain to avoid being separated from her husband. Her paintings and drawings were the subject of a fight in 2015 between the Heart Mountain Wyoming Foundation and an auction house that planned to sell the artworks.

James Ito—A graduate of the University of California, he was a leading agricultural expert at Heart Mountain. He left camp to serve in the Army and married Toshi Nagamori in 1945. He is the father of Judge Lance Ito.

Toshi Nagamori Ito—She was an incarceree at Heart Mountain who left to attend college. She married James Ito, one of the camp's leading farmers, and is the mother of Judge Lance Ito. She served on the Heart Mountain Wyoming Foundation advisory board for many years.

Fred Korematsu—His challenge of the incarceration led to the 1944 Supreme Court decision *Korematsu v. United States*, which is widely acknowledged as one of the worst Supreme Court rulings in history.

Jack Kunitomi—A Heart Mountain prisoner, he was the sports editor of the *Sentinel* and later served in the Army. He is the father of Dale and Darrell Kunitomi and Kerry Cababa, activists for the Heart Mountain Wyoming Foundation.

Sam Mihara—A neighbor of the Saito family during childhood, he is now a board member of the Heart Mountain Wyoming Foundation and travels around the country telling his story to raise money for the foundation. His grandfather died of cancer at Heart Mountain, and his father went blind there.

Jeannette Mitarai Misaka—A classmate of Setsuko Saito and William Higuchi at the Heart Mountain school, she encouraged Setsuko's later activism.

Kiyoshi Okamoto—The founder of the Fair Play Committee, he was a middle-aged Nisei who was considered a dangerous rabble rouser at Heart Mountain before he was sent to the camp at Tule Lake, California.

Harumi "Bacon" Sakatani—Before the war he was a childhood friend of Ray Uno in San Gabriel Valley, California. He also found and befriended Estelle Ishigo, who, after the war, was widowed and became a recluse in California. He is on the advisory board of the Heart Mountain Wyoming Foundation.

Carolyn Takeshita—A former incarceree, she was an instrumental member of the Heart Mountain Wyoming Foundation advisory board and co-chair of the committee that developed the exhibits at the interpretive center.

Paul Tsuneishi—A Los Angeles insurance man, he was incarcerated at Heart Mountain and then served in Army intelligence. He became one of the leading activists for redress and recognition of the courage of the draft resisters. He was on the first board of directors of the Heart Mountain Wyoming Foundation.

Satoru Tsuneishi—The father of Paul Tsuneishi. Although he had sons in the US Army, he was an early supporter of the Fair Play Committee at Heart Mountain, which opposed the draft.

Shigeru Yabu—Sent to camp as a boy, he kept a magpie named Maggie as his pet. He became one of the first members of the effort to preserve the Heart Mountain site. He is on the Heart Mountain Wyoming Foundation advisory board and is the author of a children's book about his experiences while incarcerated.

Heart Mountain Advocates

Chester and Mary Blackburn—Originally from Kansas, they moved to northwestern Wyoming after the war to homestead a farm on land that once held the Heart Mountain camp. They led local efforts to commemorate the camp.

Tom Brokaw—The longtime NBC anchorman, journalist, and author spoke at the grand opening of the Heart Mountain interpretive center and has been a good friend of the foundation.

Karen Korematsu—The daughter of Fred Korematsu, she leads the Korematsu Institute, which promotes his case and educates people about the incarceration.

Darrell Kunitomi—The son of Heart Mountain incarcerees, he is an active member of the Heart Mountain Wyoming Foundation board and observer of the incarceration's effect on the Sansei.

Eric Muller—A University of North Carolina law school professor, he wrote a book about the Heart Mountain draft resisters and co-chaired the committee to create the exhibits at the museum that sits at the former campsite.

Doug Nelson—As a young graduate student at the University of Wyoming, he did the first extensive examination of the history of Heart Mountain and wrote his master's thesis on the camp, which was turned into a Pulitzer Prize–nominated history. He later became a leader in raising money for the Heart Mountain interpretive center and currently serves as vice chair of the foundation's board.

Dave Reetz—A Powell, Wyoming, banker, he was the first head of the Heart Mountain Wyoming Foundation board, which helped lead the creation of the museum at the site.

Eric Saul—The curator of the museum at the Presidio, he created an exhibit in 1981 that honored the Nisei soldiers from World War II. The exhibit awakened Clarence Matsumura's memories of the war.

Alan Simpson—A resident of Cody, Wyoming, whose Boy Scout troop visited Heart Mountain Incarceration Center, where he befriended an incarceree Boy Scout, Norman Mineta. They became lifelong friends and reconnected as adults when they were both elected to the US Congress. He is an adviser to the board of the Heart Mountain Wyoming Foundation.

Pete Simpson—Older brother of Alan. He is currently a Heart Mountain Wyoming Foundation board member.

Patricia Wolfe—A longtime and instrumental Heart Mountain Wyoming Foundation board member, she helped recruit Shirley Ann Higuchi to join the board after Setsuko Saito Higuchi's death.

LaDonna Zall—The daughter of a pipeline worker, she watched the last train full of prisoners leave Heart Mountain in November 1945. She later became a board member of the Heart Mountain Wyoming Foundation and led the effort to collect artifacts for the interpretive center.

Officials

Karl Bendetsen—The ambitious Army colonel who developed much of the plan for the evacuation and incarceration over the objection of the FBI and Justice Department officials.

Francis Biddle—US attorney general during World War II, he fought the military's attempts to impose the evacuation and incarceration.

John DeWitt—A general, he led the Western Defense Command and argued that the evacuation and incarceration of Japanese Americans from the West Coast was a matter of military necessity.

Allan Gullion—He was the Army provost marshal in 1942 and favored the immediate removal and incarceration of Japanese Americans from the West Coast.

J. Edgar Hoover—As director of the Federal Bureau of Investigation, he led the roundup of suspected Japanese American security threats after Pearl Harbor. He opposed the wholesale evacuation and incarceration of Japanese Americans from the West Coast.

Velma Berryman Kessel—A nurse at the Heart Mountain hospital, she wrote a memoir about the conditions there and in the camp more generally.

Walter Lippmann—An influential liberal newspaper columnist, his February 12, 1942, column in favor of the evacuation swayed many who were undecided and led them to support it.

John McCloy—An assistant secretary of war, he had reservations about the evacuation but supported it because of a long-standing fear about the risk of sabotage of defense facilities.

Curtis Munson—A Detroit businessman, he was a State Department consultant who wrote a report that said Japanese Americans living on the West Coast posed a minimal security threat.

Dillon Myer—A longtime Agriculture Department official, he became the second director of the War Relocation Authority. He wanted to move as many Japanese Americans as possible out of the camps to jobs throughout the United States.

K. D. Ringle—An officer in the Office of Naval Intelligence, he determined that the Japanese Americans posed a minimal national security threat. His report was disregarded by War Department officials who favored the incarceration.

Owen Roberts—An associate justice of the Supreme Court, he led a commission that claimed it was possible that some members of Hawaii's Japanese American community had helped the Japanese before Pearl Harbor.

Franklin Roosevelt—The Democratic president who signed Executive Order 9066, which allowed the evacuation and incarceration of Japanese Americans living on the West Coast.

James Rowe—An assistant attorney general, he was a committed New Deal liberal who opposed the military's push to impose the incarceration.

Henry Stimson—The elderly secretary of war who reluctantly agreed to support the incarceration of Japanese Americans.

Earl Warren—As California's attorney general, he led the push for the evacuation and spread false claims about national security threats.

Others

William "Buffalo Bill" Cody—The famed Western adventurer and showman founded a town in his name in northwestern Wyoming and started the construction of a dam on the Shoshone River that was eventually taken over by the federal government. His irrigation project opened the door to the Heart Mountain camp.

Roger Daniels—One of the leading historians of Asians in the United States, he was Doug Nelson's thesis adviser at the University of Wyoming.

Lance Ito—A Los Angeles County Superior Court judge, he presided over the murder trial of football star O.J. Simpson in 1994 and 1995. His parents, James and Toshi, were incarcerated at Heart Mountain.

Saburo Kido—A San Francisco lawyer, he helped structure the deal that enabled the Higuchi family to buy their farm in San Jose. He was also president of the Japanese American Citizens League at the beginning of the war.

Mike Masaoka—The executive director of the Japanese American Citizens League, he worked with government officials to ease the evacuation and incarceration. He later supported civil rights laws to help the community.

Robert Matsui—An incarceree at Tule Lake as a child, he became a Democratic House member from California and a leader in the fight for redress.

Spark Matsunaga—A veteran of the 442nd Regimental Combat Team, he was a Democratic senator from Hawaii and instrumental in passing the redress law in 1988.

Floyd Mori—A former national president of the Japanese American Citizens League, he served as its executive director for many years. He led the effort to win an apology for Heart Mountain and other draft resisters.

Notes

Chapter 1. The Issei

1. James Higuchi, Chiye Higuchi biography, 1990, author's personal collection.

2. James Higuchi, "I was born on December 18, 1915, James Higuchi," February 2000, author's personal collection.

3. James Higuchi, "I was born."

4. Roger Daniels, *The Politics of Prejudice* (Berkeley: University of California Press, 1962), 1.

5. James Higuchi, Chiye Higuchi biography, 1990. California's 1913 Alien Land Law prohibited immigrants from buying and owning land, so immigrant families often put property in the names of their US-born children, who were citizens.

6. Department of Commerce, Bureau of the Census, *Fourteenth Census of the United States: 1920* (1920).

7. Department of Commerce, Bureau of the Census, *Fifteenth Census of the United States: 1930* (1930).

8. Sharon Yamato Danley, "Japanese Picture Brides Recall Hardships of American Life," *Los Angeles Times*, May 11, 1995.

9. Al (Fumio) Saito, interview by Vanessa Yuille, February 28, 2009, author's personal collection.

10. Saito, interview by Yuille.

11. Yosaburo Yoshida, "Sources and Causes of Japanese Emigration," *Annals of the American Academy of Political and Social Science* 34, no. 2, Chinese and Japanese in America (September 1909): 157–67.

12. "Japanese and Others," *San Francisco Chronicle*, April 15, 1905.

13. "Anti-Japanese League Forming," *San Francisco Chronicle*, March 8, 1905, http://ddr.densho.org/ddr-densho-69-15/. Accessed January 13, 2018.

14. Commission on Wartime Relocation and Internment of Civilians, *Personal Justice Denied* (Seattle: University of Washington Press, 2011), 30.

15. Daniel Inouye, *Journey to Washington* (Englewood Cliffs, NJ: Prentice Hall, 1967).

16. Commission on Wartime Relocation and Internment of Civilians, *Personal Justice Denied*, 30.

17. Daniel K. Inouye, interview by Tom Ikeda and Beverly Kashino, Densho Visual History Collection, Densho, June 30, 1998, http://ddr.densho.org/media/ddr-densho-1000/ddr-densho-1000-28-15-transcript-e4cf3b76da.htm. Accessed January 22, 2018.

18. Inouye, *Journey to Washington*.

19. Inouye, *Journey to Washington*.

20. Ken Ringle, "The Patriot," *Washington Post*, August 21, 2000.

21. Mark Simon, "Honoring a Man of Experience," *San Francisco Chronicle*, October 31, 2002.

22. Ringle, "The Patriot."

23. Norman Mineta, interview by Shirley Ann Higuchi and Ray Locker, July 27, 2017, author's personal collection.

24. Ringle, "The Patriot."

25. Mineta, interview by Higuchi and Locker.

26. "Building Tracks to New Beginnings: Japanese Railroad Workers in the West," Multimedia Photographs, Special Collections, Spring 2016, J. Marriott Library, University of Utah, https://newsletter.lib.utah.edu/building-tracks-new-beginnings-japanese-railroad-workers-west/. Accessed March 13, 2018.

27. Takashi Hoshizaki, interview by Tom Ikeda, Densho Visual History Collection, Densho, July 28, 2010, http://ddr.densho.org/media/ddr-densho-1000/ddr-densho-1000-290-transcript-1585f1946d.htm. Accessed May 19, 2018.

28. Harold Stanley Johnson, *Roster of the Rainbow Division* (New York: Eaton & Gettinger, 1917), 11.

29. Raymond Uno, interview by Leslie Kelen, "Interviews with Japanese in Utah: Raymond Uno," September 27, 1987, https://collections.lib.utah.edu/details?id=900074. Accessed February 26, 2018.

30. Raymond Uno, interview by Shirley Ann Higuchi and Ray Locker, July 27, 2017, author's personal collection.

31. An Act to Further Time for Naturalization to Alien Veterans of the World War under the Act Approved May 25, 1932, and for Other Purposes (Nye-Lea Act), Public Law 160 (1935): 395, https://www.loc.gov/law/help/statutes-at-large/74th-congress/session-1/c74s1ch288.pdf.

32. Amy Uno Ishii, interview by Betty Mitson and Kristin Mitchell, California State University, Fullerton Oral History Program Japanese American Project, July 9 and July 20, 1973, https://oac.cdlib.org/view?docId=ft8700334;NAAN=13030&doc.view=frames&chunk.id=Amy%20Uno%20Ishii&toc.depth=1&toc.id=0&brand=oac4. Accessed September 18, 2018.

33. Raymond Uno, interview by Kelen.

34. Raymond Uno, interview by Higuchi and Locker.

35. Richard Reeves, *Infamy: The Shocking Story of Japanese American Internment in World War II* (New York: Henry Holt, 2015), 12.

36. Curtis Munson, "Japanese on the West Coast," http://www.mansell.com/e09066/1941/41-11/Munson.html. Accessed February 12, 2018.

37. Munson, "Japanese on the West Coast."

38. Munson, "Japanese on the West Coast."

39. Daniel K. Inouye, interview by Ikeda and Kashino.

Chapter 2. Executive Order 9066

1. Reeves, *Infamy*.

2. Greg Robinson, *By Order of the President* (Cambridge, MA: Harvard University Press, 2001), 64–65, 77.

3. Robinson, *By Order of the President*, 136.

4. Reeves, *Infamy*, 43.

5. Peter Irons, *Justice at War: The Story of the Japanese Internment Cases* (Berkeley: University of California Press, 1983), 29.

6. Kai Bird, *The Chairman: John J. McCloy, the Making of the American Establishment* (New York: Simon & Schuster, 1992), 94.

7. Takashi Hoshizaki, interview by Helen Yoshida, September 26, 2016, author's personal collection.

8. Bird, *The Chairman*, 147.

9. Commission on Wartime Relocation and Internment of Civilians, *Personal Justice Denied*, 70.

10. Reeves, *Infamy*, 34.

11. Brian Niiya, "Roberts Commission Report," *Densho Encyclopedia*, http://encyclopedia.densho.org/Roberts_Commission_report/. Accessed September 18, 2018.

12. Niiya, "Roberts Commission Report."

13. Commission on Wartime Relocation and Internment of Civilians, *Personal Justice Denied*, 50, 472.

14. Lieutenant Commander K. D. Ringle, USN, "Ringle Report on Japanese Internment," https://www.history.navy.mil/content/history/nhhc/research/library/online-reading-room/title-list-alphabetically/r/ringle-report-on-japanese-internment.html. Accessed September 18, 2018.

15. Ringle, "Ringle Report."

16. Ringle, "Ringle Report."

17. Jim Newton, *Justice for All: Earl Warren and the Nation He Made* (New York: Riverhead Books, 2006), 126.

18. John H. Tolan, "National Defense Migration. Report of the Select Committee Investigating National Defense Migration, House of Representatives,

Seventy-Seventh Congress, Second Session, Pursuant to H. Res. 113, a Resolution to Inquire Further into the Interstate Migration of Citizens, Emphasizing the Present and Potential Consequences of the Migration Caused by the National Defense Program. Preliminary Report and Recommendations on Problems of Evacuation of Citizens and Aliens from Military Areas," March 19, 1942 (Washington, DC: US Government Printing Office, 1942), 28–31.

19. Commission on Wartime Relocation and Internment of Civilians, *Personal Justice Denied*, 50.

20. Bird, *The Chairman*, 237.

21. Walter Lippmann, "The Fifth Column on the Coast," *Washington Post*, February 12, 1942.

22. Bill Hosokawa, "A Concentration Camp in America—One Man's Experiences in the Heart Mountain Japanese Relocation Center near Cody, Wyoming," interview by Mark Junge, October 22, 1991, http://www.wyomingstories .com/History/(Edited)BillHosokawaInterview.htm. Accessed June 2, 2017.

23. Francis Biddle to Henry Stimson, February 12, 1942, Office of the Attorney General, Washington, DC, http://encyclopedia.densho.org/media/encyc-psms /en-denshopd-i67-00099-1.pdf. Accessed March 26, 2018.

24. "Executive Order 9066 dated February 19, 1942, in which President Franklin D. Roosevelt Authorizes the Secretary of War to Prescribe Military Areas," Code of Federal Regulations, Record Group 11, https://catalog.archives .gov/id/5730250. Accessed March 26, 2018.

25. Saito, interview by Yuille.

26. Reeves, *Infamy*, 8.

27. Raymond Uno, interview by Kelen.

28. United States War Relocation Authority, Property Receipt undated Osako Uno. Records about Japanese Americans Relocated during World War II, created 1988–1989, documenting the period 1942–1946. Record Group 210, National Archives Building, Washington, DC.

29. Mineta, interview by Higuchi and Locker.

30. President Franklin Roosevelt, "The President Requests War Declaration 125," December 7, 1941, Library of Congress, https://www.loc.gov/resource/afc 1986022.afc1986022_ms2201/?st=text&r=0.013,-0.084,0.926,0.79,0. Accessed September 5, 2018.

31. Saito, interview by Yuille.

32. Raymond Uno, interview by Shirley Ann Higuchi, Ray Locker, and Helen Yoshida, June 2, 2017, author's personal collection.

33. Harumi "Bacon" Sakatani, interview by Tom Ikeda, August 31, 2010, http://ddr.densho.org/media/ddr-densho-1000/ddr-densho-1000-298-6-tran script-b943d16d7f.htm. Accessed July 17, 2018.

34. Emily Filling notes, James Higuchi memoirs, author's personal collection.

Chapter 3. Forced Removal, Exclusion Zones, and Assembly Centers

1. US Congress, "House of Representatives, Report of the Select Committee Investigating National Defense Migration," 77th Congress, 1st Session, March 19, 1942, https://evols.library.manoa.hawaii.edu/bitstream/10524/58732/F3Item73 -1942-03-19-Report-NationalDefenseMigration-unkown_OCR.pdf. Accessed January 29, 2018.

2. Commission on Wartime Relocation and Internment of Civilians, *Personal Justice Denied*, 96.

3. "Report of the Select Committee Investigating National Defense Migration," Part 29, 11137–48.

4. "Report of the Select Committee Investigating National Defense Migration," March 19, 1942, 20.

5. Brian Niiya, Western Defense Command Public Proclamation No. 1, 1942, *Densho Encyclopedia*, http://encyclopedia.densho.org/Civilian_exclusion_orders/. Accessed September 23, 2018.

6. Robinson, *By Order of the President*, 130.

7. "Report of the Select Committee Investigating National Defense Migration," March 19, 1942, 27.

8. Ralph Carr, text of a radio address given February 28, 1942, US Congress, House, "Report of the Select Committee Investigating National Defense Migration," 11275.

9. Gabrielson to John Tolan, March 14, 1942, "Report of the Select Committee Investigating National Defense Migration," March 19, 1942, 35.

10. "Report of the Select Committee Investigating National Defense Migration," March 19, 1942, 19.

11. Western Defense Command and Fourth Army, Wartime Civil Control Administration, *Instructions to All Japanese Living on Bainbridge Island* (1942), https://cdm16855.contentdm.oclc.org/digital/collection/p16855coll4/id/13988. Accessed May 5, 2018.

12. Department of Commerce, Bureau of the Census, *Sixteenth Census of the United States: 1940* (1940).

13. C. P. Trussell, "Spy Data Sought from 1940 Census," *New York Times*, February 7, 1942.

14. Tom Clark, interview by Jerry N. Hess, October 17, 1972, and February 8, 1973, Truman Library and Museum, https://www.trumanlibrary.gov/library/oral -histories/clarktc. Accessed June 14, 2018.

15. Lori Aratani, "Secret Use of Census Info Helped Send Japanese Americans to Internment Camps in WWII," *Washington Post*, April 6, 2018, https:// wapo.st/2DtA39g. Accessed April 6, 2018.

16. United States War Relocation Authority, Form WRA-155 Reverse List of Personal Property: Yoshio Saito.

17. James Higuchi, "I was born," February 2000, author's personal collection.

18. Emily Higuchi Filling, interview by Shirley Ann Higuchi, Ray Locker, and Helen Yoshida, June 6, 2017, author's personal collection.

19. Amy (Iwagaki) Higuchi, "Before and after Pearl Harbor, December 7, 1941: September 1941 to May 1942," February 6, 1979, author's personal collection.

20. Iwagaki Higuchi, "Before and After."

21. Linda Gordon, *Dorothea Lange: A Life beyond Limits* (New York: W. W. Norton, 2010), 315.

22. Gordon, *Dorothea Lange*, 318, 319.

23. Gordon, *Dorothea Lange*, 326.

24. Dean Ryuta Adachi, "Part 3 of 5: History Is Ignored: Estelle Ishigo," May 17, 2012, http://www.discovernikkei.org/en/journal/2012/5/17/Estelle-ishigo/. Accessed August 2, 2018.

25. Sakatani, interview by Ikeda.

26. Emily Higuchi Filling, "This Is an Account," author's personal collection.

27. Mineta, interview by Higuchi and Locker.

28. Takashi Hoshizaki, interview by Tom Ikeda, Jim Gatewood, and Dana Hoshide, July 28, 2010, Densho Visual History Collection, Densho, 02:58:45, http://ddr.densho.org/interviews/ddr-densho-1000-290-15/?tableft=segments. Accessed September 19, 2018.

29. Takashi Hoshizaki, "The Tale of a Heart Mountain Conscientious Resister," *Heart: Tragedy into Triumph at Heart Mountain* (unpublished manuscript, 2014), 151.

30. Toyoko Okumura, interview by Tom Ikeda, July 6, 2008, Densho Visual History Collection, Densho, http://ddr.densho.org/interviews/ddr-janm-13-6-10/. Accessed December 5, 2017.

31. Sakatani, interview by Ikeda.

32. William Higuchi, interview by Ray Locker, July 6, 2018, author's personal collection.

33. Dr. W. Y. Hanaoka, "History of Present Disease for Fumi Saito," July 3, 1942. Records about Japanese Americans Relocated during World War II, created 1988–1989, documenting the period 1942–1946. Record Group 210, National Archives Building, Washington, DC.

34. Toshi Nagamori Ito, interview by Tom Ikeda, Densho Visual History Collection, Densho, November 9, 2010, Transcript Segment 13, http://ddr.densho.org/media/ddr-densho-1000/ddr-densho-1000-309-transcript-6e22c08ddc.htm. Accessed February 7, 2018.

35. Frank K. Omatsu, interview by Sharon Yamato, Densho Visual History Collection, Densho, October 24, 2011, http://ddr.densho.org/interviews/ddr-densho-1000-373-1/. Accessed February 7, 2018.

36. Karl Bendetsen to Milton Eisenhower, "Subject: Desirability of Rapid Relocation Center Development," April 22, 1942. CSU Japanese American Digitization Project, https://cdm16855.contentdm.oclc.org/digital/collection/p16855coll4/id/7217. Accessed July 2, 2018.

37. George Yoshinaga, interview by Alisa Lynch, Manzanar National Historic Site Collection, August 10, 2010, http://ddr.densho.org/interviews/ddr-manz-1-107-7/?tableft=segments. Accessed January 17, 2018.

38. Sakatani, interview by Ikeda.

39. Shigeru Yabu, interview by Shirley Ann Higuchi and Ray Locker, July 27, 2017, author's personal collection.

40. Frank Sumida, interview by Tom Ikeda, Densho Visual History Collection, Densho, September 23, 2009, http://ddr.densho.org/media/ddr-densho-1000/ddr-densho-1000-261-13-transcript-589fdfd125.htm. Accessed January 18, 2018.

41. Edmund Mason, "Internal Conditions, Santa Anita Assembly Center, Arcadia, California; Riot of Evacuees, August 4, 1942," File no. 100-14777, August 10, 1942, http://digitalassets.lib.berkeley.edu/jarda/ucb/text/reduced/cubanc6714_b022b07_0001_2.pdf. Accessed January 18, 2018.

42. Higuchi Filling, interview by Higuchi, Locker, and Yoshida.

43. Hoshizaki, interview by Yoshida.

44. Ike Hachimonji, interview by Martha Nakagawa, Densho Visual History Collection, Densho, November 30, 2011, https://ddr.densho.org/media/ddr-densho-1000/ddr-densho-1000-381-transcript-2146f03596.htm. Accessed January 22, 2018.

45. Sumida, interview by Ikeda.

46. Deborah Cobb, "Heart Mountain: 'Things Like This Should Never Happen Again,'" WyoFile, August 16, 2011, https://www.wyofile.com/heart-mountain-things-like-this-should-never-happen-again-2/. Accessed September 21, 2018.

47. Uno Ishii, interview by Mitson and Mitchell.

48. Estelle Ishigo, *Lone Heart Mountain* (Los Angeles: Communicart, 1972), 18.

49. Hoshizaki, interview by Yoshida.

50. Ike Hatchimonji, interview by Martha Nakagawa, Densho Visual History Collection, Densho, November 30, 2011, transcript, Segment 11, https://ddr.densho.org/media/ddr-densho-1000/ddr-densho-1000-381-15-transcript-bf831897d2.htm. Accessed December 18, 2017.

51. Raymond Uno, interview by Higuchi and Locker.

52. William Higuchi, interview by Locker.

53. Takashi Hoshizaki, interview by Shirley Ann Higuchi and Ray Locker, July 27, 2017, author's personal collection.

54. Bill Shishima, interview by Raechel Donahue, 2010, Raechel Donahue and Garrett Lindemann Collection, https://ddr.densho.org/media/ddr-densho-1011/ddr-densho-1011-1-transcript-f989f399c9.htm. Accessed January 23, 2018.

Chapter 4. A New Home in the Dust and Wind

1. Louis Warren, *Buffalo Bill's America* (New York: Random House, 2006), 8; Jeff Barnes, *The Great Plains Guide to Buffalo Bill: Forts, Fights and Other Sites* (Mechanicsburg, PA: Stackpole Books, 2014), 57, 60, 471–72, 475, and 490.

2. Karl Lillquist, *Imprisoned in the Desert: The Geography of the World War II–Era, Japanese American Relocation Centers in the Western United States* (Ellensburg: Central Washington University, September 2007), 33, https://www.cwu.edu/geog raphy/sites/cts.cwu.edu.geography/files/covercontentfigs.pdf. Accessed June 2, 2017.

3. Douglas Nelson, *Heart Mountain: The History of an American Concentration Camp* (Madison: State Historical Society of Wisconsin for the Department of History, University of Wisconsin, 1976), 10.

4. Nelson, *Heart Mountain*, 17.

5. Velma Berryman Kessel, *Behind Barbed Wire: Heart Mountain Relocation Camp* (Casper, WY: Mountain States Lithographing, 1992), 5.

6. Alice Hardesty, "To Heart Mountain," *Oregon Humanities*, December 15, 2017, 6–7, https://oregonhumanities.org/rll/magazine/harm/to-heart-mountain/. Accessed December 15, 2017.

7. Hardesty, "To Heart Mountain," 4.

8. Nelson, *Heart Mountain*, 18–19.

9. Uno Ishii, interview by Mitson and Mitchell.

10. *Heart Mountain General Information Bulletin—Series 1*, August 25, 1942, 1, https://ddr.densho.org/ddr-densho-97-75/. Accessed May 3, 2018.

11. *Heart Mountain General Information Bulletin—Series 1*, 1, 2.

12. "Center Population Now 10,767," *General Information Bulletin—Series 12*, September 17, 1942, 1, https://ddr.densho.org/ddr-densho-97-82/. Accessed May 4, 2018.

13. "Hospital Information," *General Information Bulletin—Series 7*, September 10, 1942, 4, https://ddr.densho.org/ddr-densho-97-78/. Accessed May 4, 2018.

14. "Residents Asked Not to Take Celotex," *General Information Bulletin—Series 23*, October 8, 1942, 5, https://ddr.densho.org/ddr-densho-97-93/. Accessed May 4, 2018.

15. *Heart Mountain General Information Bulletin—Series 1*, 1–2.

16. Lillquist, *Imprisoned in the Desert*, 95.

17. Raymond Uno, interview by Shirley Ann Higuchi and Ray Locker, July 8, 2018, author's personal collection.

18. *Heart Mountain General Information Bulletin—Series 1*, 2.

19. Frank Sishi Emi, "Nisei Experience/Draft Resistance Movement," interview by Alan Koch, March 11, 1993, 362, https://oac.cdlib.org/view?query=got+to +the+site&docId=ft1f59n61r&chunk.id=d0e32904&toc. depth=1&toc.id =0&brand=oac4&x=20&y=7. Accessed September 11, 2018.

20. Uno Ishii, interview by Mitson and Mitchell.

21. William Higuchi, interview by Locker.

22. "Quintet Convalesce from Operations," *Heart Mountain Sentinel*, November 28, 1942, https://www.loc.gov/resource/sn84024756/1942-11-28/ed-1/?sp=8 &r=-0.524,0.574,2.047,0.906,0. Accessed September 15, 2018.

23. Sam Mihara, interview by Shirley Ann Higuchi and Ray Locker, July 28, 2017, author's personal collection.

24. Berryman Kessel, *Behind Barbed Wire*, 9, 11.

25. Berryman Kessel, *Behind Barbed Wire*, 11.

26. "National Japanese American Student Relocation Council," *Densho Encyclopedia*, September 15, 2018, http://encyclopedia.densho.org/National_Japanese_American_Student_Relocation_Council/. Accessed September 15, 2018.

27. John J. McCloy to Mr. Clarence E. Pickett, May 21, 1942, http://webfiles.wulib.wustl.edu/units/spec/archives/digital/Throop_Japanese_19420521_p1.pdf. Accessed March 15, 2018.

28. "82 Heart Mountain Nisei Students Are Attending Colleges in Middlewest," *Heart Mountain Sentinel*, July 31, 1943, https://www.loc.gov/resource/sn84024756/1943-07-31/ed-1/?sp=8. Accessed March 15, 2018.

29. W. W. Kenville (manager at the Bank of America) to National Student Relocation Council, July 16, 1942. Records about Japanese Americans Relocated during World War II, created 1988–1989, documenting the period 1942–1946. Record Group 210, National Archives Building, Washington, DC.

30. Ronald B. Thompson (Office of the Registrar at University of Utah) to Mr. Joseph Conard (Executive Secretary, National Student Relocation Council), September 10, 1942. Records about Japanese Americans Relocated during World War II, created 1988–1989, documenting the period 1942–1946. Record Group 210, National Archives Building, Washington, DC.

31. Shirley Ann Higuchi, "On My Shoulders," August 2, 2018, filmed at the Heart Mountain Pilgrimage Digital Storytelling Workshop, https://www.youtube.com/watch?v=osqMRyxd364. Accessed August 2, 2018.

32. "Three Colonists Leave for College," *General Information Bulletin—Series 25*, October 13, 1942, 4, https://ddr.densho.org/ddr-densho-97-95/. Accessed April 27, 2018.

33. "Oberlin Vouches for Them . . .," *Oberlin Alumni Magazine* 8, no. 4 (Fall 2013): 2, http://www2.oberlin.edu/alummag/fall2013/internmentstudents.html. Accessed August 1, 2018.

34. Marjorie Matsushita Sperling, interview by Tom Ikeda, Densho Visual History Collection, Segment 20, February 24, 2010, https://ddrstage.densho.org/media/ddr-densho-1000/ddr-densho-1000-273-transcript-6f6a81a167.htm. Accessed May 7, 2018.

35. "82 Heart Mountain Nisei Students Are Attending Colleges in the Middlewest," *Heart Mountain Sentinel*, July 31, 1943, 8.

36. Saito, interview by Yuille.

37. "Recto of page 17," Hayami (Stanley) Diary, Japanese American National Museum, Calisphere, September 16, 2018, 14:31, https://calisphere.org/item/ark:/13030/tf400003cd/. Accessed September 16, 2018.

38. Raymond Uno, interview by Helen Yoshida, September 8, 2016, author's personal collection.

39. Setsuko Saito, "Jones Personality Rating Scale," March 1944. Records about Japanese Americans Relocated during World War II, created 1988–1989, documenting the period 1942–1946. Record Group 210, National Archives Building, Washington, DC.

40. Nobu Shimokochi, interview by Raechel Donahue, 2010, Segment 7, http://ddr.densho.org/interviews/ddr-densho-1011-7-7/?tableft=segments. Accessed September 10, 2018.

41. Bill Hiroshi Shishima, interview by Martha Nakagawa, Densho Visual History Collection, Densho, February 8, 2012, Segment 11, https://ddrstage.densho.org/media/ddr-densho-1000/ddr-densho-1000-393-transcript-c2c5e85bad.htm. Accessed September 10, 2018.

42. Shirley Ann Higuchi, ed., *Heart: Tragedy into Triumph at Heart Mountain* (unpublished manuscript, 2014), 8.

43. Paul Iida, "Work Starts Next Month on $140,000 High School," *Heart Mountain Sentinel*, October 24, 1942, 8, https://lccn.loc.gov/sn84024756. Accessed March 20, 2018.

44. Emily Filling notes, James Higuchi memoirs, author's personal collection.

45. Frank Emi, interview by Emiko Omori, Emiko and Chizuko Omori Collection, Densho, March 20, 1994, https://ddrstage.densho.org/media/ddr-densho-1002/ddr-densho-1002-9-3-transcript-14930acc6c.htm. Accessed June 3, 2018.

46. Eiichi Edward Sakauye, interview by Wendy Hanamura, Japanese American Film Preservation Project Collection, Densho, May 14, 2005, Segment 4, http://ddr.densho.org/interviews/ddr-densho-1005-1-4/?tableft=segments. Accessed June 3, 2018.

47. Work of the War Relocation Authority, An Anniversary Statement by Dillon S. Myer, Director of the War Relocation Authority, March 1943, https://www.trumanlibrary.gov/library/research-files/news-release-work-war-relocation-authority-anniversary-statement-dillon-s. Accessed June 5, 2018.

48. William Higuchi, interview by Locker.

49. Hatchimonji, interview by Nakagawa.

50. Sakauye, interview by Hanamura.

51. "Unauthorized Uses of Hotplates Hit," *General Information Bulletin—Series 21*, October 3, 1942, 3, https://ddr.densho.org/ddr-densho-97-91/. Accessed May 5, 2018.

52. Emily Higuchi, personal narrative, April 10, 2016, author's personal collection.

53. Caitlin Yoshiko Kandil, "A Family's Photo Trove Offers a Window into WWII Japanese-American Internment Camp Life," *Los Angeles Times*, November 8, 2015, http://www.latimes.com/socal/weekend/news/tn-wknd-et-1108-japanese-photos-20151108-story.html.

54. Ed Tokeshi, "Farm Activities Transform Barren Land," *Heart Mountain Sentinel*, August 12, 1944, 14, http://pluto.state.wy.us/awweb/pdfopener?md=1&did=11179480. Accessed March 16, 2018.

55. Heart Mountain Pilgrimage 2015, "Root Cellar Preservation," 10, http://www.heartmountain.org/pilgrimage_144_350502738.pdf. Accessed November 18, 2018.

56. "Frost Hits Farm, Slashes Yield of Crops," *Heart Mountain Sentinel*, September 11, 1943, 1, https://www.loc.gov/resource/sn84024756/1943-09-11/ed-1/?sp=1&r=-0.857,0.13,2.715,1.201,0. Accessed June 8, 2018.

57. "Volunteer Workers Save Farm Crops from Frost as Winter Threatens," *Heart Mountain Sentinel*, October 30, 1943, 1, https://www.loc.gov/item/sn84024756/1943-10-30/ed-1/. Accessed June 8, 2018.

58. "In-Patient Admission and Discharge [hospital]: Operation: Appendectomy, Setsuko Saito," July 18, 1943. Records about Japanese Americans Relocated during World War II, created 1988–1989, documenting the period 1942–1946. Record Group 210, National Archives Building, Washington, DC.

59. "In-Patient Admission and Discharge #2133," August 16, 1943. Records about Japanese Americans Relocated during World War II, created 1988–1989, documenting the period 1942–1946. Record Group 210, National Archives Building, Washington, DC.

60. Berryman Kessel, *Behind Barbed Wire*, 34.

61. Sakatani, interview by Ikeda.

62. William Higuchi, interview by Locker.

63. "Eagles Triumph over Lovell with Last Period Drive, 6–0," *Heart Mountain Sentinel*, October 30, 1943, 7, https://www.loc.gov/resource/sn84024756/1943-10-30/ed-1/?sp=8&r=-0.443,0.22,1.937,0.857,0. Accessed May 18, 2018.

64. Kerry Cababa, interview by Ray Locker, July 26, 2018, author's personal collection.

65. "Koysan Buddhist Temple Los Angeles, California," www.koyasanbetsuin.org. Accessed September 19, 2018.

66. Alan Simpson, interview by Shirley Ann Higuchi and Ray Locker, July 27, 2017, author's personal collection.

67. Norman Mineta, interview by Ronald Sarasin, September 11, 2006, https://uschs.org/wp-content/uploads/2017/03/USCHS-Oral-History-Congressman-Norman-Mineta.pdf. Accessed June 20, 2018.

68. Simpson, interview by Higuchi and Locker.

69. Julie Beck, "Two Boy Scouts Met in an Internment Camp, and Grew Up to Work in Congress," *Atlantic*, May 17, 2019.

70. *Heart Mountain General Information Bulletin—Series 1*, August 25, 1942.

71. Hosokawa, "A Concentration Camp in America."

72. Hosokawa, "A Concentration Camp in America," 11.

73. "An American's Return to the American Way of Life," *Heart Mountain Sentinel*, October 16, 1943, 6, https://www.loc.gov/resource/sn84024756/1943-10-16/ed-1/?sp=1. Accessed August 2, 2018.

74. "2,600 18–64 Men Notify Change of Address," *General Information Bulletin—Series 20*, October 1, 1942, https://ddr.densho.org/ddr-densho-97-90/. Accessed August 2, 2018.

75. "Legionnaires Ready to Aid Colonists," *General Information Bulletin—Series 7*, September 10, 1942, 3, https://ddr.densho.org/ddr-densho-97-78/. Accessed August 2, 2018.

76. Nelson, *Heart Mountain*, 32.

77. Eric Muller, "Of Coercion and Accommodation: Looking at Japanese American Imprisonment through a Law Office Window," *Law and History Review* 35, no. 2 (2017): 277–319.

78. "Temporary Block Administrative Officers Picked," *General Information Bulletin—Series 7*, September 10, 1942, 1, https://ddr.densho.org/ddr-densho-97-78/. Accessed March 2, 2018.

79. Devin M. Gonsalez, "Policing the Camp," *Kokoro Kara: Heart Mountain Wyoming Foundation* (Autumn 2017): 9–11.

80. "35 Beet Workers Leave for Montana," *General Information Bulletin—Series 12*, September 17, 1942, 1, http://ddr.densho.org/ddr-densho-97-82/. Accessed March 2, 2018.

81. "Seek Aid of High School Students for Beet Harvest," *General Information Bulletin—Series 23*, October 8, 1942, 1, https://ddr.densho.org/ddr-densho-97-93/. Accessed March 2, 2018.

82. "1128 Leave for Harvest," *Heart Mountain Sentinel*, October 24, 1942, 8, https://www.loc.gov/resource/sn84024756/1942-10-24/ed-1/?sp=8&r=-0.083,-0.164,1.31,0.579,0. Accessed May 6, 2018.

83. "Harvest Workers Assured," *Heart Mountain Sentinel*, October 24, 1942, https://www.loc.gov/resource/sn84024756/1942-10-24/ed-1/?sp=8&r=-0.083,-0.164,1.31,0.579,0. Accessed May 6, 2018.

84. "1128 Leave for Harvest."

85. Richard Drinnon, *Keeper of the Concentration Camps: Dillon S. Myer and American Racism* (Berkeley: University of California Press, 1987), 50.

86. Commission on Wartime Relocation and Internment of Civilians and United States, *Personal Justice Denied*, 202–3, 187–89.

87. "Residents Cast 2690 Votes in Charter Group Election; 10 Block Chairmen Named to Commission," *Heart Mountain Sentinel*, November 7, 1942, 8, https://cdn.loc.gov/service/sgp/sgpbatches/batch_dlc_anacostia_ver01/data/sn84024756/00237288592/1942110701/0170.pdf. Accessed May 6, 2018.

88. "Comments Concerns WPA Experience, Supervisor's Evaluation, Etc . . . for Clarence Matsumura," August 27, 1942. Records about Japanese Americans Relocated during World War II, created 1988–1989, documenting the period 1942–1946. Record Group 210, National Archives Building, Washington, DC.

89. Hoshizaki, interview by Yoshida.

90. Iyekichi Higuchi, *FWA Classification Card*, Form 85-61AB, Heart Mountain Internment Center. Records about Japanese Americans Relocated during World War II, created 1988–1989, documenting the period 1942–1946. Record Group 210, National Archives Building, Washington, DC.

91. Saito, interview by Yuille.

92. "Editorials: Christmas Greetings," *Heart Mountain Sentinel*, December 24, 1942, https://www.loc.gov/resource/sn84024756/1942-12-24/ed-1/?sp=4. March 1, 2018.

Chapter 5. Establishing Loyalties

1. Commission on Wartime Relocation and Internment of Civilians and United States, *Personal Justice Denied*, 5, 189.

2. Reeves, *Infamy*, 174.

3. The loyalty questionnaire, Ikeda Family Collection, Densho, https://encyclopedia.densho.org/sources/en-denshopd-p72-00004-1/. Accessed April 22, 2018.

4. Takashi Hoshizaki, Form WRA 152a, January 28, 1943. Records about Japanese Americans Relocated during World War II, created 1988–1989, documenting the period 1942–1946. Record Group 210, National Archives Building, Washington, DC.

5. Commission on Wartime Relocation and Internment of Civilians, *Personal Justice Denied*, 192, 192–94, 194, 413.

6. Commission on Wartime Relocation and Internment of Civilians, *Personal Justice Denied*, 192, 192–94, 194.

7. Commission on Wartime Relocation and Internment of Civilians, *Personal Justice Denied*, 192–94.

8. Commission on Wartime Relocation and Internment of Civilians, *Personal Justice Denied*, 195.

9. Commission on Wartime Relocation and Internment of Civilians, *Personal Justice Denied*, 195.

10. "Nisei to Reach Lost Battalion: Fred Yamamoto Fought to Prepare for Peace," *Heart Mountain Sentinel*, November 18, 1944, http://ddr.densho.org/ddr-densho-97-207/. Accessed July 16, 2018.

11. "Ted Fujioka Joins Army Volunteers," *Heart Mountain Sentinel*, July 3, 1943, 6, https://www.loc.gov/resource/sn84024756/1943-07-03/ed-1/?sp=6&r=-0.385,-0.133,1.874,0.829,0. Accessed March 22, 2018.

12. Ted Fujioka to Mr. Lloyd, June 24, 1943, Heart Mountain Wyoming Foundation Collections 2013.038.

13. Commission on Wartime Relocation and Internment of Civilians, *Personal Justice Denied*, 193.

14. Inouye, interview by Ikeda.

15. Reeves, *Infamy*, 173.

16. Commission on Wartime Relocation and Internment of Civilians, *Personal Justice Denied*, 178.

17. Raymond Uno, interview by Shirley Ann Higuchi, November 15, 2019, author's personal collection.

18. "Honor Clarence Uno with Military Funeral," *Heart Mountain Sentinel*, January 23, 1943, https://www.loc.gov/resource/sn84024756/1943-01-23/ed-1/?sp=1. Accessed March 1, 2018.

19. Erin Barnett, "Heart Mountain Internment Camp," *Fans in a Flashbulb*, September 28, 2011, https://fansinaflashbulb.wordpress.com/2011/09/28/heart -mountain-internment-camp/. Accessed March 5, 2018.

20. Raymond Uno, interview by Higuchi.

21. Uno Ishii, interview by Mitson and Mitchell.

22. Inouye, *Journey to Washington*, 76.

23. Inouye, interview by Ikeda and Kashino.

24. Mineta, interview by Higuchi and Locker.

25. Mike Masaoka testimony, "Congress House Select Committee Investigating National Defense Migration," Part 29, 11137, https://archive.org/stream/na tionaldefensem29unit/nationaldefensem29unit_djvu.txt. Accessed February 22, 2018.

26. "Mineta-Masaoka," *Heart Mountain Sentinel*, February 13, 1943, https:// www.loc.gov/resource/sn84024756/1943-02-13/ed-1/?sp=3. Accessed February 19, 2018.

27. Mineta, interview by Higuchi and Locker.

28. Kunisaku Mineta, application for leave clearance, February 16, 1943. Records about Japanese Americans Relocated during World War II, created 1988–1989, documenting the period 1942–1946. Record Group 210, National Archives Building, Washington, DC.

29. "Memo to Kunisaku Mineta, about Japanese-American News," January 29, 1943. Records about Japanese Americans Relocated during World War II, created 1988–1989, documenting the period 1942–1946. Record Group 210, National Archives Building, Washington, DC.

30. Elmer Shirrell to Guy Robertson, "Kunisaku Mineta approved," November 2, 1943. Records about Japanese Americans Relocated during World War II, created 1988–1989, documenting the period 1942–1946. Record Group 210, National Archives Building, Washington, DC.

31. Nelson, *Heart Mountain*, 54.

32. Hosokawa, "A Concentration Camp."

33. "Robertson Counters Allegations of Earl Best," *Heart Mountain Sentinel*, June 19, 1943, https://cdn.loc.gov/service/sgp/sgpbatches/batch_dlc_anacostia_

ver01/data/sn84024756/00237288592/1943061901/0594.pdf. Accessed March 1, 2018.

34. Hosokawa, "A Concentration Camp."

35. Nelson, *Heart Mountain*, 65, 59.

36. "Good Citizenship: An Editorial," *Heart Mountain Sentinel*, February 26, 1944, 1, https://www.loc.gov/resource/sn84024756/1944-02-26/ed-1/?sp=1. Accessed February 19, 2018.

37. Irons, *Justice at War*, 214.

38. US Congress, House of Representatives, "Report and Minority Views of the Special Committee of Un-American Activities on Japanese War Relocation Centers," 78th Congress, 1st Session, September 30, 1943, H.Rep. 717, http://www.mansell.com/eo9066/1943/43-09/IA106.html. Accessed January 15, 2018.

39. "Editorials: Looking Toward the Future II," *Heart Mountain Sentinel*, July 17, 1943, 4, http://ddr.densho.org/ddr-densho-97-137/, https://www.loc.gov/resource/sn84024756/1943-07-17/ed-1/?sp=4&r=-0.115,0.307,0.881,0.389,0. Accessed May 15, 2018.

40. US Congress, House of Representatives, "Report and Minority Views of the Special Committee," 78.

41. US Congress, House of Representatives, "Report and Minority Views of the Special Committee."

42. Estelle Ishigo, *Disloyal*, 1943, oil on canvas, 20×24 in. (50.8×60.96 cm), Japanese American National Museum, Los Angeles.

43. Commission on Wartime Relocation and Internment of Civilians and United States, *Personal Justice Denied*, 211.

44. "Zaishin Mukushima, 'Farewell,'" *Heart Mountain Sentinel*, October 2, 1943, 2, https://www.loc.gov/resource/sn84024756/1943-10-02/ed-1/?sp=2&r=-0.079,0.891,1.33,0.588,0. Accessed August 2, 2018.

45. "Takeo Takegawa, 'Farewell,'" *Heart Mountain Sentinel*, October 2, 1943, 2, https://www.loc.gov/resource/sn84024756/1943-10-02/ed-1/?sp=2&r=-0.079,0.891,1.33,0.588,0. Accessed August 2, 2018.

46. William Higuchi, interview by Locker.

47. "Tuleans Meet Guy Robertson," *Heart Mountain Sentinel*, October 23, 1943, https://www.loc.gov/resource/sn84024756/1943-10-23/ed-1/?sp=9. Accessed September 20, 2018.

48. Nelson, *Heart Mountain*, 114–15.

49. "Center Enters Important New Phase of Existence with Segregation Over," *Heart Mountain Sentinel*, October 16, 1943, 1, https://www.loc.gov/resource/sn84024756/1943-10-16/ed-1/?sp=1. Accessed August 2, 2018.

Chapter 6. Relocation

1. Dorothy S. Thomas to Joseph Willits, March 11, 1942, https://rockfound.rockarch.org/digital-library-listing/-/asset_publisher/yYxpQfeI4W8N/content

/letter-from-dorothy-swaine-thomas-to-joseph-h-willits-1942-march-11-. Accessed March 10, 2019.

2. Drinnon, *Keeper of the Concentration Camps*, 50.

3. "Future Encouraging, Says Myer: National Director Delivers Hopeful Message at Mass Meeting of Evacuees Here," *Heart Mountain Sentinel*, August 14, 1943, 1, https://www.loc.gov/resource/sn84024756/1943-08-14/ed-1/?sp=1. Accessed May 15, 2018.

4. "More Outside Employment Offers Received," *Sentinel Supplement*, Series 112, *Heart Mountain Sentinel*, August 19, 1943, 2, https://www.loc.gov/resource/sn84024756/1943-08-19/ed-1/?sp=1. Accessed March 1, 2018.

5. *Sentinel Supplement*, Series 112, *Heart Mountain Sentinel*, August 19, 1943, 2.

6. "352 in July Leave Center," *Heart Mountain Sentinel*, July 31, 1943, 1.

7. "More Job Offers Received at Outside Employment Office," *Sentinel Supplement*, Series 125, September 17, 1943, 1–2, https://cdn.loc.gov/service/sgp/sgpbatches/batch_dlc_anacostia_ver01/data/sn84024756/00237288592/1943091701/1238.pdf. Accessed March 2, 2018; "Businessmen Are Denouncing Evacuees Who Refuse Jobs," *Heart Mountain Sentinel*, July 17, 1943, https://www.loc.gov/resource/sn84024756/1943-07-17/ed-1/?sp=1. Accessed March 2, 2018.

8. "Letters to the Editor," *Heart Mountain Sentinel*, April 17, 1943, 4, https://www.loc.gov/resource/sn84024756/1943-04-17/ed-1/?sp=4. Accessed July 16, 2018.

9. Frank Emi, interview by Alan Koch, Japanese American World War II Evacuation Oral History Project: Part IV: Resisters, Online Archive of California, March 11, 1993, and February 20, 1994, https://oac.cdlib.org/view?docId=ft1f59n61r;NAAN=13030&doc.view=frames&chunk.id=d0e32904&toc.depth=1&toc.id=d0e32904&brand=oac4. Accessed July 11, 2018.

10. "An American's Return to an American Way of Life," *Heart Mountain Sentinel*, October 16, 1943, 1.

11. Joe Carroll, Employment Division to Robert M. Cullum Relocation Supervisor for War Relocation Authority, August 1, 1943. Records about Japanese Americans Relocated during World War II, created 1988–1989, documenting the period 1942–1946. Record Group 210, National Archives Building, Washington, DC.

12. Robert M. Cullum, Relocation Supervisor for War Relocation Authority to Joe Carroll, Employment Division, August 17, 1943. Records about Japanese Americans Relocated during World War II, created 1988–1989, documenting the period 1942–1946. Record Group 210, National Archives Building, Washington, DC.

13. "Release papers for Clarence Matsumura." Records about Japanese Americans Relocated during World War II, created 1988–1989, documenting the period 1942–1946. Record Group 210, National Archives Building, Washington, DC.

14. Mineta, interview by Higuchi and Locker.

15. Editorials, *Heart Mountain Sentinel*, February 26, 1944.

16. Mineta, interview by Higuchi and Locker.

17. Raymond Booth to the University of Cincinnati, January 18, 1944. Records about Japanese Americans Relocated during World War II, created 1988–1989, documenting the period 1942–1946. Record Group 210, National Archives Building, Washington, DC.

18. Alton Miller to National Japanese American Student Relocation Council, March 28, 1944. Records about Japanese Americans Relocated during World War II, created 1988–1989, documenting the period 1942–1946. Record Group 210, National Archives Building, Washington, DC.

19. Clarence Matsumura, enlistment record. World War II Army Enlistment Records, created June 1, 2002–September 30, 2002, documenting the period ca. 1938–1946. Record Group 64, https://aad.archives.gov/aad/record-detail.jsp?dt =893&mtch=1&cat=all&tf=F&q=matsumura+clarence&bc=&rpp=10&pg=1& rid=5573160. Accessed July 15, 2018.

20. "Former Resident Barred from School," *Heart Mountain Sentinel*, June 3, 1944, https://www.loc.gov/resource/sn84024756/1944-06-03/ed-1/?sp=2&st=text. Accessed July 15, 2018.

21. Arthur Hansen, "A Case Study of Heart Mountain's Draft Resisters and Military Service," *Nichi Bei Weekly*, May 11, 2018, http://www.discovernikkei.org/en /journal/2018/5/11/wyoming-samurai/. Accessed July 15, 2018.

22. "3,000 Nisei Aided by Student Council," *Heart Mountain Sentinel*, August 19, 1944, https://www.loc.gov/resource/sn84024756/1944-08-19/ed-1/?sp=7. Accessed July 16, 2018.

Chapter 7. Resistance

1. "Final Report, Japanese Evacuation from the West Coast," https://archive .org/details/japaneseevacuati00dewi, 1942, 9. Accessed June 3, 2018.

2. "Report of the Select Committee Investigating National Defense Migration," March 19, 1942.

3. Irons, *Justice at War*, 207–8.

4. Irons, *Justice at War*, 211–12.

5. "Evacuee property report: Osako Uno," War Relocation Authority, January 25, 1944. Records about Japanese Americans Relocated during World War II, created 1988–1989, documenting the period 1942–1946. Record Group 210, National Archives Building, Washington, DC.

6. "Request for transportation of property: Osako Uno," War Relocation Authority, March 24, 1943. Records about Japanese Americans Relocated during World War II, created 1988–1989, documenting the period 1942–1946. Record Group 210, National Archives Building, Washington, DC.

7. "Evacuee property report: Osako Uno," War Relocation Authority, July 19, 1944. Records about Japanese Americans Relocated during World War II,

created 1988–1989, documenting the period 1942–1946. Record Group 210, National Archives Building, Washington, DC.

8. Raymond Uno, interview by Helen Yoshida, October 18, 2016, author's personal collection.

9. "World War I Veteran's Nephews Pledge Destruction of Brother," *Heart Mountain Sentinel*, April 8, 1944, https://www.loc.gov/resource/sn84024756/1944 -04-08/ed-1/?sp=1. Accessed May 21, 2018.

10. Takashi Hoshizaki, "Kiyoshi Okamoto and the Four Franks," interview by Frank Abe, http://resisters.com/tag/resisters/, August 22, 2013, 1, 2. Accessed February 22, 2018.

11. Eric L. Muller, *Free to Die for Their Country* (Chicago: University of Chicago Press, 2001), 77, 78.

12. Guy Robertson to Dillon S. Myer, December 10, 1943. Records about Japanese Americans Relocated during World War II, created 1988–1989, documenting the period 1942–1946. Record Group 210, National Archives Building, Washington, DC.

13. Commission on Wartime Relocation and Internment of Civilians, *Personal Justice Denied*, 5, 189.

14. Guy Robertson to Dillon S. Myer, January 25, 1944. Records about Japanese Americans Relocated during World War II, created 1988–1989, documenting the period 1942–1946. Record Group 210, National Archives Building, Washington, DC.

15. Emi, interview by Koch.

16. Hoshizaki, "Tale of a Heart Mountain Conscientious Resister."

17. Hoshizaki, interview by Ikeda, Gatewood, and Hoshide.

18. "Excerpts from an FBI report on the Heart Mountain Fair Play Committee," 65, http://ddr.densho.org/ddr-densho-67-74/. Accessed July 2, 2018.

19. "Statement of United States Citizen of Japanese Ancestry: Takashi Hoshizaki," February 27, 1943. Records about Japanese Americans Relocated during World War II, created 1988–1989, documenting the period 1942–1946. Record Group 210, National Archives Building, Washington, DC.

20. Satoru Tsuneishi, "Draft Statement," July 28, 1981, Heart Mountain archives.

21. "Excerpts from an FBI report on the Heart Mountain Fair Play Committee," 65.

22. "Excerpts from an FBI report on the Heart Mountain Fair Play Committee," 7.

23. "No Rules Prohibit Nisei from Any Service Branch," *Heart Mountain Sentinel*, February 26, 1944, https://www.loc.gov/resource/sn84024756/1944-02-26 /ed-1/?sp=1. Accessed February 19, 2018.

24. Muller, *Free to Die*, 82.

25. Reeves, *Infamy*, 197.

26. Reeves, *Infamy*, 197.

27. "Excerpts from an FBI report on the Heart Mountain Fair Play Committee," 23.

28. "Leave Clearance of Kiyoshi Okamoto," Philip Glick to Assistant Director, War Relocation Authority, March 24, 1944. Records about Japanese Americans Relocated during World War II, created 1988–1989, documenting the period 1942–1946. Record Group 210, National Archives Building, Washington, DC.

29. Emi, interview by Koch.

30. Deborah Lim, "Position and Action on Resisters and the WRA Segregation Process," Conscience and the Constitution, http://resisters.com/conscience /who_writes_history/looking_back/06_limreport2e.html.

31. "ACLU Takes Issue with Okamoto," *Heart Mountain Sentinel*, April 15, 1944, https://www.loc.gov/resource/sn84024756/1944-04-15/ed-1/?sp=1. Accessed February 19, 2018; Hoshizaki, interview by Ikeda, Gatewood, and Hoshide.

32. Emi, interview by Koch.

33. Glen Hartman, Chief of Agriculture, Heart Mountain Relocation Center to Mr. K. Ichiro Hoshizaki, "Appeal for investigation of termination," April 6, 1944, Japanese American Archival Collection, California State University, Sacramento, Department of Special Collections and University Archives, https:// cdm16855.contentdm.oclc.org/digital/collection/p16855coll4/id/9775.

34. Keijiro Hoshizaki, Block 12-5-C, Heart Mountain Relocation Center to Community Council, "Poultry," April 11, 1944, Japanese American Archival Collection, California State University, Sacramento, Department of Special Collections and University Archives, https://cdm16855.contentdm.oclc.org/digital/collec tion/p16855coll4/id/9778.

35. Reeves, *Infamy*, 151–53.

36. "Triumph over Intolerance," *Heart Mountain Sentinel*, April 29, 1944, https://www.loc.gov/resource/sn84024756/1944-04-29/ed-1/?sp=4. Accessed March 1, 2018.

37. Reeves, *Infamy*, 156.

38. Hoshizaki, interview by Ikeda, Gatewood, and Hoshide.

39. Reeves, *Infamy*, 196.

40. Reeves, *Infamy*, 197.

41. Hoshizaki, interview by Ikeda, Gatewood, and Hoshide.

42. Hoshizaki, interview by Ikeda, Gatewood, and Hoshide.

43. Hoshizaki, interview by Yoshida.

44. Hoshizaki, interview by Ikeda, Gatewood, and Hoshide.

45. Hoshizaki, interview by Ikeda, Gatewood, and Hoshide.

46. Muller, *Free to Die*, 104.

47. Hoshizaki, interview by Ikeda, Gatewood, and Hoshide.

48. Muller, *Free to Die*, 111.

49. "Years of Uselessness," *Heart Mountain Sentinel*, July 1, 1944, https://

www.loc.gov/resource/sn84024756/1944-07-01/ed-1/?sp=4. Accessed September 11, 2018.

50. Emi, interview by Omori.

51. George Kawakami and Tom Muranaka, "Letter to the Editor," *Heart Mountain Sentinel*, April 17, 1943, https://www.loc.gov/resource/sn84024756/1943 -04-17/ed-1/?sp=4. Accessed July 16, 2018.

52. Muller, *Free to Die*, 120–21.

53. Muller, *Free to Die*, 122.

54. Emi, interview by Omori.

55. Hoshizaki, "Tale of a Heart Mountain Conscientious Resister."

56. Hoshizaki, interview by Ikeda, Gatewood, and Hoshide.

57. Muller, *Free to Die*, 167.

58. Takashi Hoshizaki, interview by Shirley Ann Higuchi, February 22, 2018, author's personal collection.

59. Hoshizaki, interview by Higuchi and Locker.

60. Muller, *Free to Die*, 174.

61. Hoshizaki, interview by Higuchi and Locker.

62. Hoshizaki, "Tale of a Heart Mountain Conscientious Resister."

63. Muller, *Free to Die*, 175.

64. Irons, *Justice at War*, 87.

65. Irons, *Justice at War*, 135, 136, 161, 162.

66. Lorraine Bannai, "Taking the Stand: The Lessons of the Three Men Who Took the Japanese American Internment to Court," *Seattle Journal for Social Justice*, November 1, 2005, 31.

67. Bannai, "Taking the Stand."

68. "$1261 Raised for Hirabayashi," *Heart Mountain Sentinel*, June 5, 1943, https://cdn.loc.gov/service/sgp/sgpbatches/batch_dlc_anacostia_ver01/data/sn84 024756/00237288592/1943060501/0575.pdf. Accessed September 3, 2018; "3,000 Nisei Aided by Student Council," *Heart Mountain Sentinel*, August 19, 1944.

69. Irons, *Justice at War*, 85.

70. Irons, *Justice at War*, 81, 85, 250–51, 252.

71. Irons, *Justice at War*, 311.

72. John Burling to Philip Glick, "WRA's Memorandum on Validity of Detention, dated January 1, 1944," April 24, 1944, http://ddr.densho.org/ddr-densho -67-116/. Accessed June 21, 2018.

73. John Kitasako, "Washington News-Letter," *Heart Mountain Sentinel*, October 21, 1944, https://www.loc.gov/resource/sn84024756/1944-10-21/ed-1/?sp=4. Accessed August 31, 2018.

74. *Korematsu v. U.S.*, 323 U.S. 214, https://www.law.cornell.edu/supremecourt /text/323/214. Accessed September 11, 2018.

75. *Korematsu v. U.S.*, 323 U.S. 214.

76. *Korematsu v. U.S.*, 323 U.S. 214.

77. "Supreme Court Justice Scalia Talks Eminent Domain, Internment

Camps," *Honolulu Civil Beat*, February 5, 2014, https://www.civilbeat.org/2014 /02/supreme-court-justice-scalia-talks-eminent-domain/. Accessed June 22, 2018.

78. *Ex parte Endo*, 323 U.S. 283 (1944), https://supreme.justia.com/cases/federal /us/323/283/. Accessed January 22, 2018.

79. Irons, *Justice at War*, 317.

Chapter 8. The Nisei Units

1. "Two Heart Mountaineers Killed on Italian Front," *Heart Mountain Sentinel*, July 29, 1944, https://www.loc.gov/resource/sn84024756/1944-07-29/ed-1/?sp =1. Accessed March, 2018.

2. "Cpl. Aoyama Awarded Silver Star to Be Given Posthumously to Mother," *Heart Mountain Sentinel*, November 11, 1944, https://www.loc.gov/resource/sn84 024756/1944-11-11/ed-1/?sp=1. Accessed May 21, 2018.

3. "Gen. Mark Clark Praises 100th," *Heart Mountain Sentinel*, July 29, 1944, https://www.loc.gov/resource/sn84024756/1944-07-29/ed-1/?sp=1. Accessed March 1, 2018.

4. "28 Center Draftees Honored at Sendoff Program," *Heart Mountain Sentinel*, August 19, 1944, https://www.loc.gov/resource/sn84024756/1944-08-19/ed-1/?sp =1. Accessed July 16, 2018.

5. Ted Fujioka, "Nisei Describes Conditions in Italy," *Heart Mountain Sentinel*, July 22, 1944, 5, https://www.loc.gov/resource/sn84024756/1944-07-22/ed-1/?sp =5&r=-0.239,0.089,1.57,0.695,0. Accessed May 18, 2018.

6. Daniel Inouye, "Heart Mountain Dedication Ceremony," speech, August 20, 2011, C-Span, https://www.c-span.org/video/?301340-1/heart-mountain-dedica tion-ceremony.

7. Inouye, *Journey to Washington*, 129.

8. "James Okubo Is Awarded Silver Star," *Heart Mountain Sentinel*, June 16, 1945, https://www.loc.gov/resource/sn84024756/1945-06-16/ed-1/?sp=1. Accessed September 12, 2018.

9. John Motheral, "The Luckiest Man: Chester Tanaka," *Fort Point Salvo*, June 1981, http://www.easaul.com/go-for-broke-exhibit.html. Accessed May 15, 2018.

10. Inouye, *Journey to Washington*, 133.

11. "The Price of Admission," *Heart Mountain Sentinel*, November 18, 1944, https://www.loc.gov/resource/sn84024756/1944-11-18/ed-1/?sp=1. Accessed July 16, 2018.

12. Fred Yamamoto, *Heart Mountain Sentinel*, July 28, 1945, 1, https://www .loc.gov/resource/sn84024756/1945-07-28/ed-1/?sp=1. Accessed July 16, 2018.

13. Ernest Uno to Paul Tsuneishi, April 25, 1995, Heart Mountain archives.

14. Karleen Chinen, "Nisei Soldiers of World War II Are Honored in Bruyeres and Biffontaine," *Hawaii Herald*, November 11, 1994.

15. Inouye, interview by Ikeda.

16. Inouye, *Journey to Washington*, 164.

17. Rudi Williams, "Army Secretary Lionizes 22 World War II Heroes," Armed Forces Press Service, July 10, 2000, https://archive.defense.gov/specials/medalof honor/.

18. Reeves, *Infamy*, 246.

19. Stanley Kunio Hayami and Joanne Oppenheim, Stanley Hayami, Nisei Son: His Diary, Letters and Story from an American Concentration Camp to Battlefield, 1942–1945 (New York: Brick Tower Press, 2008).

20. "Kaufering," *Holocaust Encyclopedia*, United States Holocaust Memorial Museum, https://encyclopedia.ushmm.org/content/en/article/kaufering.

21. Solly Ganor, *Light One Candle: A Survivor's Tale from Lithuania to Jerusalem* (New York: Kodansha International, 1995), 347.

22. Susan Ferris, "Somalia Stirs Memories of Nazi Camps," *Rocky Mountain News*, December 20, 1992.

23. Ganor, *Light One Candle*, 347.

24. Sheila Newlin, "I didn't know that," Manzanar Committee pilgrimage program, April 30, 2016, https://manzanarcommittee.files.wordpress.com/2016/05/2016_pilgrimage_prg_final.pdf. Accessed March 15, 2018.

25. Inouye, *Journey to Washington*, 190.

26. Inouye, *Journey to Washington*, 190.

27. David Stout, "21 Asian Americans Receive Medal of Honor," *New York Times*, May 14, 2000.

28. Jayson Jenks, "Western Student Jim Okubo Went from an 'Enemy Alien' to an American Hero," *Seattle Times*, July 25, 2017.

29. Hiro Nishimura, "Sadao S. Munemori: First Nisei Medal of Honor Recipient," Nisei Veterans Committee Foundation newsletter, October 2005.

30. Jenks, "Western Student."

31. William J. Clinton, "Remarks on Presenting the Congressional Medal of Honor to Asian-American Heroes of World War II," June 21, 2000, http://www.presidency.ucsb.edu/ws/index.php?pid=58671. Accessed May 3, 2018.

Chapter 9. Ending the Exclusion Order

1. Irons, *Justice at War*, 324.

2. Public Proclamation No. 21, Headquarters, Western Defense Command, December 17, 1944, https://www.du.edu/behindbarbedwire/pp_21.html. Accessed July 15, 2018.

3. "As They Go Forth, So Do They Prosper," *Heart Mountain Sentinel*, December 23, 1944, https://www.loc.gov/resource/sn84024756/1944-12-23/ed-1/?sp=8&r=-1.262,-0.051,3.524,1.559,0. Accessed May 15, 2018.

4. "Proclamation of Army Considered Vindication," *Heart Mountain Sentinel*, December 23, 1944.

5. Uno, interview by Higuchi and Locker.

6. "Reaction in California Shows Assorted Opinions but Many Support Nisei," *Heart Mountain Sentinel*, December 23, 1944.

7. "2 AWOL GIs Held for Fire," *Heart Mountain Sentinel*, February 10, 1945, 1, https://lccn.loc.gov/sn84024756.

8. "Myer Lashes Anti Groups on Coast," *Heart Mountain Sentinel*, January 20, 1945.

9. "Final Relocation Program Now Operating Smoothly, Advisory Group Declares," *Heart Mountain Sentinel*, February 10, 1945, https://www.loc.gov/resource/sn84024756/1945-02-10/ed-1/?sp=1. Accessed August 8, 2018.

10. "Heart Mountain Residents Visit New England," *Heart Mountain Sentinel*, February 10, 1945, https://www.loc.gov/resource/sn84024756/1945-02-10/ed-1/?sp=5. Accessed August 8, 2018.

11. Advertisement, *Heart Mountain Sentinel*, February 10, 2018, https://www.loc.gov/resource/sn84024756/1945-02-10/ed-1/?sp=2&r=-0.325,0.284,1.588,0.702,0. Accessed August 8, 2018.

12. "Farmers at $1.25 per Hour Needed, Sakauye Says," *Heart Mountain Sentinel*, February 10, 1945, https://www.loc.gov/resource/sn84024756/1945-02-10/ed-1/?sp=1. Accessed August 8, 2018.

13. Cecilia M. Tsu, *Garden of the World: Asian Immigrants and the Making of Agriculture in California's Santa Clara Valley* (Oxford, UK: Oxford University Press, 2013), 214.

14. "Come on Out the Water's Fine," *Heart Mountain Sentinel*, April 7, 1945, https://www.loc.gov/resource/sn84024756/1945-04-07/ed-1/?sp=4&r=-0.183,0.319,1.09,0.482,0. Accessed August 8, 2018.

15. "The Gates Will Swing Closed," *Heart Mountain Sentinel*, June 30, 1945, https://www.loc.gov/resource/sn84024756/1945-06-30/ed-1/?sp=4&r=-0.188,0.343,1.119,0.495,0. Accessed August 8, 2018.

16. "Project Director Urges Early Relocation Plans," *Heart Mountain Sentinel*, June 30, 1945, https://www.loc.gov/resource/sn84024756/1945-06-30/ed-1/?sp=1. Accessed August 8, 2018.

17. "Project Director Urges Early Relocation Plans"; "Three Hostels Serving as Temporary Lodgings for Seattle Relocatees"; "New Pittsburgh Hostel Opened," *Heart Mountain Sentinel*, June 30, 1945, https://www.loc.gov/resource/sn84024756/1945-06-30/ed-1/?sp=1. Accessed August 8, 2018.

18. "Farewell Notices," *Heart Mountain Sentinel*, June 16, 1945, https://www.loc.gov/resource/sn84024756/1945-06-16/ed-1/?sp=2. Accessed August 8, 2018.

19. Sakatani, interview by Ikeda.

20. Sam Mihara, interview by Shirley Ann Higuchi and Ray Locker, July 27, 2017, author's personal collection.

21. "Relocation Summary for William Higuchi," War Relocation Authority, May 7, 1945. Records about Japanese Americans Relocated during World War II,

created 1988–1989, documenting the period 1942–1946. Record Group 210, National Archives Building, Washington, DC.

22. "Physical Examination for Iyekichi Higuchi," War Relocation Authority, May 28, 1945. Records about Japanese Americans Relocated during World War II, created 1988–1989, documenting the period 1942–1946. Record Group 210, National Archives Building, Washington, DC.

23. "6-Car Relocation Special Leaves Monday with 240; Northwest Train Planned," *Heart Mountain Sentinel*, June 16, 1945, https://www.loc.gov/resource /sn84024756/1945-06-16/ed-1/?sp=1. Accessed August 9, 2018.

24. "Unemployment compensation for Iyekichi Higuchi," War Relocation Authority, July 12, 1945. Records about Japanese Americans Relocated during World War II, created 1988–1989, documenting the period 1942–1946. Record Group 210, National Archives Building, Washington, DC.

25. Robertson memo on Iyekichi Higuchi, War Relocation Authority, August 8, 1945. Records about Japanese Americans Relocated during World War II, created 1988–1989, documenting the period 1942–1946. Record Group 210, National Archives Building, Washington, DC.

26. Joe Carroll to Relocation Officer, War Relocation Authority, August 8, 1945. Records about Japanese Americans Relocated during World War II, created 1988–1989, documenting the period 1942–1946. Record Group 210, National Archives Building, Washington, DC.

27. William Higuchi, interview by Locker.

28. Emily Higuchi Filling, interview by Shirley Ann Higuchi and Ray Locker, July 7, 2018, author's personal collection.

29. William Higuchi, interview by Locker.

30. James Higuchi to William Higuchi, September 12, 1999, author's personal collection.

31. James Higuchi to William Higuchi, September 12, 1999.

32. William Higuchi, interview by Helen Yoshida, October 8, 2015.

33. George Nelson and Henry Wright, *Tomorrow's House: A Complete Guide for the Home-builder* (New York: Simon & Schuster, 1945).

34. Timken-Detroit Axle Company, pamphlet, author's personal collection.

35. Saito, interview by Yuille.

36. Yoshio Saito to Harvey Burnett, War Relocation Authority, September 30, 1945. Records about Japanese Americans Relocated during World War II, created 1988–1989, documenting the period 1942–1946. Record Group 210, National Archives Building, Washington, DC.

37. Yoshio Saito to Harvey Burnett, January 30, 1946. Records about Japanese Americans Relocated during World War II, created 1988–1989, documenting the period 1942–1946. Record Group 210, National Archives Building, Washington, DC.

38. Harvey Burnett to Yoshio Saito, February 6, 1946. Records about Japanese Americans Relocated during World War II, created 1988–1989, documenting the

period 1942–1946. Record Group 210, National Archives Building, Washington, DC.

39. Kunisaku Mineta to Mrs. Fujimura, November 23, 1945. Records about Japanese Americans Relocated during World War II, created 1988–1989, documenting the period 1942–1946. Record Group 210, National Archives Building, Washington, DC.

40. Mineta, interview by Higuchi and Locker.

41. Mark Simon, "Honoring a Man of Experience," *San Francisco Chronicle*, October 31, 2002.

42. A. S. Kell to J. Carroll, "Osako Uno," February 20, 1945. Records about Japanese Americans Relocated during World War II, created 1988–1989, documenting the period 1942–1946. Record Group 210, National Archives Building, Washington, DC.

43. Joe Carroll to Osako Uno, September 11, 1945. Records about Japanese Americans Relocated during World War II, created 1988–1989, documenting the period 1942–1946. Record Group 210, National Archives Building, Washington, DC.

44. Uno, interview by Higuchi and Locker.

45. Inouye, *Journey to Washington*, 192.

46. Defense Logistics Agency, "History of the Hart-Dole-Inouye Federal Center," https://www.defensemwr.com/battlecreek/about/hart-dole-inouye-history. Accessed May 22, 2018.

47. Inouye, *Journey to Washington*, 208.

48. Ganor, *Light One Candle*, 6.

49. Sheila Newlin, interview by Shirley Ann Higuchi and Ray Locker, June 7, 2017, author's personal collection.

50. Hoshizaki, interview by Higuchi.

51. Emi, interview by Koch.

52. George Joel to Kiyoshi Okamoto, April 22, 1946. Records about Japanese Americans Relocated during World War II, created 1988–1989, documenting the period 1942–1946. Record Group 210, National Archives Building, Washington, DC.

53. Susan Yamamura, "Minoru Tamesa: The Quiet Man Who Came to Dinner," Discover Nikkei, April 11, 2017, http://www.discovernikkei.org/en/journal/2017/4/11/minoru-tamesa-1/. Accessed June 19, 2018.

54. Amy Fujimoto, "Ben Wakaye: A True American," *Conscience and Constitution* website, 1998, https://resisters.com/study/Ben_Wakaye.htm. Accessed July 15, 2018.

55. Brian Niiya, "Guntaro Kubota," *Densho Encyclopedia*, July 8, 2015, https://encyclopedia.densho.org/Guntaro%20Kubota/. Accessed June 6, 2018.

56. Brian Niiya, "Paul Nakadate," *Densho Encyclopedia*, January 13, 2016, https://encyclopedia.densho.org/Paul%20Nakadate/. Accessed June 6, 2018.

57. Harry Truman, "Remarks upon Presenting a Citation to a Nisei Regiment,"

July 16, 1946, Presidential Papers of the United States, http://www.presidency
.ucsb.edu/ws/?pid=12457. Accessed June 6, 2018.

58. Bannai, "Taking the Stand," 31.

59. Uno, interview by Higuchi and Locker.

60. Hoshizaki, interview by Higuchi and Locker.

61. Mineta, interview by Higuchi and Locker.

Chapter 10. Moving Forward

1. William Higuchi, interview by Locker.

2. Higuchi Filling, interview by Higuchi and Locker.

3. James Higuchi, "Iyekichi Higuchi and Chiye Shiki's Family Tree," *Memoirs of James and Amy Higuchi* (2000), author's personal collection.

4. Uno, interview by Higuchi and Locker.

5. Lily Yuri Tsurumaki, interview by Diana Emiko Tsuchida, May 13, 2018, https://www.tessaku.com/oral-histories/2018/05/13/lily-yuri-tsurumaki. Accessed July 12, 2018.

6. John Higuchi, interview by Ray Locker, July 7, 2018, author's personal collection.

7. Kathleen Saito Yuille, interview by Shirley Ann Higuchi, Ray Locker, and Helen Yoshida, June 6, 2017.

8. William Higuchi, interview by Yoshida.

9. William Higuchi, interview by Yoshida.

10. William Higuchi, interview by Locker.

11. Mineta, interview by Sarasin.

12. Mineta, interview by Sarasin.

13. Inouye, *Journey to Washington*, 203, 207, 231, 241, 252.

14. Inouye, *Journey to Washington*.

15. Uno, interview by Higuchi and Locker.

16. John Osmundsen, "Hamsters Go Around with Flies in Polar Biological Clock Tests," *New York Times*, January 15, 1961.

17. Hoshizaki, interview by Higuchi.

Chapter 11. Creating a Memorial

1. Ruth Blackburn Pfaff, interview by Ray Locker, July 27, 2017, author's personal collection.

2. Mary Blackburn, "First Drawing—Blackburn," *Modern Pioneers*, ed. Winifred Sawaya Wasden (Powell, WY: Northwest College Production Printing, 1998), 23–29.

3. Blackburn Pfaff, interview by Locker.

4. Mary Blackburn, "First Drawing—Blackburn," 23–29.

5. Larry Jones, "Modern Day Homesteading in Wyoming," *American Society of Arms Collectors Bulletin* 75 (Fall 1996): 62–63.

6. LaDonna Zall, interview by Shirley Ann Higuchi, Ray Locker, and Helen Yoshida, June 2, 2017, author's personal collection.

7. Michael Millstein, "Interned Japanese Took Wyoming Desert to Heart," *Billings Gazette*, July 18, 1999.

8. Millstein, "Interned Japanese."

9. Leslie Colin Tribble, "His Heart Is on the Land," *Yellowstone Valley Woman*, June 6, 2016.

10. Chester Blackburn to Dan Iritani, February 26, 1989, Park County Library Historical Files.

11. Blackburn to Iritani, February 26, 1989.

12. Mary Blackburn to Park County Historical Society, "History of Heart Mountain Memorial," June 5, 1984, Park County Library Historical Files.

13. Blackburn to Iritani, February 26, 1989.

14. Alan Simpson to Chester and Mary Blackburn, November 8, 1984, Park County Library Historical Files.

15. Norman Mineta, remarks, Heart Mountain Ceremony to Honor WWII Soldiers, Powell, Wyoming, June 21, 1986, Heart Mountain archives.

16. John Collins to Alan Simpson, August 6, 1991, Park County Library Historical Files.

17. Powell Valley Chamber of Commerce to Mary Ruth Blackburn, September 12, 1991, Park County Library Historical Files.

18. Chester Blackburn to David Reetz, November 30, 1991, Park County Library Historical Files.

19. "Chester A. Blackburn," *Cody Enterprise*, April 22, 1996.

20. Takashi Hoshizaki, interview by Shirley Ann Higuchi and Ray Locker, July 27, 2018, author's personal collection.

21. Board of Directors and Advisory Board, Heart Mountain Wyoming Foundation, March 7, 1998.

22. Sperling, interview by Ikeda.

23. Douglas Nelson, interview by Shirley Ann Higuchi and Ray Locker, July 28, 2018, author's personal collection.

24. Sue Kunitomi Embrey to David Reetz, December 28, 2002, Heart Mountain archives.

25. Carolyn Takeshita to Patricia Wolfe, February 2, 2000, Heart Mountain archives.

26. LaDonna Zall, "Archives," in *Heart: Tragedy into Triumph at Heart Mountain* (unpublished manuscript, 2014), 84.

27. Toshiko Nagamori Ito, "Security Boots," February 25, 2000, Heart Mountain archives.

28. David Reetz, "Land Purchased," *Kokoro Kara*, Summer 2001.

Chapter 12. Acknowledging Wrongs

1. Tsu, *Garden of the World*, 212.
2. Greg Robinson, "Japanese American Evacuation Claims Act," *Densho Encyclopedia*, October 15, 2015, https://encyclopedia.densho.org/Japanese%20American%20Evacuation%20Claims%20Act/. Accessed January 16, 2018.
3. Robinson, "Japanese American Evacuation Claims Act."
4. Estelle Ishigo to Rep. Cecil King, May 14, 1952. Online Archive of California, https://oac.cdlib.org/ark:/13030/hb9m3nb8s8/?brand=oac4. Accessed June 5, 2018.
5. Warren Burger to Estelle Ishigo, July 28, 1953. UCLA, Library Special Collections, Charles E. Young Research Library, https://calisphere.org/item/ark:/13030/hb11nb3z8/. Accessed June 5, 2018.
6. "Claim of Kiyoji Murai" (RG-60) No. 146-35-1030, September 28, 1950, Adjudication of the Attorney General, Volume 1, https://www.archives.gov/files/research/japanese-americans/case-files/146-35-1030.pdf. Accessed June 29, 2018.
7. "Claim of Nizo Okano" (RG-60) No. 146-35-2392, September 27, 1950, Adjudication of the Attorney General, Volume 1, https://www.archives.gov/files/research/japanese-americans/case-files/146-35-2392.pdf. Accessed June 29, 2018.
8. Robinson, "Japanese American Evacuation Claims Act."
9. Alice Yang, "Edison Uno," *Densho Encyclopedia*, https://encyclopedia.densho.org/Edison%20Uno/. Accessed September 20, 2018.
10. Newton, *Justice for All*, 141.
11. Yang, "Edison Uno."
12. Karen Inouye, "Warren Furutani," *Densho Encyclopedia*, https://encyclopedia.densho.org/Warren%20Furutani/. Accessed September 20, 2018.
13. Diana Meyers Bahr, *The Unquiet Nisei: An Oral History of the Life of Sue Kunitomi Embrey* (New York: Palgrave Macmillan, 2007), 127.
14. Darrell Kunitomi, interview by Shirley Ann Higuchi and Ray Locker, July 18, 2018, author's personal collection.
15. Cababa, interview by Locker.
16. Phil Shigekuni, interview by Sharon Yamato, August 29, 2011, https://ddr.densho.org/media/ddr-densho-1000/ddr-densho-1000-364-transcript-85214fe590.htm. Accessed August 5, 2018.
17. Floyd Mori, "Redress and Restoration," in *Heart: Tragedy into Triumph at Heart Mountain* (unpublished manuscript, 2014).
18. Mori, "Redress and Restoration."
19. Mori, "Redress and Restoration."
20. "President Gerald R. Ford's Proclamation 4417, Confirming the Termination of the Executive Order Authorizing Japanese-American Internment During World War II," February 19, 1976, https://www.fordlibrarymuseum.gov/library/speeches/760111p.htm.

21. "Aid to Tokyo Rose and Miss Yoshimura Reflects Japanese-Americans' New Confidence," *New York Times*, February 7, 1977, https://nyti.ms/2xCPFAR.

22. "Aid to Tokyo Rose."

23. Mori, "Redress and Restoration."

24. Carolyn Sugiyama, interview by Shirley Ann Higuchi and Ray Locker, July 2, 2018, author's personal collection.

25. Sugiyama, interview by Higuchi and Locker.

26. Calvin Naito and Esther Scott, "Against All Odds: The Campaign in Congress for Japanese American Redress," Kennedy School of Government, Cambridge, Massachusetts, 1990, https://bit.ly/2xvqmBz. Accessed May 13, 2018.

27. Naito and Scott, "Against All Odds."

28. Naito and Scott, "Against All Odds."

29. Sugiyama, interview by Higuchi and Locker.

30. Jimmy Carter, "Commission on Wartime Relocation and Internment of Civilians Act Remarks on Signing S. 1647 Into Law," July 31, 1980, http://www.presidency.ucsb.edu/ws/?pid=44855.

31. Sharon Yamato, "Commission on Wartime Relocation and Internment of Civilians," *Densho Encyclopedia*, October 22, 2013, https://encyclopedia.densho.org/Commission%20on%20Wartime%20Relocation%20and%20Internment%20of%20Civilians/. Accessed June 13, 2018.

32. "Hearings Start on Internment of Japanese-Americans in '42," *New York Times*, July 15, 1981, https://nyti.ms/2Dg16EA.

33. Amy Mass, "From Prejudice and Incarceration to Reconciliation and Healing," *Heart: From Tragedy to Triumph at Heart Mountain* (unpublished manuscript, 2014), 57.

34. Mori, "Redress and Restoration."

35. "Ex-Aide Calls Japanese Internment 'Humane,'" *New York Times*, November 4, 1981, https://nyti.ms/2PVvlCx.

36. Karl Bendetsen, "Written Statement of Karl R. Bendetsen for the Commission of Wartime Relocation and Internment of Civilians," June 22, 1981, http://www.mansell.com/eo9066/1981/IA215.html. Accessed June 1, 2018.

37. Sam Roberts, "Aiko Herzig Yoshinaga, Critic of Wartime Internment, Is Dead at 93," *New York Times*, July 24, 2018, https://nyti.ms/2v6MTTa.

38. Commission on Wartime Relocation and Internment of Civilians, *Personal Justice Denied*, 459.

39. Commission on Wartime Relocation and Internment of Civilians, *Personal Justice Denied*, 463.

40. Sakatani, interview by Ikeda.

41. Bacon Sakatani, "The Hike Up Heart Mountain," in *Heart: Tragedy into Triumph at Heart Mountain* (unpublished manuscript, 2014), 102.

42. Blackburn Pfaff, interview by Locker.

43. Kunitomi, interview by Higuchi and Locker.

44. Emi, interview by Koch.

45. Emi, interview by Koch.

46. Naito and Scott, "Against All Odds."

47. Naito and Scott, "Against All Odds."

48. Grant Ujifusa, "Overwhelming Case for Mike Masaoka," Japanese American Citizens League National Convention, Las Vegas, July 15, 2015, https://wscjacl.files.wordpress.com/2015/07/aug_2015.pdf. Accessed June 22, 2018.

49. Ben Wofford, "The Forgotten Government Plan to Round Up Muslims," Politico, August 19, 2016, https://politi.co/2NXQqP9. Accessed July 31, 2018.

50. Naito and Scott, "Against All Odds."

51. Grant Ujifusa, "Remembering the 'Real Senate Redress Hero,' Spark Matsunaga," letter to Nichi Bei, September 2, 2011, https://www.nichibei.org/2011/09/remembering-the-%E2%80%98real-senate-redress-hero%E2%80%99-spark-matsunaga/. Accessed September 9, 2018.

52. Naito and Scott, "Against All Odds."

53. Paul Houston, "Japanese-Americans Ask Reparations," Los Angeles Times, August 29, 1986, http://articles.latimes.com/1986-04-29/news/mn-2249_1_internment-camps. Accessed July 30, 2018.

54. Houston, "Japanese Americans."

55. Paul Houston, "Reagan 'Rights' a Wrong, Signs Internee Reparation," Los Angeles Times, August 11, 1988, http://articles.latimes.com/1986-04-29/news/mn-2249_1_internment-camps.

56. Brian Niiya, "Lim Report," Densho Encyclopedia, https://encyclopedia.densho.org/Lim%20Report/. Accessed September 20, 2018.

57. Deborah Lim, "Position and Action on Resisters and the WRA Segregation Process," Conscience and the Constitution, http://resisters.com/conscience/who_writes_history/looking_back/06_limreport2e.html. Accessed July 19, 2018.

58. Satoru Tsuneishi, Commission on the Wartime Relocation and Internment of Civilians statement, Heart Mountain archives.

59. Michael Milstein, "Japanese Americans Revisit Their Painful Past," Los Angeles Times, October 3, 1994.

60. Paul Tsuneishi, "Paul Tsuneishi Interview," interview by Frank Abe and Frank Chin, May 19, 1995, Densho, Frank Abe Collection, http://ddr.densho.org/media/ddr-densho-122/ddr-densho-122-24-6-transcript-104a0e2821.htm. Accessed June 29, 2018.

61. The Japanese American Bar Association of Greater Los Angeles, Tak Hoshizaki, April 30, 1993, Heart Mountain archives.

62. Hoshizaki, interview by Yoshida.

63. Paul Tsuneishi to members of the Heart Mountain Wyoming Foundation Board, Mike Mackey and Clifford Uyeda, July 5, 1998, Heart Mountain archives.

64. A Resolution, Recognition of the Heart Mountain Fair Play Committee, Board of Directors, 442nd Veterans Club, August 3, 1998, Heart Mountain archives.

65. Ernest Uno to Michi Weglyn, August 6, 1998, Heart Mountain archives.

66. Frank Emi to Ernest Uno, August 12, 1998, Heart Mountain archives.

67. Tsuneishi, interview by Abe and Chin.

68. Paul Tsuneishi to Heart Mountain Wyoming Foundation board, September 5, 1998, Heart Mountain archives.

69. David Reetz to Paul Tsuneishi, February 17, 1999, Heart Mountain archives.

70. Paul Tsuneishi to Heart Mountain Wyoming Foundation board, July 16, 1999, Heart Mountain archives.

71. David Reetz, Laurel Vredenburg, John Collins, and Patricia Wolfe to Frank Abe, March 18, 1999, Heart Mountain archives.

72. Heart Mountain Wyoming Foundation Board Meeting Minutes, September 19, 1999, Heart Mountain archives.

73. Paul Tsuneishi to Barbara Uriu, January 14, 2000, Heart Mountain archives.

74. Floyd Mori, interview by Shirley Ann Higuchi and Ray Locker, September 25, 2018, author's personal collection.

75. Kenji Taguma, "Historic JACL Ceremony Recognizing WWII Resisters Called a 'First Step' in Reconciliation," *Nichi Bei Times*, May 14, 2002.

76. William Higuchi, interview by Locker.

77. John Higuchi, interview by Locker.

Chapter 13. Preservation under Duress

1. Nelson, interview by Higuchi and Locker.

2. Nelson, interview by Higuchi and Locker.

3. Nelson, *Heart Mountain*, 16.

4. Nelson, interview by Higuchi and Locker.

5. Nelson, *Heart Mountain*, 171.

6. Nelson, interview by Higuchi and Locker.

7. John Hess, "The Issei, the Nisei and Us," *New York Times*, May 10, 1976.

8. John Motheral, "Go for Broke," *Fort Point Salvo*, June 1981, http://www.easaul.com/go-for-broke-exhibit.html. Accessed August 8, 2018.

9. Motheral, "Go for Broke."

10. Motheral, "Go for Broke."

11. Motheral, "Go for Broke."

12. Gregg Kakesako, "Dachau's Liberation Burns in Memory: A 442nd Soldier Recalls Skin and Bone Prisoner in the Snow," *Honolulu Star-Bulletin*, March 21, 1993.

13. Eric Saul, "Reflections on Working with General Peers on the OSS Detachment 101 Exhibit," July 29, 2018, http://www.easaul.com/oss-detachment-101 .html. Accessed June 3, 2018.

14. Mary Battiata, "Smithsonian's Constitution Controversy," *Washington Post*, March 16, 1987.

15. Roger Catlin, "What's Changed in the 30 Years since the Smithsonian Opened an Exhibition on Japanese Internment," Smithsonian.com, February 27, 2017, https://www.smithsonianmag.com/smithsonian-institution/marking-75th -anniversary-wrong-imprisonment-120000-japanese-americans-180962278/. Accessed March 22, 2018.

16. Allen Hendershott Eaton, *Beauty behind Barbed Wire: The Arts of Japanese Our War Relocation Camps* (New York: Harper & Brothers), 3.

17. Allen Eaton to Estelle Ishigo, October 1, 1945, Ishigo (Estelle) papers, UCLA, Library Special Collections, Charles E. Young Research Library, https:// calisphere.org/item/ark:/13030/hb4s20098f/.

18. Eaton to Ishigo, October 1, 1945.

19. Eaton, *Behind Barbed Wire*, 64.

20. Arthur Ishigo to Charlie Burn, January 12, 1945, Ishigo (Estelle) papers, UCLA, Library Special Collections, Charles E. Young Research Library, https:// calisphere.org/item/ark:/13030/hb2k4008g4/. Accessed May 21, 2018.

21. LaDonna Zall, undated remarks at Northwest College symposium, Powell, Wyoming, Park County Library Historical Files.

22. Sakatani, interview by Ikeda.

23. Sakatani, interview by Ikeda.

24. Sakatani, interview by Ikeda.

25. Eve Kahn, "Art of Internment Camps Will Head to Auction," *New York Times*, March 5, 2015, https://nyti.ms/2NYPWZ5.

26. Eaton, *Beauty behind Barbed Wire*.

27. Lyman Bryson, "Exiled Art," *The Saturday Review*, June 7, 1952, https:// bit.ly/2DjEZNA.

28. Nancy Ukai, "Artifacts of Japanese Internment Tell Stories We Must Not Forget," *San Francisco Chronicle*, April 29, 2015, https://bit.ly/2poeYmG. Accessed December 8, 2017.

29. Deborah Vankin, "George Takei Helps L.A. Museum Acquire Internment Camp Artifacts," *Los Angeles Times*, May 2, 2015, https://lat.ms/2QPOh7o. Accessed December 8, 2017.

30. "Community Leaders Protest Auction of JA Camp Artifacts," April 13, 2015, http://www.rafu.com/2015/04/community-leaders-protest-auction-of-ja -camp-artifacts/.

31. Randy Kennedy, Eve Kahn, Patricia Leigh Brown, "Seller in Canceled Internment-Camp Auction Comes Forward," *New York Times*, April 17, 2015, https://nyti.ms/2OOcqZS. Accessed December 8, 2017.

32. Catherine Saillant, "Japanese Americans' Protests Halt Auction of Internment Camp Items," *Los Angeles Times*, April 16, 2015, https://lat.ms/1baVZDg. Accessed December 8, 2017.

Chapter 14. Generational Trauma and the Model Minority

1. Robert Higuchi, interview by Helen Yoshida, December 2, 2016, author's personal collection.

2. John Higuchi, interview by Locker.

3. Mass, "From Prejudice and Incarceration," 38.

4. Darrell Kunitomi, interview by Shirley Ann Higuchi, February 18, 2018, author's personal collection.

5. Mass, "From Prejudice and Incarceration," 40.

6. Nobu Miyoshi, "Identity Crisis of the Sansei and the Concentration Camp," Sansei Legacy Project, March 13–15, 1998, http://www.momomedia.com/CLPEF /sansei/identity.htm.

7. Kunitomi, interview by Higuchi.

8. Cababa, interview by Locker.

9. "Mira Mesa Driver Killed as Car Hits Wall," *Los Angeles Times*, September 29, 1986.

10. John Higuchi, interview by Locker.

11. Carl Rivkin, interview by Shirley Ann Higuchi and Ray Locker, September 25, 2018, author's personal collection.

12. John Bolton to Robert Matsui, December 1986, author's personal collection.

13. Robert Higuchi, interview by Helen Yoshida, December 2, 2016, author's personal collection.

14. *Bijarchi v. General Atomics*, A60304 Breach of Contract, San Diego, California, November 4, 1988, https://www.juralindex.com/civil/bijarchi-vs-general -atomics-case-details-01495ee1f0f4c10cd16bdda6dc7efa94.html.

15. "White House-Backed Keynoter," *New York Times*, August 27, 1968.

16. Daniel Inouye, "Democratic National Committee Keynote Address," Daniel Inouye Institute, filmed August 28, 1968, at the National Democratic Convention, video, https://dkii.org/speeches/august-26-1968/. Accessed April 7, 2018.

17. Maggie Astor, "'The Whole World Is Watching': The 1968 Democratic Convention, 50 Years Later," *New York Times*, August 28, 2018, https://nyti.ms /2ONdE7G. Accessed April 7, 2018.

18. Associated Press, "Newly Released Tapes: LBJ Urged Humphrey to Choose Hawaiian Senator Daniel Inouye as Running Mate," *Washington Post*, December 7, 2008, https://wapo.st/2xA23CL. Accessed April 7, 2018.

19. Masumi Izumi, "Repeal of Title II of the Internal Security Act of 1950

('Emergency Detention Act')," *Densho Encyclopedia*, May 12, 2014, https://bit
.ly/2OEKqb7. Accessed April 7 2018.

20. John Crewdson, "Senate Votes Inquiry on Espionage against Democrats,"
New York Times, February 8, 1973, https://bit.ly/2MQOkMh. Accessed April 7,
2018.

21. Douglas Kneeland, "Inouye Says 'Thank You, to Senators—in Hawaiian,"
New York Times, August 3, 1973, https://nyti.ms/2DrosYi. Accessed April 7, 2018.

22. Mineta, interview by Sarasin.

23. Uno, interview by Higuchi and Locker.

24. Ganor, *Light One Candle*, xxi.

25. Newlin, interview by Higuchi and Locker.

26. Ken Ringle, "The Patriot," *Washington Post*, August 21, 2000.

27. Matthew Wald, "Man in the News/Norman Yoshio Mineta, a Clinton
Holdover, a Reagan Veteran and a Departing Senator," *New York Times*, January
3, 2001.

28. Mineta, interview by Sarasin.

29. Katherine Lackey, "An Oasis of Kindness on 9/11: This Town Welcomed
6,700 Strangers amid Terror Attacks," *USA Today*, September 8, 2017.

30. Tom Brokaw, "Tom Brokaw: Friends across Barbed Wire and Politics,"
New York Times, August 11, 2017.

Chapter 15. Uncovering Setsuko's Secret

1. Uno, interview by Higuchi and Locker.

2. John Higuchi, interview by Locker.

3. Nelson, interview by Higuchi and Locker.

4. Sue Kunitomi Embrey to David Reetz, December 28, 2002, Heart Mountain archives.

5. Nelson, interview by Higuchi and Locker.

6. Inouye, "Heart Mountain Dedication Ceremony."

7. Tom Brokaw, "The Lessons of Heart Mountain," August 20, 2011, Heart
Mountain archives.

8. Mass, "From Prejudice and Incarceration," 45.

9. Mass, "From Prejudice and Incarceration," 45.

10. Sakatani, "The Hike," 108.

11. "The Rise of Asian Americans," Pew Research Center, April 4, 2013,
https://www.pewsocialtrends.org/2012/06/19/the-rise-of-asian-americans/. Accessed November 23, 2017.

12. Uno, interview by Higuchi and Locker.

13. William Higuchi, interview by Locker.

14. Daniel Inouye, "Senator Inouye on Warren Rudman," eulogy, November
29, 2012, C-SPAN, https://www.c-span.org/video/?c4231467/senator-inouye-warren
-rudman. Accessed August 8, 2018.

15. Emma Dumain, "Dole Has One Last Moment with Inouye," *Roll Call*, December 20, 2012, https://bit.ly/2DlgmA7. Accessed August 8, 2018.

16. "New Exhibit: Esse Quam Videri: Muslim Self-Portraits," *Kororo Kara*, Spring 2012, 5.

17. Shirley Ann Higuchi, "Trump Needs to Visit a Japanese American Internment Camp," *USA Today*, November 18, 2016, https://usat.ly/2PXoGVn. Accessed November 18, 2016.

Selected Bibliography

Books

Bahr, Diana Meyers. *The Unquiet Nisei: An Oral History of the Life of Sue Kunitomi Embrey*. New York: Palgrave Macmillan, 2007.

Berryman Kessel, Velma. *Behind Barbed Wire: Heart Mountain Relocation Camp*. Casper, WY: Mountain States Lithographing, 1992.

Bird, Kai. *The Chairman: John J. McCloy, the Making of the American Establishment*. New York: Simon & Schuster, 1992.

Blackburn, Mary Ruth. "First Drawing—Blackburns." In *Modern Pioneers*, edited by Winifred Sawaya Wasden. Powell, WY: Northwest College Production Printing, 1998.

Bonner, Robert E. *William F. Cody's Wyoming Empire: The Buffalo Bill Nobody Knew*. Norman: University of Oklahoma Press, 2007.

Commission on Wartime Relocation and Internment of Civilians. *Personal Justice Denied*. Seattle: University of Washington Press, 2011.

Daniels, Roger. *The Politics of Prejudice: The Anti-Japanese Movement in California and the Struggle for Japanese Exclusion*. Berkeley: University of California Press, 1977.

Daniels, Roger. *Prisoners without Trial: Japanese Americans in World War II*. New York: Hill & Wang, 1993.

Drinnon, Richard. *Keeper of the Concentration Camps: Dillon S. Myer and American Racism*. Berkeley: University of California Press, 1987.

Eaton, Allen Hendershott. *Beauty behind Barbed Wire: The Arts of the Japanese in Our War Relocation Camps*. New York: Harper and Brothers, 1952.

Ganor, Solly. *Light One Candle: A Survivor's Story of Holocaust Demons and Japanese Heroes*. New York: Kodansha International, 1995.

Gordon, Linda. *Dorothea Lange: A Life beyond Limits*. New York: W. W. Norton, 2010.

Grodzins, Mortin. *Americans Betrayed: Politics and the Japanese Evacuation.* Chicago: University of Chicago Press, 1949.

Hayami, Stanley Kunio, and Joanne Oppenheim. *Stanley Hayami, Nisei Son: His Diary, Letters and Story from an American Concentration Camp to Battlefield, 1942–1945.* New York: Brick Tower Press, 2008.

Hosokawa, Bill. *Nisei: The Quiet Americans.* New York: William Morrow, 1969.

Inouye, Daniel K. *Journey to Washington.* Englewood Cliffs, NJ: Prentice Hall, 1967.

Inouye, Mamoru. *The Heart Mountain Story: Photographs by Hansel Mieth and Otto Hagel of the World War II Internment of Japanese Americans.* San Francisco: Cummings Publishing, 1997.

Irons, Peter H. *Justice at War.* Berkeley: University of California Press, 1983.

Ito, Toshi Nagamori. *Memoirs of Toshi Ito: U.S.A. Concentration Camp Inmate, War Bride, Mother of Chrisie and Judge Lance Ito.* Bloomington, IN: Anchor House, 2009.

Johnson, Harold Stanley. *Roster of the Rainbow Division.* New York: Eaton and Gettinger, 1917.

Kupfer, Charles. *Indomitable Will: Turning Defeat into Victory from Pearl Harbor to Midway.* New York: Bloomsbury Publishing, 2012.

Lillquist, Karl. *Imprisoned in the Desert: The Geography of the World War II–Era, Japanese American Relocation Centers in the Western United States.* Ellensburg: Central Washington University, 2007.

Mackey, Mike. *Heart Mountain: Life in Wyoming Concentration Camp.* Powell, WY: Western History Publications, 2000.

McGaugh, Scott. *Honor before Glory: The Epic World War II Story of the Japanese American GIs Who Rescued the Lost Battalion.* Boston: DaCapo, 2016.

Morgan, Ted. *FDR: A Biography.* New York: Simon & Schuster, 1985.

Mori, S. Floyd. *The Japanese American Story: As Told through a Collection of Speeches and Articles.* Mustang, OK: Tate Publishing, 2014.

Muller, Eric L. *American Inquisition: The Hunt for Japanese American Disloyalty in World War II.* Chapel Hill: University of North Carolina Press, 2007.

Muller, Eric L. *Colors of Confinement: Rare Kodachrome Photographs of Japanese American Incarceration in World War II.* Chapel Hill: University of North Carolina Press, 2012.

Muller, Eric L. *Free to Die for Their Country.* Chicago: University of Chicago Press, 2003.

Nelson, Douglas W. *Heart Mountain: The History of an American Concentration Camp.* Madison: State Historical Society of Wisconsin for the Department of History, University of Wisconsin, 1976.

Newton, Jim. *Justice for All: Earl Warren and the Nation He Made.* New York: Riverhead Books, 2006.

Niiya, Brian. *Japanese American History: An A-to-Z Reference from 1868 to the Present.* New York: Facts on File, 1993.

Reeves, Richard. *Infamy: The Shocking Story of Japanese American Internment in World War II*. New York: Henry Holt, 2015.

Robinson, Greg. *By Order of the President: FDR and the Internment of Japanese Americans*. Cambridge, MA: Harvard University Press, 2003.

Steel, Ronald. *Walter Lippmann and the American Century*. New York: Little, Brown, 1980.

Tateishi, John. *And Justice for All: An Oral History of the Japanese American Detention Camps*. Seattle: University of Washington Press, 1984.

Tsu, Cecilia. *Garden of the World: Asian Immigrants and the Making of Agriculture in California's Santa Clara Valley*. Oxford: Oxford University Press. 2013.

Warren, Louis. *Buffalo Bill's America*. New York: Random House, 2006.

Weglyn, Michi Nishiura. *Years of Infamy: The Untold Story of America's Concentration Camps*. New York: Morrow Quill, 1976.

Yamamoto, Eric K., Margaret Chon, Carol L. Izumi, Jerry Kang, Frank H. Wu. *Race, Rights and Reparations: The Law and the Japanese American Internment*. Gaithersburg, MD: Aspen Law & Business, 2001.

Archival Collections

CSU Japanese American Digitization Project. California State University Fullerton. http://digitalcollections.archives.csudh.edu/digital/collection/p16855coll4.

Densho Encyclopedia. https://encyclopedia.densho.org.

Densho Heart Mountain Sentinel Collection. Densho Digital Repository. https://ddr.densho.org/.

Densho Visual History Collection. http://densho.org/visual-history-program/.

Earl Warren History Project. Regional Oral History Office. University of California at Berkeley. https://www.lib.berkeley.edu/libraries/bancroft-library/oral-history-center/projects/warren.

Heart Mountain Wyoming Foundation Archives. https://heartmountain.org/collections/research/.

Japanese Americans. The U.S. National Archives and Records Administration. https://www.archives.gov/research/japanese-americans.

Japanese-American Internment Camp Newspapers, 1942 to 1946. Library of Congress. https://www.loc.gov/collections/japanese-american-internment-camp-newspapers/.

Index